# Solidarity without the State?

This book presents the first comprehensive history of the interplay of public and private provision that made the Swiss "three-pillar" pension system into a model for the World Bank and other pension reformers during the last two decades of the twentieth century. Through a study of business federations', private pension lobbyists', and insurance companies' archives, Matthieu Leimgruber charts the century-long battle waged over the boundaries of state and private pensions. He shows how a distinctive path towards social provision has led Switzerland apart from its western European neighbors and has laid the foundation for a pension fund industry rivalling that of the United States and the United Kingdom. Through this comparative approach, Matthieu Leimgruber is also able to question current assumptions about the strict dichotomy between "Anglo-Saxon" and "continental" models of welfare provision. This study will appeal to scholars of twentieth-century European history, economic history, political economy, and welfare economics.

MATTHIEU LEIMGRUBER is a research fellow of the Swiss National Science Foundation.

# Solidarity without the State?

## *Business and the Shaping of the Swiss Welfare State, 1890–2000*

Matthieu Leimgruber

CAMBRIDGE
UNIVERSITY PRESS

CAMBRIDGE UNIVERSITY PRESS
Cambridge, New York, Melbourne, Madrid, Cape Town, Singapore, São Paulo, Delhi

Cambridge University Press
The Edinburgh Building, Cambridge CB2 8RU, UK

Published in the United States of America by Cambridge University Press, New York

www.cambridge.org
Information on this title: www.cambridge.org/9780521875400



First published 2008

Printed in the United Kingdom at the University Press, Cambridge

*A catalogue record for this publication is available from the British Library*

ISBN 978-0-521-87540-0 hardback

# Contents

# Figures

# Tables

# Abbreviations

| | |
|---|---|
| AfZ | Archiv für Zeitgeschichte (Archives for Contemporary History, Zurich) |
| AfZ-RN | Historisches Archiv Redressement National/Aktionsgemeinschaft Nationaler Wiederaufbau (historical archives of the Action for National Restoration, Zurich) |
| AfZ-SHIV | Historisches Archiv des Schweizerischen Handels- und Industrie Vereins (Zurich) (historical archives of the Swiss Trade and Industry Federation) |
| AHV | Alters- und Hinterlassenversicherung (old age and survivors' insurance) |
| BVG | Berufliche Vorsorgegesetz (federal law on occupational provision) |
| CHF | Swiss franc |
| EO | Lohn- und Verdienstersatzordnung (wage and earnings compensation scheme for military duties) |
| KUVG | Kranken- und Unfallversicherungsgesetz (federal law on sickness and accident insurance) |
| *Pensionskassenstatistik* | pension plan surveys, various publication dates<br>1925a = *Les institutions d'assurance vieillesse, invalidité et survivants* (Berne: Office fédéral des assurances sociales, 1929)<br>1925b = *Les institutions privées de prévoyance vieillesse, invalidité et survivants* (Zurich: Union centrale des associations patronales, 1929) |

| | |
|---|---|
| | 1941/1942, 1955 = *Versicherungs- und Fürsorgeeinrichtungen* (Berne: Bundesamt für Statistik)<br>1966, 1970, 1978, 1987 = *Vorsorgeeinrichtungen* (Berne: Bundesamt für Statistik)<br>1992–2006 (biennial publication) = *Die berufliche Vorsorge* (Berne: Bundesamt für Statistik) |
| SAV | Schweizerischer Arbeitgeberverband Archiv (historical archives of the Swiss Employers' Federation, Zurich) |
| SBA | Schweizerisches Bundesarchiv (Swiss Federal Archives, Berne) |
| SLA | Historisches Archiv Rentenanstalt (Swiss Life corporate archives, Zurich) |
| SNB | Schweizerische Nationalbibliothek (Swiss National Library, Berne) |
| Sozialarchiv | Schweizerisches Sozialarchiv (Swiss Social Archives, Zurich) |
| SPAHV | Studienkommission für die Probleme der Alters- und Hinterlassenenvorsorge (Study Commission on Old Age and Survivors' Provision) |
| SVPP | Schweizerischer Verband für privatwirtschaftliche Personalfürsorge (Swiss Association of Private Employee Benefits), before 1942, see SVUSAI |
| SVUSAI | Schweizerischer Verband der Unterstützungskassen und Stiftungen für Alter und Invalidität (Swiss Association of Support Funds and Foundations for Old Age and Disability), 1942 onward, see SVPP |
| VSLG | Vereinigung Schweizerischer Lebensversicherungs-Gesellschaften (Union of Swiss Life Insurance Companies) |
| Wirtschaftsarchiv | Schweizerisches Wirtschaftsarchiv (Swiss Economic Archives, Basle) |
| ZFS | Zurich Financial Services corporate archives (Zurich) |

# Acknowledgments

I have been fortunate to benefit from the support of many friends, colleagues, and institutions. Generous funding from a Fulbright scholarship, a research grant and a publication subsidy from the University of Lausanne, as well as a postdoctoral grant from the Swiss National Science Foundation, have financed my research, writing, and revision years on both sides of the Atlantic.

During my numerous archival forays, librarians and archivists have offered invaluable assistance to gather necessary sources and literature. My gratitude extends in particular to the following persons. In Zurich: Daniel Nerlich of the Archiv für Zeitgeschichte, Hans Reis of the Schweizerischer Arbeitgeberverband Archiv, Augusto Capozzi and Suzanne Schibli of the Swiss Life/Rentenanstalt corporate archives, Thomas Inglin and Christofer Stadlin of the Zurich Financial Services corporate archives. In Berne: Adrian Zimmermann of the Historisches Archiv des Schweizerischen Metall- und Uhrenarbeiterverbandes. I would also like to thank the staffs of the following libraries and archives: Nationalbibliothek and Bundesarchiv (both in Berne), Sozialarchiv (Zurich), Wirtschaftsarchiv (Basle), Bibliothèque cantonale et universitaire (Lausanne), Columbia University research libraries, and New York Public Library (both in New York).

My warmest thanks go to Hans Ulrich Jost, who has been my mentor from the first day I walked into his undergraduate lecture course to the final revisions of this manuscript. His commitment to critical historical research and his non-conformism have been a tremendous source of inspiration. Lucy apRoberts, Christoph Conrad, and Ira Katznelson have also spent hours dissecting previous versions of this work as members of my dissertation committee and have suggested numerous improvements that have made their way into this volume. Peter Baldwin's enthusiasm and kind advice have also much contributed to make this publication possible.

At every stage of the revision process, friends and colleagues have offered countless comments, feedback, and criticism. In particular,

Robin Blackburn, Giuliano Bonoli, Dominique Dirlewanger, Silja Häusermann, Martin Lengwiler, Claudine Leysinger, Robert Lieberman, Olivier Longchamp, Yves Steiner, Jean Pierre Tabin, as well as two anonymous reviewers, have helped me to steer this volume to a safe landing. Mary Nell Bockman and Chris Jackson's first-rate editing skills have greatly contributed toward improving the final version of this text. At Cambridge University Press, Michael Watson, Joanna Breeze, and Helen Waterhouse have provided amiable guidance through the intricacies of the publishing process.

Last but not least, friends, family, and loved ones have always been available during the happy, but also sometimes rough, times that I have encountered along the writing path. I thank you all from the bottom of my heart for having defused with humor my scholarly obsessions and gently reminded me that there is a life outside of the archives.

This book is dedicated to my nephew Jules, who arrived among us when this book was reaching completion.

# Introduction
# The emergence of a pension fund champion: Switzerland in the worlds of welfare

In a September 2003 article forewarning of a looming debacle in European pension systems, *The Economist* emphasized the need to shift old age provision from the first pillar of pay-as-you-go public pensions to the second and third pillars of funded occupational pensions and individual savings accounts. The weekly also listed recommendations to "cut back on the promises of the state pension system" and to "encourage" – I would say prod – people "to save for their own retirement": extending the number of contributing years needed to qualify for benefits, limiting indexing methods to price inflation, and raising the retirement age, or even scrapping it altogether to give pensioners the "free choice" to decide the timing of their retirement. Lamenting that the "transition from the first to the third pillar cannot happen overnight", *The Economist* insinuated that if individuals did not channel their savings toward individual schemes, governments should step in to introduce "an element or two of compulsion". A cartoon representing would-be pensioners escaping the "crumbling pillars" of state and corporate pensions for the alleged safe haven of individual old age provision underscored the argumentation.[1]

These proposals summarize the current welfare reform orthodoxy, which aims to redraw the boundaries between state-based pay-as-you-go pension systems and financialized forms of old age provision. The multi-pillar approach pictured in *The Economist* has been popularized in the last decade of the twentieth century by international organizations that hailed this concept as the solution to "avert the old age crisis", in the words of a famous 1994 World Bank report.[2] These "three pillars of

[1] "State pensions in Europe. The crumbling pillars of old age", *The Economist*, September 27, 2003. In pay-as-you-go pensions, payroll contributions are relied on to pay pensions directly, while pension funding relies on the interest returns of financial assets. See E. Philip Davis, *Pension funds: retirement-income security and capital markets. An international perspective* (Oxford: Clarendon Press, 1995), pp. 302, 306.

[2] *Averting the old age crisis: policies to protect the old and promote growth* (Oxford: Oxford University Press/World Bank, 1994). See also Emily S. Andrews, *Pension reform and the*

wisdom" have progressed in great strides around the globe. Privatization and free-market reform efforts have led to the development of individual pensions in countries such as Chile and Argentina and the introduction of mandatory occupational pensions in eastern Europe. Besides public pension cutbacks, the agenda of pension reform has also opened new space for private provision in countries as diverse as Sweden, Germany, France, and Italy. Despite the "mis-selling" scandal that tainted British individual retirement accounts during the 1990s, the steep losses of pension funds during the last stock market downturn of the early 2000s, and the current downsizing of corporate pensions in both the United States and the United Kingdom, the multi-pillar horizon and its accompanying financialization remain at the center of pension debates.[3]

From the World Bank to the Organization for Economic Cooperation and Development (OECD), international organizations have repeatedly singled out the Swiss three-pillar system of old age provision as a pioneer. The World Bank has designated this combination of a universal pay-as-you-go pension (first pillar), supplemented by compulsory, funded occupational pensions (second pillar) and fiscally encouraged individual savings accounts (third pillar), as a "triumph of common sense" and the "way forward for pension reform".[4] Switzerland anticipated by almost a generation the late-twentieth-century multi-pillar gospel. After the establishment of federal old age and survivors' pensions (Alters- und Hinterlassenenversicherung, AHV) in the aftermath of World War II, the three-pillar doctrine was formulated in the early 1960s and anchored in the federal constitution in 1972. It took its definitive shape in the

*development of pension systems: an evaluation of World Bank assistance* (Washington: World Bank, 2006).

[3] On the spread of the multi-pillar perspective, see Gordon L. Clark and Noel Whiteside, eds., *Pension security in the 21st century: redrawing the public–private debate* (Oxford: Oxford University Press, 2003); Martin Rein and Winfried Schmähl, eds., *Rethinking the welfare state: the political economy of pension reform* (Cheltenham: Edward Elgar, 2004); Winfried Schmähl and Sabine Horstmann, eds., *Transformation of pension systems in central and eastern Europe* (Cheltenham: Edward Elgar, 2002); Arno Tausch, ed., *The three pillars of wisdom? A reader on globalization, World Bank pensions models and welfare society* (Huntington: Nova Science Publishers, 2002). For a critique of the financialization of social provision, see Robin Blackburn, *Banking on death or, investing in life: the history and future of pensions* (London: Verso, 2002), pp. 229–35; *Age shock and pension power: the challenge of the ageing society* (London: Verso, 2007).

[4] Estelle James, "Reforming social security around the world: common problems, contrasting solutions", in *Soziale Sicherung im Alter. Informationsbedarf – heute und morgen*, ed. Robert Fluder, *et al.* (Neuchâtel: Bundesamt für Statistik, 2001), pp. 41–80; Monika Queisser and Dimitri Vittas, *The Swiss multi-pillar pension system: triumph of common sense?* (Washington: World Bank, 2000); *Reforming public pensions* (Paris: OECD, 1988), pp. 7, 109ff; Dimitri Vittas, *Swiss Chilanpore: the way forward for pension reform?* (Washington: World Bank, 1993).

decade that followed the implementation of the 1982 federal law on occupational provision (berufliche Vorsorgegesetz, BVG) that introduced both a mandatory second pillar and voluntary third-pillar retirement accounts.

Echoing praise from foreign commentators, Swiss economists have emphasized the flexibility of the pension system and its lower reliance on the state, as well as the close integration of the second and third pillars in financial markets.[5] For social scientists, the three pillars form the core of a welfare state that may well represent "a third way" between "neo-liberal retrenchment and old statist welfare policies" and "is already set on rails toward which the European welfare train will most likely follow".[6] In the era of social policy retrenchment, privatization, and financialization of old age provision, Switzerland's impressive pension assets (which peaked at 149 percent of the gross domestic product in 2000, see Table A.7, p. 303) offer a welcome success story for proponents of market-oriented pension reforms. While emphasizing the need to downsize the state share of social provision, a senior analyst at Swiss Re, the world's leading reinsurance company, boasted that "the Swiss pension system comes off rather well in comparison to the rotten social insurance systems of its European neighbors [and] rightly deserves the high esteem it receives from abroad: its foundations are properly laid".[7]

What are the origins and rationale of the division of labor between pay-as-you-go pensions and funded occupational provision? Is the second pillar, in the provocative words of a proponent of the people's pensions, "a social program or a for-profit business"? Were corporate pension plans, as the main pension lobby group argued in 1950, really able to "achieve social progress without statist solutions"?[8] What are the contradictions between pay-as-you-go and funded pensions? What is the contribution of individual pension solutions, or the third pillar in current parlance, in overall old age provision? As the multi-pillar option becomes the dominant norm, and Switzerland faces the challenges of welfare retrenchment

[5] Lars P. Feld, Gebhard Kirchgässner and Marcel Savioz, *Financing social security in the future: the Swiss pension system as an example* (St. Gallen: Universität St. Gallen, Volkswirtschaftliche Abteilung, 1997).

[6] Klaus Armingeon, "Institutionalising the Swiss welfare state", *West European Politics* 24/2 (2001), pp. 145–68 (quotation p. 163); Herbert Obinger, *Politische Institutionen und Sozialpolitik in der Schweiz: der Einfluss von Nebenregierungen auf Strukture und Entwicklungsdynamik des schweizerischen Sozialstaates* (Berne: Peter Lang, 1998), p. 238.

[7] Thomas Trauth, "Schweizer Sozialsystem als Vorzeigemodell? Notwendigkeit der Fokussierung auf die Kernaufgaben", *Neue Zürcher Zeitung*, October 13, 2000.

[8] Jean Steiger, *Le deuxième pilier: service social ou affaire lucrative?* (Geneva: Grounauer, 1978). See the annual report of the Swiss Association of Private Employee Benefits (Schweizerischer Verband für privatwirtschaftliche Personalfürsorge): *SVPP Jahresbericht 1950* (Zurich: SVPP, 1951), p. 14.

with an aging population and unstable stock markets, does its famed "model" really offer a rosier picture for pension reform?

In this book, I answer these questions by scrutinizing the long-term and intertwined development of social insurance and occupational provision in Switzerland. In order to answer the question of whether this pension system is truly "distinct", I also compare its path toward a multi-pillar pension system with those followed by several other countries, such as the United States, Canada, the United Kingdom, and the Netherlands, where funded pensions have long played a key role in old age provision. Charting the position of Switzerland's pension system thus challenges assumptions generally held by scholars of social policy about continental European and Anglo-Saxon welfare states.

This genealogy of the three-pillar pension system brings new understanding to the development of a welfare state that has been neglected by historians of social policy. However, this study does more than show how and why Switzerland became a model for pension reformers in the late twentieth century. The issues investigated in this book – the role of taxation in the development of occupational provision, the role of insurers in the making of social policy, and the connections between pension provision, collective bargaining, and financial markets – constitute key issues in studies of welfare states. The boundaries between public and private provision are now being redrawn, and the financialization of pensions is progressing. A critical reappraisal of these interactions can open new perspectives on the history of the welfare state.

This introduction will first review the traditional explanation of Swiss welfare development, then present the methodological building-blocks that I have used to shed light on the distinctive trajectory of the three-pillar pension system, and, finally, outline the comparative perspectives followed throughout this book.

## I

Traditional accounts of social policy development point out the distinct position occupied by Switzerland among western European welfare states. In comparison with other OECD countries of equivalent industrial development, social insurance programs were introduced belatedly (see Table 0.1). Federal pensions (AHV) came in 1947, more than a decade after the 1935 implementation of Social Security in the United States. Before the 1930s, Swiss national-level (or federal) social expenditure on unemployment, health, and pensions ranked at the bottom end of eighteen industrialized countries. Federal expenditure on old age provision hovered at 0.3 percent of the national income by 1930, a level that put the Confederation just above the United States, Finland, Italy, and

Table 0.1 *The introduction of core welfare state programs in Switzerland.*

| | Switzerland (federal level) | | OECD average |
|---|---|---|---|
| work accident | 1911 | (implemented in 1918) | 1905 |
| old age | 1947 | | 1917 |
| health | 1912 | (subsidization of health plans) | 1924 |
| | 1994 | (mandatory basic health insurance) | |
| unemployment | 1924 | (subsidization of unemployment schemes) | 1929 |
| | 1982 | (mandatory unemployment insurance) | |
| family allowances | 1952 | (only for farmers and agricultural workers) | 1944 |
| | 2006 | (federal guidelines to harmonize existing cantonal schemes) | |

*Source:* Herbert Obinger *et al.* "Switzerland: the marriage of direct democracy and federalism", in *Federalism and the welfare state: New World and European experiences*, Herbert Obinger, *et al.*, ed. (New York: Cambridge University Press, 2005), p. 2.

Japan, the only industrialized countries with no national pension program at that time. Both OECD and International Labor Organization statistics point out that Swiss social expenditure remained modest during the post-war growth decades and trailed far behind that of its western European neighbors.[9]

In sum, the trajectory of the Swiss welfare state could be summarized by its course on the social insurance development index devised by Peter Flora (see Figure 0.1). Despite a quantum leap related to the 1947 introduction of the AHV, the Swiss trajectory was at odds with those of western European welfare states. Its slow and incremental development put Swiss social policy "in line with the creeping welfare state development" that is characteristic of the North American welfare states and produced a "continental European welfare state with a liberal face".[10]

The dominant causal explanation for this has emphasized the role of political institutions such as federalism and direct democracy in the making of social policy. For scholars such as Ellen Immergut, Herbert Obinger, and Giuliano Bonoli, the high level of fragmentation of the political system between federal (national), cantonal (state), and local tiers of government has led to contentious tugs-of-war between a weak

[9] Manfred G. Schmidt, *Sozialpolitik: historische Entwicklung und internationaler Vergleich* (Opladen: Leske & Budrich, 1988), pp. 13, 118, 129, 135, 137ff, 164. On social expenditures before the 1990s, see Jens Alber, *Der Sozialstaat in der Bundesrepublik 1950–1983* (Frankfurt: Campus Verlag, 1989), p. 40; Peter Lindert, "The rise of social spending, 1880–1930", *Explorations in Economic History* 31 (1994), pp. 1–37 (pp. 10–12).

[10] Armingeon, "Institutionalising the Swiss welfare state", p. 151; Herbert Obinger, "Federalism, direct democracy, and welfare state development in Switzerland", *Journal of Public Policy* 18/3 (1998), pp. 241–63 (quotation p. 260).

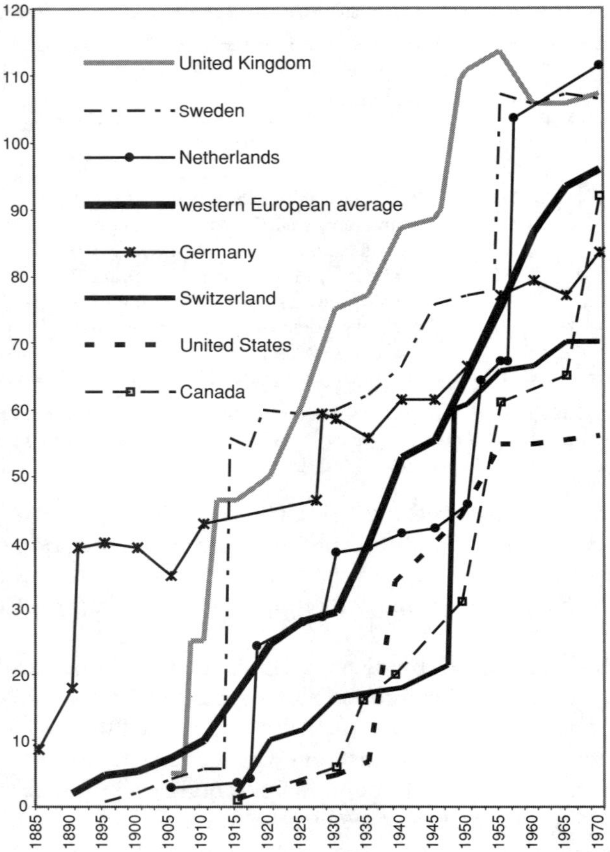


Figure 0.1 Social insurance development index, 1885–1970.
*Source:* Peter Flora and Arnold J. Heidenheimer, *The development of welfare states in Europe and America* (New Brunswick: Transaction Press, 1981), pp. 54–7, 81.

central state and regional interests opposed to centralization and emphasizing cantons' rights. The weakness of the federal state vis-à-vis cantons has also magnified the opposition of conservative forces that resisted the growth of the fiscal capacity of the Confederation. Attempts to introduce social insurance have thus led to protracted debates to secure the constitutional basis of each social policy program, as well as the financial means to implement them.[11]

[11] Ellen M. Immergut, *Health politics: interests and institutions in western Europe* (Cambridge: Cambridge University Press, 1992); Obinger, "Federalism, direct democracy, and

Extensive direct-democracy mechanisms have also considerably retarded social policy development. As we will see in Chapters 1, 2, and 3, conservative referenda demanding the repeal of social policy projects often unraveled carefully crafted policy compromises during the formative period of the welfare state. After the acceptance in 1890 of the constitutional article allowing the Confederation to legislate on social matters, universal health insurance was twice challenged by referenda (in 1900 and 1911) before being accepted by voters in 1912. A quarter-century separated the adoption of a constitutional article on old age insurance (1925) and the implementation of federal pensions (1947) that was also challenged twice by referenda (in 1931 and 1947).

The anti-centralizing resistance to social insurance, the time lag in implementation due to referenda, and the incremental development of social policy have greatly hampered the unification of social programs and led to the development of a patchwork of overlapping federal, cantonal, local, and occupational schemes. Institutional scholars have emphasized that the numerous interstices of the Swiss social security system have facilitated policy pre-emption and decentralized solutions organized by private sectors that are often subsidized by a federal state that delegates to them the organization of social provision.[12]

Recent OECD surveys remind us that taking into account private social programs can substantially modify social expenditure rankings. In Figure 0.2, countries with extensive private social provision, such as the United States, the United Kingdom, the Netherlands, Canada, and Australia, move closer to continental European welfare states when *private* social expenditure is added to the *public*. Because of the tangle of its federalized tax-system, Switzerland has yet to be included in these surveys.[13] However, *private* social programs have played a key role in the recent increase in Swiss social expenditure. At the beginning of the 1990s, Switzerland still ranked fifteenth among OECD countries in terms of *public* social spending but moved to rank fourth (behind Sweden, Denmark, and France) at the end of the decade. In a recent account, institutionalist scholars have emphasized that "with the exception of health care policy, which was transformed by the 1994 reform, [this] dramatic increase in

welfare state development"; *Politische Institutionen und Sozialpolitik in der Schweiz*; Herbert Obinger, Klaus Armingeon, Giuliano Bonoli *et al.*, "Switzerland: the marriage of direct democracy and federalism", in *Federalism and the welfare state: New World and European experiences*, ed. Herbert Obinger, *et al.* (New York: Cambridge University Press, 2005), pp. 263–306.

12 Ibid., pp. 300ff.

13 According to Willem Adema of the OECD Directorate for employment, labor, and social affairs, personal communication to the author, July 3, 2006.

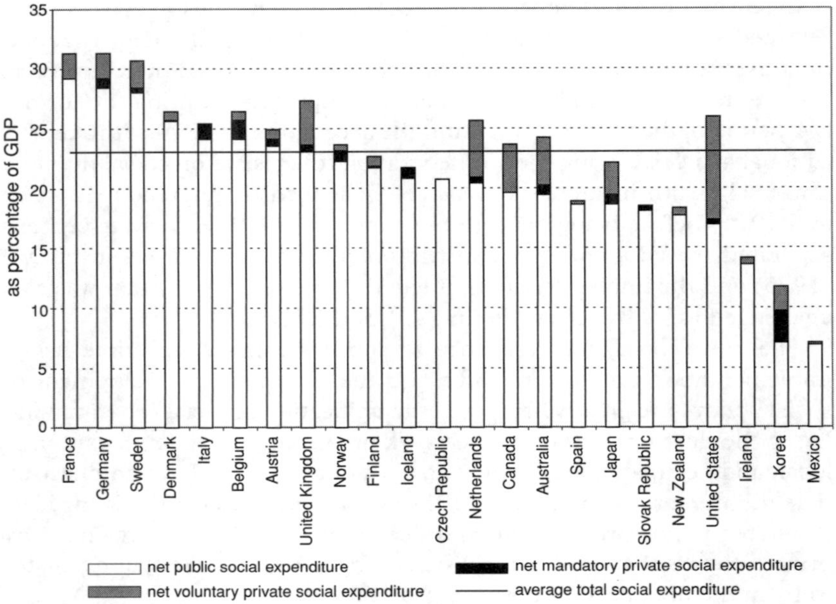


Figure 0.2 Net social expenditures in OECD countries, 2001.
*Source:* Willem Adema and Maxime Ladaique, *Net social expenditures* (Paris: OECD, 2005), p. 32.

social expenditure . . . did not result from any significant expansion of the Swiss welfare state".[14]

According to this study, closing the gap with western Europe can be mostly attributed to slow economic growth and to the impact of the 1990s crisis in unemployment insurance, but also to the maturing of compulsory second-pillar old age provision and its integration in OECD statistics as "public" social expenditure. Funded occupational pension schemes alone account for almost one-fifth of overall social security financing, while the European Union average in this domain stands well below 5 percent. As compulsory health insurance in Switzerland is provided by registered insurance companies that levy per capita premiums, the Confederation ranks just behind the United States in terms of private health spending.[15]

[14] Obinger, Armingeon, Bonoli *et al.*, "Switzerland: the marriage of direct democracy and federalism", p. 287.

[15] *Les comptes globaux de la protection sociale: résultats de 2000 – Estimations pour 2001 – Evolution depuis 1950* (Neuchâtel: Office fédéral de la statistique, 2003), pp. 62–5, 70–1, "The health of nations: a survey of health-care finance", *The Economist*, July 17, 2004.

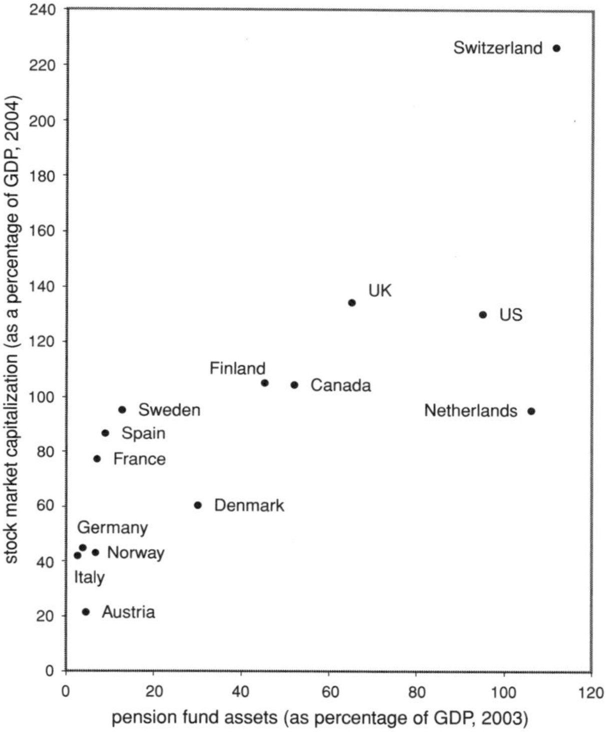


Figure 0.3 Stock markets and pension funds in Western Europe and North America, 2003–2004.
*Sources: World Development Indicators* (Washington: World Bank, 2005); "Pensions markets in focus", OECD Newsletter, December 2005.

Current developments thus undoubtedly hint at the long-term impact of private welfare arrangements in Swiss social policy.

Figure 0.3 charts the development of stock markets and funded pension assets in North America and Europe. Switzerland appears clearly as a pension fund champion: it not only overtakes the United States and the United Kingdom, the two usual suspects of Anglo-American pension fund capitalism, but also such countries as the Netherlands and Canada. This situation is far from a recent phenomenon. As we will see in Chapter 5, early postwar studies on the levels of social contributions among western European countries already pointed to the striking level of private voluntary welfare arrangements in Switzerland. At this time, funded pension assets represented one-third of the gross domestic product (see

Table A.7., p. 303), a level still unequaled by most European countries half a century later. Setting Switzerland apart from the "mechanized mass-assistance of a centralized welfare state" characteristic of continental Europe, free-market apologists praised during the 1950s the "colorful diversity of smaller and heterogeneous institutions" that made the Confederation a close relative of the American public–private welfare state.[16]

In his classic 1985 study of small European countries, Peter Katzenstein described the Swiss Confederation as a "rich man's welfare state". Characterized by the outstanding hegemony of right-wing (or, as they are called in Switzerland, bourgeois) parties and strong economic liberalism, modest social insurance expenditure and extensive private welfare schemes reinforced a "liberal capitalist" variant of democratic corporatism. Five years later, sociologist Gøsta Esping-Andersen similarly ranked Switzerland among Anglo-Saxon "liberal residual welfare states" characterized by belated development, lower de-commodification of social risk, and higher reliance on private solutions.[17] However, social scientists have neglected to explore the development of private social programs, and Switzerland remains largely absent from comparative research on the emergence of pension fund capitalism.[18] The 2003 revision of the federal law on compulsory occupational provision (BVG) has encouraged institutionalist scholars to turn their attention to recent developments of the second pillar of old age provision.[19] Yet their studies remain focused on the *public* and *state-centered* facets of the Swiss multi-tiered welfare system.

[16] Francesco Kneschaurek and Werner Eisenbeiss, "Die sozialen Leistungen der Arbeitgeber in verschiedenen OECE-Staaten", *Aussenwirtschaft* 1–2 (1958), pp. 119–41. For a discussion of this study, see also Chapter 5, Table 4.2. Wilhelm Röpke, *Grenzen und Gefahren des Wohlfahrtstaates* (Frankfurt: Schriftenreihe der Industrie- und Handelskammer Frankfurt am Main, 1955), p. 5. For a discussion of Röpke's views, see Chapters 4 and 5 of this book.

[17] Gosta Esping-Andersen, *The three worlds of welfare capitalism* (Cambridge: Polity Press, 1990), pp. 50, 83–4; Peter J. Katzenstein, *Corporatism and change: Austria, Switzerland, and the politics of industry* (Ithaca: Cornell University Press, 1984), pp. 110–12.

[18] The following studies contain only cursory mentions about Swiss occupational pensions: Clark and Whiteside, eds., *Pension security in the 21st century*; Richard Minns, *The cold war in welfare: stock markets versus pensions* (London; New York: Verso, 2001); Martin Rein and Eskil Wadensjö, eds., *Enterprise and the welfare state* (Cheltenham: Edward Elgar, 1997); Gordon L. Clark, Alicia Munnell, and Michael Orszag, eds. *The Oxford handbook of pensions and retirement income* (Oxford: Oxford University Press, 2006).

[19] Giuliano Bonoli, "Switzerland: adapting pensions within tight institutional constraints", in *Ageing and pension reform around the world: evidence from eleven countries*, ed. Giuliano Bonoli and Toshimitsu Shinkawa (Cheltenham: Edward Elgar, 2005), pp. 137–54; "The institutionalization of the Swiss multi-pillar pension system", in *Rethinking the welfare state: the political economy of pension reform*, ed. Martin Rein and Winfried Schmähl (Cheltenham: Edward Elgar, 2004), pp. 102–21; "Switzerland: the impact of direct democracy", in *West European pension politics*, ed. Ellen M. Immergut, Karen M. Anderson, and Isabelle Schulze (Oxford: Oxford University Press, 2007), pp. 203–47.

Existing historical studies of the Swiss welfare state hardly help to solve these shortcomings. Since the publication of economist Jürg Sommer's *Struggle over social insurance in Switzerland* (*Das Ringen um die soziale Sicherheit in der Schweiz*, 1978), no one has written a source-based synthesis of social policy development. Despite recent and renewed interest in this field, historical scholarship on social programs remains underdeveloped and fragmented.[20] These limitations are particularly conspicuous in the core area of the welfare state, namely old age provision. Pension researchers still have to rely on accounts written by politicians and civil servants who were direct participants in policy-making, or on descriptive studies focusing on legal and constitutional issues.[21] Again, the handful of articles and book sections devoted to the making of the AHV and its post-World War II development provide only snapshots of *state-based* old age provision.[22]

[20] Jürg Sommer, *Das Ringen um die soziale Sicherheit in der Schweiz: eine politisch-ökonomische Analyse der Ursprünge, Entwicklungen und Perspektiven sozialer Sicherung im Widerstreit zwischen Gruppeninteressen und volkswirtschaftlicher Tragbarkeit* (Diessenhofen: Rüegger Verlag, 1978). See also Alfred Maurer, "Switzerland", in *The evolution of social insurance 1881–1981: studies of Germany, France, Great Britain, Austria and Switzerland*, ed. Peter A. Köhler, *et al.* (London: St. Martin's Press, 1982), pp. 384–453. For a preliminary synthesis and discussion of the available historical literature, see Brigitte Studer, "Soziale Sicherheit für alle? Das Projekt Sozialstaat 1848–1998", in *Etappen des Bundesstaates: Staats- und Nationsbildung in der Schweiz*, ed. Brigitte Studer (Zurich: Chronos, 1998), pp. 159–86; Martin Lengwiler, *Risikopolitik im Sozialstaat: die schweizerische Unfallversicherung (1870–1970)* (Cologne: Böhlau, 2006), pp. 25–33; Sébastien Guex and Brigitte Studer, "L'Etat social en Suisse aux XIXe et XXe siècles. Notes sur quelques pistes de recherche", in *Von der Barmherzigkeit zur Sozialversicherung*, ed. Hans-Jörg Gilomen, *et al.* (Zurich: Chronos, 2002). pp. 201–12.

[21] Peter Binswanger, *Histoire de l'AVS: assurance-vieillesse et survivants suisse* (Zurich: Pro Senectute, 1987); Arnold Saxer, *Die soziale Sicherheit in der Schweiz: eine Dartstellung der Entstehung, des Aufbaus und des gegenwärtigen Standes aller Zweige der sozialen Sicherheit* (Berne: Haupt, 1970); Hans-Peter Tschudi, *Entstehung und Entwicklung der schweizerischen Sozialversicherungen* (Basle: Helbing & Lichtenhahn, 1989). Arnold Saxer was the director of the Federal Social Insurance Office during World War II. During his tenure at the Federal Council, Hans Peter Tschudi presided over the postwar development of the AHV. Peter Binswanger was a former expert of the Federal Social Insurance Office who had continued his career in the insurance sector.

[22] On the interwar period, see Bruno Dumons, "Vieillesse et Etat-providence en Suisse romande dans la première moitié du XXe siècle", *Le Mouvement social* 190 (2000), pp. 9–31; André Lasserre, "L'institution de l'assurance-vieillesse et survivants (1889–1947)", in *La démocratie référendaire suisse au 20ème siècle*, ed. Roland Ruffieux (Fribourg: Presses universitaires de l'Université de Fribourg, 1972), pp. 259–326. On World War II: Georg Hafner, *Bundesrat Walther Stampfli (1884–1965): Leiter der Kriegswirtschaft im Zweiten Weltkrieg, bundesrätlicher Vater der AHV* (Olten: Dietschi Verlag, 1986). On the postwar extension of the AHV and the gendered dimensions of social insurance, see Christine Luchsinger, *Solidarität, Selbständigkeit, Bedürftigkeit: der schwierige Weg zu einer Gleichberechtigung der Geschlechter in der AHV: 1939–1980* (Zurich: Chronos, 1995); Christine Luchsinger, "Sozialstaat auf wackligen Beinen. Das erste Jahrzent der AHV", in *achtung: die 50er Jahre! Annäherungen an eine widersprüchliche Zeit*, ed. Jean-Daniel Blanc & Christine Luchsinger (Zurich: Chronos, 1994), pp. 51–69. See also the recent contributions

If the history of the AHV is deficient, the situation is worse for the second pillar. Occupational pensions have remained an object of study for legal experts looking at the modus operandi of plans[23] or economists analyzing the financial impact of pension funds.[24] With the exception of a few outdated titles, these works give only scarce information on the evolution of private pensions before the passage of the 1982 federal law on a mandatory second pillar (BVG).[25] The history of occupational pensions remains a territory largely uncharted by historians.[26]

gathered in *Geschichte der Sozialversicherungen/L'histoire des assurances sociales* (Zurich: Chronos, 2006).

23 Jürg Brühwiler, *Die betriebliche Personalvorsorge in der Schweiz: eine Arbeits- und sozialversicherungsrechtliche Studie zum Rechtszustand nach Inkrafttreten des BVG unter besonderer Berücksichtigung des Verhältnisses zwischen Personalvorsorge und Arbeitsvertrag* (Berne: Stämpfli, 1989); Carl Helbling and Hans-Peter Conrad, *Personalvorsorge und BVG: Gesamtdarstellung der rechtlichen, betriebswirtschaftlichen, organisatorischen und technischen Grundlagen der beruflichen Vorsorge in der Schweiz* (Berne: Haupt, 2000 [1984]); Werner Nussbaum, *Das System der beruflichen Vorsorge in den USA: im Vergleich zum schweizerischen Recht* (Berne: Haupt, 1999).

24 Peter Hadorn, *Die Kapitalanlagen der schweizerischen Pensionskassen 1955–1970* (Basle: Institut für Sozialwissenschaften/Institut für angewandte Wirtschaftsforschung, 1974); Stefan Hepp, *Swiss pension funds: an emerging institutional investment force* (Berne: Haupt, 1990); Urs Oberhänsli, Robert Fluder, and Serge Gaillard, *Altersvorsorge: Kapitalschwemme oder Kapitalmangel? Untersuchung über das Spar- und Erwerbsverhalten der Rentner in der Schweiz* (Berne: Haupt, 1986); Thierry Theurillat, Olivier Crevoisier, and José Corpataux, "L'impact des caisses de pension sur les circuits de financement et de contrôle de l'économie suisse (1985–2003)", research report, Institut de sociologie/Groupe de recherche en économie territoriale (GRET), Université de Neuchâtel, 2006.

25 Wolfgang Hafner, *Im Strudel der Finanzmärkte: Pensionskassen in der Schweiz* (Zurich: Rotpunktverlag, 2004); Graziano Lusenti, *Les institutions de prévoyance en Suisse, au Royaume-Uni et en Allemagne fédérale. Placements financiers et politique sociale* (Geneva: Georg, 1989); Rudolf Rechsteiner, *Das 200-Milliarden-Geschäft. Pensionskassen in der Schweiz – Eine Einführung für Versicherte und Stiftungsräte* (Zurich: Unionsverlag, 1984); Martin Wechsler, *Die Einführung der obligatorischen 2. Säule: eine volkswirtschaftliche Analyse der problematik des Bundesgesetzes über die berufliche Alters-, Hinterlassenen-, und Invalidenvorsorge (BVG)* (Basle: Zentralstelle der Studentenschaft Zürich, 1984); Hans Gerold Wirz, *Die Personal-Wohlfahrtseinrichtungen der schweizerischen Privatwirtschaft: ihre Stellung im Steuerrecht und ihre Beaufsichtigung* (Stäfa: Buchdruckerei Stäfa, 1955).

26 For a first overview of the history of the second pillar, see Martin Lengwiler, "Das Drei-Säulen-Konzept und seine Grenzen: private und berufliche Altersvorsorge in der Schweiz im 20. Jahrhundert", *Zeitschrift für Unternehmensgeschichte* 1 (2003), pp. 29–47. I have outlined in several articles, whose findings are integrated in this volume, the role of insurance companies, pension plan associations, and tax subsidies in the making of old age provision, as well as the political elaboration of the three-pillar doctrine. See Matthieu Leimgruber, "La politique sociale comme marché: les assureurs vie et la structuration de la prévoyance vieillesse en Suisse (1890–1972)", in *Geschichte der Sozialversicherungen/Histoire des assurances sociales* (Zurich: Chronos, 2006), pp. 109–39; "Les trois piliers de la sagesse? La métaphore ternaire de la protection vieillesse en Suisse", *Aspects de la sécurité sociale* 4 (2005), pp. 2–12; "Profits de guerre, fiscalité et caisses de pension (1917–1927)", *Aspects de la sécurité sociale* 4 (2001), pp. 13–21; "Réaliser le progrès social sans solutions étatistes. Les caisses de pension face à l'assurance vieillesse et survivants (1920–1950)", in *Von der Barmherzigkeit zur Sozialversicherung*, ed. Hans-Jörg Gilomen, *et al.* (Zurich: Chronos, 2002), pp. 307–19.

This book fills in the gaps in this disparate literature by weaving together an integrated narrative of the long-term interactions between public *and* private old age provision. Two biographical profiles underscore the usefulness of such an integrated historical perspective and encapsulate in a nutshell several themes that are central here.

Federal Councilor Walther Stampfli (1884–1965) can be designated the "father of the AHV" implemented in 1947. Before his election to the executive branch in 1940, this seasoned member of the bourgeois Radical Party (the Free Democrats, or "Radicals", founded modern Switzerland in 1848) worked for two decades for the Von Roll steelworks, a leading firm that had developed extensive welfare measures. As a director of Von Roll social services, Stampfli was a member of a lobby group defending leading private pension schemes in the late 1920s. The pension system shaped under his guidance during World War II left ample room for occupational plans and *de facto* prefigured the post-1972 multi-pillar architecture. Stampfli's career, spent in the revolving doors that connect state service and business circles, is analyzed in detail in Chapters 3 and 4.

One generation later, Peter Binswanger (1916–1997), author of a standard *History of the AHV* (1987), followed a similar career straddling the first two pillars of old age provision. Before writing his much-quoted account of old age insurance, Binswanger had been involved for more than a generation in the shaping of the pension system. Hired in 1944 by the Federal Social Insurance Office, he was one of the civil servants who designed the AHV legislation. In 1955, Binswanger left the federal administration and joined Winterthur Life, one of the leading insurance companies managing group pension plans. As director of its group division and then chief executive officer, Binswanger was a key proponent of a compulsory second pillar during the 1960s. Chapter 5 explains how it was in no small part on his initiative that business federations and insurers fought to anchor the three-pillar doctrine in the federal constitution in 1972. However, Binswanger's own historical narrative does not focus solely on the AHV and barely mentions the parallel evolution of occupational benefits. The civil-servant-turned-insurance-executive keeps silent on the key inter-employer debates in which he was directly involved.

These two portraits exemplify the constant interactions that exist between social insurance and occupational provision. They also emphasize that employers, insurers, and pension lobbyists were key protagonists in the struggles to define the boundaries of these social policy areas. In order to unravel these interrelated aspects, I draw on various scholarly approaches that follow the thematic threads developed throughout this book: first, studies that detail the politics of public and private social benefits and highlight the contested boundaries between these two forms of provision; second, studies that focus on business preferences in the field of social policy and emphasize the connections between corporate social programs, social insurance, and broader economic issues such as wage-setting and collective bargaining; and last but not least, studies that underscore the pivotal role played by insurance companies as interfaces between the welfare state, employer-based provision, and financial markets.

## II

In his account of the formation of the "divided welfare state" in the United States, political scientist Jacob Hacker underscores how social insurance programs "entail significant and contested disruptions in regnant policy understandings and existing public–private boundaries". These contentious struggles can become especially protracted in decentralized political systems, such as the United States and Switzerland, where social programs face multiple institutional veto points. The decades-long path toward the establishment of federal pensions (AHV), with its succession of false starts and delays, embodies these highly visible and contentious politics. In contrast, Hacker underscores that two features of occupational social schemes are their "low visibility and low traceability".[27] Occupational schemes find their origins in the "subterranean politics" of fiscal policies, or thrive in employment relations that escape public attention. As they do not face, or skillfully avoid, political debates and institutional hurdles, private social programs are easier to implement than public ones.

As Jacob Hacker points out, the pre-emption of social insurance by private social programs has substantial effects on the development of public provision:

> When private benefits become deeply imbedded in advance of public programs . . . the prospects for major government incursion on that policy area diminish. More than simply restricting the scope for intervention, such preemption of public alternatives pushes the roster of politically viable options toward forms of government intervention that are meant to bolster or work around, rather than to challenge, private social provision.[28]

Decentralized political systems that produce belated and incremental social policy development offer a favorable configuration for private schemes that operate behind the scenes or below the radar of public

[27] Jacob S. Hacker, *The divided welfare state: the battle over public and private social benefits in the United States* (Cambridge: Cambridge University Press, 2002), pp. 43, 44–5.
[28] Ibid., p. 26.

politics. In other words, the policy stalemate faced by social insurance programs does not translate into a general stalemate for social policy. In this light, the development of Swiss old age provision can be seen as a cascading series of feedbacks between the highly contentious and public politics of social insurance and the more subterranean ones of occupational provision.

In Switzerland, delays in the implementation of federal pensions left opportunities for occupational forms of provision to develop. This private pre-emption of universal pensions meant that social insurance faced not only institutional hurdles, but also a tangle of occupational schemes that were loath to share their turf. As we will see in Chapters 2 and 3, the issue of the division of labor between the AHV and pre-existing pension plans weighed heavily in the failure or success of consecutive pension bills. After World War II, this division of labor constituted the background of the political struggle that pitted the three-pillar doctrine against the people's pensions during the 1960s (see Chapter 4). Revealing the subterranean politics of the second pillar and the fragmentation of occupational provision constitute two of my main fields of investigation.

On the issue of fiscal policy as a means to finance social programs and subsidize private welfare schemes, seminal works by Christopher Howard and Beth Stevens have underscored the existence of a "hidden welfare state" of fiscally encouraged corporate benefits alongside other publicly funded social welfare programs in the United States.[29] As pointed out by institutionalist scholars, fiscal conservative resistance to raising new taxes to finance social programs was a key factor in delaying the development of the Swiss welfare state. But these same authors do not dwell long on the fact that these same forces vigorously lobbied to safeguard and develop tax exemptions for private pension plans. From World War I on (see Chapters 2 and 3), these exemptions played a significant role in the pre-emption of social insurance by private pension providers. This lobbying for state subsidies to private welfare while at the same time resisting the state's financial provisions for social insurance can be seen throughout the century-long history of the pension system. The importance of tax breaks for pension plans has also contributed to the fragmentation of the second pillar into a multitude of company-level institutions.

[29] Christopher Howard, *The hidden welfare state: tax expenditures and social policy in the United States* (Princeton: Princeton University Press, 1997); Beth Stevens, "Blurring the boundaries: how the federal government has influenced welfare benefits in the private sector", in *The politics of social policy in the United States*, ed. Margaret Weir, *et al.* (Princeton: Princeton University Press, 1988), pp. 123–48.

Studies of Swiss political structure and power emphasize the strength of bourgeois political parties vis-à-vis the left and the high policy capacity of well-organized business interests vis-à-vis a weak central state. This privileged access and direct input in policy-making reinforce a variant of democratic corporatism described by Peter Katzenstein or André Mach as "liberal capitalist" or "liberal conservative". In a classic account, political scientist Beat Holz also showed how interactions between state and business often lead in Switzerland to the "pre-structuring" of public tasks by employers' federations, or to the implementation of public policies by a delegation of competence to private actors. The pliability of the state by business forces blurs the divide between the state and non-state spheres, and creates a tangle of intermediary "para-state" structures. In the words of political scientist Raimund Germann, "in Switzerland, the 'public' [or state] sphere is not a specific field or well-defined space, but a *variable* [sic] measuring the intensity of a shade".[30] Focusing on these shades and power relations, and on the personalities involved in the struggles on the borders between public and private provision, such as Walther Stampfli and Peter Binswanger, reveals the subterranean politics of occupational pensions.

Organized business interests played a key role in the creation, maintenance, and defense of pension plans, and this book makes extensive use of primary documents drawn from key employers' federations that articulate business preferences and strategies toward social policy and occupational schemes. These archives, briefly presented at the end of this volume, also contain abundant materials on the triangular tug-of-war between business, labor, and the state in social policy development.

Political scientist Isabela Mares has recently analyzed business social policy preferences in Germany and France by defining a "universe of social policy" whose options are organized along two axes of "risk redistribution" and "control".[31] The first explores the boundaries of coverage

[30] Katzenstein, *Corporatism and change*. In his first study of the Swiss political economy, Peter Katzenstein ironically depicted the Confederation as a capitalist paradise, see Peter J. Katzenstein, *Capitalism in one country? Switzerland in the international economy* (Ithaca: Cornell University, Western Societies Program Center for International Studies, 1980). For an updated analysis of Swiss liberal corporatism, see André Mach, *La Suisse entre internationalisation et changements politiques internes: la législation sur les cartels et les relations industrielles dans les années 1990* (Zurich: Verlag Rüegger, 2006). See also Raimund Germann, *L'amalgame public-privé en Suisse: l'administration paraétatique en Suisse* (Lausanne: IDHEAP, 1987), p. 13; Beat Hotz, *Politik zwischen Staat und Wirtschaft: verbandsmässige Bearbeitung wirtschaftspolitischer Probleme und die daraus resultierenden Konsequenzen für die Aktivitäten des Staates im Falle der Schweiz* (Diessenhofen: Rüegger Verlag, 1979).

[31] Isabela Mares, *The politics of social risk: business and welfare state development* (New York: Cambridge University Press, 2003), p. 13

for various risk pools related to sickness, old age, or unemployment: is the risk pool organized on a universal basis, for certain occupational groups, or only for workers of a specific firm? The second axis, control, measures the various "responsibilities in the administration of social insurance" retained by the state, business, or trade unions. It helps in determining why employers may favor company-based, multi-employer, or universal social insurance, and how they may react to trade union or state involvement in the management of these programs.[32] The question here is not whether capitalists simply hold antagonistic or favorable views toward social programs, but the kind of social programs that business interests will support in a specific institutional and political economic context.

Following Mares' argument, I explore the differentiated and often contradictory social policy preferences expressed by national and regional business interests, leading export sectors, and smaller domestic market-oriented firms and trades. For example, I show in Chapters 2, 3, and 4 how leading machine and metal producers were not only among the first to develop extensive corporate pensions, but were also more acquiescent toward federal pensions than entrepreneurs in other sectors with less developed schemes. They consented to the creation of basic universal pensions as long as the Confederation guaranteed the autonomy of diversified corporate schemes that enabled them to retain a skilled workforce. This combination, put forward by Federal Councilor Walther Stampfli, a veteran manager of a leading metal firm, was thus quite palatable to machine makers. In contrast, sectors such as textile manufacturing long resisted federal social insurance, as their labor-intensive profiles made them more vulnerable to the increase of social costs as a share of wages. Alongside chemicals manufacturers, textile magnates were also closer to conservative political forces that resented Radical-led federal social policy.

Given the pre-emption of old age insurance by occupational pension plans, the regulation of corporate schemes constituted a contentious issue that punctuates all the chapters of this book. If Swiss business circles welcomed state intervention in the form of tax subsidies, they consistently fought against it when it took the form of proposals to monitor pension reserves or safeguard employees' rights to pension benefits. Federal monitoring of occupational plans remained extremely limited until the 1982 law introducing a mandatory second pillar (BVG). Even after the implementation of the BVG, the control levers of pension plans remain firmly in employers' and insurers' hands. Business insistence on keeping a free hand and the resulting high level of decentralization of the second pillar

[32] Ibid., pp. 14–21.

is linked to broader interactions between social policy, corporate welfare programs, and labor relations.

Political economist Peter Swenson has contrasted the development of Swedish and American social policy by arguing that patterns of wage-setting play a key role in shaping distinctive welfare state configurations. In the Swedish case, Swenson points to the correlation between centralized wage bargaining, the strength of the left and labor, and the ensuing employers' support for comprehensive welfare measures. In contrast to this "solidarist" approach of business forces to wage-setting and social programs, Swenson describes the American configuration as a "segmentalist" case. In this case, a weaker left and decentralized wage bargaining combined to produce limited business support for social insurance and, on the contrary, continuing commitment to the extension of corporate employee benefits.[33]

In this book, I argue that Switzerland's labor relations and welfare configuration strikingly echo those in the United States and led its pension system toward a segmentalist configuration (see Chapter 1). As an export-oriented country, home to a tightly knit and disciplined business community, Switzerland may have Swedish traits, but this resemblance ends if we examine the political balance of power. Long-term Social Democratic dominance in Sweden contrasts with unbroken bourgeois dominance in Switzerland. Swiss unions are also markedly more splintered along overlapping confessional and trades fault lines, with the consequence that labor federations never equaled the centralization of powerful and well-disciplined business federations. The result of both labor fragmentation and business resolve to maintain flexible conditions for in-house wage-setting and welfare schemes is that Switzerland's collective bargaining has remained highly decentralized: industry-wide and company-wide agreements have proliferated rather than national ones, and these set the pace for collective bargaining (see Chapters 3 and 4). The fragmentation of the second pillar follows this decentralized pattern.

Historian Jennifer Klein and political scientist Marie Gottschalk have underscored that decentralized collective bargaining over corporate employee benefits has not only reinforced the "imbalance of power" in American labor relations but has also softened labor pressure in favor of social insurance. Facing relentless business resistance to the expansion of social policy, labor unions fatefully channeled their efforts toward

[33] Peter A. Swenson, *Capitalists against markets: the making of labor markets and welfare states in the United States and Sweden* (Oxford: Oxford University Press, 2002), pp. 18–44. See also Peter Swenson, "Varieties of capitalist interests: power, institutions, and the regulatory welfare state in the United States and Sweden", *Studies in American Political Development* 18 (2004), pp. 1–29.

the parallel development of occupational benefits. This led labor into an ever-tighter embrace with corporate programs and trapped unions in a genuine "institutional straitjacket" that constrained their social policy options.[34]

These dimensions are omnipresent in the Swiss case. During the protracted struggle for the AHV, the legacy of union-based forms of provision and labor distrust of state-based provision led a structurally weak labor movement to adopt forms of social partnership that were dominated by employers, who put a premium on occupational provision (see Chapters 2 and 3). After World War II, the continuing trade union attachment to occupational provision played a major role in the entrenchment of the three-pillar doctrine. At the same time, this further reduced the effectiveness of alternative proposals, such as the late 1960s people's pensions, that sought to challenge the existing division of labor between social insurance and occupational provision (see Chapter 4).

Despite an explicit focus on the role and influence of business forces and an emphasis on the cumulative weaknesses of the left and unions, my intention is not to downplay their role in social policy development. On the contrary, political and labor radicalization at the end of both world wars heralded major steps forward for social insurance by exerting strong pressure on business and the right. Socialist and Communist people's pensions challenged the three-pillar doctrine during the second half of the 1960s. However, at all these moments, business forces were able to head off redistributive social policy and safeguard private forms of provision. Among various business sectors, insurers are key to the containment of social insurance and the resilience of the division of labor between basic pensions and occupational benefits that is at the heart of the three-pillar system.

In her study of the tug-of-war between the state, labor, and business in the making of the American welfare state, Jennifer Klein designates insurers as a business faction "essential to the creation and maintenance of the private welfare system". By marketing to employers alternatives to state social programs such as group pension plans, life insurance companies contributed to the pre-emption of social insurance. At the same time, insurers were among the first to transform outright business opposition to state social programs toward a more differentiated strategy of

[34] Marie Gottschalk, *The shadow welfare state: labor, business, and the politics of health-care in the United States* (Ithaca: ILR Press, 2000), pp. 39–64; Jennifer L. Klein, *For all these rights: business, labor, and the shaping of America's public–private welfare state* (Princeton: Princeton University Press, 2003), p. 254. See also Michael K. Brown, "Bargaining for social rights: unions and the reemergence of welfare capitalism, 1945–1952", *Political Science Quarterly* 112/4 (1997–1998), pp. 645–74.

containment of social insurance by adopting a "supplementation strategy", whereby basic social insurance programs constituted a sound foundation for private supplementary forms of provision.[35]

Swiss life insurance companies have left their fingerprints on the pension debate since the 1890s and played a central role in the making of the second pillar. As their American counterparts, insurers occupied a strategic position at the "intersection of business and social service".[36] Because of the weakness of the central state, their actuarial experience was crucial during the formative period of the welfare state (see Chapter 1).

The development of group pension plans for employers began a generation before the implementation of the AHV, and their spread contributed to the fragmentation of occupational provision while entrenching the role of leading insurance companies in policy-making (see Chapters 2 and 3). Insurers shared with other employers the aims of limiting the extension of social insurance and keeping state regulation of pension schemes at a minimum level. On the other hand, insurers such as Peter Binswanger of Winterthur Life not only helped spread the three-pillar doctrine among business circles: their companies ended up being the main beneficiaries of a compulsory second pillar whose implementation opened up new opportunities for group plans (see Chapter 4).

While insurers were key proponents of fiscal conservatism and opposed the levying of taxes to finance the AHV, they supported a contributory pay-as-you-go financing structure for federal pensions (see Chapters 2 and 3). This was the result of insurers' unwillingness to see the Confederation finance the AHV through funded pension reserves, a concentration of capital in state hands that could potentially crowd out private investors and compete against funded occupational schemes (see Chapter 4). More generally, a low level of taxation was considered favorable for the development of life insurance products. The involvement of insurers in the business of social policy and their defense of private pension funding connect the history of the welfare state to that of financial interests.

To use a phrase coined by Robin Blackburn, insurance companies became key proponents of "gray capital". By gray capital, Blackburn implies that the opaque jungle of pension plans not only constitutes an area where "property rights represented by the [pension] funds represent a grey area in terms of laws and political economy", but also shapes a pension system where "funds held to finance old age is a source of vulnerability to those whose sacrifices have established them".[37] The provision of

[35] Klein, *For all these rights*, pp. 10 (quotation), 98–104.
[36] Ibid., p. 28.
[37] Blackburn, *Banking on death*, p. 15.

proper retirement benefits may well find itself in conflict with the pressure to ensure adequate profits to the business of social policy. The struggle over the boundaries of pay-as-you-go social insurance and funded pensions is a struggle over the control of savings and capital. Given Switzerland's profile as a highly developed financial center (see Figure 0.3, p. 9) this issue was at the heart of the definition of the three-pillar doctrine during the 1960s (see Chapter 4).

To sum up, this account of the making of the Swiss three-pillar system brings together two interrelated storylines: first, the belated, incremental, and highly contentious development of universal pay-as-you-go pensions and, second, the early but selective and decentralized expansion of funded occupational pension schemes. The future second pillar did not develop in splendid isolation. In the end, the autonomy and entrenchment of occupational provision depended on the failed starts of the future first pillar, generous tax breaks, and lenient state regulation of pension plans. Pension plans also thrived best when basic social insurance offered employers the foundations to build supplementary pensions on. The conflicts over the parameters of these respective areas of social policy are keys to understanding the shift from voluntary occupational pension schemes to a mandatory second pillar. This distinctive shift can be assessed by looking at the Swiss path of social policy development in a comparative context.

## III

The aim of this book is not to elaborate an umpteenth typology of welfare states. Heeding political scientist Gregory Kasza, I am keen to avoid macro-level approaches that "tend to dehumanise or simply omit the policymaking process, removing from view the practical and moral ideas that generate policies and give them substance".[38] Following historian Peter Baldwin's critique of social scientists' "obsession with ranking and hierarchy", my aim is to emphasize dynamic "family resemblances" rather than static "categorization by essences", and to trace "patterns of lineage and affiliation, resemblance and divergence, without postulating purely theoretical . . . forms".[39] In short, I use comparisons to better triangulate the position of the Swiss pension

[38] Gregory J. Kasza, "The illusion of welfare 'regimes'", *Journal of Social Policy* 31/2 (2002), pp. 271–88 (quotation p. 283).

[39] Peter Baldwin, "Can we define a European welfare state model?" in *Comparative welfare systems: the Scandinavian model in a period of change*, ed. Bent Greve (New York: St. Martin's Press, 1996), pp. 29–44 (quotation pp. 42–3). For an updated version, see also his "Der europäische Wohlfahrtsstaat: Konstruktionsversuche in der zeitgenössischen Forschung", *Zeitschrift für Sozialreform* 49/1 (2003), pp. 45–63.

system and highlight its similar or distinctive features at various moments throughout its century-long development.

The three-pillar pension system that constitutes the core of the Swiss welfare state clearly sets the Confederation apart from its immediate European neighbors. In Italy, France, Germany, and Austria, pensions developed by private firms or for specific occupational groups (miners, railroad workers, etc) were rapidly overtaken by social insurance. Battered by two world wars, inflation, and economic crises, funded occupational schemes were no match for all-encompassing pay-as-you-go social insurance that expanded after World War II. French *régimes complémentaires* offered earnings-related supplementary occupational pensions, but they were firmly integrated into the national *Sécurité Sociale* and based on pay-as-you-go structures. German, Austrian, and Italian occupational and individual pensions played a minor role in old age provision until the end of the twentieth century. Today, they are still dwarfed by universal pay-as-you-go pensions.[40] Pension funding is marginal in these countries that are situated at the antipodes of Switzerland in Figure 0.3.

If we move toward the shores of the Atlantic, the Netherlands, the United Kingdom, Canada, and the United States represent four cases in which a larger proportion of old age provision is provided through funding. Within this quadrant of Figure 0.3, the close relationship between funded pension provision, economic liberalism, and financial markets is unmistakable. For Robin Blackburn, this correlation signals the tradition of welfare systems based on "the puritan notion of industry, prudence, and individual responsibility . . . nourished by commercial and financial oligarchies from seventeenth-century Amsterdam and London to twentieth-century Boston and New York". This tradition, to which we can easily add Zwinglian and Calvinist financial centers such as Zurich and Geneva, contrasts with the "baroque idea of a well-ordered public space and beneficent, universal public power [that] still finds some echo in the elaborate state-sponsored pension schemes to be found in Germany, France, and Italy".[41]

Philip Manow has reached comparable conclusions by stressing the influence of Protestantism on European social policy development. According to him, the political influence of non-conformist Puritans infused with anti-statist and self-help ideologies in countries such as the United Kingdom, the Netherlands, and Switzerland had a retarding influence on welfare state development. By defending local and private social

[40] On supplementary pensions in France, Germany, Austria, and Italy, see the articles in Rein and Wadensjö, *Enterprise and the welfare state*.
[41] Blackburn, *Banking on death*, p. 34.

relief, political groupings such as the Dutch Anti-Revolutionary Party or the Swiss Liberal-Conservative Party contributed to the fragmentation of existing social programs, as well as to the resilience of private alternatives. In a recent reappraisal of the origins of the Dutch welfare state, sociologist Marcel Hoogenboom has also emphasized how patrician political forces linked to the *ancien régime* allied themselves with employers to maintain their grip on decentralized and privately organized social provision. The resilience of these "state-sanctioned" social programs delayed for decades the adoption of social insurance and bears striking resemblances to the public–private and para-statal configurations prevalent in Switzerland in the first half of the twentieth century.[42] These "belated-Protestant" welfare states thus offer a favorable context for the development of divided or multi-tier systems of old age provision.

Focusing on an almost similar set of countries, Martin Rein and John Turner have identified several pathways leading to the emergence of multi-pillar pension systems. According to this inspiring perspective, North American countries limit themselves to fiscally encourage occupational or individual pensions that act as "voluntary add-ons" to a first public pension pillar. This path contrasts with the British or Japanese models, where private pensions were granted the possibility to "contract out" from the main public scheme and thus offer "voluntary carve-outs" operating in parallel to state pensions. In either case, the connections between public and private pensions are weak and the autonomy of occupational schemes remains strong. Rein and Turner designate Sweden, Denmark, and the Netherlands as countries where supplementary pensions have expanded through industry-wide or national collective bargaining to the point where they constitute "quasi-mandatory add-ons" to the first public pension tier. Finally, only a handful of countries have introduced mandatory individual (Chile, Sweden) or occupational (Australia, Switzerland) pensions.[43] This last group can be used to identify the progression of fragmented pension systems toward more integrated and regulated configurations.

Table 0.2 is inspired by this approach and sets the Swiss path alongside those followed by "belated-Protestant" welfare states with strong pension

[42] Philip Manow, "*'The Good, the Bad, and the Ugly' – Esping-Andersen's regime typology and the religious roots of the western welfare state*", working paper, Max Planck Institute for the Study of Societies, Cologne, 2004 (available at http://www.mpi-fg-koeln.mpg.de/pu/workpapers–de.html). On the role of conservative Protestantism in the Netherlands, see Marcel Hoogenboom, *Standenstrijd en zekerheid. Een geschiedenis van oude orde en sociale zorg in Nederland, 1880–1940* (Amsterdam: Boom, 2004).

[43] Martin Rein and John Turner, "How societies mix public and private spheres in their pension systems", in *Rethinking the welfare state: the political economy of pension reform*, ed. Martin Rein and Winfried Schmähl (Cheltenham: Edward Elgar, 2004), pp. 102–21.

Table 0.2 *Pathways toward multi-pillar pension systems.*

| | | 1890–1914 | 1914–1938 | 1938–1948 | 1948–1972 | 1972–2005 |
|---|---|---|---|---|---|---|
| **Switzerland** | *(a)* | | failure of the first AHV project (1931) limited cantonal solutions | universal pay-as-you-go pensions (1947) | incremental expansion of the AHV (1st to 8th AHV revisions) | three-pillar pension system (9th to 11th AHV revisions) |
| | *(b)* | | tax exemptions for pension plans | tax exemptions for pension plans | pension plan articles (1958)<br>three-pillar doctrine (1963–1972) | mandatory second pillar (1982, BVG)<br>voluntary third pillar (1987) |
| *Total* | *(c1)* | *5% (1911)* | *18% (1930)* | *22% (1941)* | *32% (1955); 40% (1970)* | *>80% (1990->)* |
| *Public/private* | *(c2)* | *33%/1%* | *66%/11%* | *60%/16%* | *67%/26%; 72%/35%* | |
| | *(d)* | | | | **1948-> voluntary add-ons** | **1972-> mandatory add-ons** |
| **United States** | *(a)* | Civil War veterans' pensions fade out | Social Security Act (1935) | Social Security revisions (1939, 1949) | incremental expansion of Social Security | |
| | *(b)* | | tax exemptions for pension plans<br>voluntary occupational provision | tax exemptions for pension plans | Pension Disclosure Act (1958)<br>voluntary occupational provision | ERISA (1975)<br>failed projects to mandate occupational pensions (1980s)<br>attempts to create voluntary individual carve-outs (2000s) |
| *Private sector* | *(c)* | *2% (1910)* | *7% (1930)* | *8% (1941)* | *25% (1955); 38% (1970)* | *40% (1995)* |
| | *(d)* | | ***1935-> voluntary add-ons*** | | | |

| | | | | | | |
|---|---|---|---|---|---|---|
| **Canada** | *(a)* | | means-tested non-contributory pensions (1927) | | two-tier public system: basic pension (OAS, 1951)<br>Canada/Quebec pension plan (1965) | |
| | *(b)* | | tax exemptions for pension plans | tax exemptions for pension plans | <u>voluntary</u> occupational provision | voluntary registered pension plans and retirement savings plans (third pillar) |
| | *(c)* | | *<15% (1936)* | | *33–37% (1957)*<br>*39% (1970)* | *40% (1980s–1990s)* |
| | *(d)* | | ***1927-> voluntary add-ons*** | | | |
| **United Kingdom** | *(a)* | means-tested non-contributory pensions (1908) | contributory pensions (1925) | flat-rate basic pension (1946) | two-tier public system<br>basic pension<br>graduated pension (1961–1975) | two-tier public system<br>basic pension<br>SERPS (1975)<br>or Second State Pension (1998) |
| | *(b)* | | tax exemptions for pension plans | tax exemptions for pension plans | <u>contracted-out</u> occupational provision | contracted-out pension plans, APP (1988, third pillar) and Stakeholder pension (SHP, 1998) |
| | *(c)* | *5% (1900)* | *13% (1938)*<br>*80% (1930, public sector)* | | *28% (1953); 49% (1971)* | *48% (1991)* |
| | *(d)* | ***1908-> voluntary add-ons*** | | | ***1961-> voluntary carve-outs*** | |

*(cont.)*

Table 0.2 (*cont.*)

| | | 1890–1914 | 1914–1938 | 1938–1948 | 1948–1972 | 1972–2005 |
|---|---|---|---|---|---|---|
| **Netherlands** | *(a)* | | means-tested non-contributory pensions (1913–1919) | emergency pensions (1947) | universal basic pensions (1957) | |
| | *(b)* | | spread of industry-wide pension plans | | Industrial Pension Fund Act (1949)<br>Pension and Savings Fund Act (1953) | amendment to the 1953 Act (1973) |
| | *(c)* | | *12% (1938)* | | *44% (1955); 78% (1965)* | *>80% (1990s)* |
| | *(d)* | | **1913-> voluntary add-ons** | | ***1950s-> quasi mandatory add-ons*** | |

a) main developments of state retirement benefits; b) main developments of occupational provision; c) occupational pension coverage, in percentage of the workforce; d) role of occupational provision in the public – private pension mix

*Sources:* **Switzerland:** see appendix, Table A.4. **United States:** Jacob S. Hacker, *The divided welfare state: the battle over public and private social benefits in the United States* (Cambridge: Cambridge University Press, 2002), p. 89. **Canada:** Kenneth Bryden, *Old age pensions and policy-making in Canada* (Montreal: McGill-Queen's University Press, 1974), pp. 37–40; Ann Shola Orloff, *The politics of pensions: a comparative analysis of Britain, Canada and the United States* (Madison: University of Winsconsin Press, 1993), pp. 240–68; Keith Banting and Robin Boadway, eds. *Reform of retirement income policy: international and Canadian perspectives* (Kingston: School of Policy Studies, 1997), p. 101. **United Kingdom:** Pat Thane, *Old age in English history: past experiences, present issues* (Oxford: Oxford University Press, 2000), p. 254; Tony Lynes, "The British case", in *Enterprise and the welfare state*, ed. Martin Rein and Eskil Wadensjö (Cheltenham: Edward Elgar, 1997), p. 323. **Netherlands:** Jost van Genabeek, "Collectieve pensioenregelingen 1800–2000", in *Studies over zekerheidsarrangementen risico's, risicobestrijding en verzekeringen in Nederland vanaf de Middeleeuwen*, ed. Jacques van Gerwen and Marco van Leeuwen (Amsterdam: NEHA, 1998), p. 894; Dutch National Bank (http://www.statistics.dnb.nl) and Central Statistical Office (http://statline.cbs.nl).

funds. This rough overview, whose temporal divides correspond to the chapters of this book, charts several paths toward multi-tiered pension systems and indicates the extension of occupational pension coverage.

Table 0.2 underscores that Switzerland's belated introduction of federal pensions made it the last country of this sample where occupational provision could be described as a "voluntary add-on" to basic national pensions. In the United Kingdom (1908), the Netherlands (1913), and Canada (1927), means-tested non-contributory retirement benefits preceded postwar universal pensions. This was not the case in the United States or, a decade later, in Switzerland. In both countries, the breakthrough of the first national-level pensions introduced in 1935 and 1947 were based on a pay-as-you-go financing structure. Besides fiscal conservative pressure that limited the prospects for tax-based social provision, the United States and Switzerland benefitted from their laggard status and introduced from the beginning contributory basic pensions.

During the postwar period, the division of labor between public pensions and occupational provision took various forms as countries focused on supplementing basic old age provision with second pension tiers. The most homogeneous second pillar could be found in the Netherlands, where industry-wide pension plans that had emerged during the interwar era rapidly constituted the core of a "quasi-mandatory" occupational tier of pension provision. In contrast, Switzerland's highly decentralized single-employer and group pension plans remained voluntary. Furthermore, the belated and meager development of social insurance in the Netherlands was transformed in the aftermath of World War II, as it became a European leader in social spending.

By 1961, British pension plans had fought back attempts to develop a second tier of public pensions by obtaining "contracting-out" options: occupational plans could replace the new graduated pension and thus constitute "voluntary carve-outs" that supplemented basic pensions. Competing Labour and Conservative pension reforms led to an overlapping system of state-based basic and earnings-related pensions operating alongside occupational and individual supplementary plans. As we will see in Chapters 2 and 3, contracting-out was considered in Switzerland during the 1930s and the 1940s as a way to safeguard occupational plans. However, the failure of the 1931 AHV project and the initial modesty of AHV benefits made this issue less pressing and boosted the "voluntary add-ons" option. Major features of the postwar British welfare state such as its National Health Service and, until the 1980s, the strength of its nationalized sector had no equivalent in Switzerland. For these reasons, the British pension configuration can be distinguished from the three-pillar system.

In North America, the voluntary path had two variants: a more generous one in Canada, where voluntary occupational and individual retirement plans supplement a two-tier public pension system; and a more basic one in the United States, where Social Security remains the foremost provider of old age provision. In both countries, pension coverage peaked at around 40 percent of the workforce (though higher levels were reached for workers in the public sector and large, private corporations). Switzerland may have remained on this path in the absence of a serious challenge to occupational provision. This challenge, in the form of the late 1960s people's pensions proposals, spurred on the development of the three-pillar doctrine, which geared the Swiss pension system toward a multi-pillar configuration whose explicit aim was to contain pay-as-you-go social insurance and develop and preserve opportunities for funded pension plans. The four chapters of this book will analyze at length the genealogy of this distinctive trajectory with its branching points and critical junctures.

Chapter 1 delves into the protracted struggle for sickness and accident insurance and analyzes the role of federalism and referendum politics in early social policy. Before World War I, the issue of old age insurance remained largely off the political agenda. Yet the period witnessed the first steps toward occupational pensions and the first interventions of insurers in the business of social policy. The dynamics, actors, and developments presented in this opening chapter constitute a dress rehearsal for the politics of old age provision that unfurled in the next half-century.

In Chapter 2, I retrace the contentious politics of state pensions and the take-off of occupational pensions during World War I and the interwar decades. After the demise of the first attempt to implement the AHV in 1931, stalemate in the area of social insurance contrasted with the consolidation of private provision. These first skirmishes and contrasted outcomes prefigured the multi-tiered pension system that emerged during the 1940s.

The path-breaking introduction of the AHV during World War II is the focus of Chapter 3, where I analyze how the war context both disrupted the institutional hurdles that challenged social insurance and bolstered the development of occupational provision. The war decade marked a watershed in the history of old age provision: the boundaries of the victorious AHV were delineated to safeguard pre-existing occupational schemes, and the postwar social settlement reinforced the entrenchment of a public – private pension system.

Chapter 4 surveys the parallel and contrasted development of social insurance and occupational pensions during the postwar growth decades. I emphasize here the formulation of the three-pillar doctrine, the growing financial role of pension assets and the struggle that pitted the people's pensions against the three-pillar doctrine. The 1972 victory of the latter signaled the containment of social insurance and the reaffirmation of the role of occupational provision.

In the epilogue, I present a broad overview of the implementation of the three-pillar system and underscore the permanence of the divided politics of pension provision in the first decade of the new millennium. In the conclusion, I assess the main findings of this study and their potential impact for further explorations of the history of social policy.

# 1 The dress rehearsal for pension politics (1890–1914)

During the last quarter of the nineteenth century, such Swiss laws as the abolition of child labor, the federal regulation of industrial factories (Fabrikgesetz, 1877), and liability law reform (Haftpflichtgesetz, 1881) were considered in Europe to be innovative social policy measures. Significant fractions of the bourgeois Radical elites who had established the modern Confederation in 1848 were, at least rhetorically, in favor of social insurance. Support for social reform was especially strong on the left wing of the Radical or Free Democratic Party (Freisinnige Demokratische Partei), which was committed to developing the social and economic infrastructure of the federal state. In 1886, three years after the introduction of Chancellor Bismarck's social insurance programs in Germany, Radical politicians who dominated the Federal Council (executive branch) and leading members of the Grütli Society (precursor of the Socialist Party, founded in 1888) called for the development of social policy. In 1890, the Federal Assembly enacted a constitutional amendment that set the legal foundation for the introduction of social insurance programs.[1]

Given this favorable context, it seemed that Switzerland, like its German and Austrian neighbors, would soon introduce ground-breaking legislation covering such risks as sickness, accident, disability, and old age. However, from this point on, social policy debates veered away from this tentative Bismarckian path. Two decades after the 1890 constitutional amendment, the Confederation had introduced only accident insurance, while health policy remained limited to the subsidization of

[1] Bernard Degen, "Haftpflicht bedeutet den Streit, Versicherung den Frieden: Staat und Gruppeninteressen in den frühen Debatten um die schweizerische Sozialversicherung", in *Wissenschaft und Wohlfahrt: moderne Wissenschaft und ihre Träger in der Formation des schweizerischen Wohlfahrtstaates während der zweiten Hälfte des 19. Jahrhunderts*, ed. Hansjörg Siegenthaler (Zurich: Chronos, 1997), pp. 137–54 (pp. 139–42); Matthias Kunz and Pietro Morandi, "Zwischen Nützlichkeit und Gerechtigkeit: zur Entwicklung der sozialpolitischen Debatte in der Schweiz im Lichte ihrer Argumente", in *Krisen und Stabilisierung: die Schweiz in der Zwischenkriegszeit*, ed. Sébastien Guex and Brigitte Studer (Zurich: Chronos, 1998), pp. 145–61.

existing mutual benefit societies. The 1911 federal law on sickness and accident insurance (Kranken- und Unfallversicherungsgesetz, KUVG) was a pale shadow of the first insurance bill that had been accepted by the Federal Assembly but defeated in a referendum in 1900.

Such issues as the scale and scope of social insurance, as well as the role of existing private providers, constituted key points of friction, not only for the KUVG but also for the shaping of federal pensions that unfolded during the first half of the twentieth century. The KUVG debates thus represent a dress rehearsal for the politics of pensions. The first section of this chapter depicts how the Swiss institutional setting, characterized by federalism and referendum politics, and the shift toward conservatism that marked the 1890s both contributed to the failure of the first KUVG. In this context, the road for a rapid implementation of social policy "from above", as had been the case in the German and Austrian monarchies, was not possible. I also underline here how mutual benefit societies, insurance companies, and business interests leveraged opposition to social insurance and geared social policy development toward a configuration that reinforced the position of decentralized, private forms of provision. The second section highlights the distinctive roots of Swiss social policy by comparing it with developments taking place in Sweden and the United States. Although the issue of retirement occupied a marginal place during the first debates on social insurance, the third section surveys its emergence in the decades preceding World War I and underscores the early interplay between public and private pension provision.

## Sickness insurance and work accident compensation: the first public–private mix

The 1890 constitutional amendment authorizing the Confederation to introduce social insurance was fraught with ambiguities. While giving a green light to the study of the KUVG, the Federal Assembly crossed out from the amendment a paragraph that mentioned the potential introduction of old age pensions or disability benefits. In his history of social policy, Jürg Sommer notes that after the passing of this amendment the "chances of introducing other branches of social insurance before the implementation of the KUVG sank practically to zero".[2] The vague declaration of intent left unresolved both the scale of future social insurance and its financing. From the outset, the path toward social insurance was

[2] Jürg Sommer, *Das Ringen um die soziale Sicherheit in der Schweiz: eine politisch-ökonomische Analyse der Ursprünge, Entwicklungen und Perspektiven sozialer Sicherung im Widerstreit zwischen Gruppeninteressen und volkswirtschaftlicher Tragbarkeit* (Diessenhofen: Rüegger Verlag, 1978), p. 89.

thus marked by incrementalism and fragmentation. As the struggle for the KUVG lasted for the next twenty years, it accordingly delayed the realization of old age insurance. This situation, where the introduction of a non-binding declaration of principle is followed by protracted political battles to define the reach of social insurance programs, would recur throughout the twentieth century.

The debate over the KUVG unfolded during a period of political and socio-economic turbulence, marked by the aftermath of the Great Depression of the 1870s and major political reorientations. At the turn of the century, Radicals were confronted with the increasing combativeness and organization of the working class, as well as the opposition of the Catholic Conservatives, who used referenda to contest Radical dominance. In order to respond to this two-sided challenge, the grand old party of the bourgeoisie lurched rightward and developed new alliances with its former adversaries. In 1891, the Radicals integrated the Catholics into the executive branch that they had previously monopolized.[3] This same period was also characterized by the emergence of a distinctive bourgeois bloc (Bürgerblock). This coalition of right-wing parties, key business federations, and farmers' associations formed the basis of Switzerland's "liberal-conservative" version of democratic corporatism.[4] Together with trade tariffs and the nationalization of railroads, social policy was one of the most controversial issues of this reorientation period, during which the progressive dimensions of the 1848 Confederation, a beacon of political and economic liberalism in the middle of Europe, were fading. The road toward the implementation of the KUVG soon resembled a minefield, and the ambiguity of the 1890 constitutional amendment was only the first of the pitfalls that lay ahead for social insurance.

In her comparative study of health politics, Ellen Immergut depicts the first version of the KUVG accepted by the Federal Assembly in 1899 as "more progressive than either German social insurance or contemporary legislation in France, Britain, and Scandinavia". Based on universal

[3] Cédric Humair, *Développement économique et Etat central (1815–1914): un siècle de politique douanière suisse au service des élites* (Berne: Peter Lang, 2004), pp. 617–735; Leonhard Neidhart, *Plebiszit und pluralitäre Demokratie: eine Analyse der Funktion des schweizerischen Gesetzesreferendums* (Berne: Francke Verlag, 1970), pp. 65–76.

[4] Recent studies have confirmed Peter Katzenstein's seminal theses on Swiss corporatism while underlining that this analysis emphasized the interwar period too much and neglected the pre-1914 decades as a formative period. See Thomas David and André Mach, "Institutions and economic growth: the successful experience of Switzerland (1870–1950)", research paper no. 2006/101, United Nations University – World Institute for Development Economics Research, 2006; André Mach, *La Suisse entre internationalisation et changements politiques internes: la législation sur les cartels et les relations industrielles dans les années 1990* (Zurich: Verlag Rüegger, 2006), pp. 55–112.

coverage, the so-called Lex Forrer, named after Ludwig Forrer (1845–1921), the left-liberal Radical (Linksfreisinn) National Councilor who was in charge of drafting the bill, envisioned the creation of public health plans that would operate on an equal footing with existing mutual benefit societies.[5] Yet, the Lex Forrer already bore the brunt of a decade of fierce political bargaining. By the end of the 1890s, a multi-faceted opposition to health and accident insurance had emerged. The law was contested by business forces and also provoked the ire of mutual benefit societies, fiscal conservatives, and federalists favoring cantons' rights over the development of the central state.

Federal accident insurance was strongly opposed by insurers. From the late 1870s onward, and notably after the introduction of the 1881 liability law, companies such as Zurich Unfall (Zurich Accident Insurance Company) and Winterthur Unfall had developed lucrative activities in this domain and did not welcome the prospect of state competition. The insurance sector carried significant weight in social policy debates. If the first Swiss insurance companies were relative latecomers by international comparison, their expansion was bolstered by economic and industrial development during the second half of the nineteenth century. At the turn of the century, the insurance sector was already among the most developed in western Europe and, parallel to the emergence of social legislation, was experiencing a phase of consolidation. The introduction in 1885 of a pioneering law on private insurance (Versicherungsaufsichtgesetz) led to a rationalization of the sector, strengthened actuarial knowledge and practices, and spurred the diversification and expansion of Swiss firms into foreign markets. Tellingly, the establishment in 1886 of a Federal Private Insurance Office (Eidgenössiches Versicherungsamt) preceded by a generation the 1913 foundation of the Federal Social Insurance Office (Bundesamt für Sozialversicherung), which underlined the lead enjoyed by commercial insurance.[6]

However, private accident insurance proved costly for employers and was marred by contentious litigation. National Councilor Ludwig Forrer, who had been involved as a lawyer in many such cases, famously declared in 1899 to the Federal Assembly that "liability law means strife; social

[5] Degen, "Haftpflicht bedeutet den Streit, Versicherung den Frieden", pp. 142–8; Ellen M. Immergut, *Health politics: interests and institutions in western Europe* (Cambridge: Cambridge University Press, 1992), p. 148. On Ludwig Forrer, see Walter Labhart, *Bundesrat Ludwig Forrer 1845–1921* (Winterthur: Stadtbibliothek Winterthur, 1973).

[6] Stefan Karlen, Lucas Chocomeli, Kristin D'haemer *et al.*, *Schweizerische Versicherungsgesellschaften im Machtbereich des Dritten Reichs* (Zurich: Chronos, 2002), pp. 53–65. On the foundation of the Federal Social Insurance Office, see Jakob Graf and Jean-François Charles, "Historique, tâches et organisation de l'Office fédéral des assurances sociales", *Revue des caisses de compensation* (1988), pp. 3–52.

insurance means peace".[7] This statement echoed the rallying cry of the left-liberal wing of the Radical Party in favor of social insurance, as well as a growing consensus among employers that more homogeneous and less contentious solutions had to be found regarding accident compensation.[8] Although the steering committee (Vorort) of the Federation of Trade and Industry (Schweizerischer Handels- und Industrieverein), the main business organization, favored unified practices for work accident compensation, social insurance remained controversial.

Among textile manufacturers, silk producers, whose high value-added exports depended on labor-intensive production processes, were particularly opposed to the levying of employers' contributions that they considered damaging to their international competitiveness. Capital-intensive industries such as metals and machine-making were more favorable to social policy. In contrast to silk producers, these entrepreneurs focused on the containment of social insurance costs rather than direct opposition. Diverging views on the KUVG echoed the division between free-trade producers of luxury goods who were proponents of Manchesterian liberalism and minimum state intervention and newer manufacturing sectors that favored protectionist trade policies and a measured intervention of the Confederation in economic affairs. During the 1890s, employers succeeded in lowering their share of KUVG financing and consequently increasing the amount that had to be covered by the federal state. As pre-1914 state revenues were drawn in large part from customs duties, which free traders, fiscal conservatives, and federalists opposed increasing, opponents of the development of the financial capacity of the Confederation found themselves in the vanguard of the resistance against Ludwig Forrer's proposals.[9]

Virulent opposition to the KUVG could also be found among existing health providers. Around 1900, Switzerland boasted no fewer than 2,000 mutual benefit societies (gegenseitige Hilfsgesellschaften) in a population of 3.3 million. Global estimates of coverage should be considered with

[7] Quoted in Degen, "Haftpflicht bedeutet den Streit, Versicherung den Frieden", p. 145.

[8] Joseph Jung, *Die Winterthur: eine Versicherungsgeschichte* (Zurich: NZZ Verlag, 2000), pp. 34, 165; Martin Lengwiler, *Risikopolitik im Sozialstaat: die schweizerische Unfallversicherung (1870–1970)* (Cologne: Böhlau, 2006), pp. 61–9; Karl Lüönd, *La passion de l'avenir: 125e anniversaire de la Zurich. Histoire et vision d'un groupe multinational* (Zurich: NZZ Verlag, 1998), p. 59.

[9] On the divisions between free-trading and protectionist business fractions, see Humair, *Développement économique et Etat central*, pp. 338–407. On business opposition to the first Lex Forrer and financing controversies, see Erich Gruner, *Arbeiterschaft und Wirtschaft in der Schweiz 1880–1914* (Zurich: Chronos, 1988), pp. 640–51 (volume III); René Knüsel and Félix Zurita, *Assurances sociales: une sécurité pour qui? La Loi Forrer et les origines de l'Etat social en Suisse* (Lausanne: Mémoires et documents de l'Institut de science politique, 1979), pp. 120–39.

caution: given the meagerness of sickness benefits, it was not uncommon for individuals to be affiliated to more than one relief institution. Yet this vast network of mutual benefit societies covered approximately 15 percent of the population (in comparison with around 24 percent in the United Kingdom and 12 percent in France). Mutualism encompassed workers' and confessional sickness schemes, open schemes that operated on a local or regional basis, and finally factory-based plans. If the total number of mutual benefit societies had doubled since 1880, the pace of this development was markedly different among the various categories mentioned above. Factory-based plans witnessed the highest rate of expansion (their number almost quadrupled) and represented, in 1903, a quarter of overall coverage, as against 44 percent for open schemes and 19 percent – down from 37 percent in 1880 – for workers' mutual benefit societies, while confessional schemes remained marginal outside of local Catholic strongholds.[10]

Mutualist interests opposed the introduction of social insurance for several reasons. Local elites and Catholic organizations that used mutual benefit societies for political patronage resented the rationalization of self-organized philanthropy that was envisioned by KUVG experts who considered mutualism an outdated institution.[11] Similar fears were voiced by the declining workers' mutual benefit societies and fueled uneasiness toward social insurance among the skilled workers and craftsmen who constituted the core membership of these societies. Proponents of mutual benefit societies were most influential in French-speaking western Switzerland, where the federalist, free-trading, and fiscally conservative Liberal-Conservative Party led the opposition to social insurance. During the 1890s, the unceasing lobbying of the Federation of Mutual Benefit Societies (Fédération des sociétés de secours mutuels, founded in 1893)

[10] Hans Ulrich Jost, "Swiss cooperatives and mutual aid associations", in *Social security mutualism: the comparative history of mutual benefit societies*, ed. Marcel van der Linden and Michel Dreyfus (Berne: Peter Lang, 1996), pp. 329–42; David Muheim, "Caisses privées et assurances sociales: retour sur les premiers projets d'assurance maladie (1893–1912)", *Aspects de la sécurité sociale* 2 (2003), pp. 21–8; David Muheim, "Mutualisme et assurance maladie (1893–1912). Une adaptation ambiguë", *Traverse* 2 (2000), pp. 79–93. See also Gruner, *Arbeiterschaft und Wirtschaft in der Schweiz 1880–1914*, pp. 1359–61 (volume II/2). The 1880 and 1903 surveys elaborated by statistician Hermann Kinkelin are summarized in Tadeusz Von Dymowski, *Die Alters- und Invaliden-Versicherung in der Schweiz: eine Studie über die Sozialversicherung* (Zurich/Leipzig: Rascher, 1915), p. 141; Alfred Gutknecht, "Versicherungswesen, d: die gegenseitigen Hilfgesellschaften", in *Handwörterbuch der schweizerischen Volkswirtschaft, Sozialpolitik und Verwaltung*, ed. Naum Reichesberg (Berne: Verlag Encyclopädie, 1911), pp. 1249–61. On the issue of double counts, see Degen, "Haftpflicht bedeutet den Streit, Versicherung den Frieden", p. 139.

[11] Lengwiler, *Risikopolitik im Sozialstaat*, pp. 51–8.

pressured the Federal Assembly into abandoning the idea of setting up public health plans. The resistance to the consolidation of health provision was then one of the main causes that led to the whittling-down of social insurance. In contrast, medical associations did not fully organize themselves before the early years of the twentieth century, and doctors played a secondary role in the first KUVG debates.[12]

The accident and health insurance legislation that was finally accepted by an overwhelming majority of the Federal Assembly in October 1899 thus stood on shaky ground. The KUVG had accumulated contradictions, and resentment was strong against Ludwig Forrer's heavy-handed approach toward existing sickness schemes. The Lex Forrer was challenged by referendum and failed to clear the hurdle of the popular vote: on May 20, 1900, 70 percent of voters (58 percent in cities such as Zurich, Basle, and Geneva, but 82 percent in western Switzerland) rejected the law that could have constituted the cornerstone of federal social insurance.[13] Several labor organizations, either motivated by the fear that the Lex Forrer would compete with declining workers' mutual benefit societies or disappointed by its shortcomings, gathered signatures for the referendum, and parts of the working-class electorate voted against the KUVG.

The success of the referendum against the Lex Forrer also signaled the consolidation of the new "reactionary vanguards" that had emerged in the 1890s. Staunchly federalist Liberal-Conservatives, anti-statist and mutualist interests from western Switzerland, Catholic hard-liners, insurers, and silk manufacturers from Basle and Zurich constituted a resolute front against social insurance. In the very ranks of the ruling Radical Party, conservative factions balked at the social reform proposals elaborated by Ludwig Forrer, while large parts of the newly formed Farmers' Federation (Bauernverband) and the Federation of Small Employers and Trades (Gewerbeverband) remained at best lukewarm or even hostile

[12] Muheim, "Caisses privées et assurances sociales", pp. 26–7. On the Liberal-Conservative party and social policy, see Thomas David and Janick Marina Schaufelbühl, "Protestant philanthropy and the welfare state in Switzerland (1850–1914)", in *Religion, Wohlfahrt und Philanthropie in den europäischen Zivilgesellschaften, 1800–2000*, ed. Rainer Liedtke and Klaus Weber (Paderborn: Ferdinand Schöningh, forthcoming 2007). On the medical profession and social insurance, see Soun de Riedmatten, Daniel Rosetti, and Catherine Fussinger, "La création de l'assurance maladie: un danger pour le corps médical? (1893–1911)", *Revue Historique Vaudoise* 103 (1995), pp. 247–92.

[13] Neidhart, *Plebiszit und pluralitäre Demokratie*, pp. 146–51. For vote results, see Heiner Ritzmann-Blickenstorfer and Hansjörg Siegenthaler, eds., *Historisch Statistik der Schweiz – Statistique historique de la Suisse – Swiss Historical Statistics* (Zurich: Chronos, 1996), Table X10.

toward the KUVG.[14] The referendum finally shattered a proposal that had already been emptied of its most progressive dimensions by private health providers and by employers' determination to lower their share of the financial costs of social insurance.

The decade that followed the 1900 vote and preceded the acceptance of the second version of the KUVG was characterized by policy retrenchment. Health insurance was reduced to its bare essentials. Universal coverage was replaced by the subsidization of existing mutual benefit societies, and affiliation to these institutions remained voluntary and based on the payment of per capita premiums. The second version of the KUVG crafted by Ludwig Forrer, who had been elected to the Federal Council in 1903, thus left ample space for private health providers. In contrast, compulsory affiliation to a centralized institution remained at the heart of the new draft of the industrial work accident insurance scheme.[15]

Once again, employers were sharply divided on the issue of social insurance. Leading machine and metal manufacturers still supported compulsory accident insurance for industrial workers. However, dissent was again voiced by textile manufacturers and insurers against a federal monopoly. After an unruly assembly of the Federation of Trade and Industry held in the spring of 1911, textile manufacturers and Basle chemical companies led a small majority of the employers' federation affiliates into a stern rejection of the KUVG bill that had been accepted by an overwhelming majority of the Federal Assembly. This decision was taken against the advice of the Vorort and of metal and machine makers, both of which defended a more pragmatic approach toward social reform that avoided putting employers at odds with the Radical parliamentary majority. Finally, the second anti-KUVG campaign was initiated by dissenting employers, enabling the Vorort to remain above the fray. According to historian Hans Peter Schmid, this episode represented "the last attempt to influence the [Federation of Trade and Industry] by means of its delegates' assembly".[16] From 1911 onward, strong opposition to

14 On the concept of reactionary vanguards, see Hans Ulrich Jost, *Les avants-gardes réactionnaires: la naissance de la nouvelle droite en Suisse 1890–1914* (Lausanne: Edition d'En Bas, 1992), pp. 42–4. On the 1900 referendum, see Degen, "Haftpflicht bedeutet den Streit, Versicherung den Frieden", pp. 148–9; Immergut, *Health politics*, p. 145; Knüsel and Zurita, *Assurances sociales*, pp. 150–70. On farmers and trade interests, see Werner Baumann, *Bauernstand und Bürgerblock: Ernst Laur und der Schweizerische Bauernverband 1897–1918* (Zurich: Orell Füssli, 1993), pp. 102, 119–21; Alfred Gutersohn, *Das Gewerbe in der schweizerischen Wirtschaftspolitik: der schweizerische Gewerbeverband 1879–1954* (Zurich: Schweizerische Gewerbeverband, 1955), pp. 98–9.

15 Immergut, *Health politics*, pp. 148–52; Neidhart, *Plebiszit und pluralitäre Demokratie*, pp. 156–71.

16 Hanspeter Schmid, *Wirtschaft, Staat und Macht: die Politik der schweizerischen Exportindustrie im Zeichen von Staats- und Wirtschaftskrise (1918–1929)* (Zurich: Limmat Verlag,

social insurance persisted among employers. As will be seen in the following chapters, the Vorort was careful to avoid a public flare-up of such differences of opinion. The reinforcement of the internal discipline of business federations helped to contain displays of disunity.

The second version of the KUVG, this "liberal skeleton law with little state intervention",[17] was again challenged by a referendum set up by a conservative coalition. Zurich Unfall played a leading role in the mobilization against the KUVG and used its national network of agents and offices to gather signatures and distribute propaganda materials. However, this time, working-class districts voted clearly in favor of the KUVG, and the leadership of the Farmers' Federation, whose constituencies were not affected by mandatory accident insurance, spoke in favor of the law. Opposition in western Switzerland remained strong but was insufficient to defeat the KUVG again. The second Lex Forrer was finally accepted in February 1912 by a small majority of voters (54 percent, with larger majorities in urban areas).[18]

The second KUVG has been described as a "prototypical example of democratic, concordance-based, and disciplined decision-making".[19] The success of the law had important symbolic value for the Radicals, as it reaffirmed their leadership in social policy. Yet, this second draft had been hollowed out. During both anti-KUVG campaigns, the defense of cantons' rights and resistance to the increase in federal expenditure overlapped with free-trading positions, insurers' refusal to abandon profitable markets, and defense of traditional philanthropy and mutualism. However, the effectiveness of the second anti-KUVG coalition was blunted by the fact that the insurance bill had been weakened in order to safeguard private health provision. The referendum forces were also dampened by the attitude of the Vorort, which wanted to avoid a frontal attack against a social reform that had been, after all, enacted by the main bourgeois party. The 1912 vote constituted in the end a pyrrhic victory for the left-liberal wing of the Radical Party personified by Ludwig Forrer. The

1983), pp. 97 (quotation), 151–8. On the referendum committee, see Referendumskommittee gegen die Kranken- und Unfallversicherungsgesetz 1912, file HS 245, Wirtschaftsarchiv.

17 Herbert Obinger, "Federalism, direct democracy, and welfare state development in Switzerland", *Journal of Public Policy* 18/3 (1998), pp. 241–63 (quotation p. 253).

18 Baumann, *Bauernstand und Bürgerblock*, pp. 241–2; Lüönd, *La passion de l'avenir*, pp. 83–91. For vote results, see Ritzmann-Blickenstorfer and Siegenthaler, eds., *Swiss Historical Statistics*, Table X10.

19 Franz Horvath and Matthias Kunz, "Sozialpolitik und Krisenbewältigung am Vorabend des Ersten Weltkrieges", in *Zwischen Konflikt und Konkordanz: Analyse von Medienereignissen in der Schweiz der Vor- und Zwischenkriegszeit*, ed. Kurt Imhof, *et al.* (Zurich: Seismo Verlag, 1993), pp. 61–108, 87.

two Federal Councilors who would shape pension politics between 1918 and 1948, Edmund Schulthess during the interwar years and Walther Stampfli during World War II, did not belong to this reformist faction but to its business wing (Wirtschaftsfreisinn), and were keen to preserve elbow room for private providers of social benefits.

The acceptance of the KUVG heralded the arrival of federal social insurance, but also the fragmentation of social provision. After the defeat of compulsory health insurance, mutual benefit societies continued their activities and consolidated their position through mergers as primary providers of health coverage. After 1912, successive attempts to extend the scope of federal intervention in health insurance and to introduce universal, compulsory coverage was either prematurely aborted or resulted in minor revisions that did not challenge the architecture of the system. On all of these occasions, the entrenchment of private health providers and the resistance of the medical profession proved to be insuperable obstacles for overhauling health insurance. From the interwar period, the introduction of cantonal health insurance programs contributed to increased coverage. Yet as Ellen Immergut noted shortly before the 1994 introduction of compulsory basic health insurance: "[T]he consequence of past legislative failure is a private insurance system that, although highly regulated, is fragmented, pluralistic, and decentralized".[20] Today, even after the passage of this law, private health providers are still responsible for ensuring basic health coverage.

The implementation of industrial work accident compensation, the first federal social insurance program, was also marked by incrementalism and the preservation of opportunities for private providers. Delaying tactics from employers and the outbreak of World War I held back the establishment of the Swiss Accident Insurance Fund (Schweizerische Unfallversicherungsanstalt, SUVA) until 1918. Following a corporatist model previously implemented in Germany, the SUVA functioned as a public but not state-run institution managed by a tripartite board composed of federal, business, and trade union representatives. Paul Usteri-Escher, the first president of the board and a leading Senator of the business wing of the Radicals, characterized this configuration as an "institution set up

[20] Immergut, *Health politics*, p. 156. See also Jens Alber and Brigitte Bernardi-Schenkluhn, *Westeuropäische Gesundheitssysteme im Vergleich: Bundesrepublik Deutschland, Schweiz, Frankreich, Italien, Grossbritannien* (Frankfurt: Campus Verlag, 1992), pp. 186–91; Martin Lengwiler and Verena Rothenbühler, *Macht und Ohnmacht der Ärzteschaft. Geschichte des Zürcher Ärzteverbands im 20. Jahrhundert* (Zurich: Chronos, 2004), pp. 45–68; Rachel Vuagniaux, "Le 'médecin libre' contre le 'bolchevisme médical': le *Bulletin professionnel des médecins suisses* et les premières tentatives de révision de la LAMA (1920–1951)", *Aspects de la sécurité sociale* 3 (2002), pp. 2–9.

by the state, but operating outside of the state bureaucracy". Indeed, the SUVA was largely independent of the jurisdiction of the Federal Social Insurance Office established in 1913.[21] Moreover, federal accident insurance at first extended to only a few manufacturing sectors. Until the 1980s, the SUVA covered approximately half of workers, while the rest were covered by cantonal schemes or insurance companies. Filling the gaps left by this fragmented coverage and developing supplementary accident compensation enabled insurers to minimize the losses that followed the nationalization of industrial work accident insurance. Finally, companies relied increasingly on foreign markets to recoup losses sustained in Switzerland. In 1912, Zurich Unfall opened its first branch in the United States, an environment that remained, as the next section makes clear, more favorable to private accident insurance providers.[22]

## Pioneers and laggards: early social policy in comparative perspective

The decades leading up to 1914 laid the foundations of social policy. In an oft-repeated sequence, work accident compensation proposals were followed by debates on health, pensions, and unemployment insurance. From the outset, various solutions were put forward to address the social question: universal tax-based pensions in Denmark, contributory schemes limited to the working class in Germany, or tax-based means-tested pensions for the elderly poor in the United Kingdom and France.[23] The variety of these early social programs makes it difficult to clearly rank the pioneering versus the laggard countries. Yet the legacy of these early social insurance programs helps in understanding the subsequent trajectories of welfare states. An overview of the KUVG debates thus confirms that Switzerland's distinctive institutional configuration, notably the hurdles of federalism and the veto mechanism of referendum politics, played a key role in blocking and watering down early social policy proposals. It is crucial to understand how these institutional factors were linked to economic issues and how organized interests exploited this institutional

[21] Lengwiler, *Risikopolitik im Sozialstaat*, pp. 102–4, 132–42, 219–26. On German accident insurance, see Isabela Mares, *The politics of social risk: business and welfare state development* (New York: Cambridge University Press, 2003), pp. 65–85. Paul Usteri-Escher is quoted in "60 Jahre SUVA", *SUVA Bulletin*, November 1977.

[22] Lüönd, *La passion de l'avenir*, p. 102.

[23] Peter Baldwin, *The politics of social solidarity: class bases of the European welfare state 1875–1975* (Cambridge: Cambridge University Press, 1990), pp. 55–106; Daniel T. Rodgers, *Atlantic crossings: social politics in a progressive age* (Cambridge: Belknap Press, 1998), pp. 209–35; Manfred G. Schmidt, *Sozialpolitik: historische Entwicklung und internationaler Vergleich* (Opladen: Leske & Budrich, 1988), pp. 117–28.

framework to shape or circumscribe the development of social policy. By contrasting early Swiss social policy with developments that were taking place in the United States and Sweden, this section argues that fragmented political systems enhance business influence on social policy and that the early entrenchment of private social benefits are linked to the emergence of specific labor market regimes.

Much time has been spent debating America's "belated welfare state" development. Authors have underscored the influence of a weak central state and political parties, along with the difficulty of building successful political coalitions in favor of social insurance in a federal political system. The decentralized nature of the American political system also reinforced the ability of business interests to challenge social policy. Republican political majorities and courts were closely attuned to business interests and hostile to redistributive social programs, and tended to defeat proposals for universal social insurance. As a rule, social insurance had no chance of being implemented, except in areas where business was either supportive or simply acquiescent. The only breakthroughs were social programs such as work accident compensation that were – as in Switzerland – supported by significant business sectors, or modest maternal welfare measures that did not challenge market activities.[24]

In the United States, employers and insurers were eager to oppose social insurance programs that they considered unwelcome competition and to set up voluntary alternatives that could deflect state intrusion into labor relations.[25] Between 1911 and 1920, work accident compensation programs spread on the state level and replaced costly and contentious legal procedures. As in Switzerland, insurers opposed state-organized schemes, and accident compensation remained a major market for private companies. By the late 1930s, half of the work accident insurance market was again under their control, a proportion that remained unchanged into the late 1990s. Insurance companies and doctors also successfully

[24] Daniel Béland, *Une sécurité libérale? La politique des retraites aux Etats-Unis* (Paris: LGDJ, 1999), pp. 21–56; Jacob S. Hacker and Paul Pierson, "Business power and social policy: employers and the formation of the American welfare state", *Politics & Society* 30/2 (2002), pp. 277–325 (pp. 287–95); Ann Shola Orloff, "The political origins of America's belated welfare state", in *The politics of social policy in the United States*, ed. Margaret Weir, *et al.* (Princeton: Princeton University Press, 1988), pp. 37–80.

[25] On American welfare capitalism, see Sanford M. Jacoby, *Modern manors: welfare capitalism since the New Deal* (Princeton: Princeton University Press, 1997), pp. 11–34; Jennifer L. Klein, *For all these rights: business, labor, and the shaping of America's public-private welfare state* (Princeton: Princeton University Press, 2003), pp. 19–39; Steven A. Sass, *The promise of private pensions: the first hundred years* (Cambridge: Cambridge University Press, 1997), pp. 56–87; Andrea Tone, *The business of benevolence: industrial paternalism in Progressive America* (Ithaca: Cornell University Press, 1997).

opposed the introduction of universal health insurance at the state or federal level.[26]

Pensions for Civil War veterans are often described as the American equivalent of early European old age provision schemes. This program favored old-stock white citizens over recent immigrants and played a key role in the patronage politics of the Republican Party. Besides their use for patronage, pension expenditures constituted a means to deflate budget surpluses resulting from trade tariffs favored by protectionist manufacturing sectors but attacked by fiscal conservatives. As the share of trade tariffs in federal revenues decreased at the beginning of the twentieth century, business resistance to social insurance rose, and social policy again faced high hurdles. As the population of veterans declined in the early 1900s, the program faded away, and veterans' pensions did not constitute a foundation for extending old age provision measures.[27] On the eve of World War I, institutional fragmentation and conservative opposition blocked social policy at the federal level in both Switzerland and the United States. In both countries, the adverse conditions faced by social insurance programs were reinforced by the structure of labor markets and industrial relations.

In his study of Swedish and North American welfare regimes, Peter Swenson underlines that specific economic contexts led, in these two countries, to the adoption of diverging strategies of labor market governance that lent great weight to employers' preferences in the domain of social policy. The following two paragraphs outline this line of argumentation.

Swedish employers' federations were confronted in the first decade of the twentieth century by the fact that Swedish productivity was lagging behind its main European competitors and that high American wages acted as a magnet for growing numbers of Swedish emigrants. In order to increase wages and productivity without endangering the international competitiveness of their export-oriented economy, Swedish businessmen developed a "solidarist" labor market strategy designed to even out wages and lessen the competition for scarce labor through the

[26] Jacob S. Hacker, *The divided welfare state: the battle over public and private social benefits in the United States* (Cambridge: Cambridge University Press, 2002), pp. 193–202; Christopher Howard, "Workers' compensation, federalism, and the heavy hand of history", *Studies in American Political Development* 16 (2002), pp. 28–47 (p. 33); Rodgers, *Atlantic crossings*, pp. 245–49. On health insurance, see Colin Gordon, *Dead on arrival: the politics of health care in twentieth-century America* (Princeton: Princeton University Press, 2003).

[27] Hacker and Pierson, "Business power and social policy", p. 289; Theda Skocpol, *Protecting soldiers and mothers: the political origins of social policy in the United States* (Cambridge: Harvard University Press, 1992), pp. 102–51.

gradual centralization of wage negotiations. Employers' associations following this strategy tried to counter unions' attempts to increase wages in individual firms through the use of massive coordinated lockouts. Within their own ranks, business federations focused on dampening competition for scarce labor by discouraging individual employers or manufacturing sectors from developing social measures that disrupted collective bargaining. Peter Swenson underlines that solidarism could be implemented in part because of "Sweden's small size and the cohesiveness of its capitalist class," which enabled disciplined and well-organized business federations to favor national-level wage agreements. The early steps of solidarism geared up Swedish employers to support universal social insurance programs that were considered useful complements to centralized bargaining.[28]

Such steady and early business support for coordinated labor market regulation was absent in the United States. Given the fragmentation of their industry and peak federations, the size of the domestic market, and the continuous influx of immigrant labor, business associations were neither able to prod unruly employers into line nor to tame combative trade unions. In contrast to Swedish business circles, American employers chose another path to regulate the labor market. They relied both on aggressive anti-union measures and a "segmentalist system of decentralized wage-setting" that left room for "above standard wages and a widening variety of social benefits". This mix of high wages and corporate welfare measures favored the development of private provision and discouraged homogeneous social policy measures.[29]

Testing Swenson's approach on the Swiss case reveals a peculiar blend of Swedish and North American traits. As in Sweden, Switzerland's cohesive business elites were highly attuned to the international competitiveness of their small, export-oriented economy. However, unlike their Scandinavian counterparts, Swiss employers did not face the acute problem of emigration and labor shortages. On the contrary, from 1890 onward, wage increases were held down by a rapid influx of foreign workers. On the eve of World War I, foreigners represented 14 percent of the Swiss population, a level that was to be reached again only during the 1960s. In contrast to Swedish ore or lumber, Switzerland exported more value-added products: at that time manufactured goods represented over 90

[28] Peter A. Swenson, *Capitalists against markets: the making of labor markets and welfare states in the United States and Sweden* (Oxford: Oxford University Press, 2002), pp. 71–98.

[29] Ibid., pp. 47–60. On American employers' federations, see Colin Gordon, "Why no corporatism in the United States? Business disorganization and its consequences", *Business and Economic History* 27/1 (1998), pp. 29–46.

percent of exports, and overall productivity was higher than in Sweden.[30] With a more diversified economy and access to cheaper foreign labor, Swiss employers had more elbow room than their Swedish counterparts and did not push toward an early centralization of wage bargaining; rather, an American-style segmentalism reigned in industrial relations.

Key business associations founded in the first decade of the twentieth century, such as the Swiss Employers' Federation (Zentralverband schweizerischer Arbeitgeberorganisationen, hereafter Arbeitgeberverband), which collaborated closely with the Vorort, explicitly refused to engage in collective bargaining. Export-oriented sectors were keen to retain flexible wage-setting mechanisms in the face of international competition. They were unwilling to negotiate with unions that they did not consider able to ensure the implementation of collective agreements among the rank and file. Before the late 1930s, collective bargaining was confined to domestic trades, covered few workers, and did not spread to leading manufacturing industries.[31] Unlike Swedish employers, Swiss business federations always supported the right of individual employers to develop voluntary welfare schemes. This segmentalist labor market strategy geared Swiss old age provision toward a trajectory that echoed the path of social policy development in the United States.

## The first uncertain steps toward old age provision

Both the limitations of the 1890 constitutional amendment and the struggle over health and accident insurance conspired to keep federal pensions off the political agenda. Before World War I, old age coverage was the preserve of cantonal and municipal schemes and of pioneering occupational plans. This section presents a quantitative and qualitative assessment of this patchwork and retraces the early involvement of life insurance companies in pension provision.

Around 1900, very few of the 2,000 mutual benefit societies in operation explicitly provided coverage for old age, and genuine pension plans were rare. There were 147 such plans in 1903, a number that had changed

[30] Thomas David, "Croissance économique et mondialisation: le cas de la Suisse 1870–1914", in *Globalisierung – Chancen und Risiken: die Schweiz in der Weltwirtschaft 18.–20. Jahrhundert*, ed. Hans-Jörg Gilomen, *et al.* (Zurich: Chronos, 2004), pp. 145–70 (pp. 151, 158–60); Angus Maddison, *L'économie mondiale 1820–1992* (Paris: OCDE, 1995), p. 267.

[31] Bernard Degen and Markus Kübler, "Die Gewerkschaften zwischen Integration und Ausgrenzung", in *Krisen und Stabilisierung: die Schweiz in der Zwischenkriegszeit*, ed. Sébastien Guex and Brigitte Studer (Zurich: Chronos, 1998), pp. 127–43 (pp. 134–6); Robert Fluder *et al.*, *Gewerkschaften und Angestelltenverbände in der schweizerischen Privatwirtschaft* (Zurich: Seismo Verlag, 1991), pp. 213–16.

little since the 1860s. Occupational old age coverage reached – including double counts – at most 6 percent of the non-farm workforce at the dawn of the twentieth century. In 1911, just before the vote on the second Lex Forrer, 5 percent of the non-farm workforce was affiliated to 100 "core" pension plans (see Tables A.1, p. 290, and A.2, p. 295).[32] This proportion was broadly comparable to coverage in the same period by British occupational schemes, and superior to the American coverage level (see Table 0.2, p. 24). However, if one-third of public-sector workers were already affiliated to pension plans, the proportion of those insured was a paltry 1 percent in the private sector (see Table A.2).

From the 1880s onward, old age pensions had become common for public employees and workers at the municipal and cantonal levels of government. Public-sector retirement benefits developed in cities that modernized their municipal administration, such as Basle, Berne, Zurich, and Geneva, where pensions covered over one-third of public employees on the eve of World War I.[33] Railroad retirement plans bolstered public-sector pension coverage. As in the United States and other European countries, Swiss railroad companies were among the first corporations to introduce old age provision schemes. In 1891, five major railroad networks operated pension plans covering almost 10,000 workers. After the nationalization of railroad companies in 1898, a development that marked a watershed in the expansion of the federal state, railroad pension plans were administered by the Confederation, and by 1918 would number more than 20,000 members.[34] Given their strategic importance and their intercantonal operations, railroad plans were also the first to be regulated by the Confederation. Well before the nationalization of railroads, federal laws enacted during the 1870s and 1880s required that these pension schemes be regularly audited and be independent of their

[32] The term "core plans" designates genuine pension plans set up by employers and public administrations, as well as group plans managed by life insurance companies. These two forms of "insurance institutions" are not comparable to more informal "relief institutions" distributing old age assistance. This distinction is discussed in the quantitative appendix of this book (see p. 289).

[33] On public-sector pension plans, see *Pensionskassenstatistik 1925a*, pp. 7–26, Dymowski, *Die Alters- und Invaliden-Versicherung*, pp. 143–61. For a case study of Canton Valais, see Joanna Vanay, "Le Valais et la vieillesse au début du 20[e] siècle: la transition de la charité vers la prévoyance", *Aspects de la sécurité sociale* 3 (2002), pp. 10–16.

[34] Railroad pension plans also distributed the lion's share of early old age benefits. In 1903, around 4,000 former rail workers received old age or disability benefits. In 1891, the five major private railroad networks had already distributed 2,000 pensions. See E. Dübi, "Transportarbeiter (XII: Wohlfahrtsinstitutionen der schweizerischen Eisenbahnerschaft)", in *Handwörterbuch der schweizerischen Volkswirtschaft, Sozialpolitik und Verwaltung*, ed. Naum Reichesberg (Berne: Verlag Encyclopädie, 1911), pp. 1066–74 (p. 1067).

founding firms, and that employees' benefits should be protected in the event of bankruptcies.[35]

In contrast to railway workers, federal civil servants and postal workers were reduced to setting up their own mutual relief funds and, not unlike their counterparts in the United States, had to wait until the aftermath of World War I to benefit from state pensions. Before then, proposals to grant benefits were turned down, first in 1867 by the Federal Assembly and then in 1891 after a referendum campaign led by farmers' associations opposed to the development of the federal bureaucracy. The whole issue came to a standstill during the KUVG debates. Civil servants' petitions and federal authorities' claims that the lack of pensions delayed the modernization of the federal administration could not prevail.[36] The belated development of pension provision was due to the conservative opposition encountered by social policy and the underdevelopment of federal bureaucracy before World War I. Political campaigns against the alleged privileges enjoyed by federal employees would also resurface during the interwar years and again serve as rallying points for opponents of social policy.

Before 1914, the western Switzerland cantons of Neuchâtel and Vaud had set up voluntary retirement programs. However, these schemes, which were favored by local Liberal-Conservative elites opposed to mandatory social insurance, were more akin to state-encouraged individual saving accounts than genuine pensions and invariably covered a minute proportion of the population. Several other cantons tried to follow suit, but none of these projects had been implemented by the outbreak of the war.[37] These cantonal schemes replicated commercial insurance products aimed at skilled workers and the middle class. Moreover, while most public-sector pension plans were administered by cantonal or city governments, some were outsourced to insurance companies. With the delayed introduction of pensions for federal civil servants, this blurring of

[35] Karl Greiner, "Die Personalversicherung als Ergänzung der staatlichen Sozialversicherung", *Schweizerische Zeitschrift für Volkswirtschaft und Statistik* (1930), pp. 362–85 (quotation p. 362).

[36] Felix Roch, "Gründung einer Alters-, Invaliden-, Witwen- und Waisenkasse für das Personal eidgenössischer Verwaltungen", *Schweizerische Blätter für Wirtschaft und Sozialpolitik* (1910), pp. 321–42. See also "Message du Conseil fédéral à l'Assemblée fédérale concernant l'attribution à la Confédération du droit de légiférer en matière d'assurance-invalidité, vieillesse et survivants, et la création des ressources nécessaires à la Confédération pour les assurances sociales, du 21 juin 1919", in *Feuille Fédérale* (Berne: Chancellerie fédérale, 1919), pp. iv, 1–234 (pp. 58–64).

[37] *Pensionskassenstatistik 1941*, pp. 103–24; Bruno Dumons, "Vieillesse et Etat-providence en Suisse romande dans la première moitié du XXe siècle", *Le Mouvement social* 190 (2000), pp. 9–31; Dymowski, *Die Alters- und Invaliden-Versicherung*, pp. 92–138. By 1914, cantonal old age provision was on the political agenda in Geneva, St. Gallen, Glarus, Solothurn, Zurich, Appenzell Ausserrhoden, Argovia, Basle, Berne and Lucerne.

boundaries between the public and private sectors was a specificity that differentiated Switzerland from its neighbors.[38]

Accident insurance companies had been outspoken opponents of the KUVG. By contrast, life insurance companies had remained in the background during the fierce battles on the Lex Forrer, as they were not active in either accident compensation or health provision, the fiefdom of mutual benefit societies. However, life insurers actively promoted private alternatives to state-based insurance, a strategy that was not unique to Switzerland. As historian Jennifer Klein reminds us, "the struggle against social insurance and government intervention in the employment relation [was] the original impetus for group insurance", or collective insurance contracts covering employees for the risk of health or old age.[39] As in the United Kingdom, American and Canadian insurance companies also marketed "industrial insurance" or "life annuity" policies to encourage private savings and self-help among the working class. German insurers had also introduced these as a direct reaction to state-based accident and health insurance.[40]

In Switzerland, the location of insurers at the "intersection of business and social service" took on a peculiar dimension because of the pre-eminence of the Swiss Society for Life and Pension Insurance (Schweizerische Lebensversicherungs- und Rentenanstalt, now Swiss Life) among other companies, and its strategic position at the confluence of the financial and political establishments. This mutual firm – founded in 1857 under the leadership of Crédit Suisse – was intended both as a vessel to centralize savings in a period of industrial expansion and as a way to ensure political and social stability by encouraging life insurance and thriftiness. Zurich business elites and notables from the Radical establishment crowded onto the board of directors of Rentenanstalt.[41] This intimacy with Radical politicians meant that the company acted almost as an extension of the federal state. Because of its actuarial knowledge, the company became an essential interlocutor of the state and, from the 1880s

38 On western European public-sector retirement plans, see *Pensionssysteme im öffentlichen Dienst in Westeuropa (19./20. Jh.)*, (Baden-Baden: Nomos, 2000).

39 Klein, *For all these rights*, p. 52.

40 Rodgers, *Atlantic crossings*, pp. 209–35, 62. On Canada, see Kenneth Bryden, *Old age pensions and policy-making in Canada* (Montreal: McGill-Queen's University Press, 1974), pp. 36–7. On Britain, see Paul Johnson, *Saving and spending: the working-class economy in Britain, 1870–1939* (Oxford/New York: Clarendon Press/Oxford University Press, 1985), pp. 11–47. On Germany, see Lengwiler, *Risikopolitik im Sozialstaat*, pp. 166–7.

41 *Société suisse d'assurances générales sur la vie humaine 1857–1957*, (Zurich: Rentenanstalt, 1956). On the political connections of Rentenanstalt, see Robin Pearson, "The birth pains of a global reinsurer: Swiss Re of Zurich, 1864–1879", *Financial History Review* 8/1 (2001), pp. 27–47 (pp. 28–31); Pollux, *Versicherungs-Zauber* (Zurich: Genossenschaftendruckerei, 1945), pp. 30–3 (see Chapter 3, note 127, regarding Pollux).

onward, was systematically represented in the commission of experts on social insurance. Thanks to its insider status, Rentenanstalt would enjoy a vanguard position among employers in the field of old age provision and exert a decisive influence on the shaping of federal pensions. There are two products with social policy aims developed by insurers before 1914, group contracts and "popular life insurance", the Swiss version of industrial insurance, worth examining more closely.

Until the 1920s, Rentenanstalt was the only company to propose group life insurance contracts for public administrations and private firms. From the 1860s, these contracts, at first more similar to bundled individual life insurance policies than genuine pension plans, covered teachers in several cantons and municipalities, as well as the faculty of the Zurich-based Federal Institute of Technology. This outsourcing of public pensions to the private sector underscored the para-state functions of Rentenanstalt. In 1863, the biggest group contract of the company covered approximately 1,000 workers of the Nordostbahn, a railroad network with close links to Crédit Suisse. However, early group contracts did not attract much interest from employers, and in 1870 the Nordostbahn ended its collaboration with Rentenanstalt and set up its own company plan. Between 1890 and 1914, Rentenanstalt signed only a handful of new contracts (covering, for example, the employees of the highbrow *Neue Zürcher Zeitung* and clerks of small regional banks).[42] As we will see in Chapter 3, the growth of group pensions would take place in the aftermath of World War I.

As controversy raged around the first Lex Forrer, Rentenanstalt also introduced a product specifically aimed at the working class: the "popular life insurance" (Volksversicherung). Not coincidentally, insurers developed this new product right after the first 1893 meetings of the commission of federal experts on health and accident insurance. During these meetings, Conrad Widmer, former director of Rentenanstalt, criticized the idea of social insurance and advised the adoption of solutions relying on private providers.[43] Thanks to its close links with the Radical establishment, Rentenanstalt signed an agreement in 1894 with the federal government that enabled individual policyholders to pay their weekly Volksversicherung premiums at any post office. This public–private partnership spurred on the growth of these policies, and a second company, Basler Life, soon joined Rentenanstalt in this market. Despite their impressive

[42] Dr. Martha Gut, "Unterlagen für die Geschichte der Gruppenversicherung" [n.d., ca. 1956], pp. 1–9, file 615.642/1, Historisches Archiv Rentenanstalt/Swiss Life (Swiss Life corporate archives, Zurich, hereafter SLA). On early group insurance, see also Hans Asch, *Die Gruppenlebensversicherung: mit besonderer Berücksichtigung der Schweiz* (Berne: Stämpfli, 1930).

[43] Lengwiler, *Risikopolitik im Sozialstaat*, pp. 53–4.

expansion at the beginning of the twentieth century, Volksversicherung policies remained of secondary importance in comparison with ordinary life insurance contracts. As in the United Kingdom, these policies constituted low-cost individual savings accounts mostly used to cover burial costs.[44] Promoters of the Volksversicherung described it as a welcome "supplement" to the future KUVG. Its *raison d'être* lay in the fact that, unlike social insurance, the Volksversicherung constituted a form of "voluntary self-help free from any compulsory character", and that "state-based organization of the collectivity should not tread on territories where the use of one's own forces is sufficient". For some, Volksversicherung schemes might even render social insurance obsolete, especially if subscription to an individual savings account was made compulsory by the state.[45]

Such statements echoed similar positions held by American life insurers toward the nascent welfare state. Paul Morton, president of Equitable Life, boasted in a speech to the industry in 1909 that "insurance by the state [was] neither desirable nor necessary in this land of the greatest life insurance corporations the world has ever known".[46] Contemporary critics of the Volksversicherung replied that individual solutions did not cover the neediest cases and were plagued by hefty management costs. In addition, late payment of weekly premiums, a common occurrence during periods of illness or unemployment, could lead to the termination of contracts and loss of benefits. Behind its alleged benevolent aims, critics explained, the Volksversicherung represented above all a clever marketing instrument to siphon workers' savings into the coffers of life insurance companies.[47]

The individual solutions favored by proponents of Volksversicherung contracts constitute a red thread that can be followed throughout and beyond the twentieth century. Individual retirement accounts managed by financial institutions would be presented as an alternative to federal

44 In 1900, Rentenanstalt managed 12,000 Volksversicherung policies (4,000 at Basler Life). By 1925, the number of policies had reached 119,000 (259,000 at Basler Life). See *75 Jahre Basler Lebens-Versicherungs-Gesellschaft Basel 1864–1939* (Basle: Frobenius, 1941), pp. 16–17; Hermann Renfer, "Die Entwicklung der Volksversicherung in der Schweiz", in *Transactions of the Eighth International Congress of Actuaries held in London, 27th to 30th June 1927* (London: Layton, 1927), pp. 37–45 (volume IV).

45 Josef Litschi, "Die schweizerische Volksversicherung an der schweizerischen Lebensversicherungs- und Rentenanstalt", *Schweizerische Blätter für Wirtschaft und Sozialpolitik* (1895), pp. 677–90 (quotation p. 690); Siegfried Mehler, *Die Volksversicherung in der Schweiz* (Leipzig: Deichert, 1906).

46 Quoted in Klein, *For all these rights*, p. 21.

47 Albin Drexler, "Die kapitalistische und die sociale Versicherungsökonomie", *Schweizerische Blätter für Wirtschaft und Sozialpolitik* (1898), pp. 594–612, (1st part), 34–41 (2nd part), 58–705 (3rd part).

pensions, albeit with little success, during the 1931 and 1947 referenda campaigns against old age insurance. At the beginning of the third millennium, self-help has made an impressive comeback: third-pillar savings accounts – to use late-twentieth-century terminology – are again presented as an attractive alternative to collective forms of pension provision organized by the state or employers.

Before World War I, life insurance companies tried to pre-empt the development of social insurance and to occupy terrain left vacant because of protracted social policy struggles. With the development of the Volksversicherung and group life insurance, we can discern the emergence, in a still tentative form, of the strategy that would unfold after World War I. First, social insurance had either to be resisted, as it might constrict insurers' markets, or be pre-empted through the development of private alternatives. However, if social insurance programs were finally introduced, they had to be contained at a minimum level to leave space for supplementary forms of provision set up by private providers. Insurers' statements acknowledging the necessity for social insurance but affirming at the same time the need to pre-empt it and to limit its scale and scope were to become recurrent during the following decades, especially when the issue of federal pensions and employer-based occupational plans became increasingly intertwined.

On the eve of World War I, private firms were lagging behind public administrations in pension provision. As mentioned above, barely 1 percent of the total private workforce was covered by core pension plans in 1911. Coverage was higher in the printing trade, where labor and management had developed jointly managed pension schemes, as well as in local transport firms that followed the trend set by the federal railways (see Table A.5, p. 299). In retailing, pension coverage spread after the creation, in 1909, of a multi-employer pension plan by the Consumers' Cooperatives Union (Verband schweizerischer Konsumvereine). Yet pensions were still rare in the textile industry, the traditional sector of nineteenth-century industrialization: in 1912, fewer than one in ten Zurich textile firms provided some kind of old age benefit.[48] Pension plans in textile or machine-making firms covered at most 1 percent of their respective workforce. However, before the war, leading metal and machine-making entrepreneurs had developed welfare funds and other relief schemes that constituted a step toward the establishment of genuine pension plans (see Table 1.1). In 1898, eighteen retirement welfare funds

48 Albert Hablützel, *Die Angestellten- und Arbeiter Wohlfahrtseinrichtungen der zürzerischen Maschinen- und Textilindustrie* (Winterthur: Buchdruck Winterthur, 1929); Hans Handschin, *Die Sozialleistungen des V. S. K. und seiner Verbandsvereine zugunsten ihrer Angestellten* (Basle: Verband schweiz. Konsumvereine, 1940).

Table 1.1 *Old age provision in leading metal and machine-making firms, 1880s–1920s.*

| | |
|---|---|
| Brown & Boveri | **1900** two welfare funds (Wohlfahrtsfonds) for white-collar and blue-collar workers<br>**1923–1924** support fund (Unterstützungsfonds) for blue-collar workers, pension plan (Pensionskasse) for white-collar employees |
| Escher Wyss | **1830–1850s** various relief schemes (Hilfskassen) to provide "against illness and destitution, old age, disability and loss of income during military duties"<br>**1925** old age, survivors' and disability plans for white-collar employees |
| Sulzer | **1871** group life contracts with Rentenanstalt<br>**1920** pension plan and group contracts for white-collar employees |
| Von Roll | **1868** Hilfskasse for sickness, death, and old age<br>**1897** Pensionskasse for overseers, foremen, and white-collar employees<br>**1918–1920** Pensionskasse for white-collar employees, and assistance fund for old age and disability personnel |
| Schweiz. Lokomotiv- und Maschinenfabrik (SLM), Landis & Gyr (L&G), Georg Fischer (GF), Rieter, Aluminum Industrie (AIAG) | **before 1914** various relief schemes (all companies)<br>**1919** Pensions- und Unterstützungskasse (SLM)<br>**1920** Pensionskasse (L&G)<br>**1920s** Pensionskasse for white-collar employees and savings plans for blue-collar workers (GF, Rieter, AIAG) |

*Sources:* **Brown & Boveri:** K. Stoll, "Die Alters- und Invalidenvorsorge für die kaufmännische Angestellten in der Schweiz", *Schweizerische Blätter für Wirtschaft und Sozialpolitik* (1904), p. 142; Karl Sachs, *50 Jahre Brown Boveri: 1891–1941* (Baden: Brown Boveri, 1941); Mario König, Hannes Siegrist and Rudolf Vetterli, *Warten und Aufrücken: die Angestellten in der Schweiz, 1870–1950* (Zurich: Chronos, 1985), pp. 103–5. **Escher Wyss:** Hans-Peter Schär, *Aufbau und Bedeutung privater Pensionskassen in der Schweiz* (Winterthur: Keller, 1958), p. 18. **Sulzer, SLM:** Albert Hablützel, *Die Angestellten- und Arbeiter Wohlfahrtseinrichtungen der zürzerischen Maschinen- und Textilindustrie* (Winterthur: Buchdruck Winterthur, 1929), p. 31. **Von Roll:** Walter Bieber, *Die sozialen Einrichtungen der solothurnischen Industrie* (Olten: Dietschi, 1946), p. 23; André Kienzle, *Es gibt nur ein Gerlafingen! Herrschaft, Kultur und soziale Integration in einer Standortgemeinde des Stahlkonzerns Von Roll, 1918–1939* (Zurich: Chronos, 1997), p. 338 (note 97). **Landis & Gyr:** Hans Gerold Wirz, *Die Personal-Wohlfahrtseinrichtungen der schweizerischen Privatwirtschaft: ihre Stellung im Steuerrecht und ihre Beaufsichtigung* (Stäfa: Buchdruckerei Stäfa, 1955), p. 53. **Georg Fischer, Rieter, Aluminium Industrie:** Rudolf Vetterli, *Industriearbeit, Arbeiterbewusstsein und gewerkschaftliche Organisation*, pp. 132–9; Gerold Ermatinger, *Kapital und Ethos: Die sozialen und kulturellen Taten des schweizerischen Privatkapitals im 19. und 20. Jahrhundert* (Zurich/Leipzig: Rotapfel Verlag, 1936), pp. 47, 79; Mario König *et al.*, *Warten und Aufrücken*, p. 507 (note 68).

(Wohlfahrtsfonds) operated in the banking sector, with 1 million Swiss francs (CHF) in assets. The first genuine pension plan in banking was set up in 1887 by the Banque cantonale vaudoise (state bank of Canton Vaud), followed in 1913 by the private Basler Handelsbank. Coverage remained low in the banking sector before World War I.[49] In contrast, pensions were well-developed among insurance companies. Most had set up formalized retirement schemes that covered two-fifths of the workforce by 1911 (see Table A.5, p. 299).

Employer pension schemes contributed to the modernization of business benevolence that is generally described as welfare capitalism or "company-based social policy" (betriebliche Sozialpolitik).[50] Like their European and North American counterparts, Swiss entrepreneurs developed these institutions to bind a workforce to their firms and to "contribute to the creation of a culture of industry".[51] The term "rooting workers" is used repeatedly in contemporary depictions of employer social programs. As historian Geneviève Billeter points out in her study of metal and machine-making entrepreneurs, the aim of these selective social measures was to "form squads of loyal workers" because "employers of course prefer[ed] the commitment to the workshop and its four walls to the development of class consciousness".[52] Early arguments in favor of employee benefits emphasized that pensions could be used to reduce labor turnover or to boost workers' productivity.[53]

Pension schemes were also used to fight off labor organizations. For example, the creation in 1898 of a fund for older workers (Alterszulagenkasse) by the metal firm Georg Fischer had as much to do with the

[49] Hans Lyner, *Die Personalfürsorge im schweizerischen Bankwesen* (Wald: W. Hess, 1930), pp. 14–17. Crédit Suisse and Basler Handelsbank concentrated more than half of banking pension assets (respectively 43 and 12 percent). See "Pensions-, Unterstützungs-, Invaliden- und sonstige Hülfsfonds der schweizerischen Bankinstitute", *Schweizerische Blätter für Wirtschaft und Sozialpolitik* (1900), p. 355.

[50] Jacoby, *Modern manors: welfare capitalism since the New Deal*, pp. 11–34; Sylvie Schweitzer, ed., *Logiques d'entreprises et politiques sociales des XIXe et XXe siècles* (Lyons: Centre Jacques Cartier, 1993); Thomas Welskopp, "Betriebliche Sozialpolitik im 19. und frühen 20. Jahrhundert: eine Diskussion neuerer Forschungen und Konzepte und eine Branchenanalyse der deutschen und amerikanischen Eisen- und Stahlindustrie von den 1870er bis zu den 1930er Jahren", *Archiv für Sozialgeschichte* 34 (1994), pp. 333–74.

[51] Hans Gerold Wirz, *Die Personal-Wohlfahrtseinrichtungen der schweizerischen Privatwirtschaft: ihre Stellung im Steuerrecht und ihre Beaufsichtigung* (Stäfa: Buchdruckerei Stäfa, 1955), p. 109.

[52] Geneviève Billeter, *Le pouvoir patronal* (Geneva: Droz, 1985), pp. 26–7. See also Gruner, *Arbeiterschaft und Wirtschaft in der Schweiz 1880–1914*, p. 1364 (volume II/2).

[53] Arnold Guise, *Die Alters- und Invalidenfürsorge im schweizerischen Handel und in der schweizerischen Industrie: nach Material gesammelt von der Technischen Gesellschaft Baden* (Brugg: Effingerhof, 1916); Johann Jakob Kummer, "L'assurance des employés c'est-à-dire l'application de l'assurance dans la prévoyance en faveur des employés et de leur famille", *Schweizerische Zeitschrift für Volkswirtschaft und Statistik* (1889), pp. 421–42.

determination to use social measures as a "corporate weapon against labor organizations" as with employer benevolence. Retirement benefits constituted the answer by Georg Fischer's board of directors to the creation of a workers' mutual aid society. The bonus fund served primarily to placate the workforce when the company was expanding and wanted to avoid labor strife. A few years after this, the board reduced without notice the endowment of the fund. While acknowledging the positive role of pension benefits in labor relations, the board of directors admitted candidly that financing them was not necessary, as labor unrest was receding.[54]

Discretionary benefits remained the norm. Among eighty-two large firms surveyed by the Baden Technical Society at the outbreak of World War I, half answered that they had set up some kind of old age assistance, but only five of them had set up a pension plan. Only a dozen welfare institutions had formal statutes. Moreover, employers often refused to introduce financing schemes that relied on payroll contributions, in order to deflect workers' demands for a voice in pension plan management.[55] Commenting on this progress, Arnold Guise of the Baden Technical Society assessed it as "unfortunately rather unsatisfactory . . . [and] even less satisfactory if we consider that only the large firms have been surveyed". In the end, deplored Guise, "only a negligible percentage of private personnel" enjoyed pension coverage.[56] Further surveys undertaken before the war similarly noted that workers' rights to benefits depended on employers' goodwill and could be terminated without further notice or denied to striking or dismissed employees. Considered as corporate gratuities, occupational benefits were reserved for those handpicked by management and, apart from packages offered to high-ranking employees, seldom went beyond "alleviating deprivation".[57]

Opponents of corporate pension plans pointed out that workers had to be wary of the "unhealthy chains of entrepreneurs' charity", as such schemes offered no guarantees for employees. In this context, a secretary

[54] Rudolf Vetterli, *Industriearbeit, Arbeiterbewusstsein und gewerkschaftliche Organisation: dargestellt am Beispiel der Georg Fischer AG (1890–1930)* (Göttingen: Vandenhoeck & Ruprecht, 1978), pp. 132–9 (quotation p. 32).

[55] Guise, *Die Alters- und Invalidenfürsorge*, pp. 37–9.

[56] According to a 1917 conference quoted by "Message du Conseil fédéral à l'Assemblée fédérale concernant l'attribution à la Confédération du droit de légiférer en matière d'assurance-invalidité, vieillesse et survivants, et la création des ressources nécessaires à la Confédération pour les assurances sociales, du 21 juin 1919", p. 44.

[57] Hans-Peter Schär, *Aufbau und Bedeutung privater Pensionskassen in der Schweiz* (Winterthur: Keller, 1958), p. 19 (quotation); K. Stoll, "Die Alters- und Invalidenvorsorge für die kaufmännische Angestellten in der Schweiz", *Schweizerische Blätter für Wirtschaft und Sozialpolitik* (1904), pp. 137–45 (1st part); 79–91 (2nd part) (quotation pp. 142–3).

of the railroad workers' union argued that corporate benefits were not based on a right to social welfare but remained marked by the "odium of charity". Negative depictions of employer-based welfare schemes as "bogus", a "scourge", or a "menace" were not uncommon.[58] Some critics urged workers' organizations to set up union-based provision in order to counteract the employers. However, retirement benefits were rare among trade union mutual benefit societies that focused on sickness, unemployment, and strike benefits. In 1911, only twenty-five membership-based retirement schemes, set up mainly by transport workers or printing shops, were in operation. Labor welfare schemes found their origins in the long tradition of fraternal self-help.[59] They not only considered employer-based schemes competitors, but also were often distrustful of social insurance programs enacted by a bourgeois state that showed little sympathy for labor interests. By emphasizing their autonomy in the area of social provision, trade unions put obstacles on the difficult path to the introduction of social insurance and, as the following chapters show in more detail, found themselves increasingly gravitating toward social schemes controlled by employers.

Early pension plans often lacked actuarial rules and formal statutes. As mentioned earlier, railroad pension schemes had been subjected to federal supervision in the late 1870s. In 1888, the Federal Council refused to extend this measure to other pension plans because of their limited and local development. In 1903, statistician Hermann Kinkelin, one of the key experts in the KUVG debate, pointed to the weak financial foundations of retirement schemes. However, his call for a regulation of pension plans modeled on the federal law on private insurance found no echo. Similarly, the issue of occupational plans was only superficially touched by the 1914 revision of the federal law on industrial factories.[60] Pension plan regulation remained the prerogative of cantonal or local authorities but remained, at best, minimal. This absence of regulation reflected the

[58] Bernhard Kaufmann, *Arbeiterwohlfahrtseinrichtungen in kritischer Beleuchtung* (Zurich: Buchhandlung des schweizerischen Grütlivereins, 1905), p. 21; Schär, *Aufbau und bedeutung privater Pensionskassen*, p. 17.

[59] Hermann Dommer, "Das Kassenwesen von fünf ausgewählten Gewerkschaften 1904–1913", in *Arbeiterschaft und Wirtschaft in der Schweiz 1880–1914*, ed. Andreas Balthasar, *et al.* (Zurich, 1988), pp. 1299–338; "Message du Conseil fédéral à l'Assemblée fédérale concernant l'attribution à la Confédération du droit de légiférer en matière d'assurance-invalidité, vieillesse et survivants, et la création des ressources nécessaires à la Confédération pour les assurances sociales, du 21 juin 1919", pp. 74–6. See also *Pensionskassenstatistik 1941*, pp. 304–5.

[60] Hans Christen, "Die finanzielle Lage der Pensionskassen", *Schweizerische Zeitschrift für Volkswirtschaft und Statistik* (1938), pp. 40–68, p. 42; Karl Greiner, *Aufbau und Finanzierung der Alters- und Hinterbliebenenversicherung in den Kantonen* (Zurich: Orell Füssli, 1935), p. 362.

underdevelopment of pension plans before World War I. However, despite the subsequent expansion of occupational schemes, lax regulation would remain the norm for most of the twentieth century. Corporate resistance to state intrusion into employer-based welfare would play a key role in delaying the implementation of pension plan regulation.

In the early days of pension provision, Switzerland diverged from countries that had already introduced statutory pensions such as Germany, Austria, and Denmark, but also from France, Sweden, the United Kingdom, and the Netherlands, which had set up non-contributory means-tested pensions before World War I. The intervention of the Confederation in pension provision remained limited. Decentralized forms of old age provision were slowly on the rise, but their development remained patchy. With the exception of public administrations and a handful of pioneering firms, the overwhelming majority of workers were still unaffiliated to a pension plan. Instead, individual forms of provision – such as Volksversicherung contracts or cantonal voluntary retirement schemes – provided meager coverage against the hazards of old age.

During the first decade of the twentieth century, the transformation of industrial production, changes in family structure, and increasing life expectancy all contributed to growing debates on the necessity of old age provision. However, as the protracted struggles on the KUVG and the resistance to pensions for federal civil servants highlighted the obstacles confronting social insurance, proponents of pensions hesitated as to which path to follow. Those who advocated private solutions envisioned an extension of coverage based on company plans and reliance on the expertise of life insurance companies. Critics of "capitalist insurance" relentlessly attacked employer-based schemes and advocated instead non-profit solutions based on cooperative or trade union structures.[61]

In 1908, the Zurich section of the Socialist Party considered old age and disability insurance a "social necessity" that ought to replace inadequate poor relief and voluntary solutions. However, the conservative resistance displayed during the constitution of the KUVG made the federal path seem risky. Socialists advocated the introduction of pensions in cantons where the left held more parliamentary power than in the Federal Assembly. The same year, a conference of cantonal relief works administrators also spoke in favor of a standardization of the assistance measures for the elderly poor that were then set up in a haphazard way by local and

[61] Guise, *Die Alters- und Invalidenfürsorge*; Kummer, "L'assurance des employés". For a critique of "capitalist" insurance, see Albin Drexler, "Die Alters-, Invaliden- und Hinterlassenen-Versicherung auf genossenschaftlich-sozialer Grundlage", *Schweizerische Blätter für Wirtschaft und Sozialpolitik* (1913–1914), pp. 449–81 (1st part), 544–62 (2nd part).

cantonal authorities. However, for the author of a 1915 study underlining the "laggardness" of Switzerland in old age provision, this was not enough: the cantonal path led to an "alarming fragmentation" of provision that could be solved only by a federal scheme.[62]

Key questions related to the organization, financing, and scope of old age pensions were still largely unclear, and the issue of retirement had yet to become a major policy debate. The terms of the debate around old age provision were radically reshaped after 1914. The social and political impact of World War I opened a new phase of social policy development that would span three decades and whose outcome would culminate in 1947 with the implementation of federal pensions. The establishing of old age insurance and the parallel development of occupational pensions are detailed in the next two chapters of this study. Several elements that had marked the dress rehearsal for social policy, such as the fragmentation of old age provision, federalist opposition to social insurance, and referendum politics, would continue to play a key role in pension debates. Moreover, both the growing importance of corporate schemes and the involvement of insurers in policy-making would bring to the fore the issue of the division of labor between social insurance and occupational provision.

62 Dymowski, *Die Alters- und Invaliden-Versicherung*, pp. 123–4 (relief works conference), 206, 210 (quotation); T. H. Graf, "Ueber Alters- und Invalidenversicherung", *Schweizerische Blätter für Wirtschaft und Sozialpolitik* (1909), pp. 11–23 (1st part), 49–58 (2nd part).

# 2 Laying the foundations of a divided pension system (1914–1938)

Among the industrialized countries, Germany, Austria, France, the United Kingdom, Australia, New Zealand, Sweden, and Denmark had introduced universal or means-tested pension schemes before 1914. During the interwar decades, Belgium, Italy, Canada, the Netherlands, Norway, and the United States followed suit. By 1935, when the Social Security Act was introduced in the United States, Switzerland was one of the only European industrialized countries without national-level pensions.[1] Yet, old age and survivors' insurance (Alters- und Hinterlassenenversicherung, AHV) constituted a very contentious item on the Swiss postwar political agenda. After a decade of political debate, the law introducing federal pensions was challenged by a referendum and defeated in 1931. The demise of the Lex Schulthess – named after its Radical architect, Federal Councilor Edmund Schulthess – postponed the introduction of pensions until the aftermath of World War II.

The struggle for the AHV was carried out in the public arena and endured a conflict-ridden and protracted policy-making process. In contrast, occupational provision began its expansion behind the scenes, in particular in the interstices of the tax code, and its evolution was rarely the focus of public controversies. This subterranean process coexisted with the highly contentious politics of social insurance. The first two sections of this chapter are devoted to these diverging trajectories.

In the aftermath of the war, political upheavals put the issue of social insurance at the top of the agenda. However, the path toward the implementation of the AHV was soon blocked by a conservative political rollback, even as business efforts to develop occupational provision came to fruition. Spurred on by tax exemptions, employers' responses to worker militancy, and modernization of corporate welfare measures, the growth of occupational plans led to the emergence of a politically active pension lobby. Stalemate and failure in the realm of social insurance contrasted

[1] Manfred G. Schmidt, *Sozialpolitik: historische Entwicklung und internationaler Vergleich* (Opladen: Leske and Budrich, 1988), pp. 117–36.

with the expansion of occupational provision. The third and fourth sections below argue that controversies over the boundaries between federal pensions and existing occupational plans contributed significantly to the final demise of the Lex Schulthess in 1931.

The fifth section presents an overview of social policy during the Depression, when occupational provision continued its expansion, albeit at a slower pace, while the development of social insurance was stuck in neutral. The fates of these two areas of insurance provision constituted a key moment in the history of the pension system. The respective legacies of occupational provision and the first unsuccessful attempt to introduce federal pensions set the trajectory of the pension system toward a multi-pillar configuration. The sixth and final section of this chapter elaborates on the comparative perspectives introduced in the preceding chapter and, in particular, discusses the similarities between the trajectories followed by the Swiss and American pension systems. Although proposals for Swiss social insurance came to a standstill at the very moment when the Social Security Act 1935 – the "big bang" of social policy in the United States – was enacted, both countries continued to be characterized by divided pension systems.

## Seven lean years: the gridlock of social insurance in the aftermath of World War I

Despite being a non-belligerent country, Switzerland was profoundly affected by the socio-economic and political upheavals of World War I. For workers, the wartime years were synonymous with inflation, wage freezes, decreasing standards of living, and, especially in the second half of the conflict, social misery. Food shortages and problems in the distribution of basic commodities were widespread in urban centers. The deterioration of living conditions emphasized the lack of preparation by the political authorities for the protracted war situation, and was particularly severe for the families of mobilized soldiers, reliant on insufficient soldiers' pay and means-tested assistance to compensate for lost wages. At the end of the war, around one-sixth of the population was eligible for the relief measures set up in haste by federal, cantonal, and local authorities.[2]

[2] As we will see in Chapter 4, a federal insurance scheme to offset income loss during military service was only introduced in 1940. On World War I assistance measures for soldiers, see Karl Attinger, *Les caisses de compensation militaires: le régime des allocations pour perte de salaire institué par l'Arrêté du Conseil Fédéral du 20 décembre 1939 et ses répercussions* (Zurich: Sihl, 1946), pp. 1–5. On World War I and the interwar period, see Hans Ulrich Jost, "Menaces et repliement (1914–1945)", in *Nouvelle histoire de la Suisse et des Suisses*

In contrast to urban workers, farmers profited from the skyrocketing prices of agricultural products on the domestic market during the war, while exporters of machines, chemical products, watch-related products (timers and fuses), and textiles (especially clothing manufacturers) profited handsomely from their positions as neutral suppliers to both sides. Export dynamism was so great that the balance of trade was positive in 1916, an exceptional occurrence for the Swiss economy. Corporate profits were also on the rise, and dividends paid in 1917 by joint-stock companies were 20 percent higher, in inflation-adjusted terms, than in 1913. Inaugurating a pattern that would be confirmed during World War II, Switzerland was only nominally "neutral", and its economy was deeply embedded in the wartime context.[3]

Deteriorating living conditions led to political radicalization and popular protests. Working-class mobilization culminated in November 1918 in an unprecedented general strike. Old age and survivors' insurance featured among the political and social demands of the joint strike committee, or Olten Committee, formed by members of the Socialist Party and the Trade Union Confederation (Gewerkschaftsbund). The Federal Council refused to negotiate and troops occupied the main cities, which led the Olten Committee to call off the strike after a few days.[4] Although the reforms demanded in the general strike were wide-ranging, this flare-up of class struggle was modest in comparison with the civil wars and revolutionary situations that raged in neighboring Germany, Austria-Hungary, and Italy. However, the general strike constituted the sharpest political conflict since the 1847 civil war and sent profound shockwaves through the political system. In the tense months that followed November 1918, the stabilization of the political situation by the ruling bourgeois parties followed a two-pronged strategy of appeasement and repression.

(Lausanne: Payot, 1986), pp. 683–769. On the wartime deterioration of living conditions, see Willi Gautschi, *Der Landesstreik 1918* (Zurich: Chronos, 1988 [1968]), pp. 27–43.

[3] On war profits, farmers, and the war economy, see Werner Baumann, *Bauernstand und Bürgerblock: Ernst Laur und der Schweizerische Bauernverband 1897–1918* (Zurich: Orell Füssli, 1993), pp. 310–16; Sébastien Guex, *La politique monétaire et financière de la Confédération suisse 1900–1920* (Lausanne: Payot, 1993), pp. 365, 73. The surge in exports did not benefit all manufacturing sectors: luxury textile goods such as embroidery and ribbons suffered losses during the war. On the distinctive position of neutral Switzerland during the two world wars, see Hans Ulrich Jost, "La Suisse, un pays neutre en guerre", in *Le XXe siècle des guerres*, ed. Pietro Causarono and Valeria Galimi (Paris: Editions de l'Atelier, 2004), pp. 150–7.

[4] Other demands included the introduction of proportional representation and the eight-hour workday (both introduced in 1919), universal women's suffrage (belatedly introduced in 1971), army reform, the establishment of a national work service to reduce unemployment, the regulation of foreign trade and of farm products in order to ensure food supplies to the urban working class, and finally the payment of public debts by wealthy citizens. See Gautschi, *Der Landesstreik 1918*.

The organization of vigilante groups, the rise of virulent anti-Socialism, and the trials of the leading organizers of the general strike reflected, on the one hand, the uncompromising attitude of a bourgeoisie that deemed the strike a dangerous revolutionary insurgency; on the other hand, Radical and Catholic Conservative politicians quickly announced social and political reforms to defuse worker unrest: in early 1919, social insurance, the eight-hour workday, and the introduction of a proportional electoral system were the main items on the political agenda. Switzerland's situation in 1918 fits into Charles S. Maier's classic study of the "recasting of bourgeois Europe" in the aftermath of the war, when "each country had to find a new and precarious equilibrium, based less on the revival of traditional ideological prescriptions than upon new interest group compromises or new forms of coercion".[5]

These postwar social policy proposals were warmly greeted by the Socialists, but also by moderate bourgeois parliamentarians. National Councilor Christian Rothenberger, a left-liberal Radical from Basle, described old age insurance as a "means to restore confidence in capitalism among those who were tempted by socialism and class struggle".[6] By June 1919, the Federal Council had drafted an initial pension bill according to which the entry generation (people over 60 years old at the time of the introduction of the AHV) would receive a CHF 300 annual pension at the age of 65 without having to make contributions. After a long maturation period, the insurance scheme – financed by individual contributions of around CHF 40 a year – would have pensions amounting to around one-fifth of a skilled worker's wages.[7] Federal and cantonal budgets would cover the early deficits of the scheme, but new fiscal revenues had to be levied to ensure its long-term financing.

As policy-makers debated the AHV legislation, the political landscape was still in turmoil, and working-class militancy remained high. In the

[5] Charles S. Maier, *Recasting bourgeois Europe: stabilization in France, Germany and Italy in the decade after World War I* (Princeton: Princeton University Press, 1975), p. 4. On this two-sided strategy in Switzerland, see Ruedi Brassel-Moser, *Dissonanzen der Moderne: Aspekte der Entwicklung der politischen Kulturen in der Schweiz der 1920er Jahre* (Zurich: Chronos, 1994), pp. 75–85; Hanspeter Schmid, *Wirtschaft, Staat und Macht: die Politik der schweizerischen Exportindustrie im Zeichen von Staats- und Wirtschaftskrise (1918–1929)* (Zurich: Limmat Verlag, 1983), p. 140.

[6] Quoted in André Lasserre, "L'institution de l'assurance-vieillesse et survivants (1889–1947)", in *La démocratie référendaire suisse au 20ème siècle*, ed. Roland Ruffieux (Fribourg: Presses universitaires de l'Université de Fribourg, 1972), pp. 259–326 (p. 268). This author wrongly designates Rothenberger as a member of the Socialist Party.

[7] Ibid., pp. 263–9; Jürg Sommer, *Das Ringen um die soziale Sicherheit in der Schweiz: eine politisch-ökonomische Analyse der Ursprünge, Entwicklungen und Perspektiven sozialer Sicherung im Widerstreit zwischen Gruppeninteressen und volkswirtschaftlicher Tragbarkeit* (Diessenhofen: Rüegger Verlag, 1978), pp. 132–3.

midst of revolutionary uprisings in neighboring Germany and Austria-Hungary, citywide general strikes paralyzed Zurich and Basle in the summer of 1919. In October, the first national elections organized according to proportional representation provoked yet another political upheaval. The grand old party of the bourgeoisie, the Radicals, lost 43 of the 103 seats they held in 1917 in the lower house of the Federal Assembly (Nationalrat, or National Council), as parts of their constituencies departed to the newly formed and staunchly anti-socialist Farmers', Artisans', and Burghers' Party (Bauern-, Gewerbe- und Bürgerpartei). Thanks to proportional representation, the Socialist Party became the second strongest in the National Council, adding nineteen seats to the twenty-one it held in 1917. However, the 1919 elections were not followed by a left turn in Swiss politics: the Socialist Party had only one seat in the second chamber of the Federal Assembly (Ständerat, or Council of States) and was still barred from the executive branch. During the interwar period, the bourgeois bloc always maintained a more than two-thirds majority of parliamentary seats and firmly controlled the legislative and executive branches. The conservative leanings of the Farmers', Artisans', and Burghers' Party also contributed to the containment of the left.[8]

The two key protagonists of the pension debate in the executive branch personify the contrasted responses of the bourgeoisie to the challenge of the general strike – a strategy of appeasement and social reform on the one hand and an aggressive conservative roll-back on the other. Edmund Schulthess (1868–1944), head of the Economic Affairs Department from 1912 to 1935, was the leading architect of social insurance during the interwar years. Before his election to the executive branch, this seasoned Radical politician had long worked as a lawyer for the engineering firm Brown & Boveri. His corporate background underscored the fading of the left-liberal wing of the Radical Party, personified by Ludwig Forrer, and the reinforcement of its business wing (Wirtschaftsfreisinn). During the war, Schulthess had been in charge of the implementation of the federal law on sickness and accident insurance (KUVG) and had supervised the war economy. Schulthess considered the introduction of the AHV as an absolute necessity in a time of social and political crisis. He was determined to forge a social insurance scheme, although this would necessitate concessions from the bourgeoisie.[9]

If the June 1919 pension legislation drafted by Edmund Schulthess symbolized a window of opportunity for social reform, the election of

[8] Brassel-Moser, *Dissonanzen der Moderne*, pp. 85–92.

[9] Hermann Böschenstein, *Bundesrat Edmund Schulthess: Krieg und Krisen* (Berne: Haupt, 1966), pp. 165–75.

the Catholic Conservative Jean-Marie Musy (1876–1952) to the Federal Council in December 1919 clearly embodied a counteracting conservative roll-back. Attempts to build a solid consensus in favor of pensions were immediately challenged by the postwar consolidation of the bourgeois bloc. With close links to the banking and financial establishment, Musy belonged to the business wing of the Catholic Party and was also known for his anti-Socialism. His staunch denunciation of the 1918–1919 strikes had contributed to his election. During his long tenure at the Finance Department (1920–1934), Musy vigorously defended cantonal rights and unceasingly tried to delay and derail the AHV by opposing the development of federal taxation. His resolve to pursue austerity measures to balance budgets and his fiscal conservatism left little room for new social policy expenditures.[10] The clashes between the divergent political conceptions defended by these two key politicians would hinder the development of the AHV until the defeat of the Lex Schulthess in 1931.

When social and political unrest ebbed, the pension debate shifted from vague promises to hard bargaining, as bourgeois politicians and business circles appeared less and less willing to accept social reform. The postwar financial crisis of the federal state and the economic recession of the early 1920s also reinforced the uncompromising attitude of the right toward the AHV. Between 1920 and 1922, the AHV was shuttled back and forth between the two chambers of the Federal Assembly. During this period, "Musy's reluctance and steadfast opposition" played a "determining role in the slowdown of debates" and encouraged other conservative and federalist opponents of social reform to step up delaying tactics.[11]

The main opponents of the AHV could be found within the ranks of the Catholic Conservative Party, the western Switzerland and Basle-based Liberal-Conservatives, and the new Farmers', Artisans', and Burghers' Party. Months were spent in skirmishes over the organizational structure and benefits of the AHV. If the first drafts envisioned a national insurance scheme covering the whole population, the issue of either narrowing the scope of pensions to certain occupational groups or of limiting the role of the Confederation to the subsidizing of existing cantonal or employer-based pension schemes resurfaced repeatedly during political discussions. To maintain their hold over local old age provision, Catholic Conservatives and federalist defenders of cantonal rights also steadfastly expressed their preference for decentralized, means-tested assistance rather than national-level social insurance.

[10] Guex, *La politique monétaire et financière de la Confédération suisse*, pp. 262–3; Chantal Kaiser, *Bundesrat Jean-Marie Musy: 1919–1934* (Freiburg: Universitätsverlag Freiburg, 1999), pp. 128–39.

[11] Lasserre, "L'institution de l'AVS", p. 270.

The financing issue was no less daunting. By linking the issue of AHV financing to the stabilization of the federal budget, fiscal conservatives fought on two fronts: they tried to keep in check potential social expenditure and, more generally, to oppose increases in federal revenues and to roll back wartime emergency fiscal measures. Attempts to introduce a federal inheritance tax in order to finance pensions were repeatedly turned down by the Federal Assembly and were even hijacked by Jean-Marie Musy, who claimed that the priority for new taxes should be to balance federal budgets. In 1922, the banking establishment, employers' federations, and bourgeois political parties mobilized to crush a Socialist initiative proposing a special tax on wealth (Vermögensabgabe), a hated remnant of the general strike, that could have contributed to the financing of the AHV. By 1924, an initiative launched in 1919 by National Councilor Christian Rothenberger (Radical), who envisioned financing pensions with the proceeds of a tax on war profits, was the only proposal based on direct taxation that had not yet been rejected in the postwar fiscal conservative roll-back. Supported by the left, the Rothenberger Initiative was opposed by the bourgeois bloc in the Federal Assembly, received no support from the Radical leadership, and was attacked by business federations. For bourgeois parties and employers, the only new revenues for social insurance that would be acceptable were taxes on tobacco and alcohol that put the costs of the AHV on the shoulders of the whole population and did not focus on wealthier citizens. However, a first attempt to introduce an alcohol tax was defeated in June 1923 by a referendum launched by farmers' organizations.[12]

After the first parliamentary debates, prospects for a rapid implementation of the AHV plummeted, and high hopes for social reform were replaced with disillusionment and gridlock. In the conservative context of the postwar years, the stumbling-blocks of the political system were restored, and social insurance proposals were reduced to a pale shadow of the first drafts introduced in 1919. After seven lean years, nothing was settled on the AHV front. In 1924, the constitutional article enabling the Confederation to legislate in the domain of pensions had still to be put to the vote, and no bill would be presented until 1929. Before examining this second phase of policy-making, I will leave the stormy debates that characterized social insurance to focus on the more opaque politics

[12] Leonhard Neidhart, *Plebiszit und pluralitäre Demokratie: eine Analyse der Funktion des schweizerischen Gesetzesreferendums* (Berne: Francke Verlag, 1970), p. 199; Luca Pellegrini, "L'assurance vieillesse, survivants et invalidité: ses enjeux financiers entre 1918 et 1925", in *Geschichte der Sozialversicherungen/Histoire des assurances sociales* (Zurich: Chronos, 2006), pp. 79–108; Schmid, *Wirtschaft, Staat und Macht*, pp. 221–30, 271–6. On the campaign against the wealth tax, see file 68.100/18, Vermögensabgabe 1922, SLA. See also Arbeitgeberverband Vorstand, November 6, 1922, pp. 97–100, SAV.

of occupational provision. In this parallel realm of social provision, the dynamics were different: the steady expansion of occupational provision contrasted with the stalemate over federal pensions.

## Seven fat years: tax exemptions and the pension lobby

Before discussing the dynamics of occupational provision, it is useful to chart its quantitative development during the interwar period. The number of core pension plans increased ten-fold between 1911 and 1930. Four out of five of the 1,145 plans in operation on the eve of the Depression (there had been 343 such plans in 1920) were in the private sector. During the same period, the number of workers covered by old age provision rose four-fold (see Table A.1, p. 290, and Table A.2, p. 295). Altogether, these core plans covered 18 percent of the total non-farm workforce in 1930 (compared with 11 percent in 1920 and only 5 percent in 1911). The reach of Swiss occupational provision during the interwar period was slightly higher than the levels in the Netherlands, Canada, the United States, and the United Kingdom (see Table 0.2, p. 24). Unsurprisingly, the level of coverage differed markedly in the public and private sectors. Core plans covered only 7 percent of the private workforce in 1920 and 11 percent in 1930. By contrast, overall coverage in the public sector jumped from 38 to 66 percent, primarily because of the postwar establishment of two pension plans for railroad workers, postal workers, and federal civil servants. The number of workers affiliated to private plans did not overtake the number of those insured by public plans before 1930: there were then 124,000 workers insured by the private sector, as against 112,000 in public-sector plans. The two federal pension plans – the Pensions- und Hilfskasse der Konföderation (PHK) and the Eidgenössische Versicherungskasse (EVK) – alone covered more than 60,000 people.[13]

Leading manufacturing and financial sectors were in the vanguard of occupational old age provision. From the 1920s on, pension plans covered two-fifths of the workforce in chemicals, banking, and insurance. Among metal and machine-making firms, another manufacturing powerhouse, coverage surpassed the 25 percent mark by 1930 (see Table A.5, p. 299). Over one-third of all insured workers in the private sector were affiliated to pension plans in these industries. Coverage was also above average in the utilities and in transport firms that were managed in concert with regional and local authorities, and mimicked the dynamics of public-sector plans. A second tier including textile and clothing firms,

[13] W. Grütter and A. Alder, "Pensionskassen", in *Handbuch der schweizerischen Volkswirtschaft* (Berne: Benteli, 1939), pp. 221–5.

food-processing companies, commerce and retail firms, paper and rubber manufacturers, and the printing trade hovered just above or below the average level of coverage. Finally, manufacturing or service sectors characterized by low capital intensiveness, such as wood and stone products, the building trade and tourism, all trailed far behind the others in terms of coverage. In watch-making, a key export sector divided into a multitude of small firms, occupational schemes remained rare. They would become more widespread after the rationalization and concentration of production that followed the war and accelerated during the Depression.

Several factors underlay the selective expansion of private occupational pensions during the second half of World War I and its immediate aftermath. First, wartime labor shortages and heightened labor militancy spurred the development of pension plans, notably in capital-intensive sectors. Second, the war heralded the introduction of tax exemptions for occupational provision, a factor that had lasting consequences on its long-term development. Third, the modernization of corporate social activism gave birth to a pension lobby determined to defend occupational schemes that accumulated financial assets, enabled employers to improve industrial relations, and were used to further workforce management aims. Last but not least, in the aftermath of the war a market for group pensions developed by life insurers opened up.

After 1912, the subsidization of mutual benefit societies to aid the sick and the nationalization of industrial work accident insurance contributed to a shifting of employers' welfare efforts toward old age benefits. As the war-induced export boom unfolded and the labor market tightened, employers had ever-stronger incentives to develop these benefits in order to retain skilled workers. In a survey published in 1916, Arnold Guise of the Baden Technical Society argued that well-designed corporate welfare measures facilitated the economic mobilization of the workforce, especially in dynamic export sectors. With nationalist undertones, Guise also pointed out that the prewar reliance of the industry on a foreign workforce had allegedly "forced young Swiss men of all occupations to earn their bread abroad" and that their "brave strength [was] lost to the country". Since the beginning of the war, continued Guise, this situation had changed. As many foreigners left for neighboring countries to serve in their respective armies, "the Swiss element [was] again strongly represented". For Guise, it was then clearly "in the interest of firms to retain this Swiss workforce" by providing company-based benefits.[14]

[14] Arnold Guise, *Die Alters- und Invalidenfürsorge im schweizerischen Handel und in der schweizerischen Industrie: nach Material gesammelt von der Technischen Gesellschaft Baden* (Brugg: Effingerhof AG, 1916), pp. 3, 5 (quotation).

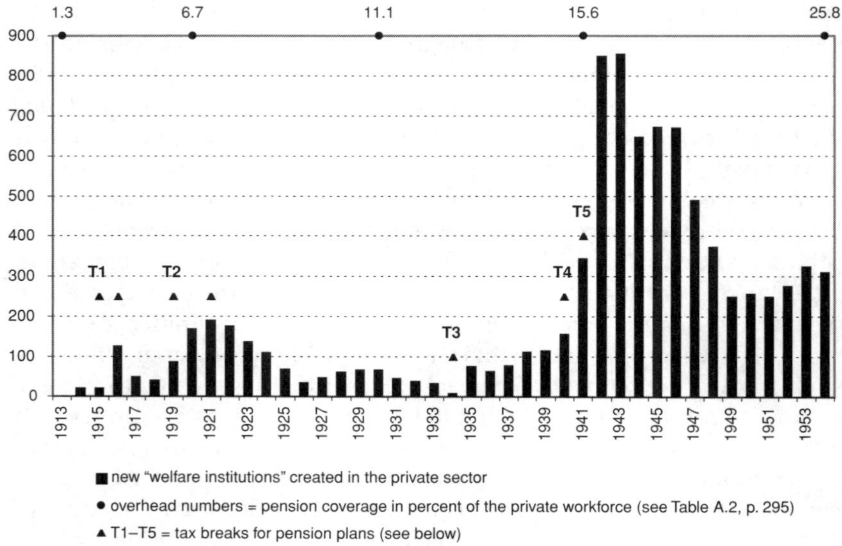


Figure 2.1 New welfare institutions in the private sector, 1913–1954.
*Source:* Hans Gerold Wirz, *Die Personal-Wohlfahrtseinrichtungen der schweizerischen Privatwirtschaft* (Stäfa: Buchdruckerei Stäfa, 1955) p. 21.
*Note:* The welfare institutions (Wohlfahrtseinrichtungen) surveyed in Figure 2.1 encompass corporate schemes covering health, unemployment and old age benefits. These numbers do not coincide with federal pension surveys. However, as pension schemes represented a large proportion of these welfare institutions this data can be used to chart the expansion of private old age provision.

Fiscal measures including tax exemptions for occupational pension plans:

(T1) special war tax (Kriegssteuer, 1915) and tax on war profits (Kriegsgewinnsteuer, 1916)
(T2) revision of the special war tax (1919) and the tax on war profits (1921)
(T3) emergency crisis tax (Krisenabgabe, 1934)
(T4) tax on war profits (Kriegsgewinnsteuer, 1940) and sacrifice for national defense (Wehropfer, 1940)
(T5) revision of the tax on war profits and sacrifice for national defense (1941)

If it is difficult to confirm or deny this argument, it is true that selective welfare measures helped to ensure that key categories of workers identified with corporate values. In late September 1918, right before the general strike, another strike led by impoverished and radicalized Zurich bank employees was immediately followed by a generalization of

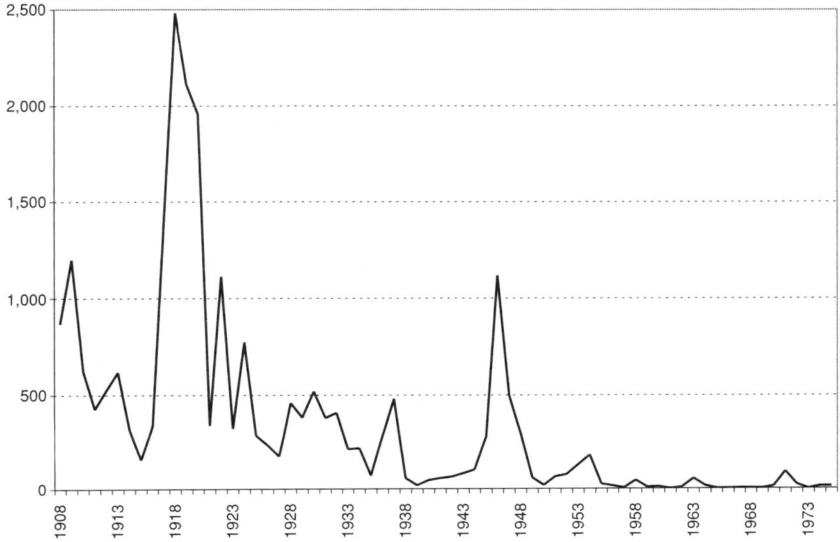


Figure 2.2 Number of strikers per 100,000 workers, 1907–1976.
*Source:* Peter Flora, Jens Albert and Richard C. Eichenberg, eds. *State, economy, and society in western Europe 1815–1975* (Frankfurt/London: Campus/Macmillan, 1983), volume 2, pp. 705ff.

pension schemes in the banking sector. As social tensions rose, preferential retirement benefits offered useful "golden chains" to divide white-collar and blue-collar workers.[15] The annual rate of creation of new welfare institutions (Figure 2.1) runs parallel to the evolution of labor conflict (Figure 2.2). The expansion of corporate welfare benefits was concomitant with the upsurge in labor militancy that took place during the second half and immediate aftermath of the war.

The early 1920s was a formative period for the inner core of the future second pillar, as the few hundred pension plans created were among the largest and richest in the private sector. Indeed, the steeper *quantitative* rise in welfare institutions during the 1940s was *qualitatively* different from the interwar expansion of occupational provision. As I will show in Chapter 3, corporate social activism was much more pre-emptive during World War II. The early 1940s increase in employer-based benefits was related to an eagerness by business to avoid social unrest that could have led to a repeat of the 1918 general strike. Moreover, the thousands

[15] Mario König, Hannes Siegrist, and Rudolf Vetterli, *Warten und Aufrücken: die Angestellten in der Schweiz, 1870–1950* (Zurich: Chronos, 1985), pp. 103–5.

of pension plans created during World War II were concentrated among less important firms. This second phase of expansion signaled the consolidation and widening of occupational provision.

Preferential tax treatment granted to corporate welfare programs had a profound impact on the expansion of private pension plans. Figure 2.2 underlines the coincidence between the first peaks in the creation of welfare institutions and the introduction and revisions of the war taxes levied by the federal government. The fiscal foundations of occupational provision confirmed the importance of pension plans in large firms and underscored key interactions between public policies and private social measures.

Because of the rise of ordinary and extraordinary spending, such as mobilization costs and emergency relief measures, the federal government had begun a major overhaul of its revenues. A new war tax (Kriegssteuer) was introduced in December 1915, to be followed in 1916 by taxes targeting war profits (Kriegsgewinnsteuer) and financial operations (Stempelsteuer). This new taxation was introduced to fight the catastrophic deterioration of federal public finances and to control war profits that attracted the growing hostility of the impoverished working class.[16] In order to deflect conservative and business opposition to these new levies, the Federal Council introduced several measures that mitigated their impact. The war tax exempted monies that were earmarked by private companies for welfare purposes, and its 1920 revision enabled firms to deduct voluntary contributions to welfare funds from the profits subjected to taxation. Similar provisions were introduced in the tax on war profits and its subsequent revisions in 1918 and 1921. This hastily implemented tax relief outsourced in a sense the development of social welfare to the corporate sector and spurred on in particular the establishment of several hundred pension plans.

By 1929, according to the final report on the tax on war profits established by the Federal Revenues Administration, around 1,300 firms had benefitted from exemptions, whose total amount, CHF 241 million, equaled nearly one-third of total returns of the tax (CHF 761 million). The overwhelming majority of monies exempted had been devoted to the creation of pension plans. Their geographical repartition also underlined the pre-eminence of leading manufacturing regions such as Zurich and Basle, which together received almost half of the total exemptions. Large corporations in export-oriented industrial sectors – especially textile mills, metal and machine-making firms, and chemical plants – were

[16] Guex, *La politique monétaire et financière de la Confédération suisse*, pp. 327–419. Declared war profits amounted to more than CHF 2 billion in nominal terms between 1915 and 1920 (p. 373).

granted the lion's share of the exemptions.[17] A 1917 survey estimated that the pension assets of 68 leading manufacturing and financial firms had already reached CHF 30 million.[18] Between 1916 and 1927, the Rieter textile machines factory deposited CHF 1.3 million in its new welfare fund (Wohlfahrtsfonds). The pension assets of the Von Roll steelworks doubled in nominal terms during the 1920s, surpassing CHF 15 million in 1929. The Gesellschaft für Chemische Industrie Basel (CIBA), a leading chemical firm, set up in 1916 a new pension plan for its managerial and white-collar staff with an endowment that reached CHF 4.5 million by the late 1920s.[19]

In its 1929 report, the Federal Revenues Administration complained that it had insufficient means at its disposal to monitor the allocation of exempted monies, to enforce tax rules, and to fight tax avoidance maneuvers. In order to be granted exemptions, firms had to ensure a strict legal distinction between the monies devoted to welfare schemes and those subjected to the tax on war profits. However, the federal administration was deluged with exemption demands and was often unable to check compliance with these guidelines for several months, or even years, opening the way for the use of pension assets for self-financing purposes at affordable rates, or to straightforward tax evasion. The report gave no estimate of

[17] CHF 190 million had been devoted to pension and welfare plans, whereas the remaining monies were divided between corporate housing measures (CHF 29.2 million), sickness plans (CHF 4.6 million), and various relief measures (CHF 17.4 million). Among cantons, Zurich (27 percent of total exemptions) and Basle (19 percent, City and Country) were followed by Solothurn (10 percent), Berne and Argovia (7 percent each), and Schaffhausen and St. Gallen (6 percent each). See K. Böschenstein and H. Held, "Bericht über die Durchführung der Eidgenössischen Kriegsgewinnsteuer", Berne, Eidg. Steuerverwaltung, 1929, file E6300 (B) 1969/255/7, SBA. Thanks to Sébastien Guex (University of Lausanne) for providing me with this report. See also Heiner Ritzmann-Blickenstorfer and Hansjörg Siegenthaler, eds., *Historisch Statistik der Schweiz – Statistique historique de la Suisse – Swiss Historical Statistics* (Zurich: Chronos, 1996), Table U10a; "Impôt sur les bénéfices de guerre", in *Rapport du Conseil Fédéral à l'assemblée fédérale sur sa gestion en 1927* (Berne: Chancellerie fédérale, 1927), pp. 492–500; Max Wolfensberger, *Die Wohlfahrtsfonds industrieller Unternehmungen im schweizerischen Recht* (Laupen: Polygraphische Gesellschaft, 1927), pp. 16–17.

[18] *Le Mois: Société de Banques Suisses*, 1917, quoted by "Message du Conseil fédéral à l'Assemblée fédérale concernant l'attribution à la Confédération du droit de légiférer en matière d'assurance-invalidité, vieillesse et survivants, et la création des ressources nécessaires à la Confédération pour les assurances sociales, du 21 juin 1919", in *Feuille Fédérale* (Berne: Chancellerie fédérale, 1919), pp. 1–234 (p. 38) (volume IV).

[19] On Rieter, see Albert Hablützel, *Die Angestellten- und Arbeiter Wohlfahrtseinrichtungen der zürzerischen Maschinen- und Textilindustrie* (Winterthur: Buchdruck Winterthur, 1929), pp. 31, 54. On the CIBA, see Gerold Ermatinger, *Kapital und Ethos: die sozialen und kulturellen Taten des schweizerischen Privatkapitals im 19. und 20. Jahrhundert* (Zurich/Leipzig: Rotapfel Verlag, 1936), pp. 90–5. On Von Roll, see André Kienzle, *Es gibt nur ein Gerlafingen! Herrschaft, Kultur und soziale Integration in einer Standortgemeinde des Stahlkonzerns Von Roll, 1918–1939* (Zurich: Chronos, 1997), p. 338 (note 97).

the extent of fraud but clearly hinted that abuses had occurred. The Federal Revenues Administration pointed out that a stricter definition and enforcement of exemptions alone would have added more than CHF 50 million in revenues. It emphasized that exemptions for welfare purposes should be capped in the future to avoid the creation of gaping tax loopholes. However, this report and its conclusions remained confidential, and there was little public debate over these tax exemptions.[20]

Switzerland was not the only country to introduce preferential tax treatment for pension plans. Similar measures were also taken during the early 1920s in the United States and the United Kingdom. In his study of American fiscal debates, Christopher Howard shows that early links between fiscal policy and pension plans constituted the foundation of a "hidden welfare state". The origin of these tax exemptions is difficult to trace, as "they were enacted with little debate or justification". However, as in Switzerland, they were introduced at a time when "conservative Republicans were determined . . . to lower the excess profits tax on corporations and surtaxes on individuals" that had been introduced during World War I. Howard concludes that although "business elites were not instrumental in creating the tax expenditure for employer pensions . . . policy makers were attentive to business interests". At the beginning of the 1920s, the newly formed British Conference of Superannuation Funds successfully lobbied the Treasury to obtain exemptions from income tax.[21] If the introduction of tax exemptions had obvious similarities on both sides of the Atlantic, scholars agree that "tax factors were not the engine driving the pension machine" in the United States or the United Kingdom before the 1940s.[22] In Switzerland, tax exemptions triggered and fueled a genuine boom in corporate pension plans within the context of high war profits in an economy that was spared

[20] K. Böschenstein and H. Held, "Bericht über die Durchführung der Eidgenössischen Kriegsgewinnsteuer", pp. 44–50. For examples of these legal loopholes, see Matthieu Leimgruber, "Profits de guerre, fiscalité et caisses de pension (1917–1927)", *Aspects de la sécurité sociale* 4 (2001), pp. 18, 20. The final report on the war profits tax was not even circulated among the federal administration; see Guex, *La politique monétaire et financière de la Confédération suisse*, p. 439.

[21] On American tax exemptions, see Christopher Howard, *The hidden welfare state: tax expenditures and social policy in the United States* (Princeton: Princeton University Press, 1997), pp. 60–3; Steven A. Sass, *The promise of private pensions: the first hundred years* (Cambridge: Cambridge University Press, 1997), pp. 101–12. On British tax exemptions, see Leslie Hannah, *Inventing retirement: the development of occupational pensions in Britain* (Cambridge: Cambridge University Press, 1986), pp. 19–21; Michael Moss, *The building of Europe's largest mutual life company: Standard Life 1825–2000* (Edinburgh: Mainstream, 2000), p. 200. See also Gøsta Esping-Andersen, *The three worlds of welfare capitalism* (Cambridge: Polity Press, 1990), p. 89.

[22] Hannah, *Inventing retirement*, p. 21 (quotation); Howard, *The hidden welfare state*, p. 115.

wartime destruction and characterized by heightened social tensions and resurgent fiscal conservatism.

Given the belated introduction and lax enforcement of wartime taxation, exemptions for corporate welfare measures continued throughout the 1920s. Employers saw the tax privileges hastily granted by the state during the war as an inalienable right that should suffer no governmental interference. Contemporary accounts underlined that these measures were considered a legitimate means to counter the overhaul of allegedly "confiscatory" fiscal policies. For economist Graziano Lusenti, pension plans were used not so much as "social institutions" as "agents in global corporate strategies aiming at reducing global costs and limiting fiscal expenses".[23] If business circles welcomed state incentives in the area of occupational provision, they resisted new tax levies to pay for social insurance. As previously mentioned, employers opposed the use of proceeds from the tax on war profits for the future AHV and ferociously attacked the Socialist-backed tax on wealth. When the economy was hit by a severe recession in 1921, business federations also spoke resolutely against a "too rigorous interpretation and application" of the federal guidelines regulating tax exemptions.[24] This appeal to leniency came at a time when exemptions enabled employers to build up financial reserves that could be used for self-financing purposes during a period of uncertain economic prospects. The exploitation of tax privileges was part of the postwar fiscal conservative agenda.

In 1925, occupational pension assets reached 12 percent of gross domestic product. Although early estimates did not include group pension reserves managed by insurers (more on this subject later), private pension assets (CHF 394 million) were clearly dwarfed by public ones (CHF 587 million) because of the size of the two Confederation pension plans (see Table A.7, p. 303). Global estimates do not fully account for the concentration of private pension assets. In the banking sector, where coverage spread rapidly in the early 1920s, pension assets reached CHF 110 million by 1928. Two-thirds of these assets were then in the hands of the eight largest financial institutions, while the largest pension plan of the sector – most probably a plan set up by Crédit Suisse, Schweizerisches Bankverein, or Schweizerische Bankgesellschaft – held CHF 30 million

23 "Aus der Praxis der Pensionsfonds-Einrichtungen", *Schweizerischer Versicherungs-Zeitschrift*, February 15, 1918; Graziano Lusenti, *Les institutions de prévoyance en Suisse, au Royaume-Uni et en Allemagne fédérale: placements financiers et politique sociale* (Geneva: Georg, 1989), p. 89.

24 "Die Sicherstellung der Zuwendungen für Wohlfahrtszwecke", *Schweizerische Arbeitgeber Zeitung*, June 24 (1st part), July 1 (2nd part), and July 8, 1922 (3rd part).

in assets.[25] This development bolstered employers' resolve to resist state and labor demands to monitor new corporate welfare institutions.

White-collar trade unions, whose members were among the main beneficiaries of the postwar surge in occupational provision, repeatedly asked the Federal Council to monitor pension plans or at least to make sure that monies derived from tax exemptions were properly used by private firms. In 1923, National Councilor Karl Brodtbeck, a Socialist, summarized employees' demands before the Federal Assembly: employers should guarantee rights to benefits, accept workers' participation in the management of plans, and safeguard pension assets in cases of bankruptcy.[26] Inaugurating a repeated trend, pension plan regulation was put on standby or brushed aside. In 1928, the Federal Council stated that it was not among its prerogatives to investigate the tax on war profits, as its revenues were monitored by the cantons, and that such a complex issue would best await the revision of the Code of Obligations (Obligationenrecht) that regulated private contracts.[27]

Fiscal policy had triggered the first pension boom and raised employers' consciousness about the potential advantages of pension reserves. Opposition to a federal law on pension plans and delaying tactics, as well as the fragmentation of regulation at federal and cantonal levels, came together to encourage the subterranean nature of the politics of corporate employee benefits. The financial foundations of corporate plans would be consolidated and confirmed when further preferential fiscal measures were introduced during the 1930s and World War II. By contrast, the privileges of the "hidden welfare state" were to remain out of public scrutiny for decades.

If the financial strength of pension plans was quietly on the rise, coverage obviously remained selective and benefits modest. Given their more stable job status, white-collar employees and skilled workers employed in key manufacturing and financial sectors had the best chances to be covered by "core" pension plans (Versicherungseinrichtungen),

[25] Hans Lyner, *Die Personalfürsorge im schweizerischen Bankwesen* (Wald: W. Hess, 1930), p. 17. See also Ermatinger, *Kapital und Ethos*, pp. 99–112.

[26] König, Siegrist, and Vetterli, *Warten und Aufrücken*, pp. 103–5; Lyner, *Die Personalfürsorge im schweizerischen Bankwesen*, p. 33. See also "Die Krise und die Wohlfahrteinrichtungen in Fabriken", *Metallarbeiterzeitung*, April 21, 1921; *Soziale Informationen*, no. 6–7, May/June 1921, p. 30; "Vereinigung schweizerischer Angestelltenverbände an die Mitglieder des Ständerates, Bundesversammlung, Bern, betreffend Obligationenrecht: Revision der Titel XXIV bis XXXIII (Sicherstellung der Wohlfahrtsfonds)" [n.d., ca. June 1931], file M Private Wohlfahrtseinrichtungen Arbeitnehmerfürsorge (1921–1939), Wirtschaftsarchiv.

[27] K. Böschenstein and H. Held, "Bericht über die Durchführung der Eidgenössischen Kriegsgewinnsteuer", p. 49. See also Karl Greiner, "Die Personalversicherung als Ergänzung der staatlichen Sozialversicherung", *Schweizerische Zeitschrift für Volkswirtschaft und Statistik* (1930), pp. 362–85, pp. 380–5.

while less skilled and auxiliary workers (many of them women) often had to content themselves with more informal "relief institutions" (Fürsorgeeinrichtungen). Yet, while corporate pension plans "reinforced pre-existing differences in the material situation of different groups", they did not generally "inaugurate new privileges for white-collar employees". More frequently, they "contributed to blur the divide between workers and employees in corporations that put above all a premium on fidelity to the firm rather than on the type of job contract".[28]

It is difficult to estimate average pensions for the immediate postwar period, as the number of pensioners was still low, and benefit recipients often belonged to managerial staff or a thin stratum of skilled workers and employees.[29] By my calculations, pensions in public-sector plans amounted to almost two-thirds of the average wage of a skilled worker, as against one-third in the private sector. However, private banks and insurance firms offered pensions hovering around public levels (between 44 and 64 percent of average wages), while pensions in manufacturing sectors were much lower (between 15 and 30 percent; see Table A.6, p. 301).

Employers' paternalism and discretionary practices in the area of employee benefits remained prevalent. For Gewerkschaftsbund secretary Max Weber, "workers' welfare in large firms still follow[ed] traditional lines", and corporate schemes constituted a "severe hindrance for unions fighting for better work conditions, as workers feared to lose employee benefits as soon as they uttered a word of protest".[30] In a comment on "the problem of the aging worker", turbine manufacturer Oscar Sulzer welcomed the recent development of occupational pensions but cautioned that entrepreneurs should not promise benefits that would jeopardize the sound financing of pensions. Sulzer did not mention the substantial reserves accumulated due to tax exemptions, but argued that besides frugal pensions, firms should set up special workshops for elderly workers in tune with the best traditions of paternalist benevolence. Would-be pensioners could continue to work part-time and earn incomes

28 Firms such as Georg Fischer, AIAG, Von Moos, or Rieter set up after World War I old age savings plans (Alterssparkasse) for their blue-collar workers and a pension plan (Pensionskasse) for their employees. Only white-collars received genuine pensions, while workers received generally old age relief or lump sums. See König, Siegrist, and Vetterli, *Warten und Aufrücken*, p. 105.

29 In 1925, private-sector pension plans paid only 4,840 old age pensions, 1,267 disability pensions, and 1,740 survivors' pensions. By comparison, the federal railways already paid 3,416 pensions to elderly invalids, as well as 4,500 survivors' pensions. See *Pensionskassenstatistik 1925b*, annex VI, Karl Greiner, *Aufbau und Finanzierung der Alters- und Hinterbliebenenversicherung in den Kantonen* (Zurich: Orell Füssli, 1935), p. 369.

30 Max Weber, "Wohlfahrtspflege in der schweizerischen Industrie", *Gewerkschaftliche Rundschau*, January 1928, pp. 7–13 (quotation p. 13).

higher than in-house pensions.[31] This avoided overburdening pension plans and enhanced employers' reputations, while enabling corporations to continue employing aging workers at lower cost.

In 1918, an insurance executive pointed out that the long-term viability of the new pension plans was untested and that occupational provision still remained largely uncharted territory.[32] Yet, as the skirmishes continued over the issue of social insurance, the foundations of a corporate pension system were being laid. The emergence of a pension lobby, as well as the growth of group pension plans, accompanied this reorganization and modernization of corporate welfare measures.

The aftermath of the general strike saw various attempts at defusing social tensions. Besides the introduction of old age provision and the subsidizing of existing unemployment funds (implemented in 1924), Federal Councilor Edmund Schulthess proposed the establishment of a national Economic Council (Wirtschaftsrat) to foster cooperation between business and labor. Welcomed by domestic, market-oriented sectors that had been destabilized by the war and the 1921 economic crisis, these attempts foundered, as the main employers' federations refused to be constrained by such a corporatist framework. On the Catholic-conservative side of the political spectrum, conservatives bolstered by Jean-Marie Musy's election to the Federal Council addressed class and labor issues from the perspective of their own social doctrines. The end of World War I also coincided with the spread in Europe of Taylorist methods imported from the United States. Swiss employers joined in the fray by advocating a renewal of production methods and personnel management, with promises of rejuvenated corporate welfare measures constituting major facets of efforts to raise productivity and efficiency.[33] Such measures offered a hopeful horizon for entrepreneurs in a period of economic, social, and political turmoil.

During the 1920s, reform-minded employers organized Social Conferences that were part of the broad strategy of class reconciliation that

[31] Oscar Sulzer, "Das Problem des alternden Arbeiters", *Schweizerische Arbeitgeber Zeitung*, May 1, 1926.

[32] Walter Zollinger (Zurich Unfall), "Fürsorgeeinrichtungen für Angestellte und Arbeiter", *Neue Zürcher Zeitung*, October 18, 1918.

[33] On corporatist proposals, see Schmid, *Wirtschaft, Staat und Macht*, pp. 121–5; Quirin Weber, *Korporatismus und Sozialismus: die Idee der berufsständischen Ordnung im schweizerischen Katholizismus während der Zwischenkriegszeit* (Freiburg: Universitätsverlag Freiburg, 1989), pp. 46–51. On the scientific management movement, see Rudolf Jaun, *Management und Arbeiterschaft: Verwissenschaftlichung und Rationalisierung der Arbeitsverhältnisse in der Schweiz 1873–1959* (Zurich: Chronos, 1986), pp. 67–75; Matthieu Leimgruber, *Taylorisme et management en Suisse romande 1917–1950* (Lausanne: Antipodes, 2001), pp. 13–40.

followed the general strike. These conferences dealt with issues ranging from unemployment benefits to new forms of remuneration, as well as the role of corporate welfare programs. Private organizations such as the Association for People's Welfare (Schweizerischer Verband Volksdienst, hereafter Volksdienst) formed the backbone of the corporate-sponsored social offensive.[34] For the economist Jakob Lorenz, one of the leading advocates of the Volksdienst, pre-emptive corporate social reforms had a "prophylactic role" to play in the troubled times that followed the war. This disillusioned Socialist, who acted as a bridge between business reform milieus and Catholic social doctrine, was convinced that encouraging "social reform as a principle" among employers would help capitalism to avoid reactive, or "curative", social reforms:

> Social reform resulting from class struggle gives way to a damaging social situation, in which political parties are pitted against each other and try to resolve social problems under the pressure of an imminent danger. In this situation, social reform works as a cure. Social reform as a principle, however, works as a prophylactic. Its task consists in pre-empting social struggle, so as not only to avoid a damaging social situation, but also to resolve as much as possible the roots of [social problems].[35]

This social activism at the corporate level redoubled the efforts undertaken by Federal Councilor Edmund Schulthess to defuse social and political tensions, notably by making the AHV a key issue on the post-war political agenda. Tellingly, the newsletter of the Volksdienst, *Soziale Informationen*, kept a regular tally of new pension plans and praised them as living proof of "corporate social consciousness".[36] Once again, corporate social activism followed similar trends in the United States, where welfare capitalism "buttressed the business offensive of the 1920s", and in France and Germany, where a "technocratic vision of social peace" also spread among large firms eager to combine welfare measures and Taylorist rationalization.[37] Corporate-sponsored social reform lost some momentum as the threat of workers' mobilization subsided and

34 Jakob Tanner, *Fabrikmahlzeit: Ernährungswissenschaft, Industriearbeit und Volksernährung in der Schweiz* (Zurich: Chronos, 1999), pp. 273–331.

35 Jakob Lorenz, *Zur Einführung in die Arbeiterfrage unter besonderer Berücksichtigung schweizerischer Verhältnisse* (Zurich: Orell Füssli, 1921), p. 5. During the 1930s, Jakob Lorenz (1883–1946) became a leading proponent of conservative, and even fascist, corporatist measures. See Markus Zürcher, "Jakob Lorenz: vom Sozialisten zum Korporationentheoretiker", in *Intellektuelle von rechts: Ideologie und Politik in der Schweiz 1918–1939*, ed. Aram Mattioli (Zurich: Orell Füssli, 1995), pp. 219–38.

36 "Alters- und Invalidenversicherung durch die Industrie", *Soziale Informationen*, February 15, 1921.

37 Martin Fiedler, "Betriebliche Sozialpolitik in der Zwischenkriegszeit: Wege der Interpretation und Probleme der Forschung in deutsch-französischen Vergleich", *Geschichte und Gesellschaft* 22 (1996), pp. 350–75 (quotation p. 367); Colin Gordon, *New Deals:*

employers faced the economic crisis of the early 1920s. The Social Conferences nevertheless helped to raise business awareness about the advantages of employment-based benefits and were an incubator for the first association devoted to the defense of private pension schemes.

In September 1921, the fourth Social Conference devoted its attention to the challenges of social legislation for private employee benefits. Gathered in the "welfare house" of the synthetic textile manufacturer Viscosa in Emmenbrücke, company owners and managers acknowledged the tremendous growth in pension plans since the introduction of the tax on war profits. They unanimously stressed the importance of safeguarding occupational provision at a time when the introduction of social insurance was expected in the short to mid-term. Putting in perspective the results of his 1916 survey of corporate welfare schemes, Arnold Guise of the Baden Technical Society pointed out that despite their expansion, postwar pension plans remained selective, favored white-collar over blue-collar workers, and did not offer adequate benefits. Guise also assessed negatively the "increasing fragmentation" of occupational provision and urged his audience to create regional or industry-wide pension plans in order to solve such issues as the lack of portability rights (the transfer of pension contributions and benefits between successive employers) which hindered labor mobility.[38]

Arnold Guise's appeals in favor of the orderly expansion of private benefits were characteristic of Taylorist and "industrial betterment" experts. By the mid-1920s, multi-employer plans covered small regional savings banks and electricity utilities.[39] However, they remained of marginal importance in comparison with the company plans that dominated occupational provision in leading manufacturing and financial sectors. Employers' use of pension schemes as fiscal refuges and tools for personnel management ran counter to rationalization proposals that were aimed at homogenizing pension provision. This situation differed markedly from

*business, labor, and politics in America, 1920–1935* (Cambridge; New York: Cambridge University Press, 1994), p. 253.

38 "Protokoll der IV. Sozialkonferenz für die schweizerische Industrie", *Soziale Informationen*, November 1921, pp. 35–9. The Federal Private Insurance Office also criticized the lack of portability rights in company pension plans and advised instead the creation of industry-wide and group pension plans. See *Die privaten Versicherungsunternehmungen in der Schweiz in 1916* (Berne: Eidgenössisches Versicherungsamt, 1917), p. 53*.

39 Efforts to set up a multi-employer pension plan for small railroad companies would not succeed before 1933. See *50 ans de la Caisse de pensions ASCOOP 1933–1983* (Berne: ASCOOP, 1983); Jakob Bertschinger, *Caisse de pension des centrales suisses d'électricité, rapport jubilaire 1922–1947* (Zurich, 1947); Marzio Sailer, *Les 50 ans de la Caisse de prévoyance des banques et caisses d'assurances suisses* (Bellinzona: [Caisse de prévoyance de banques et caisses d'épargne suisses], 1973). See also Arbeitgeberverband geschäftsleitende Ausschuss, January 11, 1923, p. 191, SAV.

that in the Netherlands, where industry-wide pension plans set up during the interwar decades constituted the core of the expansion of occupational provision.[40]

The fourth Social Conference was followed by the creation, in January 1922, of the Swiss Association of Support Funds and Foundations for Old Age and Disability (Schweizerischer Verband der Unterstützungskassen und Stiftungen für Alter und Invalidität, SVUSAI). Until 1925, the SVUSAI was part of the social research department of the Volksdienst headed by Jakob Lorenz and was presided over by Hans Wirz, the social welfare secretary of the Tobler chocolate factories. The statutes of this association, comprising a handful of leading firms, supported "the rational expansion and encouragement of relief measures" as well as "the defense of the common interests of (employers' plans) and the fostering of mutual contacts between them". The rationalization of pension provision envisioned by Arnold Guise ranked low on the SVUSAI agenda, and the first public meetings of the association asked federal and cantonal authorities to expand tax exemptions for pension plans. In 1925, a second version of the SVUSAI statutes specified that the defense of the common interests of pension plans was especially important "in issues regarding public social insurance and fiscal policy".[41]

The protracted social policy debates that had characterized the aftermath of World War I and the upsurge in occupational provision left time for the pension lobby to regroup.[42] The emergence of the pension

[40] Jost van Genabeek, "Collectieve pensioenregelingen 1800–2000", in *Studies over zekerheidsarrangementen: risico's, risicobestrijding en verzekeringen in Nederland vanaf de Middeleeuwen*, ed. Jacques van Gerwen and Marco van Leeuwen (Amsterdam: NEHA, 1998), pp. 883–905.

[41] On the foundation and first activities of the SVUSAI, see "Zusammenschluss von Unterstützungskassen und Stiftungen", *Soziale Informationen*, November 1922; "Verband der Unterstzützungskassen und Stiftungen für das Alter", *Neue Zürcher Zeitung*, December 5, 1923; "Besteuerung von Wohlfahrtsfond", *Schweizerische Arbeitgeber Zeitung*, December 1, 1923. For the 1925 statutes, see Werner Ammann, *Die Altersfürsorge des Bundes und die Durchführung in den Kantonen* (Basle: Helbing & Lichtenhahn, 1934), p. 4. See also Félix Lotz, *30 Jahre Verbandstätigkeit: Referat an der Hauptversammlung der Schweizerischer Verband für Personalfürsorge privatwirtschaflicher Unternehmungen vom 28. April 1952 in Basel* (Zurich: SVPP, 1952). Sources on the SVUSAI are located in file V Schweiz 3234, SNB. See also the papers of the successor of the SVUSAI, the Schweizerischer Verband für privatwirtschaftliche Personalfürsorge (SVPP), founded in 1942, file V Schweiz 2435, SNB. The Swiss Association of Pension Funds (Association suisse des institutions de prévoyance, ASIP) is the direct descendant of the SVUSAI/SVPP and remains the mouthpiece of leading pension plans in current social policy debates. See: http://www.asip.ch (November 2006).

[42] In 1922 and 1923, similar pension lobby groups had been founded in Germany (Verband Deutscher Privatpensionskassen) and the United Kingdom (Association of Superannuation and Pension Funds). See Hannah, *Inventing retirement*, p. 20; P. Koch, "Zur Geschichte der betrieblichen Altersversorgung in Deutschland", in *Jubiläumsschrift*

lobby echoed the situation that had prevailed around 1900, when private providers of health benefits had formed coalitions to face the challenge of the KUVG. However, the SVUSAI differed markedly from the associations of mutual benefit societies that had played a role in the derailment of the Lex Forrer. The political weight of mutualism had been clearly centered in western Switzerland, from where its proponents had fought a rearguard defense of traditional philanthropy that overlapped with federalist opposition to social insurance. By contrast, this hotbed of anti-KUVG activism was never at the center of the pension lobby. From the outset, the SVUSAI's profile was unambiguously corporate: its core membership originated from the manufacturing and financial centers of Basle and Zurich and represented the interests of large and richly endowed pension plans. These differences also point to the qualitative difference between old age pensions and health provision. From the 1920s, the issue of planning for retirement mobilized far more assets and actuarial expertise than the twisting jungle of mutual benefit societies. Moreover, the philanthropic and patronage preoccupations of not-for-profit mutualism differed from the personnel and financial issues that absorbed the attention of corporate pension plans. Alongside the SVUSAI, insurers selling group contracts formed the second arm of the nascent pension lobby, reinforcing its corporate profile.

Group life insurance contracts, a rare occurrence before 1914, directly benefitted from wartime tax exemptions. As the federal administration was unable to cope with the groundswell of inquiries originating from firms eager for tax exemptions, it often advised entrepreneurs to contact life insurers to solve practical issues related to the creation and management of pension schemes. This was a godsend for the marketing of group pension products.[43] The development of group contracts coincided with a decisive expansion period for insurers. The 1920s witnessed both dramatic growth and diversification: new companies were founded, and life insurance thrived as Swiss companies took over whole market segments previously occupied by German competitors battered by the consequences of war, economic crisis, and hyperinflation.[44] The

*zum 50-jährigen Bestehen der ABA Arbeitsgemeinschaft für betriebliche Altersversorgung* (Heidelberg: ABA, 1989), pp. 1–18.

43 K. Böschenstein and H. Held, "Bericht über die Durchführung der Eidgenössischen Kriegsgewinnsteuer", p. 50. See also *Société suisse d'assurances générales sur la vie humaine 1857–1957* (Zurich: Rentenanstalt, 1956), p. 218; Walter Zollinger, *Die Kollektivversicherung als Alters-, Invaliden- und Hinterbliebenenfürsorge* (Zurich: Separatabdruck aus "Unsere Banken", 1926).

44 Stefan Karlen, Lucas Chocomeli, Kristin D'haemer, *et al.*, *Schweizerische Versicherungsgesellschaften im Machtbereich des Dritten Reichs* (Zurich: Chronos, 2002), pp. 53–66. In 1910, Swiss insurance companies controlled only 43 percent of their domestic market. In the aftermath of the war, this share rose to 64 percent in 1920 and 95 percent

combination of fiscal incentives, corporate social activism, and the general expansion of life insurance activities led insurers to quickly recognize the potential for group contracts.

By 1918, Rentenanstalt, which was then the sole provider of these contracts, had begun a systematic propaganda effort to promote them. In December 1921, the first issue of a Rentenanstalt newsletter on group contracts described how life insurers envisioned their role as providers of old age benefits. This pamphlet argued that, by setting up pension schemes, entrepreneurs fulfilled a moral mission. Providing benefits for superannuated workers – and especially for loyal white-collar employees – also ensured the stability, loyalty, and finally the "amortization" of the labor force. To reconcile these moral and personnel management missions, Rentenanstalt then promoted its group plans – based on solid actuarial expertise and sound financial assets – as the best deal for socially conscious firms. The newsletter also urged its corporate readership to consider group insurance in a wider political context. In a period of sharp class conflicts, the pre-emptive development of old age provision was seen as a deterrent against the encroachment of the state. "From the point of view of the private sector", insisted Rentenanstalt, "voluntary welfare activities are preferable to social insurance. To encourage the former is in the interest of commercial and manufacturing circles. The more firms can decide to take upon themselves the costs of social provision, the less it becomes necessary to envision state-based solutions that might end up burdening production costs."[45] This text reiterated the pre-emption rhetoric that had characterized the prewar development of people's life insurance (Volksversicherung) and extended it to the postwar expansion of corporate pension plans.

In 1924, Rentenanstalt set up a new group insurance division. Other firms such as Basler Life, Vita (a 1922 offshoot of the Zurich insurance company), and Winterthur Life (founded in 1923) soon followed suit.[46] By 1930, group premiums amounted to 10 percent of overall life insurance premiums, and ten companies – with Rentenanstalt and the three companies mentioned above dominating the market – were proposing group contracts (see Figure 2.3 and Figure 2.4). Competition in the group market was particularly sharp: while independent consultants peddled their services to firms eager to set up new pension plans, insurers

in 1925. See Peter Borscheid, "Vertrauensgewinn und Vertrauensverlust: das Auslandsgeschäft der deutschen Versicherungswirtschaft 1870–1945", *Vierteljahrschrift für Sozial- und Wirtschaftsgeschichte* 88 (2001), pp. 311–45 (pp. 333–7).

45 *Rentenanstalt: Blätter für Angestellten- und Arbeiterfürsorge*, December 1921, p. 8.

46 Karlen, Chocomeli, D'haemer *et al.*, *Schweizerische Versicherungsgesellschaften*, p. 60; Karl Lüönd, *La passion de l'avenir: 125ᵉ anniversaire de la Zurich: histoire et vision d'un groupe multinational* (Zurich: NZZ Verlag, 1998), p. 110.

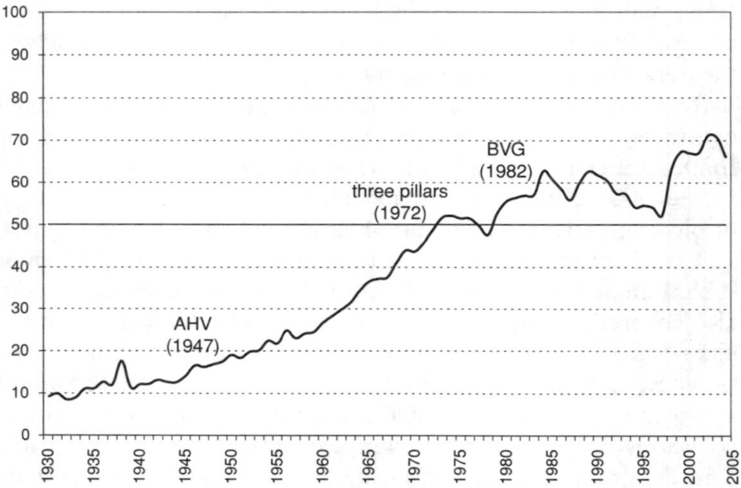


Figure 2.3 Group insurance premiums as a percentage share of overall life insurance premiums, 1930–2005.

vied with each other to attract new customers. Stressing the actuarial challenges of implementing pensions, insurers presented group contracts as a safe and convenient alternative to company-level plans. They even denounced entrepreneurs who accumulated war profits in opaque pension plans that were used as mere "business reserves": instead they urged them to choose the "ideal solution" of group contracts that smoothed over labor conflicts and sweetened the bitter pill of wage losses incurred by workers during the postwar economic crisis.[47] Employers' newsletters such as the *Schweizerische Arbeitgeber Zeitung* added momentum to the expansion of group plans by publishing monthly lists of new group contracts signed by life insurance companies. In the context of heightened competition and in reaction to the rapid spread of group plans, the Federal Private Insurance Office introduced minimum rules for contracts in 1931. From that point, its annual reports distinguished group contracts from other life insurance activities.[48]

The expansion of group contracts among smaller firms contributed to the increasing fragmentation of occupational provision. By 1930, group plans represented two-thirds of all core pension plans – as against

[47] "Die Gruppenversicherung", *Schweizerische Zeitschrift für Privat- und Sozialversicherung*, September 1924, pp. 73–5.

[48] Markus Roth, "Die rechtliche Natur der Gruppenversicherung in der Schweiz", Dissertation der juristischen Fakultät, Universität Bern, 1935, p. 12.

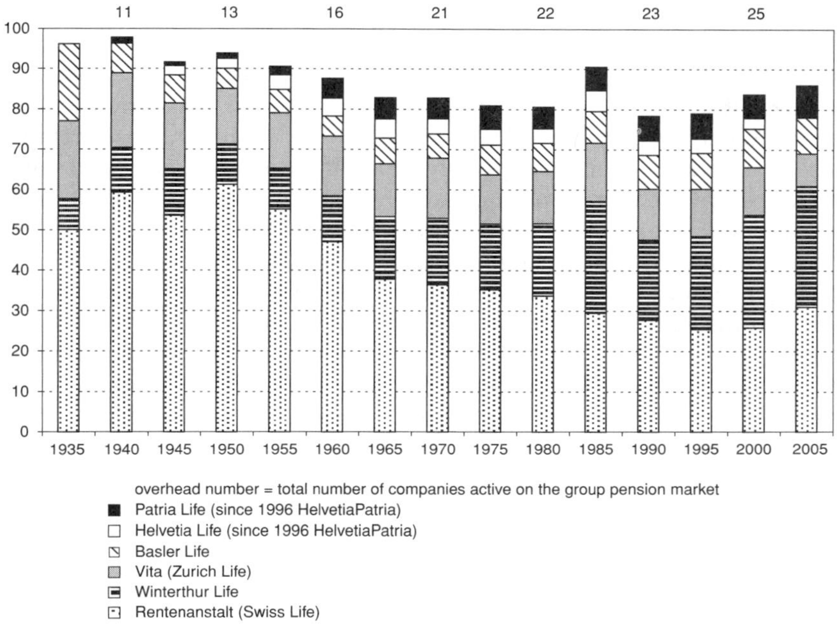


Figure 2.4 Percentage share of the group pension market controlled by leading insurance companies, 1935–2005.
*Source for Figures 2.3 and 2.4: Die privaten Versicherungsunternehmungen in der Schweiz* (Bern, Bundesamt für Privatversicherung: 1931–2006).

one-third in 1920 (see Table A.1, p. 290). In 1924, two-thirds of the group contracts managed by Rentenanstalt included fewer than thirty policies, with a dozen contracts with larger firms containing the bulk of existing policies.[49] Public administrations had occasionally outsourced pension provision to Rentenanstalt at the end of the nineteenth century. However, the majority of group plans founded during the interwar era were in the private sector. Small and medium-sized businesses that lacked the actuarial capacity to organize company-level plans turned to insurance companies to set up pension schemes, whereas larger firms used group contracts to create special plans for their managers and directors.

[49] Hans Asch, *Die Gruppenlebensversicherung: mit besonderer Berücksichtigung der Schweiz* (Berne: Stämpfli, 1930), p. 8. See also "Personal-Fürsorge: Selbstversicherung oder Anschluss an eine Versicherungsgesellschaft?", *Schweizerische Arbeitgeber Zeitung*, September 9 (1st part) and September 16 (2nd part) 1922. On group plans, see Werner Friedli, "Über den Zusammenschluss kleiner Pensionskassen", *Schweizerische Zeitschrift für Volkswirtschaft und Statistik* (1921), pp. 291–6, as well as Rentenanstalt, "Jahresbericht Kollektivversicherungen" for the years 1923–1930, file 676.21/1, SLA.

As with other employers, insurers were eager to seize the opportunity of tax exemptions for welfare purposes. Confronted by relentless attempts from Rentenanstalt to secure them, an irritated civil servant from the Federal Revenues Administration had to remind the company in 1920 that: "When the legislature [had] set up . . . an exceptional preferential tax treatment in order to spur benevolent initiatives, its intention was not to transform the duty of paying taxes into a total or even partial illusion because of exemptions."[50] In contrast to the fiscal privileges that fueled the development of the "hidden welfare state", federal taxes to finance social insurance programs found no support among insurance companies. In the early 1920s, insurers actively participated in the bitter fight against the Socialist proposal for a special tax on wealth that might have been used to finance federal pensions. More generally, insurers held that "irrational fiscal measures" such as the taxation of financial transactions (Stempelsteuer) endangered the "civilizing role" of the insurance sector.[51] Life insurance companies systematically assessed the development of the AHV according to the needs of corporate pension plans and in particular of their own group contracts.

Prominent firms such as Rentenanstalt increasingly realized that the fates of both areas of old age provision were linked. In a celebration of popular life insurance (Volksversicherung), Georg Schärtlin, director of Rentenanstalt, emphasized in 1919 that social insurance would be welcome as long as it stimulated "a widening and deepening of the idea of insurance and the encouragement of self-provision".[52] Before World War I, group provision had remained in the shadow of Volksversicherung contracts. After the war, the situation was reversed. If the latter steadily continued its development, group contracts would now be the insurers' weapon of choice in the struggle over the contested boundaries of old age provision. The emergence of occupational provision immediately interfered, or rather interacted, with social policy debates. How would private pension plans and life insurance companies react toward the AHV? What would be the respective roles attributed to the envisioned federal pensions and to existing occupational plans? These issues constituted a major point of contention during pension debates.

50 Federal Revenues Administration to Rentenanstalt executive board, July 20, 1920, file 68.100/17, Kriegsgewinnsteuer 1914–1918, SLA. See also file 68.100/16, Kriegssteuer 1914–1918, SLA. For examples of opposition to wartime taxation at the Zurich insurance company, see Lüönd, *La passion de l'avenir*, p. 101.

51 "Das Kulturprogramm des Versicherungswesen", *Schweizerische Zeitschrift für Privat- und Sozialversicherung*, August 1924, pp. 15–17.

52 Georg Schärtlin, *25 Jahre Volksversicherung der Schweizerischen Lebensversicherungs- und Rentenanstalt in Zürich (1894–1918)* (Zurich: Fretz, 1919), p. 15.

## Early skirmishes on the boundaries of old age provision (1923–1925)

The conservative reaction that followed the general strike hindered a rapid implementation of social insurance, and increasing gridlock soon characterized the politics of pensions. As the AHV found itself in disarray in the Federal Assembly, Edmund Schulthess briefly considered a pension system based solely on occupational or private providers as a means of extricating old age provision from its financial and political logjam. These debates revealed the unfeasibility of such solutions, while underlining insurers' awareness that hybrid solutions, where social insurance would coexist with occupational plans, might well constitute the best configuration for marketing group plans and ensuring the development of private pensions.

Because of the resistance exercised by conservative political forces, labor circles doubted whether social insurance could be implemented at the federal level. In 1923, the leadership of the Gewerkschaftsbund, dismayed by the protracted progress of pension legislation, contemplated the idea of organizing social insurance on a union basis or in partnership with employers. This would have led to the replacement of universal old age coverage with industry-wide occupational schemes. Despite their expansion, union-based old age schemes remained rudimentary and were found in the transport sector, the printing trade, and the metal and machine-making sector. More akin to savings and relief schemes, these plans did not bear comparison with those of large public administrations and leading firms.[53] The Metalworkers and Watchmakers' Union (Schweizerische Metall- und Uhrenarbeitnehmer-Verband) was one of the labor organizations that tried to challenge corporate welfare schemes on their own terrain. "In order to bind metalworkers and watchmakers to the union and to win new labor conflicts", declared Metalworkers secretary Konrad Ilg to the central committee of his union, "we must have at our disposal insurance institutions similar to those of our opponents."[54]

[53] *Pensionskassenstatistik 1941*, pp. 73ff. The under-development of trade union old age provision can be contrasted with more extensive measures existing in the domain of sickness or unemployment benefits: Bernard Degen and Markus Kübler, "Die Gewerkschaften zwischen Integration und Ausgrenzung", in *Krisen und Stabilisierung: die Schweiz in der Zwischenkriegszeit*, ed. Sébastien Guex and Brigitte Studer (Zurich: Chronos, 1998), pp. 127–43 (p. 130).

[54] Minutes of the Central Committee of the Metalworkers' Union, quoted in *Unsere Zukunft hat Geschichte: ein Jahrhundert im Gewerkschaftskampf gegen materielle Not, für Gerechtigkeit und Menschenwürde. Eine Festschrift zum hundertjährigen Bestehen des schweizerischen Metall- und Uhrenarbeitnehmer-Verbandes* (Berne: SMUV, 1988), p. 43.

Such declarations appealed to the legacy of mutualism in which many labor organizations found their roots. However, the Metalworkers' Union's efforts to set up a real pension plan (Alterskasse) did not lead to satisfactory results. Before 1938, the union could field only a modest old age relief scheme (Altersfürsorgekasse) that paled beside large corporate plans.[55] While spending a lot of energy and resources on union-based provision, the Metalworkers' Union neglected or even showed hostility toward social insurance programs that they saw as competing against union-based plans. By turning their backs on social insurance and simultaneously pressing employers to accept joint management procedures, labor organizations found themselves trapped in the corporate dynamics they were trying to challenge. Trade union entanglement in employer-dominated occupational provision significantly restrained labor leverage in the area of social insurance. In the end, the prospect of jointly managed occupational pensions found a limited echo among the affiliates of the Gewerkschaftsbund, and no support from employers' federations unwilling to let trade unions participate in the management and organization of welfare schemes.[56]

In contrast to the trade unions' inconclusive attempts to bypass the AHV or to compete with corporate welfare schemes, insurers occupied a strategic position in both the development of occupational provision and the AHV policy-making process. Federal Councilor Edmund Schulthess systematically invited life insurers to the deliberations of the commissions of federal experts that shaped the AHV. This integration enabled the state to benefit from actuarial expertise, but also defused the potential opposition of insurance companies to the scheme. On the other hand, it gave insurers a privileged vantage point from which they could keep an eye on the AHV and make sure that federal pensions would not compete with private provision.

At the same time that unions were considering the option of union-based or joint labor–employers' pension alternatives to the AHV, Federal Councilor Edmund Schulthess envisioned organizing old age insurance on a private basis. The Federal Council had already gone on record in 1919 as saying that multiple pension providers would constitute a very complicated solution. However, financial prospects for the AHV

55 Ernst Wütrich, "Die Sozialversicherungen des Schweizerischen Metall- und Uhrenarbeiterverbandes", *Schweizerische Zeitschrift für Sozialversicherung* (1963), pp. 215–28.

56 Marco De Nicolo, *Die Sozialpolitik des Schweizerischen Gewerkschaftsbundes (1880–1960)* (Winterthur: P. G. Keller, 1962), pp. 92–6. On metal producers' and machine makers' refusal to set up jointly managed pension plans, see Robert Fluder *et al.*, *Gewerkschaften und Angestelltenverbände in der schweizerischen Privatwirtschaft* (Zurich: Seismo Verlag, 1991), p. 582.

had reached a nadir after the June 1923 failure of the alcohol tax. During the summer following this vote, Edmund Schulthess proposed to remove disability benefits from the AHV or to limit the scope of pensions to workers who were not covered by occupational schemes. Convinced that this substantial downsizing could save the AHV, Schulthess asked life insurance companies if they would help the Confederation to organize basic pension coverage by setting up a privately organized and publicly subsidized institution. This would have enabled the Federal Council to overcome resistance to financing the AHV through general revenues or new taxes. Insurers welcomed the abandonment of disability benefits and offered the suggestion that these could be provided through decentralized health plans. With its focus on bare essentials, opting-out possibilities for existing occupational plans (which constituted, in historian André Lasserre's words, "the price to pay to ensure the collaboration of private funds"), and limited public financing, this revised and whittled-down proposal was a pale shadow of what had first been promised in 1919.[57]

The Union of Life Insurance Companies convened in May 1924 to discuss this issue. During the meeting, Georg Schärtlin of Rentenanstalt reminded his colleagues that social insurance had always been an issue of the utmost importance for insurers. He explained that the key question was not whether or not the AHV had to be realized, but how pensions were to be shaped so that they did not hinder the activities of life insurance companies.[58] Edmund Schulthess' proposal was deemed impractical, since a state-controlled pension institution might overshadow group and company pensions, and its large financial reserves raised the specter of an unwelcome concentration of capital in the hands of the Confederation.

Insurance companies were highly resistant to a hybrid public–private pension institution that might be modeled on the Accident Insurance Fund (SUVA) set up in 1918. According to Alfred Georg, an executive of Genevoise Assurances, insurers had to turn down any proposal that would burden them with the organization of basic coverage. The basic AHV benefits distributed this way would be deemed "scandalous" by

[57] "Konferenz des Volkswirtschaftsdepartments über die allfällige Mitwirkung der Gesellschaften an der Durchführung der AHV", July 4, 1923, file 310.31, SLA, and "Konferenz des Bundesamt für Sozialversicherung mit Vertretern von privaten Versicherungsgesellschaften", September 10 to September 11, 1923. See also Böschenstein, *Bundesrat Edmund Schulthess*, pp. 166–8; Greiner, "Die Personalversicherung", pp. 372ff; Lasserre, "L'institution de l'AVS", pp. 280–2, 393 (note 88).

[58] Minutes of the meeting of the Konferenz der Direktoren der schweizerischen Lebensversicherungs-Gesellschaften (hereafter KDSL), May 23, 1924, p. 8, file Q127 206, ZFS.

the working class, and reproaches about the shortcomings of the scheme would not be directed at the Confederation, but at insurance companies: "The envisioned institution would find itself in an untenable situation: as a recipient of federal subsidies it would be strictly controlled by the Confederation, and its possibilities to make profits would be limited. People would then say that private companies are unable to manage social insurance, and state monopoly would appear as the way toward salvation."[59] To the insurance companies, ensuring basic pensions on a private basis seemed a highly problematic, even dangerous, option.

Yet, contrary to the opinion of western Switzerland insurers, whose companies were minor players in the group market and stood against the AHV,[60] Georg Schärtlin of Rentenanstalt argued that insurers could not afford to break away from the AHV commission. On the contrary, Schärtlin insisted, insurance companies had to "safeguard [their] freedom of movement; but besides this caveat we should give a positive answer [to the Federal Council]".[61] Other leading providers of group contracts (Vita, Winterthur Life, Basler Life) agreed that continuing to collaborate with Edmund Schulthess offered a useful position to keep in check any challenge to private old age provision. Life insurers followed this two-pronged approach to the AHV. While continuing to advise and support Schulthess in his efforts, they took pains to contain the scale and scope of federal pension benefits in order to safeguard occupational provision.[62]

In its answer to the Federal Council, the Union of Life Insurance Companies opposed state-based funded pensions and warned against any intrusive regulation of private plans. Insurers reiterated their preferences for modest pensions financed by contributions on a pay-as-you-go basis (i.e. where annual payroll contributions broadly cover annual expenses) and consumer taxes.[63] The Union also hinted that insurers would gladly burden themselves with basic coverage if the Confederation allowed the

[59] Ibid., p. 9.

[60] Life insurers from western Switzerland were close to the Liberal-Conservative party. As a leading member of the Geneva Chamber of Commerce, Alfred Georg had actively participated in the 1911 referendum against the KUVG and opposed the AHV. See Alfred Georg, *Contre l'étatisme et la bureaucratie: souvenirs de luttes 1894–1927* (Geneva: Imprimeries du Journal de Genève, 1936).

[61] KDSL, May 23, 1924, p. 10, file Q127 206, ZFS. [62] Ibid.

[63] Emile Marchand, *A propos de l'introduction des assurances sociales en Suisse: contribution à l'étude des diverses possibilités pour la répartition des charges* (Berne: Stämpfli, 1921); "Message complémentaire du Conseil fédéral à l'Assemblée fédérale concernant l'assurance-vieillesse, invalidité et survivants, du 23 juillet 1924", in *Feuille Fédérale* (Berne: Chancellerie fédérale, 1924), volume II, pp. 717–78 (pp. 740–6). See also "Ein Vorschlag und ein Weg", *Schweizerische Zeitschrift für Privat- und Sozialversicherung*, August 1924, pp. 24–7.

creation of a pension consortium entirely funded and managed by life insurance companies. Such a consortium would then organize basic coverage according to federal regulations but would be authorized to earn profits. This proposal was turned down by Edmund Schulthess, as it implied surrendering the AHV to business interests.

In conclusion, insurance companies were not keen to organize highly regulated basic old age provision that would bring little profit. In tune with fiscal conservatives, they also opposed the accumulation by the federal state of funds that might compete with financial institutions in capital markets, preferring a pay-as-you-go system. Of course, the opposition to state-based funding contrasted with employers' and insurers' determination to preserve their own pension schemes. Commenting on the uncertain contours of the AHV in the fall of 1924, a Rentenanstalt newsletter pointed out that whatever solutions might be chosen for the AHV, "a large part of provision, arguably its core part, should remain in the hands of private providers". Another insurance journal reminded the industry that state pensions were not by definition inimical to insurers and could prove less harmful than sharp interfirm competition. Besides, the same journal noted, "in every country that has introduced social insurance . . . private insurance products and social insurance benefits have not been at each other's throats but have encouraged and even complemented each other".[64] From the 1920s, the division of labor between the state and private providers of old age provision always constituted a thorny issue. The boundaries between pay-as-you-go and funding or between basic and supplementary pensions would be debated until the introduction of the AHV in 1947 and remain controversial during the decades following World War II as the three-pillar doctrine was formulated.

Swiss insurers' debates on the organization of pensions had echoes on the other side of the Atlantic. Aware of the potential shortcomings of existing private plans and, notably, of their often-fragile financial foundations, American life insurance companies enjoined employers to adopt modern and actuarially sound forms of private provision. This proposed rationalization of occupational pensions was meant to deter state involvement, but also to guarantee a selective system of employment-based social benefits while serving insurers' own interests in the development of group products. Historian Steven Sass explains that "cooperation [between corporations and insurance companies] and preemption of government were hallmarks of corporate thinking in the 1920s", and that insurers

[64] *Rentenanstalt: Blätter für Angestellten- und Arbeiterfürsorge*, no. 8, September 1925, p. 9, "Die Sozialversicherung und ihr Nutzen für die Privatversicherung", *Schweizerische Zeitschrift für Privat- und Sozialversicherung*, August 1924, pp. 15–17.

were eager to win "a government pension mandate", so that "several percent of national income would, for the foreseeable future, flow to the nation's insurance industry". However, a 1923 conference convened by New York-based Metropolitan Life to convince large corporations of this idea ended in a fiasco. Business executives were not ready to abandon to insurers control over company pension plans that played a major role in the management of the workforce and in lowering their tax expenditures.[65]

On both sides of the Atlantic, life insurers were realizing the limits of solutions that relied exclusively on private pension schemes. Their companies turned to another strategy. Instead of opposing or pre-empting social insurance, insurers perceived that abandoning basic benefits to the state would enable private providers to focus on supplementary provision. The concluding section of this chapter will return to the development of this notion in the United States during the 1930s. In Switzerland, early attempts to delineate the respective areas covered by the AHV and existing pension plans remained inconclusive. Worse still, as we will see in the next section, haggling over this issue would contribute to the failure of the Lex Schulthess.

When citizens voted in December 1925 on the constitutional amendment on old age insurance, the first AHV draft had been whittled down to the bone. In addition, Edmund Schulthess omitted financing details in order to overcome Federal Councilor Jean Marie Musy's continuing obstruction and to oppose the Rothenberger Initiative that envisioned financing the AHV with the tax on war profits. Launched in 1919 by Christian Rothenberger, a Radical politician keen to dampen class struggle through social reform, the initiative was opposed by a united front of insurers, employers, and bourgeois parties. In July 1925, the Rothenberger Initiative was rejected by 58 percent of voters.[66] This defeat cleared the path for the constitutional amendment on the AHV, which was accepted by two-thirds of voters in December 1925. The principle of social insurance had survived, but this victory was ambiguous: neither organizational nor financial issues were resolved. The constitutional article stated that the proceeds of tobacco and alcohol taxes would be earmarked for social insurance, but no consensus had yet been reached on

[65] Sass, *The promise of private pensions*, pp. 69–79 (quotation p. 71). See also Jennifer L. Klein, *For all these rights: business, labor, and the shaping of America's public–private welfare state* (Princeton: Princeton University Press, 2003), pp. 27–39.

[66] KDSL, September 23, 1925, p. 6, file Q127 206, ZFS. On the business campaign against the Rothenberger Initiative, see Vorort Vorstand, April 29 and May 27, 1925, file 1.5.3.6, AfZ-SHIV. For vote results, see Ritzmann-Blickenstorfer and Siegenthaler, eds., *Swiss Historical Statistics*, Table X10.

the level of AHV contributions and benefits.[67] As had been the case with health and accident insurance during the late 1890s, the constitutional amendment was only a very tentative step toward the implementation of social insurance.

Tellingly, the steering committee (Vorort) of the Federation of Trade and Industry declined to join the campaign in favor of the constitutional amendment and adopted a neutral stance during the final weeks preceding the vote. The Arbeitgeberverband also shared this wait-and-see attitude and, as preparation for coming debates on the implementation of the law, launched a survey of existing private pension plans.[68] As the contours of the AHV were still unclear, some employers feared that their pension plans would either have to face the competition of a federal scheme or might be constrained by state regulation.

In October 1925, the SVUSAI pension lobby complained that the current AHV drafts did not contain clear answers on these key issues. According to Walther Stampfli, social secretary of the Von Roll steelworks and future "father of the AHV" during World War II, employers who had set up pension plans should be allowed to opt out from the future AHV. Other members of the SVUSAI representing Basle employers worried that the introduction of meager federal pensions would lead to the creation of supplementary cantonal schemes that might compete with occupational plans.[69] Although insurers did not raise such objections, they were quick to denounce the alleged inferiority of social insurance in comparison with private provision. In correspondence with federal authorities on the taxation of insurance contracts, insurers Georg Schärtlin (Rentenanstalt) and Alfred Georg (Genevoise Assurances) thus complained that such taxes were "incompatible with the general interest of the nation and seem highly paradoxical at a time when we are about to throw tens of millions [of Swiss francs] into the bottomless pit of social insurance to reach moral and material benefits that bear no comparison with those accomplished by private forms of provision".[70]

67 Lasserre, "L'institution de l'AVS", pp. 282–92.

68 Vorort Vorstand, November 27, 1925, p. 10, file 1.5.3.6, AfZ-SHIV; Arbeitgeberverband Vorstand, November 5, 1925, pp. 84–8, SAV. On the pension plan survey, see Arbeitgeberverband geschäftsleitende Ausschuss, November 20, 1925, p. 49, SAV.

69 "Industrielle Alters- und Invalidenfürsorge und allgemeine Alters- und Hinterbliebenen-Versicherung", *Schweizerische Arbeitgeber Zeitung*, October 24, 1925. Besides Walther Stampfli, the key speakers at this meeting were Hans Wirz, social secretary of the Tobler chocolate factory and president of the SVUSAI, Paul Scherrer, chief executive at the CIBA chemical corporation, and Hermann Henrici, secretary of the Basle Chamber of Commerce.

70 Alfred Georg to Federal Councillor Jean-Marie Musy, October 14, 1925. See also Georg Schärtlin to Hans Giorgio, director of the Federal Social Insurance Office, September 24, 1925, both letters in file 317/21, SLA.

Yet, insurers did not share the worries of the SVUSAI about a potential crowding-out of emerging corporate plans. We have to remember that the development of group insurance, as was the case with popular life insurance earlier, represented for them an interesting diversification, but not the core, of their business. As they were constantly in contact with Edmund Schulthess and the federal administration, life insurers also had more guarantees that their group contracts would not be threatened by a public scheme whose outlines remained blurry, but which nevertheless seemed to be geared toward very low benefits. Employers who were part of the SVUSAI did not enjoy the same access to AHV deliberations and were likely to be more preoccupied with the potential impact of social insurance on their pension schemes. In other words, when proponents of corporate employee benefits looked at the AHV, they considered it from the limited standpoint of their own pension plans – and not from a more global perspective, as insurers did – which contributed to their more sanguine attitude toward social insurance. When the outlines of the AHV became clearer, the reluctance of many SVUSAI affiliates to support social insurance only hardened.

## The demise of the Lex Schulthess (1926–1931)

During the second half of the 1920s, the AHV underwent several versions, and the final bill that emerged in 1929 still faced fierce opposition. Studies of social policy have usually explained the demise of the Lex Schulthess by pointing to the divisions between Edmund Schulthess' push for social reform and Jean-Marie Musy's fiscal conservatism, or by emphasizing the relentless opposition of federalist and conservative politicians.[71] Pensions finally reached the popular vote at the worst of times, for they coincided with the Depression. When the Federal Assembly accepted the pension law in June 1931, opponents of social insurance seized the opportunity to launch a referendum against it. In the context of deteriorating economic conditions, the Lex Schulthess failed to pass the referendum hurdle in December 1931. Alongside fiscal conservatism and plain opposition to social insurance, the definition of the boundaries between the AHV and occupational pension plans emerged as one of the main obstacles to the Lex Schulthess. Focusing on this issue enables us to understand employers' opinions of social insurance, and to underscore the role of the pension lobby in the defeat of the Lex Schulthess. After 1931, occupational provision could continue its expansion without

[71] Lasserre, "L'institution de l'AVS", pp. 293–315; Sommer, *Das Ringen um die soziale Sicherheit*, pp. 140–58.

being constrained by a state program. This configuration had long-term consequences for the development of the pension system.

The drafts of the pension legislation bore the imprint of the discussions that had taken place with insurers and took into account the uncertain financial revenues available for the AHV. Beginning in 1926, the AHV was envisioned as a basic pension whose modest benefits would have to be supplemented by additional pension schemes. These two components had very different organizational and financing structures. The universal basic pension (Grundversicherung) would be set up by the Confederation. As direct taxes and contributions linked to wage levels were ruled out by the bourgeois majority as too redistributive, basic pensions were to be financed by consumer taxes on tobacco and alcohol (representing half the financing needs), flat-rate contributions (one-third), and the returns on the accumulation of contributions in a reserve fund. In its initial 1926 version, supplementary pensions (Zusatzversicherung) would have provided earnings-related benefits financed by a 2 percent levy on payrolls. Existing public and private occupational pension plans, as well as regional schemes set up by cantonal authorities, were envisioned as insurance providers.[72] As we will see below, this second component attracted the ire of the pension lobby.

The Socialists greeted these AHV drafts with dismay. The left criticized the downward trend of proposed basic benefits, which were openly described by the Federal Council as "minimum provision" and averaged 10 percent of a skilled worker's wages.[73] However, the Socialists had only narrow room to maneuver, as any proposal to upgrade AHV benefits faced problems. In December 1929, the election to the Federal Council of a member from the Farmers', Artisans', and Burghers' Party reinforced the right wing of the bourgeois bloc and further endangered Schulthess' efforts to put together a solid consensus in favor of the AHV. Jean-Marie Musy's budgetary intransigence and the offensive by farmers' associations to obtain lower contribution levels limited the financial means available to the AHV. Catholic and federalist opposition to the idea of federal pensions represented another formidable obstacle. The left continued to support the pension bill, despite its meagerness, out of fear that its implementation might otherwise be postponed indefinitely. Although some trade unions continued to explore the idea of setting up pensions on an occupational basis, they adopted the same cautious stance

72 Lasserre, "L'institution de l'AVS", pp. 294–8, 301–4. See also "Message du Conseil fédéral à l'Assemblée fédérale relatif à un projet de loi sur l'assurance-vieillesse et l'assurance survivants, du 29 août 1929", *Feuille Fédérale* (Berne: Chancellerie fédérale, 1929), volume II, pp. 264, 273, 344.

73 Sommer, *Das Ringen um die soziale Sicherheit*, p. 147.

as the Socialists. The small Communist Party was the only dissenting voice on the left that relentlessly criticized and attacked the paucity of the Lex Schulthess.[74]

The dual pension system that emerged between 1926 and 1929 left "a large role for private initiative" and was meant to "placate employers who had set up pension plans and who feared the higher costs that might have been induced by too rigid a state scheme".[75] However, the first version of the supplementary component stipulated that firms with more than three employees would have to either set up pension plans or join a public supplementary scheme, which challenged the voluntary character of occupational provision. Federalists defending cantonal rights also denounced the fact that this draft left no role for the cantons in the implementation of the AHV. Because of such resistance, this early draft was replaced in 1928 by cantonal supplementary schemes with opting-out possibilities. The final version of the supplementary scheme outlined in Article 29 of the 1929 AHV bill did not contain any binding language. It only stated that cantons could "create or support other old age provision schemes" and that "no contributions [could] be imposed on employers".[76]

In a 1929 report on occupational pensions, the Federal Social Insurance Office underscored that the AHV would constitute a "modest supplement to the benefits of existing occupational schemes".[77] This notion, whereby selective occupational provision instead of social insurance was designated the basis of retirement pensions, closely echoed insurers' notion that "state pensions will only represent a complement added on to individual savings and, especially for workers, to the sums obtained through the provident institutions set up by employers".[78] This statement by Emile Marchand, a prominent Rentenanstalt executive, pointed to the interrelatedness of state and occupational old age provision, and formulated, albeit in reverse order, the shape of the future three-pillar pension system. For a contemporary study of group contracts, the "reciprocal relation" between "state-based social insurance and group life insurance" meant that "their development and design are mutually dependent on each other". However, "the supplementation and perfection of social insurance [would] always remain the task of group insurance".[79] This second quotation accurately describes the situation that finally emerged in 1947, when the AHV was explicitly designed as a basic pension that

74 Lasserre, "L'institution de l'AVS", pp. 299, 302–4. 75 Ibid., p. 295.

76 Ibid., p. 304. 77 *Pensionskassenstatistik 1925a*, p. 46.

78 Emile Marchand, "L'assurance sur la vie par groupe, en Suisse", in *Transactions of the Eighth International Congress of Actuaries held in London, 27th to 30th June 1927* (London: Layton, 1927), pp. 57–65 (volume III), p. 57.

79 Asch, *Die Gruppenlebensversicherung*, p. 18.

left space for supplementary occupational schemes. Yet, despite the fact that occupational plans always covered a smaller proportion of the population than universal pensions, life insurers and employers systematically promoted individual and employment-based solutions over "state-based social insurance".

If employers' federations appreciated Edmund Schulthess' conciliatory stance toward entrepreneurs, some of their members were more reluctant to support this hybrid pension architecture. In January 1929, a meeting of the Federation of Trade and Industry accepted the AHV bill presented by the Federal Council in its broad outlines, but focused on two problematic issues. Limiting the amount of budgetary transfers devoted to the AHV was the Vorort's first concern. Thanks to Federal Councilor Musy's intransigence and the modesty of envisioned benefits, this goal seemed relatively easy to reach. The status of existing pension plans represented a more divisive issue. A few weeks before the Vorort meeting, the Basle Economic Alliance (Basler Volkswirtschaftsbund) had petitioned both the Vorort and the Swiss Employers' Association (Arbeitgeberverband) to consider this proposal: if employers could prove that they offered benefits that were equal or superior to the basic AHV pension, they should be allowed to opt out. This proposal had found support in the textile industry and in western Switzerland, but the Arbeitgeberverband, the second main business federation, strongly opposed it, as it opened a breach in the universal character of the AHV, hindered pension portability, and might fuel demands to introduce strict regulation of pension plans. For the main business federations, the concessions granted to private plans were deemed sufficient, and the belated proposal of the Basler Volkswirtschaftsbund was turned down.[80]

Basle employers were not the only ones to be concerned about the coming AHV. In 1925, the SVUSAI had already criticized the unclear role devolved to occupational schemes and opposed the creation of cantonal old age provision. In a fall 1928 letter to the federal authorities, the association proposed wide-ranging changes to the basic pension, notably the reintroduction of a system based on multiple providers that included existing occupational plans and would provide differentiated levels of benefits.[81] In fact, these two lobbying efforts were closely related.

[80] Vorort Vorstand, January 25, 1929, pp. 1–4, file 1.5.3.7, AfZ-SHIV; Arbeitgeberverband Vorstand, January 15, 1929, pp. 2–9, SAV.

[81] "Entwurf zu einem Bundesgesetz über Alters-, Hinterlassenen- und Invalidenversicherung. Abänderungsvorschläge des Schweizerischen Verbandes der Unterstützungskassen und Stiftungen für Alter und Invalidität zum Vorentwurf des Eidg. Volkswirtschaftsdepartementes vom August 1928", open letter of the SVUSAI [n.d., ca. fall 1928], file V Schweiz 3234, SNB. According to correspondence

Understanding the common ground between Basle employers and the association representing leading private pension plans, as well as the dialectic between regional and federal social policy debates, is key to understanding which employers were opposed to the Lex Schulthess. To do that, a review of late 1920s social policy debates in Basle is needed here.

The patrician elites of the Rhine city, the second pole of Swiss capitalism after Zurich, constituted a natural breeding-ground for anti-AHV activism. Local silk manufacturers had already figured among the most vocal opponents of the KUVG around 1900. The fact that these manufacturers faced mounting difficulties in the postwar decade only hardened their opposition to social schemes that could lead to an increase in labor costs. In contrast, the chemical and pharmaceutical industries, dominated by Sandoz, CIBA, and Geigy (all nowadays part of Novartis), had emerged as the most dynamic export sector of the postwar period. These employers had all developed pension plans during the war and were known for both their conservative leanings and their refusal to negotiate collective bargaining agreements with trade unions. The giants of the chemical sector and silk manufacturers were the key players in business associations, such as the Basler Volkswirtschaftsbund – an organization founded in 1918 to coordinate bourgeois forces in a period of acute social tensions. Both sectors also had intimate links to the local branch of the Liberal-Conservative Party, the only one active in a German-speaking canton. Liberal-Conservatives played a prominent role in Basle politics and, like their counterparts in western French-speaking cantons, were a gathering-point for die-hard opponents of social insurance.[82]

Basle textile firms and chemical firms were heavily represented in the SVUSAI, where they accounted for almost one-third of its membership. The SVUSAI itself was presided over by Hans Bächtold, active in Basle philanthropic circles and secretary of the joint employers–workers'

between members of the future anti-AHV referendum committee, the SVUSAI proposition had been first presented to the Radical Party, which had refused to take it into account, as it clearly torpedoed Edmund Schulthess' efforts to introduce a universal basic pension at the federal level. This episode is recounted in Prof. Jakob Steiger to National Councilor Hans Hoppeler (Evangelical Party), March 24 1930, file II/16.6, Nachlass Rudolf Grob, AfZ.

82 On Basle employers, see Christian Simon, "Arbeiterkommission und Gesamtarbeitsvertrag in der chemischen Industrie: Aspekte der industriellen Beziehungen in Basel während des Zweiten Weltkrieges", *Vierteljahrschrift für Sozial- und Wirtschaftsgeschichte* 78 (1991), pp. 39–80 (pp. 42–6). On the foundation of the Basler Volkswirtschaftsbund, see *Jahresbericht 1925/1926* (Basle: Basler Volkswirtschaftsbund, 1927), p. 31, file D11, Wirtschaftsarchiv. On Basle patrician elites, see Philipp Sarasin, *Stadt der Bürger: struktureller Wandel und bürgerliche Lebenswelt. Basel 1870–1900* (Basle/Frankfurt am Main: Helbing & Lichtenhahn, 1990).

association of the ribbon-manufacturing sector (Verband Arbeiter und Arbeitgeber der Basler Bandfabriken), and Paul Scherrer, chief executive at the CIBA chemical corporation.[83] The confluence of the Basler Volkswirtschaftsbund and the SVUSAI explains their parallel lobbying efforts. However, these two business outfits were not only keen to obtain opting-out provisions from the basic pension but were also very hostile to the cantonal supplementary schemes envisioned by Edmund Schulthess.

Handing over supplementary benefits to the cantons placated federalist forces. Moreover, when the scheme was outlined in 1928, only five cantons (Geneva, Vaud, Neuchâtel, Glarus, and Appenzell) had set up voluntary or compulsory old age assistance schemes, and only a handful among them planned to follow suit before the implementation of federal pensions.[84] However, as the AHV continued its protracted journey through the political system, this issue had become a key preoccupation for the Basler Volkswirtschaftsbund. In December 1928, a coalition of Socialists and Radical politicians (given the local pre-eminence of the Liberal-Conservatives, the Basle Radical Party held centrist positions) had introduced in the cantonal assembly a bill proposing means-tested assistance benefits for the elderly. This proposal was characteristic of an urban canton depicted by historian Josef Mooser as a "welfare city" (Wohlfahrtsstadt) during the interwar era. Due to the sharp class conflict and intense political competition between the left – the Basle branch of the Communist Party was the strongest in Switzerland – and the right, the Rhine city was a pioneer in health policy, unemployment compensation, and the monitoring of working conditions and wages.[85]

Basle employers considered the cantonal old age assistance plan a challenge to their in-house welfare measures. The newly founded special commission on social policy of the Basler Volkswirtschaftsbund – which included several SVUSAI members and insurers – opposed the assistance scheme as soon as it was introduced in the cantonal

[83] The oldest register of SVUSAI members I have located contains the names of the 120 members of the association in December 1933. We can use it as an indicator of the SVUSAI social base for the late 1920s; see the appendix of Ammann, *Die Altersfürsorge des Bundes*. For a list of the SVUSAI board, see "An die Nationalrätliche Kommission zur Beratung des Bundesgesetzes über die AHV", open letter of the SVUSAI, Basle, November 12, 1929, file V Schweiz 3234, SNB. See Bächtold's obituary in "Hans Bächtold (1884–1941)", *National Zeitung*, August 31, 1941. Other board members included Walther Stampfli of the Von Roll steelworks in Gerlafingen, C. A. Buss of the Saurer truck factory in Arbon, and Ad. Schluep of Viscosa in Emmenbrücke.

[84] On cantonal old age schemes, see *Pensionskassenstatistik 1941*, pp. 111–14.

[85] Josef Mooser, "Konflikt und Integration – Wirtschaft, Gesellschaft und Politik in der "Wohlfahrtsstadt"", in *Basel – Geschichte einer städtischen Gesellschaft*, ed. Georg Kreis, *et al.* (Basle: Christoph Merian Verlag, 2000), pp. 226–66, pp. 251–2. See also *Jahresbericht 1925/1926* (Basle: Basler Volkswirtschaftsbund, 1927), p. 31, file D11, Wirtschaftsarchiv.

assembly.[86] Extolling the solidity of local corporate welfare schemes (a survey underlined that Basle pension schemes accounted for 9 percent of all private plans in operation in Switzerland, but 17 percent of overall pension assets), the Volkswirtschaftsbund warned against any state solution that would compete with existing pension plans and damage economic competitiveness. Following a classic line of reasoning, the Basle employers underscored that "social insurance only benefits the insured when it does not lower economic competitiveness in foreign markets, when it does not force manufacturing firms to leave the country, and when it does not hinder the creation of new businesses".[87] Until it was passed in a referendum in March 1931, the cantonal old age assistance program provoked heated debates. Thanks to the resistance and the lobbying of the Basler Volkswirtschaftsbund, local business elites succeeded in their attempts to secure opt-outs for employers' plans. The Basle scheme did not pay benefits before the 1940s and covered only workers unaffiliated to existing pension plans.[88]

The cantonal debate revealed the close links between Basle employers and the SVUSAI. It also provided a model strategy, deployed by these same actors against federal pensions. In November 1929, during parliamentary debates about the Lex Schulthess, the SVUSAI sent a second open letter to federal authorities exhorting them to allow opt-outs from the basic pension. The SVUSAI also suggested that cantonal supplementary insurance should remain the prerogative of existing occupational schemes and refused "bureaucratic" solutions. Underscoring the necessity of state support for private provision, namely the extension of tax exemptions, the association finally warned that any bill that might be detrimental to existing pension schemes would provoke fierce opposition – in other words, might face a referendum.[89]

[86] Max Flury, *25 Jahre Basler Volkswirtschaftsbund 1918–1943* (Basle: Basler Volkswirtschaftsbund, 1943), p. 81. See also *Jahresbericht 1931/1932* (Basle: Basler Volkswirtschaftsbund, 1933), p. 12, file D11, Wirtschaftsarchiv.

[87] *Die Alters-, Invaliditäts- und Hinterbliebenenfürsorge privater Unternehmungen im Kanton Baslestadt* (Basle: Gasser AG, 1928), p. 3.

[88] On the Basle old age assistance scheme, see Charles Stirnimann, *Der Weg in der Nachkriegszeit 1943–1948: ein Beitrag zur politischen Sozialgeschichte des "Roten Basle"* (Basle/Kassel: Friedrich Reinhardt Verlag, 1992), pp. 326–32. On the opt-outs negotiated by the Basler Volkswirtschaftsbund, see Greiner, "Die Personalversicherung", pp. 372–7, and *Jahresbericht 1933/1934* (Basle: Basler Volkswirtschaftsbund, 1935), file D11, Wirtschaftsarchiv.

[89] "An die Nationalrätliche Kommission zur Beratung des Bundesgesetzes über die AHV", open letter of the SVUSAI, Basle, November 12, 1929, p. 14, file V Schweiz 3234, SNB. Similar views were held by Jakob Steiger, a Basle economics professor who would play a key role in the 1931 referendum campaign against the Lex Schulthess; see Jakob Steiger, *Die finanzpolitische Seite der obligatorischen schweizerischen Alters- und Hinterlassenenversicherung* (Basle: Helbing and Lichtenhahn, 1929).

The Basler Volkswirtschaftsbund, which hinted that Article 29 of the AHV law devoted to cantonal supplementary schemes might turn out be the "fateful paragraph" of the Lex Schulthess, expressed similar concerns. The business league pointed out that the benefits envisioned by the local assistance scheme they were fighting in Basle were lower than for future cantonal schemes as determined by the Federal Social Insurance Office.[90] The fact that the Vorort had not lent a sympathetic ear to their demands left both Basle employers and the SVUSAI eager to pursue their lobbying efforts through other channels. Both the campaign against the Basle assistance scheme and the debate on the AHV bill were a wake-up call for the SVUSAI, whose following doubled in a few months and reached 100 members in late 1929. The association was the meeting-point for leading pension plans: its members accounted for half of the total pension assets of the private sector (see Table A.7, p. 303).

Edmund Schulthess and the Federal Social Insurance Office refused to budge on the issue of opting out from the basic universal pension. The idea of a blanket tax exemption for occupational plans was also met with much skepticism and rapidly lost steam. Given the divided positions of their affiliates on these two issues, business federations decided against pursuing them.[91] The SVUSAI nevertheless did not call off its efforts and continued to press for favorable tax status for occupational provision at the cantonal level, where its members had more leverage.[92]

On the other hand, cantonal supplementary schemes were hotly debated in the National Council, and business federations used substantial resources to avoid, in the words of a Vorort member, "the crowding-out of private welfare by social insurance".[93] Last-minute fights surrounded Article 29 of the bill: employers lobbied to erase from it any language suggesting that existing pension plans could be forced to participate in the financing of cantonal supplementary schemes. The article also mentioned that taxes should not cover more than half of financing needs for such measures, an attempt to hamper Socialists from introducing tax-financed old age assistance in cantons or cities where they occupied stronger positions than at the federal level.[94] In July 1930, after being

[90] *Jahresbericht 1929/1930* (Basle: Basler Volkswirtschaftsbund, 1931), pp. 33–8, file D11, Wirtschaftsarchiv.

[91] Vorort Vorstand, February 27, 1930, file 1.5.3.7, AfZ-SHIV; Arbeitgeberverband Vorstand, January 11, 1930, SAV.

[92] A report of the SVUSAI describes such actions in the cantons of Bern, Argovia, and Schaffhausen. See *Zur Frage der Besteuerung der privaten Stiftungen, Fonds und Kassen für Alter, Invalidität und Tod*, (Basle: Helbing und Lichtenhahn, 1931), pp. 2–3.

[93] Vorort Vorstand, November 26, 1929, p. 3, file 1.5.3.7, AfZ-SHIV.

[94] Ibid., January 16, February 27, and May 27, 1930, file 1.5.3.7, AfZ-SHIV. See also Lasserre, "L'institution de l'AVS", pp. 306–8. By 1932, the "red" municipalities of Basle,

amended to protect employers' preferences, Article 29 was deemed to be satisfactory and depicted as a "welcome improvement" by both the Vorort and the Arbeitgeberverband. The Basler Volkswirtschaftsbund continued nevertheless to oppose the AHV, for example during the 1930 general assembly of the Swiss Chamber of Commerce.[95]

When the Lex Schulthess finally reached the Council of States (Senate) in the second semester of 1930, it faced a last stand by the Catholic and federalist opposition to the AHV. The opponents of social insurance proposed a counter-project based on a decentralized system of means-tested old age assistance and envisioned a long transition period before the payment of any pension benefits. The Federal Council opposed with determination this counter-proposal that unabashedly demanded the dismemberment of the Lex Schulthess. Rentenanstalt insurance executives even helped Edmund Schulthess in this fight by writing the official reply debunking it.[96]

Federal Councilor Jean-Marie Musy attacked the Lex Schulthess in early 1931. In a breach of the collegiality principle that normally governed the proceedings of the executive branch, Musy publicly criticized the AHV as financial adventurism and proposed to exclude public employees from universal basic coverage. This measure, in line with Musy's austerity framework, would have lowered pension expenditure, but infuriated civil servants. At the urging of the Basler Volkswirtschaftsbund, the Vorort also proposed last-minute corrections to Article 29 of the AHV bill.[97] Once again, Schulthess did not budge. The other members of the Federal Council backed his position, and the two chambers of the Federal Assembly accepted the Lex Schulthess in June 1931 almost unanimously.

After more than a decade of bargaining, Federal Councilor Schulthess had finally succeeded in shaping a social insurance bill. However, the consensus reflected in the vote of the Federal Assembly was fragile, and the AHV had been emptied of much of its substance. The months that followed showed that this hollow shell could not withstand the referendum. Immediately after the passage of the bill, a group of die-hard conservatives launched a referendum, collecting the bulk of the signatures in western Switzerland. The anti-AHV committee also simultaneously launched an initiative that proposed compulsory individual retirement accounts instead of federal pensions, an all-private solution that would

Zurich, Biel, and Berne had introduced limited old age assistance measures. See Emil Klöti, "Die kantonale Ergänzungsversicherung als zweite Etappe", *Gewerkschaftliche Rundschau*, November 1931, pp. 371–6.

95 Vorort Vorstand, July 4, 1930, file 1.5.3.7, AfZ-SHIV. See also Schmid, *Wirtschaft, Staat und Macht*, p. 230.

96 Lasserre, "L'institution de l'AVS", p. 309.

97 Vorort Vorstand, January 23 and February 27, 1931, file 1.5.3.7, AfZ-SHIV.

have opened a lucrative market for financial institutions. On the other side of the political spectrum, the Communist Party began a second referendum campaign that attacked the "anti-social" tobacco taxes meant to make up the public share of AHV financing.[98] Scornfully described by Edmund Schulthess' biographer as a "scattered opposition", the anti-AHV referendum crystallized the resentment of a rather eclectic conservative coalition that "represented a final manifestation of the steadfast opponents of the federal liberal state":

> In the wake of early Frontism and other "restoration movements",[99] [the referendum] served as a rallying-point for various groups that declared war on "the System" dominated by the Radicals and their exponent, [Federal Councilor] Schulthess. You could find among them corporatist doctrinaires, religious zealots, "anti-state" activists and political mavericks [as well as] leading western Switzerland journalists [and] ultra-conservative Catholics.[100]

The Federal Council was at first confident that it could easily win against the anti-AHV and anti-tobacco tax referenda, as all major political parties, trade unions, and business federations backed the Lex Schulthess. However, direct democracy often magnifies the impact of splintered oppositions. In this sense, the 1931 vote can be considered a replay of the momentous failure of health insurance in 1900. Moreover, the anti-AHV front was more than a chance encounter of "political mavericks". The referendum committee had difficulty finding high-profile personalities willing to publicly lead the assault against the Lex Schulthess, but it could count on support from the highest political circles. Federal Councilor Jean-Marie Musy not only spoke publicly against the pension bill but also secretly backed the referendum. During the 1920s, Musy had actively participated in early efforts at organizing the informal networks of conservative free-marketers who were now opposed to the AHV. His personal assistants were discreetly, but directly, involved in the referendum.[101]

98 André Rauber, *Histoire du mouvement communiste suisse (XIXe siècle–1943)* (Geneva: Slatkine, 1997), pp. 185–6.

99 The term "Frontism" (Frontismus) designates far-right and fascist "fronts" that emerged during the 1930s in Switzerland. Some of these groups had connections with a broader "restoration movement" (Erneuerungsbewegung) that encompassed national-conservative tendencies and free-market lobbies. On these interrelated dimensions, see Christian Werner, *Für Wirtschaft und Vaterland: Erneuerungsbewegungen und bürgerliche Interessengruppen in der Deutschschweiz 1928–1947* (Zurich: Chronos, 2000), pp. 38–49.

100 Böschenstein, *Bundesrat Edmund Schulthess*, p. 169; Lasserre, "L'institution de l'AVS", p. 316.

101 Prof. Jakob Steiger to Rudolf Grob, March 25 1931, file II/17.36, Nachlass Rudolf Grob, AfZ. On 1920s free-market networks, see Werner, *Für Wirtschaft und Vaterland*, pp. 66–7.

If the anti-AHV committee could count on Basle and western Switzerland employers, support for the referendum was not unanimous in the pension lobby. The president of the SVUSAI, Hans Bächtold, was staunchly opposed to the law but did not want to appear at the head of the referendum committee. In a post-referendum report, the SVUSAI stated disingenuously that they never had any intention of "sabotaging" the law and that the association "did not mount any resistance to the law and did not participate in any action directed against [federal pensions]".[102] Basle members of the pension lobby were among the opponents of the AHV, but prominent business executives who had previously signed SVUSAI appeals, such as Walther Stampfli from the Von Roll steelworks, declared their support. Machine makers and metal producers had been more supportive of social insurance than textile or chemical manufacturers and had already backed the Lex Forrer. Like Edmund Schulthess, Walther Stampfli belonged to the business wing of the Radicals. In July 1929, he sponsored a proposal for a cantonal AHV scheme in the Solothurn parliament and was to become the political architect of the 1947 federal pensions during his tenure at the Federal Council.[103] However, even employers who were in favor of the AHV adopted a wait-and-see attitude. Von Roll stopped paying contributions to its retirement plan after 1929 and waited for the result of the vote on the Lex Schulthess before developing new corporate welfare measures.[104]

Finally, the deterioration of the economic situation did not bode well for the AHV. As the shockwaves of the Depression spread from the United States to Europe, a growing unease over social insurance was discernible among employers. Looking across the border, Swiss employers found many examples that fueled second thoughts about social insurance. In the summer of 1930, strikes were launched in France in response to employers' resistance to the implementation of state old age pensions, while the economic downturn meant deficits in financing social insurance in the Weimar Republic.[105]

Six weeks before the December 1931 vote, the Vorort discussed whether business federations should publicly back the Lex Schulthess. Several employers' representatives warned that convening a general

102 See Prof. Jakob Steiger to Alfred Georg (Genevoise Assurances), October 12, 1930, file II/16.6, Nachlass Rudolf Grob, AfZ. On the SVUSAI ex-post denials, see Ammann, *Die Altersfürsorge des Bundes*, p. 6.

103 Georg Hafner, *Bundesrat Walther Stampfli (1884–1965): Leiter der Kriegswirtschaft im Zweiten Weltkrieg, bundesrätlicher Vater der AHV* (Olten: Dietschi Verlag, 1986), p. 153.

104 Kienzle, *Es gibt nur ein Gerlafingen*, pp. 177–9, 338 (note 97).

105 Schmidt, *Sozialpolitik*, pp. 40–54; Dominique Simon, "Le patronat face aux assurances sociales: 1920–1930", *Le Mouvement social* 137 (1986), pp. 7–27.

assembly to vote on this issue might prove tricky, as many Vorort affiliates had either cold feet or were staunchly opposed to the law. Half-hearted support or, worse, a split vote on the question – as had been the case in 1900 during the debates on the Lex Forrer – would harm Federal Councilor Schulthess.[106] The Vorort was careful not to appear publicly divided. The assembly of the Swiss Chamber of Commerce finally backed the Lex Schulthess a few days before the vote, but the looming economic crisis may have swayed many employers into a last-minute rejection of the AHV.

To claim that employers' federations' support was at best lukewarm is not exaggerated if we consider the official position of the Arbeitgeberverband on the Lex Schulthess. In late November 1931, the second main business federation emphasized the disadvantages of the law and described employers' contributions to the AHV as a "tax on entrepreneurs". The Arbeitgeberverband finally enjoined its affiliates to support the Lex Schulthess but emphasized that, if approved, the implementation of social insurance should take into account the "economic situation" of the country. In the context of the Depression, some Arbeitgeberverband members proposed a postponed implementation of the AHV if it passed the referendum hurdle.[107]

The Lex Schulthess was finally defeated on December 6, 1931. Only 40 percent of voters and the three cantons of Zurich, Basle, and Neuchâtel accepted it. On the same day, to Edmund Schulthess' dismay, the Communist-led referendum against the revision of the tobacco tax was also accepted by an extremely narrow margin. Some commentators have argued since the 1930s that the anti-AHV campaign could be described, in the words of the *Neue Zürcher Zeitung*, as a "referendum originating from the two opposite extremes of the political spectrum". However, the small Communist Party was mostly present in the few urban regions that voted in favor of the AHV *and* accepted the tobacco tax revision.[108] By contrast, both referenda tended to score highest in the rural Catholic Conservative strongholds of central Switzerland and in western Switzerland, where traditional hotbeds of federalist opposition to

[106] Vorort Vorstand, October 30, 1931, file 1.5.3.8, AfZ-SHIV.

[107] "Der Zentralverband der Arbeitgeber und die Abstimmungsvorlage vom 6. Dezember 1931", *Schweizerische Arbeitgeber Zeitung*, November 21, 1931. See also Arbeitgeberverband geschäftsleitende Ausschuss, March 17, 1931, p. 78 and October 29, 1931, pp. 90–4, SAV.

[108] *Neue Zürcher Zeitung*, June 23, 1931 quoted in Sommer, *Das Ringen um die soziale Sicherheit*, p. 152. The result of the vote on the tobacco tax was close: 425,449 voters (50.1 percent) supported the Communists' referendum, while 423,523 (49.9 percent) voted against it. See Ritzmann-Blickenstorfer and Siegenthaler, eds., *Swiss Historical Statistics*, Table X10.

centralist policies had already contributed to the 1900 demise of the Lex Forrer.

The morning after this vote, the *Neue Zürcher Zeitung*, the newspaper of the Radical establishment, spoke of a "catastrophic defeat" for Edmund Schulthess. Opponents of the law, such as the Liberal-Conservative *Gazette de Lausanne*, declared triumphantly that "armed with its unwavering common sense, the people . . . have once and for all buried a dangerous law inspired by Socialist and German ideas".[109] In more sober terms, the *Schweizer Arbeitgeber Zeitung* stated that the rejection of the Lex Schulthess was directly related to the deterioration of the economic situation. The business federation newsletter emphasized that the whole AHV debate had taken a wrong turn since the 1922 Socialist attempt to tax wealth to finance social insurance. Commenting on the same result, the Basler Volkswirtschaftsbund bluntly declared that, as the Lex Schulthess was now off the agenda, the Confederation had its hands free to take urgent measures to fight unemployment and the looming economic crisis.[110]

### A lost decade? Social policy during the Depression

All in all, the 1930s were a fundamentally conservative decade. Switzerland did not experience major political upheavals, so the balance of power between parties remained stable, and the bourgeois bloc kept a tight grip on the executive and the Federal Assembly. Between 1931 and 1941, the Socialists steadily held between one-fifth and a quarter of all seats in the National Council, but had only a tiny representation in the Council of States and none in the Federal Council. Switzerland's bourgeois bloc formed the opposite of the Swedish center-left coalition of 1932 under the aegis of the Social Democratic Party. Stirrings on the far right, notably the rise of domestic Frontist movements and of fascism in neighboring Germany and Italy, prodded the Swiss left into line. The 1935 revision of the Socialist program, the marginalization of the Communists, centrist openings to middle-class and farmer constituencies in order to counter the rise of Frontist movements, and the acceptance of defense-spending increases signaled the retreat of the left in the national consensus dominated by the bourgeois parties.[111] During the Depression, economic policy remained geared toward austerity, wage reductions, and the defense

109 *Neue Zürcher Zeitung* and *Gazette de Lausanne*, December 7, 1931, both quoted in Sommer, *Das Ringen um die soziale Sicherheit*, pp. 157–8.

110 "Un fossé?", *Schweizerische Arbeitgeber Zeitung*, December 22, 1931; *Jahresbericht 1931/1932* (Basle: Basler Volkswirtschaftsbund, 1933), p. 27, file D11, Wirtschaftsarchiv.

111 Pietro Morandi, *Krise und Verständigung: die Richtlinienbewegung und die Entstehung der Konkordanzdemokratie, 1933–1939* (Zurich: Chronos, 1995).

of a strong currency. As an alternative to the deflationary policies of the federal government and employers, the Gewerkschaftsbund-sponsored Crisis Initiative (Kriseninitiative) unsuccessfully proposed an alternative interventionist economic policy. This initiative was defeated in June 1935 after a bitter political campaign, and it was only after the 1936 devaluation of the Swiss franc that economic prospects began to improve. The "farewell to class struggle" of the 1920s continued after the defeat of the Crisis Initiative.[112]

Increasing appeasement also marked industrial relations. After confidential negotiations, the Metalworkers' Union and the Federation of Machine Manufacturers and Metal Producers signed in 1937 the famous Peace Agreement (Friedensabkommen). This collective-bargaining agreement focused on a commitment from both sides not to resort to strikes or lockouts during labor disputes. Described by employers as "free advertising toward foreign countries for Swiss industry", this agreement was controversial among workers and was not comparable to the extensive labor peace that characterized industrial relations after World War II.[113] The Peace Agreement underscored the social partnership stance adopted by Konrad Ilg, the authoritarian leader of the Metalworkers' Union, to the detriment of more combative forms of labor action. During the 1930s, Ilg put a premium on maintaining jobs and export capacity in the metal and machine-making sector. This strategy pushed the largest industrial union into a stand-alone attitude that contributed to fragmenting union power and undermining the leverage of the Gewerkschaftsbund. After 1936, Konrad Ilg also distanced himself from the Socialist Party and defended union autonomy instead of unity of action with the main left-wing party.[114]

112 Bernard Degen, *Abschied vom Klassenkampf: die Partielle Integration der schweizerischen Gewerkschaftsbewegung zwischen Landesstreik und Weltwirtschaftskrise (1918–1929)* (Basle/Frankfurt a.M.: Helbing & Lichtenhahn, 1991). On the 1936 devaluation, see Philipp Müller, "La bataille pour le franc: la Suisse entre déflation et dévaluation (1931–1936)", in *Franc suisse, finance et commerce*, ed. Philipp Müller, *et al.* (Lausanne: Antipodes, 2003), pp. 7–145.

113 According to a 1937 article of the *Werkzeitung*, quoted in Geneviève Billeter, *Le pouvoir patronal* (Geneva: Droz, 1985), p. 100. On the 1937 Peace Agreement, see Bernard Degen, "Der Arbeitsfrieden zwischen Mythos und Realität", *Widerspruch* Spezialheft "Arbeitsfrieden – Realität eines Mythos" (1987), pp. 11–30; Degen and Kübler, "Die Gewerkschaften zwischen Integration und Ausgrenzung". Until this date, relations between the Metalworkers' Union and employers of the metal and machine-making sector had been tense. After refusing for many years to negotiate directly with the union, employers had accepted such negotiations only after securing pledges from the metalworkers that they would rein in their combative locals (branches); see Fluder *et al.*, *Gewerkschaften und Angestelltenverbände*, pp. 213–16.

114 Oskar Scheiben, "Konrad Ilgs Weg nach Rechts", *Widerspruch* Spezialheft "Arbeitsfrieden – Realität eines Mythos" (1987), pp. 11–30.

The Peace Agreement can be contrasted with the 1938 Basic Agreement signed in Sweden between the main trade union confederation (LO) and the employers' federation (SAF).[115] Although both of these cross-class alliances were intended to strengthen the international standing of their respective export-oriented economies, the Swedish agreement constituted a decisive step toward a centralization of collective bargaining at the national level that had begun early in the century and had no equivalent in Switzerland. The 1937 Peace Agreement concerned only one leading export sector and left untouched such issues as the setting of wages, which remained largely decentralized on a company-by-company basis. Tellingly, the Arbeitgeberverband did not recognize the Gewerkschaftsbund as a negotiating partner until 1939.[116] In both countries the agreements reflected business interests, but the Swiss one was more conservative. In Sweden, the dominance of a red–green social-democratic and farmer alliance that could count on a strong and unified labor movement contrasted with the Swiss situation. There, a weaker Socialist Party and fragmented labor movement were ensconced in a constraining framework set by a strong bourgeois bloc composed of the political parties of the right, business federations, and farmers' organizations.

The 1938 Basic Agreement represented a key stage in the development of solidarist wage policies, whereby Swedish employers' federations consented, albeit grudgingly, to the expansion of social insurance in order to even out pay levels and discouraged their members from setting up firm-based corporate welfare measures. Such a strategy was completely foreign to Swiss employers' federations, which always asserted the employers' right to develop voluntary welfare schemes. Key unions such as the Metalworkers' Union were also reluctant to support social insurance and continued to favor union-based or jointly managed occupational benefits.[117] In Switzerland, the company pension plans of leading manufacturing and financial companies dominated occupational provision.

In conclusion, this combination of decentralized employee benefits and collective bargaining was similar to the segmentalist profile of North American industrial relations and occupational provision. I will

[115] Peter A. Swenson, *Capitalists against markets: the making of labor markets and welfare states in the United States and Sweden* (Oxford: Oxford University Press, 2002), pp. 99–120; Mario Telo, *Le New Deal européen: la pensée et la politique sociales-démocrates face à la crise des années trente* (Brussels: Editions de l'université de Bruxelles, 1988), pp. 180–92.

[116] Degen and Kübler, "Die Gewerkschaften zwischen Integration und Ausgrenzung", p. 141.

[117] Jürg Siegenthaler, *Die Politik der Gewerkschaften: eine Untersuchung der öffentlichen Funktionen schweizerischen Gewerkschaften nach dem Zweiten Weltkrieg* (Berne: Francke, 1968), pp. 53–4.

elaborate in the next section on the similarities between Switzerland and the United States.

The Depression not only dealt the final blow to the foundering Lex Schulthess. Deflationary policies, the growing collaboration between employers and key trade unions, and continuing conservative opposition to social insurance compounded this defeat and halted the development of social policy. During the 1930s, federal authorities confined themselves to subsidizing means-tested assistance for the elderly poor distributed by the Pro Senectute charity, and supported decentralized unemployment schemes organized by employers' associations, trade unions, and regional authorities. Social assistance and the delegation of social welfare tasks to private institutions thus dominated social policy.[118] The tobacco and alcohol taxes that were earmarked for the AHV accumulated in a special fund that reached CHF 200 million in 1934, but were used instead to reduce the budgetary deficit of the Confederation. The Federal Council even stopped paying interest into the fund to rein in its growth.[119] Social policy continued its uneven development at the regional level as several cantons expanded health insurance coverage and developed relief works for the unemployed. By 1941, the handful of existing cantonal old age insurance and assistance schemes covered only 200,000 persons, or 5 percent of the total population. These figures were lower than the total number of workers covered by occupational pension plans a decade before.[120]

Throughout the 1930s, occupational provision continued to fill the space left vacant by the failure of the Lex Schulthess. As noted previously, coverage was high in the public sector. In 1937, the two pension plans for federal employees and railway workers alone accounted for half of the overall public-sector coverage, while the next four largest accounted for one-fifth of overall coverage.[121] As most public-sector pensions had been founded a generation before private ones and offered

118 Bernard Degen, "Zur Geschichte der Arbeitslosigkeit in der Schweiz: eine historische Skizze", *Widerspruch* 25 (1993), pp. 37–46. Founded in 1917, Pro Senectute received annual grants from the Confederation during the 1930s and distributed means-tested assistance to the elderly poor. See Margret Klauser and Peter Rinderknecht, *75 ans d'histoire Pro Senectute Suisse: de l'oeuvre d'assistance à une organisation moderne et professionnelle de services. Chronique des années 1917–1992* (Vevey: Pro Senectute, 1992).

119 Peter Binswanger, *Histoire de l'AVS: assurance-vieillesse et survivants suisse* (Zurich: Pro Senectute, 1987), pp. 22–3; Hafner, *Bundesrat Walther Stampfli*, p. 369.

120 Binswanger, *Histoire de l'AVS*, pp. 23–4, *Pensionskassenstatistik 1941*, 124. On the development of cantonal health insurance, see Martin Lengwiler and Verena Rothenbühler, *Macht und Ohnmacht der Ärzteschaft: Geschichte des Zürcher Ärzteverbands im 20. Jahrhundert* (Zurich: Chronos, 2004), pp. 45–68.

121 Besides these two federal pension plans, the largest cantonal retirement schemes were those of Zurich, Basle, and Berne. See Hans Christen, "Die finanzielle Lage der

more generous pension benefits, they included the majority of pensioners. The Depression and austerity policies destabilized their budgets, which made them the target of conservative political campaigns. During the 1930s, free-market lobby groups established with the support of the main business federations – such as the Action for National Restoration (Redressement National) or the League of Non-Subsidized Persons (Bund der Subventionslosen) – used campaigns to cut public-sector wages and social benefits as trial runs for similar attacks in the private sector. Fiscal conservatives and free-marketers specifically railed against the alleged retirement privileges enjoyed by civil servants and denounced the "billion deficit" of the Confederation pension plans. The financial reorganization of these plans was turned down in December 1939 after a bitter referendum campaign led by these "mercenaries of the business federations".[122] Referendum politics loomed menacingly over social policy proposals, which stymied a reopening of the AHV debate.

If pensions were commonplace but under attack in the public sector, consolidation, cost control, and selective expansion were the watchwords of their evolution in the private sector. In the aftermath of the defeat of the Crisis Initiative, a 1936 pamphlet entitled *Capital as Ethic* (*Kapital als Ethos*) extolled the virtues of corporate social measures and buried calls for state intervention in economic affairs under a forbidding enumeration of the social commitment of individual corporations. Ironically, this underlined the fragmentation of employer-based social benefits.[123] In the same vein, a secretary of the Arbeitgeberverband appealed to employers to continue developing "voluntary provision" despite the Depression in order to "relieve" the state from the costly burden of providing social welfare.[124] The development dynamics of occupational provision remained largely below the radar of public debate and were still largely motivated by the advantages that pension plans had for employers in terms of workforce management or tax exemptions.

Pensionskassen", *Schweizerische Zeitschrift für Volkswirtschaft und Statistik* 1938), pp. 40–68 (p. 62).

122 Heinz Dickenmann, *Das Bundespersonal in der Wirtschaftskrise 1931–1939* (Zurich: Zentralstelle der Studentschaft, 1983), pp. 175–222; Werner, *Für Wirtschaft und Vaterland*, pp. 207–11; Hans Ulrich Jost, "Die Söldner der Wirtschaftsverbände", *Die Weltwoche*, July 6, 2000. Insurance executives were well represented at the foundation meeting of the Redressement national; see Jürg Frischknecht, Peter Haffner, Ueli Haldimann *et al.*, *Die unheimlichen Patrioten: politische Reaktion in der Schweiz. Ein Aktuelles Handbuch* (Zurich: Limmat Verlag, 1987), pp. 139–43.

123 Ermatinger, *Kapital und Ethos*.

124 Friedrich Bernet, *Entlastung der öffentlichen Verwaltung durch soziale Massnahmen der privaten Betriebe* (Zurich: Emil Rüegg, 1938).

In 1933, the general assembly of the pension lobby SVUSAI discussed how firms could cope with a graying workforce in a period of economic crisis. The debate rapidly centered on ways to use pension plans to renew the workforce without overburdening firms with welfare obligations. The SVUSAI advised its members to favor savings plans and other relief efforts that offered more flexibility to employers than company and group pension plans. The SVUSAI also urged its members to avoid paying pensions with high replacement rates that could, according to the president of the association, "undermine the thriftiness of those insured".[125] The use of pension plans to regulate unemployment has been analyzed in the case of the Von Roll steelworks. Between 1930 and 1937, Von Roll annual pension expenses almost tripled as the directors of the firm – including future Federal Councilor Walther Stampfli and his mentor Ernst Dübi, the corporate mastermind of the 1937 Peace Agreement – used the company pension plan even more extensively than its unemployment fund as a buffer to ease redundancies and renew the foundry workforce in an orderly manner.[126]

As private pension plans focused on the day-to-day management of the economic crisis, the activities of the pension lobby gradually declined. From 1937 to its rebirth in 1942 in the midst of renewed debates on the AHV, the SVUSAI held no general assemblies. Yet, the association remained a magnet for leading firms. In 1937, eighty-three of its affiliates (or less than 10 percent of all core private plans) made up three-quarters of all contributions to corporate plans, paid one-third of private pension benefits, and accounted for more than half of the total pension assets of the private sector.[127] Most of the expansion of occupational pensions took place during the second half of the decade, after the attenuation of the Depression. In 1934, new tax exemptions for pension plans and other corporate social measures were introduced in the emergency crisis tax (Krisenabgabe) levied by the federal authorities.[128] These exemptions contributed to the recovery of the annual rate of creation of new corporate

[125] Erwin Gisi, *Das Problem der älteren Angestellten: Krise und Pensionsversicherung* (Basle: Helbing & Lichtenhahn, 1933), p. 12.

[126] Kienzle, *Es gibt nur ein Gerlafingen*, p. 186. Von Roll pension expenditures rose to CHF 2.8 million by 1937. In 1934, the overall assets of the extensive social measures (pensions, widows' benefits, family allowances, and unemployment benefits) of the firm were superior to its market capitalization of the firm. See Ermatinger, *Kapital und Ethos*, p. 75.

[127] Grütter and Alder, "Pensionskassen", p. 225. See also the appendix of this book, Table A.7 (p. 303).

[128] Hans Gerold Wirz, *Die Personal-Wohlfahrtseinrichtungen der schweizerischen Privatwirtschaft: ihre Stellung im Steuerrecht und ihre Beaufsichtigung* (Stäfa: Buchdruckerei Stäfa, 1955), p. 150.

welfare institutions, which had dropped in 1934 to its lowest level since 1913 (see Figure 2.1 p. 66). However, before World War II this rate remained markedly below its heyday of the early 1920s.

After the failure of the Lex Schulthess, insurers proclaimed that it was employers' and insurers' duty to pursue efforts to develop pensions and to promote "self-insurance" among the workforce.[129] However, Rentenanstalt concluded a declining number of contracts until the second half of the 1930s, and the Depression all but halted the selling of group insurance in foreign markets. For the market leader in group pensions, expansion was replaced by the consolidation of existing contracts and the streamlining of "midget plans" subscribed to by small employers.[130] When the group insurance market recovered around 1936, the issue of pension regulation made a comeback. This renewed interest came about due to the contradictory demands raised by labor organizations and insurers. In the early 1920s, white-collar unions had repeatedly asked the Confederation to safeguard pensioners' rights and to monitor the opaque functioning of pension plans. These demands fizzled out and were conveniently buried in the 1936 revision of the Code of Obligations (Obligationenrecht), which clarified that in order to be eligible for tax exemptions, pension plans had to be separate from the general accounts of firms, but offered no guarantees for pensioners' rights or workers' participation in the management of plans. This totally "insufficient and incomplete" revision left unanswered the issues raised by white-collar unions, which in 1938 reiterated their demands for proper federal supervision of pension plans.[131]

Insurers supported regulation primarily because they were keen to stifle potential competition. The Union of Life Insurance Companies was especially worried by the development of multi-employer pension plans by utilities, transport firms, local banks, and the Consumers'

[129] According to the 1932 annual report of Vita (Zurich Life), quoted in *25 Jahre "VITA"* (Zurich: VITA Versicherungen, 1947).

[130] "Jahresbericht Kollektivversicherungen", Rentenanstalt, 1934, file 671.21/1, SLA (quotation). See also Guido Nonella, *Die Gruppenversicherung als Personal-Fürsorge-Einrichtung* (Berne: Peter Lang, 1950), pp. 13–15.

[131] Jürg Brühwiler, *Die betriebliche Personalvorsorge in der Schweiz: eine Arbeits- und sozialversicherungsrechtliche Studie zum Rechtszustand nach Inkrafttreten des BVG unter besonderer Berücksichtigung des Verhältnisses zwischen Personalvorsorge und Arbeitsvertrag* (Berne: Stämpfli, 1989), p. 89 (quotation). See also Hermann Reber, *Die Fonds zu Wohlfahrtszwecken nach dem schweizerischen Obligationenrecht* (Interlaken: Otto Schlaefli, 1943), p. 17; Wirz, *Die Personal-Wohlfahrtseinrichtungen*, pp. 119–21. See also Martin Lüpold, "Corporate Governance in der Krise? Der Einfluss der Wirtschaftskrise auf die Aktienrechts-Revision von 1936", paper presented at the conference "Les entreprises dans les crises économiques du 20ème siècle", Société suisse d'histoire économique et sociale, Neuchâtel, November 2004, pp. 6–8.

Cooperatives Union. Insurers deplored the close links these plans had with trade unions, and resented the fact that these plans could attract new clients without having to comply with the federal law on private insurance.[132]

As the market for group contracts recovered in the second half of the 1930s, life insurers first tried unsuccessfully to settle the issue through informal contacts with business-friendly Federal Councilors. The Union of Life Insurance Companies then brought the issue to the Federal Insurance Court, but lost the case in 1938. After briefly considering the option of paying one of their corporate clients to reintroduce the issue to the Court, in June 1939 life insurers contacted a prominent Radical Senator, Gottfried Keller, who agreed to file a parliamentary motion expressing concerns about the financial viability of pension plans that were not covered by the federal law on private insurance.[133] Although the Union of Life Insurance Companies claimed that its aim was not to encourage state meddling with corporate welfare, the issue of the regulation of pension plans and the monitoring of their financial situation resurfaced at the end of the 1930s.[134] When the war broke out, the whole debate was temporarily postponed, before flaring up again around 1945. Yet, as will be explained in the following chapters of this study, decades would pass before the enactment of proper regulation of corporate social provision. The same business circles that relentlessly denounced the financial crisis of public-sector pension plans were much less eager to open their own account ledgers to public scrutiny and went to great lengths to hold off state regulation of occupational schemes.

If the 1930s constituted a lost decade for federal social policy, the situation was more nuanced for occupational provision. All in all, corporate welfare remained unscathed by the Depression. Apart from a handful of early pioneers, most of the private occupational plans had been created in the early 1920s, and their limited coverage and discretionary

[132] For the first mention of this issue, see KDSL, May 25, 1923, file Q127 206, ZFS. See also Rentenanstalt, "Jahresbericht Kollektivversicherungen", Rentenanstalt, 1933–1934, file 671.21/1, SLA.

[133] On these informal contacts, see KDSL to Federal Department of Justice and Police, October 31, 1935, and Federal Department of Justice and Police to KDSL, December 31, 1936, both in file 316.4/1, SLA. On the judicial hearings, see KDSL, March 19, 1937, April 29, 1938, and January 13, 1939, all documents in file Q127 206, ZFS. For contacts with Senator Keller, see KDSL, July 14, 1939, file Q127 206. See also Paul Matthey, "Les entreprises d'assurance non soumises à la surveillance de la Confédération", *Schweizerische Versicherungszeitschrift* (1938), pp. 364–7, and "Die eidgenössische Betriebszählung 1939 und die Staatsaufsicht über die kleinen Versicherungsinstitutionen", *Schweizerische Versicherungszeitschrift* (1939), pp. 47–50.

[134] KDSL, September 26, 1940, file Q127 206, ZFS. See also Hans Christen, "Zur Frage einer Beaufsichtigung der Pensionskassen", *Neue Zürcher Zeitung*, February 1, 1940.

nature meant they had low pension commitments. Documentation is lacking on the impact of the Depression on specific occupational plans. Although the Federal Private Insurance Office pointed out in its 1939 annual report that "it is no secret that the financial situation of numerous autonomous [i.e. single-employer] pension plans raises serious misgivings", large private occupational plans seemed to have escaped major difficulties.[135] As railroad companies had been nationalized, their large pension commitments and deficits now burdened the Confederation and not private employers. Despite the 1936 devaluation of the Swiss franc, the long-term stability of the currency and the strength of financial institutions had also protected pension plans from the currency depreciations and galloping inflation that had wiped out savings and discredited funded provision in neighboring countries such as France and Germany.

## Stalemate vs. big bang: interwar social policy in comparative perspective

The politics of social insurance had followed a path of attrition that led from the high expectations of 1918 to the defeat of 1931. After the demise of the Lex Schulthess, the Confederation financed assistance measures to support destitute elderly people, but the extent of state intervention remained limited. The shock of the Depression did not trigger a renewed discussion on old age insurance. On the contrary, the window of opportunity for federal pensions remained shut. If there was a growing awareness among employers, and especially insurers, that the AHV could provide a basis on top of which private supplementary provision might be developed, the division of labor between social insurance and occupational plans remained unresolved after the 1931 vote.

What might have happened to corporate pension plans if the Lex Schulthess had cleared the referendum hurdle? It is plausible that the introduction of federal pensions in 1931, given the economic crisis, might have hindered the development of occupational plans. Given employers' insistence on introducing, as in Basle, opt-outs for pension plans, the Swiss pension system may have continued in a highly decentralized way, with overlapping cantonal and occupational schemes supplementing a basic AHV. It can also be argued that the minimum pension benefits envisioned by the Lex Schulthess and the persistence of means-tested assistance, combined with a delayed implementation of federal pensions

[135] Report quoted in Nonella, *Die Gruppenversicherung*, p. 89. Hans Gerold Wirz points out that cantonal authorities were confronted with several small pension plan failures, but he does not name these firms. Wirz, *Die Personal-Wohlfahrtseinrichtungen*, pp. 296–8.

due to the Depression, might have accelerated the unfolding of the supplementation idea that had begun to emerge during the 1920s.

This hypothesis may be tested by a comparison with the system of old age provision that took shape in the United States during the Depression. At first glance, the legacy of interwar social policy on the other side of the Atlantic seems diametrically different from the Swiss case: the groundbreaking introduction of the Social Security Act (SSA) 1935 contrasts with the demise of the Lex Schulthess in 1931. The momentum toward the adoption of Social Security began as Schulthess' efforts foundered and the AHV was set aside for another decade. The interwar evolution of social policy in the United States followed a path leading to a genuine "big bang" of social policy, rather than the attrition or stalemate that characterized Swiss policy. However, despite the apparently divergent outcomes, both countries were laying the foundations of divided pension systems.

After the demise of proposals for health insurance in the aftermath of World War I in the United States, old age insurance was confined to the state level. Congress discussed the idea of federal pensions in the late 1920s, but no bills ever made it to the floor before the Depression.[136] The gravity of the economic crisis revealed the shortcomings of existing federal and state social measures, and, in contrast to Switzerland, economic turbulence fueled the debates that led to the Social Security Act in 1935. The SSA – encompassing not only pensions, but also unemployment insurance and means-tested assistance – represented the backlog of measures that had got bogged down in the political system during the preceding decades.

Furthermore, the political upheaval of the 1930s was not limited to the victory of a more interventionist Democratic government, but also witnessed the emergence of grassroot mobilizations in favor of retirement pensions. These "welfare populisms" fueled popular expectations and kept political pressure for social insurance at a high level.[137] Yet, the financing structure of American pensions, their limited scope and slow implementation, as well as the emerging division between basic social insurance and supplementary occupational benefits, prefigured the development of the Swiss pension system during the 1940s.

In the United States, the financing of Social Security through payroll contributions anticipated the generalization of pay-as-you-go systems in post-World War II European retirement schemes. The adoption of this

[136] Daniel Béland, *Une sécurité libérale? La politique des retraites aux Etats-Unis* (Paris: LGDJ, 1999), pp. 49–55.
[137] Klein, *For all these rights*, pp. 66–9.

financing system underlined President Roosevelt's familiarity with contributory pension schemes and life insurance actuarial models. However, more crucial than the intellectual influence of private insurance, financing pensions through earmarked payroll contributions supplemented by a reserve fund was designed to make Social Security a "self-supporting" scheme that would not depend on general state revenues. According to political scientist Julian Zelizer, this choice represented a "conservative method of public finance" devised to defuse resistance to the new federal taxes necessary to finance pensions.[138]

Secondly, Social Security pensions were implemented incrementally. Their constitutionality was challenged before the Supreme Court, and large sectors of the population – from agricultural workers to federal employees – were not included in Social Security at the beginning. The first pensions were paid out only in 1940, and state-level means-tested assistance long remained the norm. The opposition of Southern states to universal social programs that challenged the system of racial apartheid weighed heavily in this. The exclusion of farm workers denied millions of African-Americans Social Security benefits and made them dependent on racially biased state assistance programs.[139] The real implementation of social insurance did not occur before the 1939 and 1949 Social Security amendments. While the former dramatically increased the scope of the scheme, the latter almost saved from oblivion federal pensions that had stagnated during World War II.[140]

Finally, the Depression and the introduction of the SSA did not lead to the end of corporate welfare. On the contrary, the slow implementation of federal pensions left time for corporate interests to consolidate their plans. In Steven Sass' words, the "socialization of basic old age benefits" was not detrimental to employers. On the contrary:

> The most clear-sighted business people also understood that a significant private institution remained possible only with the socialization of basic old age pension benefits. Government would handle pension functions separable from the firm – retiring aged labor from the workforce and assuring these people a basic standard of living. Remaining to the sponsors was the pension function that they themselves

[138] Julian E. Zelizer, *Taxing America: Wilbur D. Mills, Congress and the state, 1945–1975* (Cambridge: Cambridge University Press, 1998), pp. 55–61.

[139] Ira Katznelson, *When affirmative action was white: an untold history of racial inequality in twentieth-century America* (New York: W. W. Norton, 2005), pp. 25–52; Robert C. Lieberman, *Shifting the color line: race and the American welfare state* (Cambridge, MA: Harvard University Press, 1998), pp. 23–67; Jill S. Quadagno, "From old-age assistance to Supplemental Security Income: the political economy of relief in the South, 1935–1972", in *The politics of social policy in the United States*, ed. Margaret Weir, *et al.* (Princeton: Princeton University Press, 1988), pp. 235–63.

[140] Zelizer, *Taxing America*, pp. 66–78.

most valued – attaching workers to organizational careers and then releasing these highly-paid personnel in an orderly fashion.[141]

According to Jennifer Klein, the development of the SSA witnessed the emergence of a configuration where "the acceptance of welfare capitalism in the core of the welfare state . . . limited the ideological space in which the welfare state could expand".[142] By the end of the 1940s, a divided, or bifurcated, pension system combining public and private provision was solidly entrenched. Among "clear-sighted business people", insurance companies played an important role popularizing this perspective within the business community.

For insurers, the SSA and its basic pay-as-you-go pensions clearly represented a lesser evil compared with proposals by welfare populists or the left wing of the New Deal coalition. Insurers were also reluctant to support in the Senate the Clark Amendment, a conservative attempt to safeguard private provision by securing opt-outs for existing occupational plans. Insurers were among the first to realize that the attempts to dilute the SSA might backfire and lead to stricter regulation of employers' plans. Together with large corporations that had developed in-house pension plans, leading insurance companies withdrew their support of the Clark Amendment and moved to "conceptualize the government's national pension program as a foundation upon which they could build".[143]

The issue of business influence in the making of American social policy tends to lead to polarized conclusions. Scholars emphasizing the pro-business dimension of the New Deal depict some corporate representatives as the vanguard behind-the-scenes shapers of the SSA, while some institutionalist scholars deny any role in policy-making to business circles, crippled as they were by the Depression.[144] Recent scholarship has moved from this Manichean debate and focused instead on the differentiated attitudes of business forces in the entangled histories of the two areas of provision. Peter Swenson and Colin Gordon emphasize, for example, that the SSA provided a regulatory impulse that stabilized corporate plans unbalanced by the crisis. Consequently, federal social policy gathered more business support than might have been expected.[145] For example, the Depression struck the economy at a time when the first

141 Sass, *The promise of private pensions*, p. 101.
142 Klein, *For all these rights*, p. 79.
143 Ibid., p. 92.
144 For a sample of this polarized debate, see Edwin Amenta and Sunita Parikh, "Capitalists did not want the Social Security Act: a critique of the capitalist dominance thesis", *American Sociological Review* 56 (1991), pp. 124–9; G. William Domhoff, *State autonomy or class dominance? Case studies on policy making in America* (New York: Aldine de Gruyter, 1996), pp. 117–76.
145 Gordon, *New Deals*, pp. 240–79; Swenson, *Capitalists against markets*, pp. 191–220.

significant group of workers reached retirement. The financial crisis of railroad retirement plans, which represented at the time around half of private-sector occupational pension coverage, and their subsequent rescue by the federal government in 1934 constituted a major step toward the passing of the SSA.[146] In contrast, Swiss railroad plans had been taken over by the federal state long before, and other corporate plans still faced very low pension commitments, significantly reducing their exposure to the economic crisis.

To sum up, the United States set up, in 1935, a basic pension system based on a pay-as-you-go structure. Yet, because of the strength of Southern opposition, federal pensions were only gradually phased in. Until the late 1940s, means-tested assistance left ample room for the development of private pension schemes, and the foundations of the pension system laid during the Depression were consolidated only at the end of World War II. These foundations were based on a division of labor between basic social insurance and supplementary occupational provision. The Swiss situation followed a very similar trajectory.

First, as we will see in the next chapter, the implementation of the AHV was also carried out in two phases. In Switzerland, the large exogenous shock that triggered the development of social insurance was not the Depression, but World War II. The war not only added new urgency to social policy, but also lowered the institutional hurdles of federalism and referendum politics that had hindered social insurance during the interwar years. The breakthrough for Swiss social insurance occurred in two stages: the first focused on the introduction of an innovative income-substitution insurance scheme for mobilized soldiers in 1940; and the second on the rapid implementation of federal pensions between 1944 and 1948. Despite the contrast between the failure of 1931 in Switzerland and the big bang of Social Security in 1935 in the United States, the quantum leap from modest assistance programs to social insurance took place in both countries during the mid-1940s.

Second, the opportunity of pay-as-you-go financing had also been discussed in Switzerland during the interwar period, and fiscally conservative insurers had been among its central supporters. However, the debates on the Lex Schulthess had focused on flat-rate individual contributions and not on the payroll deductions that formed the basis of pay-as-you-go in the United States. The emphasis on universal basic pensions based on a "self-supporting" financing structure constituted a key dimension of the

[146] Jill S. Quadagno, *The transformation of old age security: class and politics in the American welfare state* (Chicago/London: Chicago University Press, 1988), pp. 72–5; Sass, *The promise of private pensions*, pp. 92–4.

Swiss pension debate during World War II and was also influenced by prevailing fiscal conservatism. Like the United States, the Swiss "welfare laggard" leapfrogged earlier tax-based or means-tested solutions that had been developed in the Netherlands, the United Kingdom, and Canada (see Table 0.2, p. 24).

Finally, in response to the AHV, Swiss insurance companies developed supplementation strategies because of their financial interests in group contracts. They supported the 1925 constitutional amendment on social insurance and the Lex Schulthess because they estimated that federal pensions would not compete directly with employer-based provision. However, the dual system of basic federal provision and supplementary regional schemes proposed by the Federal Council had blurred the line between social insurance and occupational provision, and attracted the hostility of the pension lobby and the business community. Supplementation remained unresolved by the time of the 1931 defeat of the Lex Schulthess.

In 1938, the Swiss Society for Statistics and Political Economy devoted its annual meeting to the economic impacts of the "graying of the population". Reminding attendees that "elderly poverty" had now become a "mass phenomenon", Werner Ammann of the Pro Senectute charity argued that this issue had to be urgently addressed by the authorities. Yet, in line with conservative business interests, Ammann did not envision a universal pay-as-you-go pension system but only means-tested assistance measures supplemented by pension schemes. In contrast, Emile Marchand of Rentenanstalt spoke in favor of pay-as-you-go, but feared that the "issue of social insurance could not be solved" in the near future, and that Switzerland would still have to wait "many years" before the implementation of federal pensions.[147] However, it was precisely during World War II that a clear-cut supplementation strategy made its breakthrough in Switzerland. During the war, both the executive branch and the Federal Social Insurance Office took great pains to avoid a potentially damaging entanglement of social insurance and occupational schemes. The 1947 pension system that will be the focus of the next chapter thus avoided the pitfalls of the interwar period.

[147] See Werner Ammann, "Die Auswirkungen der Ueberalterung auf die Altersversicherung und –fürsorge", *Schweizerische Zeitschrift für Volkswirtschaft und Statistik* 1938), pp. 184–95. For Emile Marchand's comment, see p. 196.

# 3 No monster like the Beveridge Plan The wartime breakthrough of social insurance (1938–1948)

The July 1947 landslide vote in favor of the AHV ended decades of missed opportunities for social insurance. The introduction of federal pensions is often depicted as a major innovation that symbolized the solidarity of the people's community (Volksgemeinschaft) forged during the course of World War II. The popular enthusiasm that welcomed the introduction of the AHV was the polar opposite of the social and political tensions that culminated in the 1918 general strike. The AHV also constituted a key aspect of a postwar settlement designed to maintain political and social stability during the difficult transition from war to peace. A century after the establishment of the modern Swiss Confederation in 1848, the introduction of the AHV had an epochal dimension, and public opinion surveys several decades after the vote still registered that the introduction of federal pensions was widely seen as "the most significant political event of the twentieth century" in Switzerland.[1]

This chapter spans a decade that spills over the boundaries usually set for World War II. The decade 1938–1948 encompassed the early organization of the war economy in the late 1930s, intense manufacturing and financial activities in a western European political economy dominated by Nazi Germany, and finally Switzerland's reorientation in a postwar international order dominated by the Allies.[2] As had been the case a generation earlier, the war experience was unique for Switzerland: the country did not take part in military operations, and its population and productive capacities did not endure the staggering suffering and destruction inflicted on its neighbors. The two temporal markers of this decade of war also have their significance for the development of social policy. While 1938 signaled the first parliamentary motion on the AHV presented to the Federal Assembly after the 1931 defeat of the Lex Schulthess,

[1] Peter Binswanger, *Histoire de l'AVS: assurance-vieillesse et survivants suisse* (Zurich: Pro Senectute, 1987), p. 9.

[2] Hans Ulrich Jost, *Politik und Wirtschaft im Krieg: die Schweiz 1938–1948* (Zurich: Chronos, 1998). *Switzerland, National Socialism, and the Second World War: report of the Independent Commission of Experts Switzerland – Second World War* (Zurich: Pendo Verlag, 2002).

January 1948 saw payment of the first AHV pensions six months after the momentous July 6, 1947 vote.

The first two sections of this chapter outline two facets of the war economy. First, the 1940 insurance scheme designed to offset losses in wages and earnings during military duties is described. This program constituted a trial run for the AHV and was implemented in an institutional setting where wartime executive dominance and technocratic structures enabled its rapid introduction. The second facet, occupational pension plans, were spurred on by tax exemptions and industrial relations that put a premium on collaboration between labor and capital. These simultaneous developments proved that a smooth cohabitation was possible between basic social insurance and occupational schemes.

The third and fourth sections discuss the blueprints for postwar social reforms that emerged as the "New Europe" dominated by Nazi Germany was rolled back by Allied victories. I examine how the political and geopolitical shifts in the period 1941–1943 enhanced the prospects of success for social insurance while narrowing its potential scale and scope. In the fourth section, I underline in particular how Federal Councilor Walther Stampfli, the Radical "father of the AHV", shaped federal pensions into the epitome of postwar consensus and sidelined alternative reform proposals.

The fifth and sixth sections focus on the shaping of the AHV and on the division of labor between the two areas of old age provision between 1944 and 1948. Beginning with the strategies followed by employers' federations, life insurance companies, and the pension lobby to limit the scope of federal pensions, I then review how the Federal Council molded an ironclad cross-class alliance in favor of social insurance that prevented a repeat of the failure of 1931. This section then describes the unsuccessful attempt to shatter this almost unassailable social program through referendum politics and discusses the limited leverage of the left during pension debates, as well as the entanglement of key industrial unions with corporate social programs. The seventh and final section assesses the standing of the Swiss postwar social insurance breakthrough in a wider international context.

## Protecting soldiers and preserving social peace (1938–1941)

After the lost decade of the 1930s, social insurance made its comeback to the political agenda as the economy was recovering from the Depression and benefitting from German rearmament. In late 1938, as the Federal Council raised federal subsidies for means-tested old age assistance,

National Councilor Arnold Saxer, a left-liberal Radical who in the spring of that year had filed a parliamentary motion asking the executive branch to develop federal pensions, was designated the new director of the Federal Social Insurance Office (Bundesamt für Sozialversicherung). Saxer's explicit mandate was to carry out preliminary studies on the feasibility of social insurance.[3] However, as a new war was breaking out in Europe, official concern for old age provision was eclipsed by such issues as the preparation of the war economy, whose basic structures were set up in December 1938 by Federal Councilor Hermann Obrecht (1882–1940). A radical like his predecessor, Edmund Schulthess, whom he replaced as head of the Economic Affairs Department in 1935, Obrecht was a key member of the Wirtschaftsfreisinn and close to economic elites.[4] Federal social policy focused at first on the protection of citizen-soldiers through an insurance scheme that would compensate for losses in wages and earnings occasioned by the fulfillment of military duties (Lohn- und Verdienstersatzordnung, also dubbed Erwerbersatzordnung or EO). Retracing the origins of the EO offers an insight into the politics of military and economic mobilization and points to how it constituted a trial run for the AHV.

Ensuring wage compensation during national service and regular militia training duties had been discussed sporadically during the interwar years and was considered crucial to integrating the labor movement in national defense efforts, as well as to homogenizing unequal compensation and assistance measures set up by individual employers and city councils. As the prospect of full-scale war mobilization drew closer, the memory of the lack of proper compensation for military duties that had sharpened social and political tensions during World War I resurfaced and reinforced these concerns. The trauma of the 1918 general strike greatly influenced the mindset of the economic and political elites that presided over the implementation of the EO. This scheme represented not only a welcome rationalization of existing welfare measures, but was also a key element of national solidarity meant to safeguard social stability on the home front. Finally, the rationalization of soldiers' compensation

[3] Georg Hafner, *Bundesrat Walther Stampfli (1884–1965): leiter der Kriegswirtschaft im Zweiten Weltkrieg, bundesrätlicher Vater der AHV* (Olten: Dietschi Verlag, 1986), p. 367. During the interwar years, Arnold Saxer (1896–1975) had led both the St. Gallen embroidery manufacturers' association and the National Association of Free Workers (Landesverband schweizerischer freier Arbeiter). This trade union, founded in the aftermath of the general strike, was dominated by left-liberal Radical politicians advocating class reconciliation. See Robert Fluder *et al.*, *Gewerkschaften und Angestelltenverbände in der schweizerischen Privatwirtschaft* (Zurich: Seismo Verlag, 1991), p. 69.

[4] Hermann Böschenstein, "Hermann Obrecht 1882–1940", in *Le Conseil Fédéral*, ed. Urs Altermatt (Yens: Cabédita, 1993), pp. 395–9.

echoed the policy of Spiritual National Defense (geistige Landesverteidigung) developed by the Federal Council. Designed as a bulwark against authoritarian propaganda and infused with nationalist and militaristic values, this program extolled people's community (Volksgemeinschaft) and the readiness of citizen-soldiers to defend the motherland against foreign invasion.[5]

This conjunction of factors was incubated in a favorable institutional context. The expansion of administrative capacity that coalesced into the war-economy apparatus relied heavily on private-sector executives and reinforced the collaboration between the federal administration and business federations. Labor was integrated into these tightly knit public–private partnerships, albeit as a junior partner: Socialist and trade union representation in the "war-economy militia system" remained limited and subordinate. The granting of emergency powers to the Federal Council also greatly strengthened the executive. Together, executive dominance and technocratic structures bypassed the legislative branch, political parties, and direct-democracy mechanisms.[6]

In the fall of 1939, Federal Councilor Hermann Obrecht gave his benediction to an EO project that had been drafted by the Employers' Federation (Arbeitgeberverband) and endorsed by trade unions and the Federal Office for Industry, Trades, and Labor (Bundesamt für Industrie, Gewerbe, und Arbeit). The program was also welcomed by trade sectors and small employers who rarely offered compensation for military service.[7] Passed on to the Federal Council, the EO was then implemented by emergency decree in December 1939. Mobilization for war enabled the Federal Council to follow a "direct executive road" that bypassed the objections that could be raised in the Federal Assembly against the program and insulated it from referendum politics. This policy-making

[5] Jost, *Politik und Wirtschaft im Krieg*, pp. 40–4.

[6] Hafner, *Bundesrat Walther Stampfli*, pp. 226–35; Jakob Tanner, *Bundeshaushalt, Währung und Kriegswirtschaft: eine finanzsoziologische Analyse der Schweiz zwischen 1938 und 1953* (Zurich: Limmat Verlag, 1986), pp. 286–93.

[7] Alfred Gutersohn, *Das Gewerbe in der schweizerischen Wirtschaftspolitik: der schweizerische Gewerbeverband 1879–1954* (Zurich: Schweizerische Gewerbeverband, 1955), pp. 230–2; Jürg Sommer, *Das Ringen um die soziale Sicherheit in der Schweiz: eine politisch-ökonomische Analyse der Ursprünge, Entwicklungen und Perspektiven sozialer Sicherung im Widerstreit zwischen Gruppeninteressen und volkswirtschaftlicher Tragbarkeit* (Diessenhofen: Rüegger Verlag, 1978), pp. 178–86. See also Karl Attinger, *Les caisses de compensation militaires: le régime des allocations pour perte de salaire institué par l'Arrêté du Conseil Fédéral du 20 décembre 1939 et ses répercussions* (Zurich: Sihl, 1946), pp. 19–51. Despite its publication date, this study, based on extensive research in employers' federation archives, offers excellent insights into the making of the EO. For an overview of the project, see Arbeitgeberverband geschäftsleitende Ausschuss, September 26, 1939, pp. 113–17, and Arbeitgeberverband Vorstand, October 19, 1939, pp. 26–53, SAV.

process can be described as an exemplary case of the pre-structuring of state tasks by economic forces, followed by its implementation by the federal government.[8]

The EO scheme was financed by a 4 percent levy on wages supplemented by federal outlays and a reserve fund. The implementation of the EO relied on equalization funds managed by employers' associations, a solution favored by the Arbeitgeberverband, as it limited state and labor involvement in the administration of the program. This distinctive public–private structure was inspired by French employers' mutual schemes set up during the interwar period to distribute family allowances.[9] As economist Jürg Sommer noted, the EO was a "unique opportunity". What is more, the "positive experiences acquired by means of the financial system and organizational structure of the EO could be used, after years of social policy stagnation, to usher in the further expansion of social insurance".[10] The EO success story opened up the way for the AHV. However, the expansion of social insurance was by no means a certainty in 1940. At the very moment when the EO sailed unhindered through the political system, the financial reorganization of the pension plans of the Confederation was successfully challenged in December 1939 by a referendum launched by conservative free-market circles. The simultaneity of this roll-back of state retirement benefits further underscores the distinctive nature of the military insurance scheme. The breathtaking speed of its implementation reminds us that the protracted log-rolling that is typical of Swiss politics can be replaced by striking rapidity in specific contexts.

The EO was an instant success and generated impressive money flows. In 1940, payroll contributions amounted to CHF 230 million, and equalization funds distributed CHF 170 million in benefits to soldiers, or several times the amount (in inflation-adjusted terms) that had been disbursed for similar purposes by the Confederation during World War I.[11] Figure 3.1 shows that the EO and military accident and disability benefits constituted the lion's share of federal social policy expenditure, while means-tested assistance for the elderly poor financed by the

[8] Beat Hotz, *Politik zwischen Staat und Wirtschaft: verbandsmässige Bearbeitung wirtschaftspolitischer Probleme und die daraus resultierenden Konsequenzen für die Aktivitäten des Staates im Falle der Schweiz* (Diessenhofen: Rüegger Verlag, 1979), pp. 27–44; Ellen M. Immergut, *Health politics: interests and institutions in western Europe* (Cambridge: Cambridge University Press, 1992), p. 155 (quotation).

[9] Attinger, *Les caisses de compensation militaires*, pp. 19–51; *La politique sociale de la Confédération* (Berne: Centrale fédérale de l'économie de guerre, 1946), pp. 71–98; Immergut, *Health politics*, p. 280 (note 38); Susan Pedersen, *Family, dependence, and the origins of the welfare state: Britain and France, 1914–1945* (Cambridge: Cambridge University Press, 1993), pp. 224–91.

[10] Sommer, *Das Ringen um die soziale Sicherheit*, p. 208.

[11] Ibid., p. 186 (note 2).

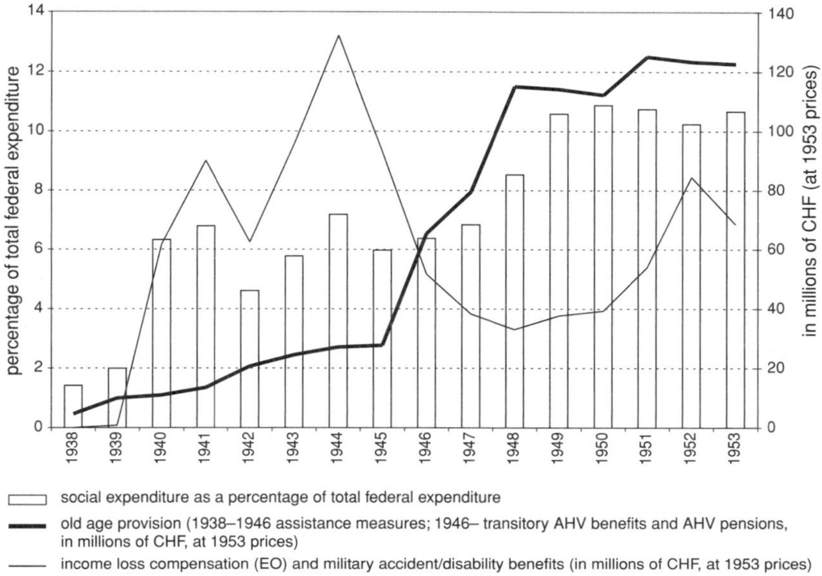


Figure 3.1 Federal social expenditure, 1938–1953.
*Source:* Heiner Ritzmann-Blickenstorfer and Hansjörg Siegenthaler, eds., *Historisch Statistik der Schweiz – Statistique historique de la Suisse – Swiss Historical Statistics* (Zürich: Chronos, 1996), Table U8b.

Confederation trailed far behind. All in all, federal social policy expenditure tripled after the introduction of the income compensation scheme. EO reserves swelled and soon overtook the stagnating funds resulting from the taxation of tobacco and alcohol that were earmarked for federal pensions.[12]

The EO played a major role in smoothing over wartime class relations, because all male citizen-soldiers, from factory workers to bank managers, as well as the self-employed and farmers, received benefits. Foreign workers and women who did not serve in the army also paid the levy, but they did not receive benefits, which strengthened gender divides. Right after the outbreak of hostilities, the EO ensured the orderly entry of the Swiss economy into the new wartime context. The EO also contributed to the easing of both labor shortages and bottlenecks at key moments of the

[12] While the EO reserve fund reached CHF 440 million in 1943, the revenues of tobacco and alcohol taxes earmarked for the AHV increased from CHF 216 million to CHF 236 million between 1938 and 1942. In inflation-adjusted terms, this meant a loss of 21 percent. Sébastien Guex, *L'argent de l'Etat: parcours des finances publiques au 20ème siècle* (Lausanne: Réalités Sociales, 1998), pp. 94–5; Hafner, *Bundesrat Walther Stampfli*, p. 369.

conflict. Full mobilization of the army at the beginning and end of World War II coincided with uncertain economic prospects. In this context, men carrying out militia duties covered by the EO avoided layoffs or unemployment. For example: the partial demobilizations that followed the lull in military operations on the western front in June 1940 enabled militiamen to return to their workplaces, maintaining the productive capacities of the export-based economy.[13]

The strength of the EO scheme pointed to the potential of payroll contributions – the pay-as-you-go system – for financing social insurance. Its success triggered a debate on whether EO monies earmarked for soldiers' benefits could also be used to finance job-creation programs and unemployment benefits, or even to introduce new social insurance programs. In June 1940, the Trade Union Confederation (Gewerkschaftsbund) demanded that the EO form the basis of a postwar AHV. In contrast, the powerful Metalworkers' and Watchmakers' Union (Schweizerischer Metall- und Uhrenarbeitnehmer-Verband) envisioned using EO monies to support existing unemployment schemes.[14] At first, employers' federations were reluctant to support either option. After Hermann Obrecht's unexpected resignation for health reasons in the summer of 1940, his successor at the Economic Affairs Department, Walther Stampfli, also expressed strong reservations about social insurance and claimed repeatedly that the priority of the Federal Council was to stabilize the economy and provide jobs, not to introduce old age pensions.[15]

Elected to the executive branch by the Federal Assembly during the tense summer that followed the June 1940 armistice between France and Germany, Walther Stampfli (1884–1965) had led a dual career. While climbing the corporate ladder at the Von Roll steelworks, Stampfli had become a seasoned member of the Radical Party, first in the Solothurn cantonal parliament and then in the National Council. The 1940 election of this veteran politician and business executive, who followed in Edmund Schultess' and Hermann Obrecht's footsteps, personified the choice of the ruling elites to maintain close economic and financial relationships with their traditional German partners while defending the autonomy of Swiss manufacturing and financial interests during the war. The

[13] Tanner, *Bundeshaushalt, Währung und Kriegswirtschaft*, pp. 36–40, 286ff.

[14] Marcela Hohl, *Die wirtschaftspolitischen Vorstellungen von Max Weber (1897–1974) und sein Einfluss auf die Tätigkeit des Schweizerischen Gewerkschaftsbundes* (Diessenhofen: Rüegger Verlag, 1983), pp. 319–21.

[15] Vorort Vorstand, November 4, 1940, file 1.5.3.11, AfZ-SHIV; Otto Steinmann, "Künftige Aufgaben der Lohnersatzausgleichkassen", October 30, 1940, memorandum added to the October 22, 1940, minutes of the Arbeitgeberverband geschäftsleitende Ausschuss, SAV. See also Hafner, *Bundesrat Walther Stampfli*, pp. 367–71.

narratives about the "armed neutrality" of a "besieged democracy" during World War II fail to account for a manufacturing and financial center for which armed conflict did not mean simply disruption, but the opening of profitable opportunities.[16] As Walther Stampfli's biographer reminds us, "war in the twentieth century also means economic war, and on this, for Switzerland, hot front, Stampfli was the General".[17] Ironically, unlike General Henri Guisan, the commander-in-chief of the federal army, this economic general has not left a deep imprint in popular memory. Yet, Stampfli's steering of the war economy and management of foreign economic and financial relations can be considered without exaggeration as the true Swiss wartime defense policy.

Despite his early uncompromising stance against social insurance, Stampfli was to shape the political consensus in favor of the AHV during his tenure at the Federal Council (1940–1947). As mentioned in the preceding chapter, Stampfli was well-versed in corporate social provision and had supervised the reorganization of Von Roll welfare measures in the aftermath of the general strike. While publicly backing the Lex Schulthess in 1931, Walther Stampfli had belonged to the board of the Association of Support Funds and Foundations for Old Age and Disability (SVUSAI) and signed appeals that criticized the AHV. As a veteran politician and prominent executive of a manufacturing sector that had always acquiesced on the issue of social insurance, Stampfli had the standing to become the "father of the AHV" and the architect of the division of labor that would emerge at the end of the war between basic social insurance and supplementary occupational provision. Finally, his trajectory from corporate circles to the executive branch emphasized again the dense intertwining of the state and the business community.

Walther Stampfli's course is similar to that of Marion Folsom, a prominent Eastman Kodak executive who played a key role in the making of American social policy and who is designated by historian Sanford Jacoby a proponent of "a welfare state imbued with market values and intertwined with private alternatives".[18] Folsom was a veteran organizer

[16] Georg Kreis, "Etat démocratique en Etat de siège", *Revue d'histoire de la deuxième guerre mondiale* 121 (1981), pp. 71–82. On Swiss business strategies during World War II and the long-term partnership between German and Swiss capitalism, see Daniel Bourgeois, *Business helvétique et Troisième Reich* (Lausanne: Editions Page deux, 1998); Dominique Dirlewanger, Matthieu Leimgruber, and Gian Franco Pordenone, "L'Allemagne a-t-elle encore besoin de la Suisse? Le capitalisme helvétique en Europe (1890–1970)", in *Bienvenue en Euroland! De l'Europe de Maastricht à l'euro* (Lausanne: Antipodes, 1998), pp. 97–136.

[17] Hafner, *Bundesrat Walther Stampfli*, p. 225.

[18] Sanford M. Jacoby, "Employers and the welfare state: the role of Marion B. Folsom", *Journal of American History* 80 (1993), pp. 525–56 (quotation p. 552).

of corporate welfare schemes and advised President Roosevelt during the making of the Social Security Act 1935. After repeated involvement in social policy debates, Folsom was nominated in 1953 to head the Department of Health, Education, and Welfare during the Eisenhower administration. Folsom was an advocate of supplementation, according to which business supported basic social insurance programs as long as they left room for company benefits. With Walther Stampfli at the economic wheel, we have in Switzerland a Folsom-like figure who occupied a commanding position in the executive branch, enabling him to directly implement this concept.

Besides their stern refusal to transform EO benefits into old age pensions, business circles readied themselves for a potential resurgence of demands for social insurance. In early 1940, the Federal Social Insurance Office contacted the Union of Life Insurance Companies and solicited its expertise to help the federal administration in the drafting of a new AHV project. After a short discussion, insurance executives agreed that it was "suitable to collaborate, without commenting on either the opportunity of the envisioned solutions or on its core principles. If we abstain, [the Confederation] would act without us, and we could then expect the worst."[19] While maintaining contacts with the federal administration, insurance executives kept a watchful eye on social insurance through other channels.

In the fall of 1940, the Redressement National and the Arbeitgeberverband convened in Zurich, as part of a brainstorming on postwar economic prospects, a study group on old age insurance (hereafter Untergruppe Altersversicherung). Discussing the postwar period in 1940 might seem premature. However, after the Blitzkrieg and the Battle of Britain, the prospect of a stabilized western Europe under German domination did not seem such a distant and unwelcome possibility for business circles that had long entertained close links with German capitalism. The Untergruppe Altersversicherung drew its members from Zurich business and financial circles that were heavily represented in the Redressement National.[20] Otto Steinmann, secretary of the Arbeitgeberverband and drafter of the EO law, Werner Ammann, secretary of the Pro Senectute charity, and Ernst Röthlisberger, founding member of the Redressement

[19] Konferenz der Direktoren der VSLG, January 26, 1940, p. 23, file Q127 206, ZFS.

[20] For the minutes of meetings, see Untergruppe Altersversicherung der Arbeitsgemeinschaft für die wirtschaftliche Gestaltung der Nachkriegszeit (hereafter, Untergruppe Altersversicherung), file 5.3.2.4/I, AfZ-RN. Executives from the Zurich insurance company were also heavily implicated in the famous "Petition of the 200" that demanded Switzerland's "adaptation" to the European order dominated by the Third Reich; see Stefan Karlen, Lucas Chocomeli, Kristin D'haemer *et al.*, *Schweizerische Versicherungsgesellschaften im Machtbereich des Dritten Reichs* (Zurich: Chronos, 2002), pp. 207–8.

National and director of the group division of Vita (Zurich Life), were the main animators of the Untergruppe Altersversicherung.[21] During the first meeting of this group, Röthlisberger enumerated the motivates for a reappraisal of the AHV issue among business circles:

> The study of this question imposes itself today not only because, since the rejection of the Lex Schulthess, the graying of the population has continued . . . [but also because] the pauperization of the nation has increased as a consequence of war, and the will to self-organized old age provision seems to be paralyzed to a large extent. Therefore, we must also study the issue of old age insurance, because the 1939–1941 provisory federal program for the assistance of the elderly will soon come to an end.[22]

The study group started by churning out a series of reports examining current public assistance measures and the situation of life insurance and private pension plans, as well as foreign social programs. This first round of discussions revealed that social insurance was not under consideration.

Röthlisberger's provisory theses on the opportunity of a federal pension scheme envisioned public provision strictly as a supplement to existing pension plans and individual savings. According to his fiscal conservative preferences, the Confederation had to ensure that EO funds would remain out of bounds and limit its involvement in pension provision to the introduction of compulsory individual retirement accounts managed by public or private institutions.[23] Other insurers linked to the Redressement National held similar views. For Paul Pfeil of Winterthur Life, a "fair solution" had to be based on a "dual design" ordained along "a modest means-tested insurance scheme and a vigorous encouragement of individual old age provision through compulsion, tax exemptions, free choice of the insurance carrier . . . [as well as] public subsidies for existing pension plans".[24] This preference for private alternatives to universal social insurance was self-serving, as the management of individual retirement accounts would open up new markets to insurance

21 For biographical information on Ernst Röthlisberger (1894–1967), see Peter Brechtbühl (general director of Vita), "Abschiedsansprache", August 23, 1967, ZFS. Thanks to Thomas Inglin (Zurich Financial Services) for providing me with this document.

22 Untergruppe Altersversicherung Sitzung, September 3, 1940, p. 1, file 5.3.2.4/I, AfZ-RN.

23 Ernst Röthlisberger, "Anregungen für den Aufbau einer allgemeinen schweizerischen oder kantonalen Altersversicherung", Untergruppe Altersversicherung, Beitrag 18 [n.d., ca. 1941]. See also "Provisorischen Thesen zur Frage einer schweizerischen sozialen Alters- und Hinterlassenenversicherung", Untergruppe Altersversicherung, Beitrag 15 [n.d., ca. 1941] file 5.3.2.1, AfZ-RN. Röthlisberger had first outlined these guidelines at the February 1940 general assembly of the Redressement National. See Ernst Röthlisberger, *Richtlinien für die künftige Gestaltung der Altersversicherung und -Fürsorge in der Schweiz* (Zurich: Schweizer Druck- und Verlagshaus, 1941).

24 Paul Pfeil, "Altersversicherung ja – aber wie?" *Die Schweiz: Jahrbuch der Neuen Helvetischen Gesellschaft* (1940/1941), pp. 150–6 (quotation p. 155).

companies and banks. The punch line of Röthlisberger's final report was unmistakable: "The exploitation of the idea of social insurance for political means must be confronted vigorously and without delay."[25]

During the spring of 1941, this warning was translated into action as the Untergruppe Altersversicherung took a leading role in a successful referendum campaign against an old age insurance scheme drafted by the Zurich cantonal authorities.[26] The referendum committee was chaired by right-wing personalities, and had the full organizational and financial support of business circles. Its main propaganda leaflet denounced the "meagerness" of the scheme and the fact that means tests would lead to a "politicization" of welfare. For its detractors, the proposal undermined individual savings, competed with existing pension plans, and accumulated monies that could be used for state-controlled investment. The referendum committee also depicted the scheme as an ominous first step toward further social expenditures and disingenuously warned that cantonal social programs might delay the implementation of a federal AHV.[27] Less than eighteen months after the successful campaign against the financial reorganization of the Confederation pension plans, and despite the ground-breaking introduction of the EO, the defeat of the Zurich cantonal scheme in May 1941 underlined that social insurance still faced daunting obstacles.

Yet, the sheet of ice that held back the AHV thawed more rapidly than the Untergruppe Altersversicherung could ever have imagined. As explained in the third section of this chapter, a sudden acceleration of social policy debates followed the Zurich referendum. Before outlining this new phase, an explanation of the other area of old age provision is needed. It was precisely at the time when the prospects for social insurance seemed most uncertain that an unprecedented boom of occupational provision developed. In addition to the EO program, this expansion of corporate benefits constituted the second facet of the wartime mobilization and stabilization of the labor market. When the AHV came back on the political agenda, so did the issue of the integration or combination of the two sectors of old age provision.

[25] Ernst Röthlisberger, "Provisorischen Thesen zur Frage einer schweizerischen sozialen Alters- und Hinterlassenenversicherung".

[26] Untergruppe Altersversicherung, Sitzung, December 5, 1940, file 5.3.2.4/I, AfZ-RN.

[27] "Altersversicherung bezw. Altersfürsorge im Kanton Zürich auf Grund der Gesetzvorlage vom 10. März 1941" [s.d., ca. April 1941], file 5.3.3.2, AfZ-RN. Ernst Röthlisberger had drafted this leaflet. Insurers and the League of Non-Subsidized Persons (Bund der Subventionslosen) supported the referendum but were careful not to appear publicly to do so. See unsigned letter to Ernst Röthlisberger and other members of the referendum committee, May 8, 1941, file 5.3.3.2, AfZ-RN.

## Corporate social benefits and the war economy

In an August 1940 letter, insurance executive Ernst Röthlisberger argued that occupational provision represented "a valuable and not-to-be neglected tool to reinforce the export capacity of industry":

> For trade and industry, a properly organized old age and disability provision offers an appropriate means to replace an elderly or prematurely unemployable workforce; such measures also guarantee the necessary renewal of the workforce. On the other hand, corporate provision helps the employer to build a stock of skilled and faithful workers, in other words to maintain and foster the quality of work which is so essential for Switzerland. Adequate provision also creates a tighter bond between employer and labor and thus has a welcome social function.[28]

At the beginning of the war, the last pockets of unemployment dried up under the combined effect of mobilization of the army and the increase in exports. Corporate benefits evolved within the context of labor relations transformed by the war economy. Once again, fiscal policy, competition for scarce labor, and corporate attempts to prevent labor unrest and foster social peace contributed to the expansion of occupational provision. Although the two pension surveys covering the years 1941 and 1955 contain little information on corporate pension plans during the wartime years that preceded the introduction of the AHV, available data nevertheless makes clear that this was a key moment for them.

In contrast, new public-sector pension plans were mostly set up during the war in small communes, which brought no significant change in terms of coverage: more than two-thirds of public-sector workers were affiliated to pension plans from the 1930s into the mid-1950s. In the private sector, the number of core pension plans rose tremendously between 1941 and 1955. Yet, pension coverage still trailed behind the public sector, increasing from 11 percent in 1930 to 16 percent in 1941, and finally 26 percent in 1955 (see Table A.2, p. 295). Banks, insurance companies, machine manufacturers, and chemical producers confirmed their lead in the field of occupational provision, and their pension coverage rate continued to overtake the private-sector average (see Table A.5, p. 299).

During World War II, existing pension plans in leading firms and large public administrations were shored up, and countless new small and medium-sized plans were created. But it was only at the end of the conflict that the growth rate of pension coverage accelerated dramatically. Many

[28] Ernst Röthlisberger to John Brunner, secretary of the Swiss Office for the Development of Foreign Trade (Schweizerische Zentralstelle für Handelsförderung), August 29, 1940, file 5.3.2.3/I, AfZ-RN.

of the thousands of new plans established during the war were either primarily for tax purposes – on average, 500 of them were founded every year between 1942 and 1946 (see Table A.1, p. 290) – or, as mentioned in Röthlisberger's assessment, they were used to placate labor relations at a time when Switzerland was deeply embedded in a European political economy dominated by Nazi Germany.

The experience of World War I encouraged employers and insurers to act more pre-emptively. In December 1939, the Union of Life Insurance Companies reminded the Finance Department that most existing pension plans had been created under the auspices of the favorable tax regime introduced during World War I. Unfortunately, the Union added, their underdevelopment in smaller businesses explained why Swiss old age provision lagged behind countries that relied more extensively on state solutions. As the Depression slowed down the expansion of occupational provision, insurers pointed out that increasing profits and a favorable tax regime could reinvigorate pension plans. For insurance executives, bolstering private provision was crucial not only because "even among the wealthiest firms, there exists almost no pension plan that does not need to be . . . financially reorganized", but also because employee benefits held down pressures for wage hikes and contributed to the stabilization of wartime labor relations. For all these reasons, the Union of Life Insurance Companies appealed to the Federal Council to reconsider its decision to limit the fiscal exemption of corporate schemes. For insurers, "the times are over when welfare measures were still more or less considered as an ex gratia luxury provided by the employer and their fiscal exemption was described as a privilege. Today, the non-exemption of corporate plans would exert a regressive, not to say reactionary, effect."[29]

In contrast to the chaotic situation that had prevailed during World War I, the orderly organization of the war economy had led to a substantial overhaul of the federal tax system.[30] Among the new fiscal levies of the Confederation introduced at the beginning of the war, two were particularly important for private pension plans: the tax on war profits, and the sacrifice for national defense (Wehropfer). While fiscal authorities did not challenge the principle of tax exemptions for pension plans, they nevertheless were keen to limit their extent. Employers were just as eager to stretch these federal tax subsidies to the limit. Despite strong protests from business federations, monies exempted from the tax on

[29] Konferenz der Direktoren der VSLG to Federal Councilor Ernst Wetter (Finance Department), December 15, 1939, file 317.2/1, SLA. See also Konferenz der Direktoren der VSLG, January 26, 1940, p. 5, file Q127 206, ZFS.

[30] Tanner, *Bundeshaushalt, Währung und Kriegswirtschaft*, pp. 177–228.

war profits for welfare purposes were capped at 15 percent of the total wage bill for new corporate plans. However, more substantial contributions to pre-war plans remained fully exempted.[31] Tax exemptions from the Wehropfer, which had been at first intended only for core pension plans (Versicherungseinrichtungen), were finally extended to the myriad informal old age relief and savings schemes (Fürsorgeeinrichtungen) that had become an increasingly important feature of corporate welfare efforts during the second half of the 1930s. Although insurers complained that, contrary to the situation that had prevailed at the end of World War I, the federal administration refused to introduce a blanket tax exemption for monies devoted to welfare purposes, fiscal policy still remained a main incentive for private pension plans.[32]

In a postwar report, the Canton Berne fiscal administration stressed that pension schemes had shot up out of the ground "like mushrooms" as tax exemptions "spurred" employers "into action" at the beginning of the war.[33] Although only 100 new private welfare institutions had been founded in 1938, 800 of them were set up right after the introduction of the tax exemptions (see Figure 2.1, p. 66). A survey undertaken by the Redressement National highlighted the trigger effect of fiscal policy on the expansion of private provision among a core group of manufacturing and financial firms. This survey underscored that profits experienced a notable compression during the first years of the war, while wages only slightly decreased in real terms (see Table 3.1). Wage freezes and inflation – which shot up over 40 percent between 1940 and 1942 – contributed to this development. On the other hand, social expenditure resulting from voluntary schemes set up by employers and fiscal costs grew by more than one-third in inflation-adjusted terms. Compulsory social expenditure more than doubled after the introduction of the EO in 1940, but was dwarfed by the expansion of the voluntary.

Life insurers explicitly marketed group products by exploiting the argument of tax exemptions. In a leaflet entitled *Modern Principles of*

31 "Die Personalfürsorge unter der Herrschaft der Kriegsgewinnsteuer: Beilage zum Bericht über die Eidg. Kriegsgewinnsteuer 1939–1946", Eidgenössische Steuerverwaltung, Berne, April 1954, p. 3, file E6300 (B) 1969/222/1, SBA. Thanks to Olivier Longchamp (University of Lausanne) for sharing this document with me.

32 Konferenz der Direktoren der VSLG, July 2, 1943, p. 20, file Q127 206, ZFS. See also Graziano Lusenti, *Les institutions de prévoyance en Suisse, au Royaume-Uni et en Allemagne fédérale: placements financiers et politique sociale* (Geneva: Georg, 1989), pp. 74–5; Hans Gerold Wirz, *Die Personal-Wohlfahrtseinrichtungen der schweizerischen Privatwirtschaft: ihre Stellung im Steuerrecht und ihre Beaufsichtigung* (Stäfa: Buchdruckerei Stäfa, 1955), p. 150.

33 According to a 1951 report quoted in Peter Hadorn, *Die Kapitalanlagen der schweizerischen Pensionskassen 1955–1970* (Basle: Institut für Sozialwissenschaften/Institut für angewandte Wirtschaftsforschung, 1974), pp. 41–2.

Table 3.1 *Wages, profits, and social expenditure in leading firms, 1938–1942.*

| *in millions of CHF (at 1942 prices)* | **1938** | **1942** | |
|---|---|---|---|
| equity capital | 1787.9 | 1315.1 | −26 percent |
| dividends, free shares, and management bonuses | 144.7 | 103.7 | −28 percent |
| wages and bonuses | 507.2 | 474.5 | −6 percent |
| taxes and other fiscal costs | 85.9 | 115.7 | +35 percent |
| **voluntary social expenditure** | **81.0** | **110.0** | **+36 percent** |
| compulsory social expenditure (EO, industrial work accident insurance, and local unemployment schemes) | 6.4 | 17.7 | +176 percent |

*Source:* Otto Steinmann, Eduard Seiler and Gustav Erhard, *Die Anteile von Arbeit, Staat und Kapital an den Erträgnissen der schweizerischen Privatwirtschaft* (Zurich: Aktionsgemeinschaft Nationaler Wiederaufbau, 1943). This survey covered 244 manufacturing firms and 15 banks that accounted for respectively one-third and one-half of the total workforce in manufacturing and banking.

*Corporate Provision*, Genevoise Assurances hinted that it was ready to "provide firms, which would like to benefit from the conditions set by the tax on war profits but would not like to bind their hands for years, with specific solutions that will free them from future obligations". According to Rentenanstalt, tax exemptions favored firms benefitting from war-related orders that had well-established pension plans.[34] Like during World War I, export-oriented firms were the main beneficiaries of tax exemptions, whose total was estimated at around CHF 100 million in 1949. This amount was much lower than the level attained during World War I and corresponded to the "disappointing" returns of the tax on war profits.[35] If business was brisk during the war, the short-term speculative operations that had fueled social tensions during World War I were not repeated. Employers focused on longer-term objectives, such as maintaining their presence in foreign markets, and were keen to lower the visibility of profits by setting up special war reserves of all kinds.[36] The early introduction of tax exemptions for pension plans and the mushrooming of expenditure on employee benefits reduced resentment against war profiteering.

34 Genfer Lebensversicherung, *Die Betriebsfürsorge nach modernen Grundsätzen* [n.d., ca. 1943], p. 7 (quotation), file M (1940–1944), Wirtschaftsarchiv. See also "Jahresbericht Kollektivversicherungen", Rentenanstalt, 1939–1942, file 671.21/1, SLA.

35 Federal Department of Justice and Police to Vorort, July 22, 1949, file 107.1, AfZ-SHIV.

36 On this practice among insurance companies, see Karlen, Chocomeli, D'haemer *et al.*, *Schweizerische Versicherungsgesellschaften*, p. 115. See also Olivier Longchamp, "Profits de guerre et fiscalité: l'impôt sur les bénéfices de guerre en Suisse durant la Deuxième Guerre Mondiale", *Traverse* 1 (2006), pp. 130–45 (pp. 130–3).

Fiscal authorities pointed out that if straightforward tax evasion and fraud were admittedly not widespread, compliance with such principles as the autonomy of pension plans vis-à-vis the founding company or sound and independent auditing practices were difficult to enforce, because federal and cantonal administrations were overburdened by more pressing issues during the war. Employers resisted state intrusions into their welfare schemes or tried to channel indirect dividends to "shareholder-executives" through special pension plans.[37] If World War I had signaled the rising importance of pension funds as reserves and tax refuges, World War II confirmed this trend and prepared the ground for the postwar evolution of pension funds into institutional investors. By 1941, occupational plan financial assets had already reached one-third of the gross domestic product (see Table A.7, p. 303).

At the very moment when private welfare institutions boomed, labor disputes dropped to an all-time low (see Figure 2.2, p. 67). Tax relief for pension plans helped to stabilize labor relations in leading export sectors, as the promise of deferred wage increases in the form of social benefits enabled firms to ease the wartime freezing of wages. This smooth and orderly transition into the war economy contrasted with the dramatic imbalances that had characterized World War I, when corporate profits soared, wages plummeted, and uncertain employment prospects and social misery had fueled the political radicalization that led to the 1918 general strike. In the machine-making sector, a heavyweight in terms of pension coverage and assets, the development of corporate benefits paralleled the 1941 renewal of the 1937 Peace Agreement. This agreement, which reaffirmed a *de facto* no-strike pledge between labor and employers, was followed by a rapid increase in welfare expenditure, notably on pensions and family allowances, in metal and machine-making firms during the war and its immediate aftermath (see Figure 3.2).

In a leaflet for its group division clients, Vita (Zurich Life) summed up the trend of occupational provision expansion. As workers' demands for income security were rising, the leaflet underscored, employers could rely on private provision to make up for the lack of social insurance. Enumerating factors related to labor relations (such as ensuring the collaboration of the workforce and facilitating its renewal in an orderly fashion), the insurance company argued that, in the context of the war-induced boom and full employment, pension plans not only offered useful tools to deflect demands for higher wages or a reduction in working hours, but also gave

[37] "Die Personalfürsorge unter der Herrschaft der Kriegsgewinnsteuer. Beilage zum Bericht über die Eidg. Kriegsgewinnsteuer 1939–1946", Eidgenössische Steuerverwaltung, Berne, April 1954, pp. 6–11, 18, file E6300 (B) 1969/222/1, SBA.

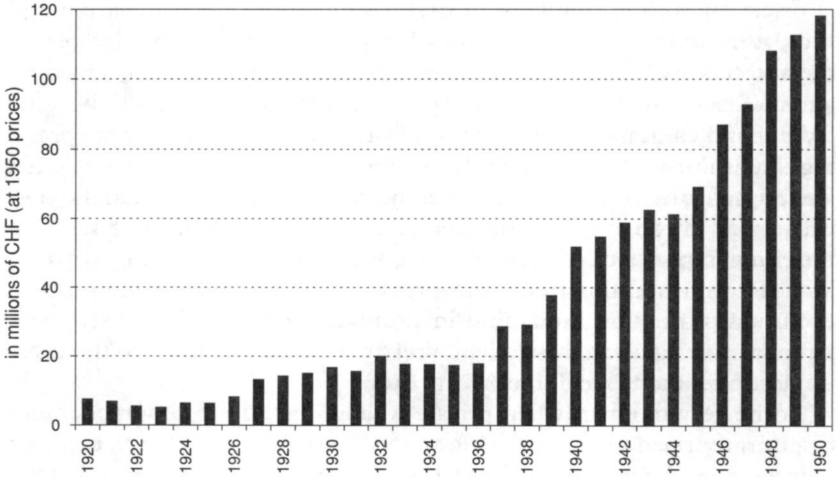


Figure 3.2 Welfare expenditure in the metal and machine-making sector, 1920–1950.
*Source:* Annual reports of the Arbeitgeberverband schweizerischer Maschinen- und Metall-Industrieller, quoted by Hans Gerold Wirz, *Die Personal-Wohlfahrtseinrichtungen der schweizerischen Privatwirtschaft* (Stäfa: Buchdruckerei Stäfa, 1955) p. 85.

firms an edge in the struggle over scarce skilled labor. In terms of benefits, the group division of Zurich Life reassured its cost-conscious customers: there was no need "to follow the bad example set by public pension plans". Benefits could be set at a low level and then be raised only at a "later stage". Finally, group contracts managed by insurance companies were a useful deterrent against labor demands to be involved in pension management, as they did not "entail the same risk as independent [i.e. company-based] welfare funds, where the statutory contributions of the employees might lead to labor demanding a say in the management of the [pension scheme], which may considerably complicate its operations".[38]

By positioning themselves between employers and employees, insurers helped to undermine the reach of joint management procedures favored by trade unions. Alongside the EO, employee benefits thus contributed toward pacifying labor relations, and their expansion often preceded the extension of collective bargaining that took place from 1944 onward.[39]

[38] *Pensionsversicherung für Angestellte und Arbeiter* (Zurich: Vita Versicherungen, 1941).
[39] From 1939 to 1944, only 132 collective agreements were signed, which brought their total number to 632. By 1946, this number had already doubled. See Ruedi Brassel and Rita Schiavi, "Kämpfend in den Arbeitsfrieden: zur Streikwelle in der

The war brought ambivalent results for providers of group pensions. According to Rentenanstalt, full employment, tax breaks, and the interest of unions in employee benefits fueled "employers' growing understanding of the value of personnel welfare". At the same time, disruptions brought by extensive military duties, uncertainties about the contours of the post-war environment, inflation, the use of pension plans to hoard reserves, the re-emergence of the AHV issue (more on this in the next section), and finally the competition that insurance companies suffered from pension consultants offering their services to private firms were all described as negative factors that discouraged firms from signing group contracts. While the sale of group contracts picked up in 1940, Rentenanstalt had to wait until the end of the war to see sales overtake late 1930s levels.[40]

The spread of group contracts further contributed to the fragmentation of occupational provision. In 1941, group plans amounted to 70 percent of all core pension plans, but covered only one-third of all private-sector workers affiliated to a pension plan (and only 2 percent in the public sector). Yet, the group market remained extremely concentrated, as over 90 percent of group premiums and reserves were controlled by Rentenanstalt and its three immediate competitors (see Figure 2.4, p. 80), All in all, if 84 percent of group plans covered firms with fewer than 51 workers, this proportion reached only 37 percent for single-employer plans. The latter represented the inner core of pension provision, accounting for 80 percent of all workers covered and over 90 percent of pension assets.[41] In other words, a few hundred large plans and four insurance companies constituted the heavyweights in a jungle of thousands of smaller plans and relief funds. By 1942, there were 1,508 relief institutions, such as savings schemes (Spareinlegerkassen) and welfare funds (Wohlfahrtsfonds), in the private sector and 400 in the public sector. These relief institutions either supplemented core pension plans or, according to the Federal Statistical Office, enabled firms to "accumulate monies for the ulterior realization of a personnel welfare plan".[42]

A survey focusing on Canton Solothurn – Walther Stampfli's political fiefdom – showed the differentiated expansion of these various forms of provision. If around one-third of the workforce subject to the federal law on manufactures was covered by core pension plans in 1943 (double the national average), only one-fifth of firms with fewer than 51 workers, but

unmittelbaren Nachkriegszeit", *Widerspruch* Spezialheft "Arbeitsfrieden – Realität eines Mythos" (1987), pp. 57–69, 63.

40 "Jahresbericht Kollektivversicherungen", Rentenanstalt, 1943, file 671.21/1, SLA.

41 *Pensionskassenstatistik 1941*, pp. 20 (coverage), 42 (group plans), 268 (assets).

42 Ibid., p. 72. Most relief institutions (Fürsorgeeinrichtungen) had been set up by private firms. Among these institutions, 1,108 welfare funds (Wohlfahrtsfonds) accounted for CHF 160 million in pension assets.

Table 3.2 *Corporate old age provision in Canton Solothurn, 1943.*

| | size of the firms (number of workers) | | |
|---|---|---|---|
| percentage of firms | **2–50** | **5–499** | **500+** |
| 1) with at least one pension plan (Pensionskasse) | 12 | 26 | 79 |
| 2) with at least one welfare fund (Wohlfahrtsfonds) | 8 | 45 | 16 |
| total (1+2) | **20** | **71** | **95** |
| 3) without any old age provision scheme | 80 | 29 | 5 |

*Source:* Walter Bieber, *Die sozialen Einrichtungen der solothurnischen Industrie* (Olten: Dietschi, 1946). This survey covered 188 firms employing 28,000 workers (or 82 percent of workers submitted to the federal law on factories). Among these firms, 76 had set up 117 occupational schemes covering 27,700 workers (including double counts). The survey was repeated in 1947 and 1957. See *Erhebungen bei dem Fabrikgesetz unterstellten Unternehmen des Kantons Solothurn über den Ausbau der freiwilligen sozialen Einrichtungen, Stand Herbst 1957* (Solothurn: Kanton Solothurn, 1959).

almost all firms with at least 500 workers, had set up some kind of old age provision. The largest corporations were most likely to have core pension plans, whereas small and medium-sized firms tended to set up informal welfare funds and relief schemes (see Table 3.2).

The case of the armaments manufacturer Oerlikon-Bührle offers insights into the transformation of corporate pensions from the Depression into World War II. After its reorganization during the 1920s, this factory, located on the outskirts of Zurich, decided to expand its rudimentary "support fund" by contracting for a voluntary group plan with Vita (Zurich Life) in 1933. However, at a time of unemployment and cost-cutting, this voluntary approach brought disappointing results: in 1938 only one-tenth of the workforce was still affiliated to the group scheme, down from over one-third four years before. A buoyant economic recovery fueled by German armament orders encouraged Oerlikon-Bührle to set up in 1939 a new pension plan that offered differentiated benefits to blue-collar workers and white-collar employees, and was supplemented by a voluntary savings plan. Before the outbreak of military operations, 40 percent of the workforce was affiliated to the pension plan, a percentage that remained constant throughout the war.[43] Oerlikon-Bührle's pension plan covered the stable and skilled part of the workforce. Employees over thirty-nine years old, married and divorced women, and widows were

[43] Hugo Binder, *Die Pensionskasse der Arbeiter der Werkzeugmaschinenfabrik Oerlikon & Bührle Co.* (Oerlikon: Oerlikon Bührle, 1945).

barred from the pension plan and could only join the voluntary savings plan.

In early 1941, as exports were booming and women were hired in larger numbers, Oerlikon-Bührle lifted compulsory affiliation for workers in the ammunition workshops, where many employees were women.[44] Such gender discrimination was common. The 1940 pension statutes of the pharmaceutical firm Sandoz stated, for example, that "auxiliary workers", or part-time women workers, were barred from joining the company pension plan.[45] The coverage gap between male and female workers was significant: two-thirds of male public-sector employees were affiliated to a core pension plan in 1941, while only two-fifths of their female counterparts were enrolled. The situation was similar in the private sector, where one-fifth of men but only one-tenth of women were covered by pension provision (see Table A.2, p. 295). The EO and occupational benefits granted to the male citizen-soldier-worker prefigured a postwar configuration where federal pensions supplemented by occupational benefits favored male breadwinners over women who received old age provision through their husbands' pensions and, when working, were seldom affiliated to occupational pension plans.

The Swiss wartime expansion of corporate benefits echoed developments that were taking place in the United States, Canada, and the United Kingdom. In particular in North America and Switzerland, the apparatus of production was preserved from the devastation of war and benefitted fully from the war-induced economic boom, positive harbingers for the development of occupational provision. Scholars have emphasized that the extension of New Deal income taxation led to a recrudescence of the use of pension trusts as tax shelters. The outbreak of World War II and the ensuing economic growth accelerated this phenomenon. Wartime tax exemptions granted to welfare measures – such as the Revenue Act 1942 – acted as a further incentive for the provision of occupational benefits. Government wage freezes also bolstered corporate welfare measures, because employer contributions to pension plans were not subject to anti-inflationary measures and acted as deferred wage

44 Ibid., pp. 10, 15.

45 On Sandoz, see Katharina Von Saal, "Frauenerwerbsarbeit während des Zweiten Weltkrieges in der Schweiz unter besonderer Berücksichtigung des Chemieunternehmens Sandoz AG", Lizentiatsarbeit des historischen Seminars, Universität Basel, 1999, p. 67. For a discussion of gender and labor relations during the war, see Sabine Christe, Nora Natchkova, Manon Schick *et al.*, *Au foyer de l'inégalité: la division sexuelle du travail en Suisse pendant la crise des années 1930 et la Deuxième Guerre Mondiale* (Lausanne: Antipodes, 2005); Béatrice Ziegler, *Arbeit – Körper – Öffentlichkeit: Berner und Bieler Frauen zwischen Diskurs und Alltag, 1919–1945* (Zurich, Chronos, 2007).

increases.[46] In the United Kingdom and Canada, tax expenditure and wartime labor relations similarly sustained the growth of employer welfare schemes. Tellingly, two-thirds of Canadian pension plans surveyed in 1947 had been created after 1939, many of them in subsidiaries of US automobile firms.[47]

The contribution of corporate welfare schemes to the overall functioning of the war economy was significant in Switzerland. The development of employee benefits and the accumulation of pension plan reserves contributed to damping down wage and price inflation. As the labor market dried up with the outbreak of the war, these plans also played a role in the distribution of skilled manpower at a time of growing scarcity. The Federal Council urged moderation in wage and price increases to keep inflation at a low level. However, beyond these general guidelines, wide latitude was given to arrangements between social partners.[48] Further studies on the combined effects of the EO and employer social programs on the labor market and the organization of the war economy would undoubtedly show how the allocation of manpower was fine-tuned in Switzerland through decentralized and self-managed arrangements that involved less state control than in other, belligerent, countries.

The wartime upsurge of occupational plans ran parallel with the implementation of the EO and, paradoxically, reinforced the possibilities for social insurance. This proved to employers that state programs were not disadvantageous to corporate schemes but, on the contrary, could offer a foundation on which to develop occupational provision. The militarized sense of solidarity and people's community (Volksgemeinschaft) brought by the EO to citizen-soldiers combined well with the inclusive factory community (Betriebsgemeinschaft) centered on male workers in the export sectors who benefitted from the expansion of occupational plans. The success of the EO offered a trial run for the AHV and inspired both its institutional and financial organization. These

46 Jennifer L. Klein, *For all these rights: business, labor, and the shaping of America's public–private welfare state* (Princeton: Princeton University Press, 2003), pp. 102–4, 83–4; Steven A. Sass, *The promise of private pensions: the first hundred years* (Cambridge: Cambridge University Press, 1997), pp. 101–12.

47 Kenneth Bryden, *Old age pensions and policy-making in Canada* (Montreal: McGill-Queen's University Press, 1974), p. 38; Michael Moss, *The building of Europe's largest mutual life company: Standard Life 1825–2000* (Edinburgh: Mainstream, 2000), pp. 217, 221.

48 Hafner, *Bundesrat Walther Stampfli*, pp. 308–36. On the economic "strategic synthesis" during World War II, see Tanner, *Bundeshaushalt, Währung und Kriegswirtschaft*, pp. 287–306.

perspectives should be kept in mind in the next section, which analyzes the social policy debates that took place in Switzerland as the Allies began to roll back the Axis powers.

## The turn of the tide: blueprints for postwar reforms (1941–1943)

In early 1941, the introduction of the AHV seemed a distant prospect. Both the Federal Council and the Federal Social Insurance Office agreed that the organization of the war economy and the stabilization of prices and wages took precedence over social insurance. The idea of old age insurance met steadfast resistance within business circles and was also opposed by labor organizations such as the Metalworkers' Union. Finally, the May 1941 defeat of old age provision in Zurich was an ominous warning sign of the referendum threat that hovered over social policy proposals. However, it was precisely in mid-1941, when a yet unchallenged Third Reich surrounded Switzerland, that debates about social insurance took a new turn. In rapid succession, no fewer than four initiatives addressing the issue of postwar social reforms were launched. By the end of 1943, federal pensions had made an impressive comeback at the forefront of the political agenda. In an address to the nation on New Year's Eve 1944, Walther Stampfli himself declared that the Federal Council had begun the drafting of a new AHV project.

Direct democracy and political pressure succeeded in opening a crack in the uncompromising attitude toward the social policy of a government dominated by the war economy apparatus. This shift unfolded at the turning-point of World War II, between the apex of the "New Europe" dominated by Germany and the shift in favor of the Allies. The comeback of the AHV also took place as EO benefits and corporate provision were decisively shaping wartime labor relations. In this new context, the AHV emerged as the symbol of a real, but limited and well circumscribed, social reform.

A new context favoring social policy emerged in the summer of 1941 as an initiative demanding the transformation of EO equalization funds into AHV funds was launched in Geneva. By early 1942, political parties, trade unions, and organizations covering a wide chunk of the political spectrum had endorsed this initiative, entitled *For a Secure Old Age* (*Gesichertes Alter*). The proposal was coordinated at the national level by the patriotic Gothard League (Gotthardbund), but was supported by the Gewerkschaftsbund, the Socialists, and several industrial and white-collar trade unions. The Radicals soon joined this grouping, followed by the centrist Alliance of Independents (Landesring der Unabhängigen), and more than two dozen civic groups and professional associations. Motions and initiatives on old age pensions launched by cantonal parliaments in Geneva and Neuchâtel were part of this upsurge of direct democracy.[49] The timing of the *Gesichertes Alter* initiative and the catch-all dimension of its organizing committee require some explanation.

At the time when signatures were being gathered for the initiative, military operations had shifted to Eastern Europe. As the eye of the storm was now hovering over Soviet Russia, a new Europe seemed to be emerging in the West under Germany's dominance. In this context, it was not fortuitous that the initiative became the hobbyhorse of the Gothard League. This movement, founded in 1940, extolled defiant patriotic values, but also "domestic renewal", an echo of slogans of the 1930s conservative "restoration movements" (Erneuerungsbewegungen). Social insurance could appeal to those who were impressed by Germany's leadership and who thought that Switzerland might play a role in this new, more disciplined, Europe.[50] The initiative also offered a platform to political forces muzzled by the technocratic war economy apparatus. By supporting *Gesichertes Alter*, labor organizations tried to give a center-left twist to the official doctrine of Spiritual National Defense that dominated the political culture. Since the initiative fit in with calls for wartime national unity launched by federal authorities, it also appealed to the Radical Party.

However, prominent forces were absent from this broad front. The Metalworkers' Union and the main employers' federations focused their efforts on employment-based provision and did not endorse *Gesichertes Alter*. Traditional opponents of social insurance, such as the Catholic and Liberal-Conservative parties, the Farmers', Artisans' and Burghers' Party, the Farmers' Federation, and the Federation of Small Employers and Trades (Gewerbeverband), were also conspicuously absent from the initiative committee or only joined it belatedly. The Catholic Conservatives launched a competing initiative in late 1941 proposing to use EO funds for the creation of extensive family-support measures. The initiative *For the Family* (*Für die Familie*) called for family allowances instead

[49] For an overview of the 1941–1943 debates on social policy, see Hafner, *Bundesrat Walther Stampfli*, pp. 371–5; Sommer, *Das Ringen um die soziale Sicherheit*, pp. 189–96. On the launch of the *Gesichertes Alter* initiative, see Christian Gasser, *Der Gotthard-Bund: eine schweizerische Widerstandsbewegung. Aus den Archiven 1940 bis 1948* (Berne: Haupt, 1984), p. 103.

[50] Christian Werner, *Für Wirtschaft und Vaterland: Erneuerungsbewegungen und bürgerliche Interessengruppen in der Deutschschweiz 1928–1947* (Zurich: Chronos, 2000), pp. 260–84. On Germany's wartime social policy, see Götz Aly, *Comment Hitler a acheté les Allemands* (Paris: Flammarion, 2005), pp. 56–64.

of individual rights to social insurance benefits and could be considered an anti-liberal and conservative alternative to federal pensions.[51]

Both initiatives gathered over 160,000 signatures, three times the amount needed for validation, and they were presented to the Federal Chancellery in the spring of 1942. Yet, the gap between direct democracy and the emergency powers delegated to the executive remained wide. In September 1942, Federal Councilor Walther Stampfli reaffirmed before the annual assembly of the Swiss Chamber of Commerce that the time was not auspicious for social insurance.[52]

As the winter of 1942–1943 brought tidings of the encircling of the Wehrmacht at Stalingrad and the Allies decisively regained the upper hand in military operations, the prospects for a postwar Europe were transformed. An Allied victory seemed more plausible than a postwar order under German domination. From this moment on, Anglo-American blueprints for postwar reform, from the Atlantic Charter to the Beveridge Report, fed popular expectations and rising pressures on the social policy front. The Beveridge Report, the key blueprint of the postwar British welfare state, was translated and distributed in Switzerland in early 1943, a few months after it had been issued in the United Kingdom in December 1942.[53] The public debate on the Beveridge Report, to be discussed in more detail below, coincided with the launch of a second batch of initiatives addressing the issue of postwar reforms. This multiplication of proposals was obviously linked to the federal elections scheduled for the fall of 1943. After the elections of 1939, which had taken place under the ominous shadow cast by the outbreak of war, political parties scrambled for positions and tried to outmaneuver each other by presenting their own blueprints for postwar society.

In December 1942, the Socialists presented a "global program of structural reforms".[54] The *New Switzerland* (*Neue Schweiz*) manifesto confirmed the centrist shift of the party that had taken place during the 1930s and preceded its integration into the governing coalition. The program called for a "social insurance plan" and the nationalization of insurance

[51] Katrin Stadler, "Die Initiative *Für die Familie* der Schweizerischen Konservativen Volkspartei von 1942 und der Gegenvorschlag von Bundesrat und Parlament", mémoire de licence de la section d'histoire, Université de Lausanne, 2003.

[52] Hafner, *Bundesrat Walther Stampfli*, p. 373.

[53] William H. Beveridge, *Der Beveridgeplan: Sozialversicherung und verwandte Leistungen* (Zurich/New York: Europa Verlag, 1943); Emil-Friedrich Rimensberger, *Qu'est-ce que le Plan Beveridge? Exposé, résumé et commenté d'après le texte original* (Neuchâtel: La Baconnière 1943).

[54] Bernard Degen, "Entre opposition et participation au Conseil Fédéral", in *Solidarité, débats, mouvement. 100 ans du Parti Socialiste suisse 1888–1988*, ed. Karl Lang (Lausanne: Editions d'En Bas, 1988), pp. 319–45 (p. 331).

companies, but its preamble also pledged party allegiance to a "strong army" and the need to "increase the productive forces" of the country. This program formed the prelude to the *Economic Reform and Labor Rights* (*Wirtschaftsreform und Rechte der Arbeit*) initiative, which proposed in early 1943 to include in the Constitution the notion that "capital [had] to be used in favor of labor, economic growth, and popular welfare".[55] Almost simultaneously, the centrist Alliance of Independents' *Right to Work* (*Recht auf Arbeit*) initiative also asked the Federal Council to introduce social insurance and take measures to ensure full employment.[56] These proposals for social reforms coincided with a modest revival of labor unrest (see Figure 2.2, p. 67).

Direct democracy and debates about postwar social policy, as well as signs of renewed labor militancy, provoked uneasiness among Radicals. In April 1943, Walther Stampfli was criticized during a party congress held in Geneva. Propelled into action by the left-liberal wing of the party, the congress proposed a fourteen-point program that called for the appeasement of class conflicts and acknowledged the need for social and economic reforms. Through this eclectic program, which included federal pensions and family allowances, and encouraged collective bargaining and the monitoring of wages by the Confederation, the grand old party of the bourgeoisie tried to reaffirm its leading role in the social field.[57]

The string of motions and petitions addressing social and economic reforms – launched in particular in the cantons of Berne, Argovia, Zurich, and Graubünden – continued unabated until the October 1943 federal elections. Although bourgeois parties still outnumbered the left in both legislative chambers by a large margin, the Socialists won thirteen seats in the Federal Assembly, bringing their total to one-quarter of all seats (as against one-fifth in 1939). In December, these electoral gains were

[55] *Die Neue Schweiz* (Zurich: Sozialdemokratische Partei der Schweiz, 1942), quoted in Charles Stirnimann, *Der Weg in der Nachkriegszeit 1943–1948: ein Beitrag zur politischen Sozialgeschichte des "Roten Basel"* (Basle/Kassel: Friedrich Reinhardt Verlag, 1992), p. 128. See also Matthias Kunz, *Aufbruchstimmung und Sonderfall-Rhetorik: die Schweiz im Übergang von der Kriegs- zur Nachkriegszeit in der Wahrnehmung der Parteipresse* (Berne: Schweizerisches Bundesarchiv, Dossier 8, 1998), pp. 16–20.

[56] The Alliance of Independents had been founded in 1935 by Gottlieb Duttweiler. This successful entrepreneur was the executive director of Migros, a leading retail chain. The following of this party was centered in Zurich. See Hans Georg Ramseier, *Die Entstehung und die Entwicklung des Landesringes der Unabhängigen bis 1943* (Zurich: Landesring der Unabhängingen, 1973).

[57] Eugen Dietschi, *60 Jahre eidgenössische Politik: ein Beitrag zur Parteigeschichte des schweizerischen Freisinns* (Berne: Freisinnig-Demokratische Partei der Schweiz, 1979), pp. 184–7; Philipp Ischer, "Die AHV-Diskussion in der FDP: die Genese des Sozialliberalismus und die Bemühung des Freisinns um Orientierung in den 1940er Jahren", in *Von der Barmherzigkeit*, ed. Hans-Jörg Gilomen, *et al.* (Zurich: Chronos, 2002), pp. 331–43; Stirnimann, *Der Weg in der Nachkriegszeit*, pp. 110–27.

followed by Ernst Nobs' nomination to the Federal Council. This former member of the 1918 general strike committee was the first Socialist to join the executive branch.[58] In a radio address to the nation on New Year's Eve 1944, Walther Stampfli announced that the Federal Council would present a new pension bill that would constitute the official counter-project to the *Gesichertes Alter* initiative. The AHV had made an impressive political comeback.

This rapid succession of events could lead one to the premature conclusion that the conjunction of direct-democracy initiatives, mounting popular support for social insurance fueled by the domestic echoes of Allied blueprints for postwar reform, labor unrest, and electoral gains for the left had coaxed Walther Stampfli into action. These dynamics did represent a genuine turn of the tide. However, the seeming inexorability of these developments is misleading. Walther Stampfli's conversion to the idea of social insurance was far from representing a sign of weakness. On the contrary, his decision to rapidly draft an official counter-proposal to the *Gesichertes Alter* initiative cut short the debate on postwar reforms, and, as historian Kurt Imhof notes, "[w]ith the exception of the AHV, the social and economic postulates and utopias of the postwar discussion were thrown in the bin".[59]

The eclectic set of initiatives and party programs mentioned above was far from representing a homogeneous pressure in favor of social insurance. In addition to the contradictory visions of postwar reform contained in these initiatives, the integration of the left in the federal executive and the strength of the war economy apparatus, as well as the influence of Spiritual National Defense, reinforced Walther Stampfli's grip on social policy debates. The "economic general" was able to handpick the long-overdue issue of the AHV and shape it within a constraining and limited framework while sidelining other reform projects.

First, political parties, and in particular those on the left, occupied a weak position in the wartime political system. The 1943 electoral gains of

[58] For election results, see Heiner Ritzmann-Blickenstorfer and Hansjörg Siegenthaler, eds., *Historisch Statistik der Schweiz – Statistique historique de la Suisse – Swiss Historical Statistics* (Zurich: Chronos, 1996), Table X6. The Socialist Party had claimed a seat in the executive branch since the end of the 1920s and had unsuccessfully launched in 1942 an initiative demanding the direct election of the Federal Council by the electorate. See Degen, "Entre opposition et participation au Conseil Fédéral", pp. 329–35; Tobias Kästli, *Ernst Nobs: vom Bürgerschreck zum Bundesrat: ein politisches Leben* (Zurich: Orell Füssli Verlag, 1995).

[59] Kurt Imhof, "Das kurze Leben der geistigen Landesverteidigung: von der "Volksgemeinschaft" vor dem Krieg zum Streit über die "Nachkriegsschweiz" im Krieg", in *Krise und sozialer Wandel: Analyse von Medienereignissen in der Schweiz der Zwischen- und Nachkriegszeit*, ed. Kurt Imhof, *et al.* (Zurich: Seismo Verlag, 1993), pp. 19–84, 83.

the Socialists came at a time when the center of gravity of decision-making had shifted markedly to the executive branch and extra-parliamentary commissions. Socialists and trade unionists occupied only marginal positions in these overlapping networks of civil servants, employers' representatives, and private-sector executives. The left's electoral gains, and especially Ernst Nobs' election to the Federal Council, appeared less a sign of the rising power of the left than a symbol of its disciplined integration into the governing coalition at the very moment when technocratic structures were bypassing parliamentary ones.[60]

As labor unrest rose again in 1943 and underground Communist cells re-emerged from hiding – the party had been declared illegal in 1940, with the assent of the Socialists – the integration of the left in the governmental coalition increasingly insulated the Socialists from working-class militancy. What is more, there was no unity on the left on the issue of social reforms. Although the Socialists and the Gewerkschaftsbund had both endorsed the *Gesichertes Alter* initiative, there was only weak trade union support for the *Neue Schweiz* program and its related initiative. Labor organizations had developed no specific proposals for social insurance and contented themselves with supporting the catch-all *Gesichertes Alter* initiative.[61] In conclusion, the governmental left lacked the leverage to influence Walther Stampfli's strategic choice in favor of a limited program of social insurance.

Secondly, the wartime doctrine of Spiritual National Defense that extolled "Swissness" spurned comprehensive welfare reforms inspired by foreign examples. It was thus easier for opponents of the Beveridge Plan to dismiss it as irrelevant than for its potential supporters to introduce it into public debate. In a context of heightened patriotism, the Beveridge Plan stirred up a great deal of public discussion, but most often was described as being totally incompatible with Swiss realities. All in all, this famous blueprint for the postwar welfare state had no impact on social policy proposals.[62] In a 1942 brochure on social policy, insurer Ernst Röthlisberger emphasized that if Switzerland could be singled out among industrialized countries because of its lack of old age pensions, this situation was not the result of laggardness. In contrast with large

60 Tanner, *Bundeshaushalt, Währung und Kriegswirtschaft*, pp. 71–5.

61 Jürg Siegenthaler, *Die Politik der Gewerkschaften: eine Untersuchung der öffentlichen Funktionen schweizerischen Gewerkschaften nach dem Zweiten Weltkrieg* (Berne: Francke, 1968), p. 54. See also Eduard Kobelt, *Die Wirtschaftspolitik der Gewerkschaften, 1920–1950: der Einfluss einzelner Gewerkschaftsverbände und Persönlichkeiten auf die Wirtschaftspolitik des Schweizerischen Gewerkschaftsbundes* (Zurich: Chronos, 1987), pp. 137–57.

62 Jean-Jacques Monachon, "Le Plan Beveridge et les débats sur la sécurité sociale en Suisse entre 1942 et 1945", in *Von der Barmherzigkeit zur Sozialversicherung*, ed. Hans-Jörg Gilomen, *et al.* (Zurich: Chronos, 2002), pp. 321–31.

countries with a mass proletariat that, according to Röthlisberger, could not avoid national social insurance, small, federalist, neutral, and allegedly "egalitarian" Switzerland did not need to move in that direction. Such a state-based solution would simply prove too costly for an economy dependent on foreign trade and would endanger the "moral roots" of the country.[63]

In January 1943, Willy Bretscher, editor-in-chief of the influential *Neue Zürcher Zeitung*, similarly downplayed appeals for social reform by urging proponents of social reforms to adopt a "significant dose" of "proven Helvetic sobriety":

> It is understandable that the Swiss debate on postwar problems is influenced by the wash of the waves of foreign trends and disputes, and it is also not surprising that certain political parties show themselves inclined to fill up the sails of their distinctive social criticism with the fresh wind that we can feel around the world, and to call in Switzerland for reforms and projects similar to those that are so much debated beyond our borders. What we should imperatively demand of these discussions about a "new Switzerland" is to throw in a significant dose of the proven Helvetic sobriety that incorporates a sense of realistic conditions and proportions.[64]

Similar rhetoric often celebrated the superiority of Swiss social policy programs by linking them to national defense efforts that had allegedly enabled the Confederation to remain untouched by the war. In an article on the Beveridge Plan, a management review stated proudly that "Scandinavian social programs . . . were introduced to the detriment of security; both Denmark and Norway have learned that fact the hard way. Switzerland has made vast sacrifices for its army and national defense, without neglecting social endeavors. Events have proven her right. [Switzerland] will continue to pursue these two essential goals: national security, social security."[65] Equating "social security" with "national security" might perhaps have made sense to male citizen-soldiers covered by the EO and working in export sectors well endowed with corporate employee benefits. However, it sounded hollow to disenfranchized female workers who paid EO contributions but seldom received any benefits, or for the elderly poor who had to rely on patchy means-tested assistance.

This constant dismissal of foreign examples and the insistence on Swiss "exceptionalism" (Sonderfall) can be contrasted with the

[63] Ernst Röthlisberger and Harald Schulthess, *Soziale Alters-, Invaliden- und Hinterbliebenenversicherung in der Schweiz und im Ausland* (Basle: Verlag für Recht und Gesellschaft, 1942), pp. 49–51.

[64] Willy Bretscher, "Der eigene Weg", *Neue Zürcher Zeitung*, January 21, 1943.

[65] "Une comparaison entre la Suisse et le Plan Beveridge", *Industrielle Organisation*, no. 1, 1945, p. 25.

situation that prevailed among European politicians and social policy experts exiled in London. Dutch or French proponents of social insurance did not intend to simply replicate British proposals. They were, however, deeply influenced by its popular impact and acknowledged Beveridge's call for comprehensive welfare measures as a positive example.[66] In contrast, when Walther Stampfli explained to the Federal Assembly in December 1943 that the AHV was now a key priority for the government, he immediately added that this social insurance scheme would be "no monster like the Beveridge Plan", but a carefully delineated system of old age benefits. The Federal Councilor was not interested in bringing into being a useless "futuristic social policy symphony".[67] By presenting the AHV as the quintessentially Swiss postwar social reform, Stampfli was able to channel popular expectations in a particular direction.

The dismissal of comprehensive reforms contrasted with the widespread acknowledgment that existing pension plans would play a major role in old age provision. Debates on the AHV had started when the boom in occupational provision was well under way. Even the *Gesichertes Alter* initiative envisioned federal pensions coexisting with tax-exempted and collectively bargained occupational schemes. The initiative committee stressed that private forms of provision should not be "inhibited" or "paralyzed", but on the contrary "encouraged" and "promoted". It also rejected the nationalization of insurance companies that was envisioned – albeit in a propagandistic way – in the *Neue Schweiz* manifesto of the Socialist Party.[68] However, deference toward occupational schemes had its limits. Confronted with the growth of corporate plans, trade unionists emphasized that "thanks to social benefits, employers can hire better personnel for lower wages than other firms that offer no such benefits. Nowadays, when people compare wage levels, they consider such benefits a substantial part of wages." In this situation, it was "[e]ven worse that corporate schemes indeed state a right to benefits, but [benefits] whose level depends on employers' discretion".[69]

Other commentators urged private firms to reconsider the way they administered their pension plans. During the 1943 Geneva congress of

[66] Paul V. Dutton, *Origins of the French welfare state: the struggle for social reform in France 1914–1947* (Cambridge: Cambridge University Press, 2002), pp. 202–8; A. C. M. Kappelhof, "'Omdat het historisch gegroeid is': de londense commissie van Rhijn en de ontwikkeling van de sociale verzekeringen in Nederland (1937–1952)", *Tijdschrift voor Sociale en Economische Geschiedenis* 2 (2004), pp. 71–91.

[67] Minutes of the National Council, December 1943 session, quoted in Hafner, *Bundesrat Walther Stampfli*, p. 376.

[68] *Gesichertes Alter: die erste soziale Tat nach Kriegsschluss* ([n.p.]: Eidg. Kommittee Gesichertes Alter, 1943), pp. 37–9.

[69] P. Sch, "Personalfürsorge", *Der öffentliche Dienst*, December 3, 1943.

the Radical Party, Alfred Schaller, a young Basle member of the left-liberal wing of the party, pointed out that employers' paternalism and discretionary attitudes were incompatible with the "new spirit" of class cooperation brought about by the war:

> The new spirit reveals itself principally because social policy is no longer made up of one-sided warranties, concessions, deals, welfare, or relief measures, but rather of predictable agreements with workers over rights, claims, and shared responsibility in the firm and its social institutions, etc. To put it more clearly: there are firms which deposit dozens of millions of francs in social and relief institutions. However, the intended social purpose of these schemes will not be met when access to their benefits is tied to vexing requirements, conditions, and degrading formalities; and when the granting of benefits or the payment of employees' contributions depends only on one-sided decisions reached by the employer or the trustees of the relief institutions. The intended social purpose will also not be met when the very same firm pays insufficient basic wages and a large share of workers' overall wages is composed of discretionary emoluments drawn from the social institutions of the firm. The intended social purpose will only be met when workers are given a guaranteed legal right to such social programs.[70]

Schaller did not ask for a reversal of the current expansion of employment-based schemes, but simply for the adoption of more collaborative and fairer practices that would reinforce the factory community (Betriebsgemeinschaft). For left-liberal members of the Radical Party, corporate plans had their role to play, together with federal social policy, in the reinforcement of social peace and political stability.

Debates about postwar social programs gave an unexpected twist to the issue of pension plan regulation. As mentioned in the preceding chapter, insurers' efforts to induce federal authorities to check potential competition in the pension market had been delayed by the outbreak of hostilities. It was only in March 1942 that Senator Gottfried Keller (Radical) presented to the Federal Assembly a motion addressing the lack of regulation of multi-employer pension plans that were not subject to the federal law on private insurance. Keller also authored an influential series of articles on the same subject in the highbrow *Neue Zürcher Zeitung*, whose publication coincided with the validation of the *Gesichertes Alter* initiative.

The resonance of Keller's motion and his articles largely overtook the limited goal of checking unwelcome competition initially set by the Union of Life Insurance Companies and offered a springboard for proponents

70 Alfred Schaller, "Grundsätze und Aufgaben schweizerischer Sozialpolitik", in *Im Dienste unseres Volkes: die politische Arbeit und die sozialen Forderungen der Freisinnig-demokratischen Partei der Schweiz* (Berne: FDP, 1943), quoted in Stirnimann, *Der Weg in der Nachkriegszeit*, p. 113.

of federal regulation of all pension plans.[71] In the autumn of 1942, the Federation of Employees reiterated its demands for a federal registry of welfare foundations, as well as rules to safeguard employees' rights to benefits and ensure labor involvement in the management of pension plans.[72] For the main white-collar trade union these demands constituted logical counterparts to the tax privileges granted to employers.

The convergence of the wartime boom of occupational provision, renewed interest in social insurance, and criticism of corporate schemes led to the re-emergence of the pension lobby. In the spring of 1942, the SVUSAI held its first meetings since 1937. The first declarations of the renamed Swiss Association of Private Employee Benefits (Schweizerischer Verband für privatwirtschaftliche Personalfürsorge, SVPP) showed its distrust for "anonymous state welfare".[73] The SVPP's aims were to "defend the interests of [pension plans] in the coming struggles in the domain of social provision" and to help private relief institutions "to hold their ground against statist trends and currents hostile to the factory community [Betriebsgemeinschaft]".[74]

In March 1943, the SVPP pronounced itself against any state regulation of occupational plans or, as proposed by the *Gesichertes Alter* initiative, the subordination of pension plans to federal social insurance. The constituency of the association (136 plans in 1943, against 120 in 1933) was still composed of large pension plans that covered around one-third of workers affiliated to core private pension plans. Compared

71 Gottfried Keller, "Zum Pensionskassen-Problem", *Neue Zürcher Zeitung*, article series published on July 31 (1st part), August 3 (2nd part), August 5 (3rd part), and August 6 (4th part), 1942. See also Hans Christen, "Soll eine Pensionskasse nach soliden versicherungstechnischen Grundsätzen geführt werden?" *Schweizerische Versicherungszeitschrift* (1943), pp. 193–213; Hans F. Moser, "Ein eigenartige Aufsicht", *Schweizerische Versicherungszeitschrift* (1943), pp. 283–4; Wirz, *Die Personal-Wohlfahrtseinrichtungen*, pp. 119–21. Konferenz der Direktoren der VSLG, September 25, 1942, p. 25, file Q127 206, ZFS. Arbeitgeberverband geschäftsleitende Ausschuss, August 28, 1942, p. 36, SAV.

72 "Bundesgesetz über Personalfürsorgestiftungen und -Fonds", law project presented at the October 31, 1942 general assembly of the Federation of Employees, file 368/28, Sozialarchiv. Employers were strongly opposed to this law project; see Arbeitgeberverband geschäftsleitende Ausschuss, February 25, 1943, pp. 68–9, SAV. See also Dr. Max Greiner, "Private Personalfürsorge-Stiftungen und -Fonds", *VSA Mitteilungsblatt*, October 1944. This article revealed that only one-third of 338 pension plans surveyed by the Federation offered explicit vesting rights to insured workers or employees.

73 Federal Social Insurance Office to Federal Private Insurance Office, February 16 and December 14, 1942, file E3340 (B) 1985/102/268, SBA.

74 *Geschäftsbericht 1942* (Zurich: SVPP, 1943), p. 4, file E3340 (B) 1985/102/253, SBA. See also Hermann Büchi (Wirtschaftsförderung), "Projekte zu einer schweiz. Altersfürsorge", conference held at the March 9, 1943 general assembly of the SVPP, and "Was geschieht mit den privaten Personalfürsorgekassen", internal report of the Wirtschaftsförderung, September 19, 1945, both documents in file I/3.22.1, #16, Dokumentationsarchiv Wirtschaftsförderung, AfZ.

with the 1930s, the SVPP membership was more diverse. The center of the association, originally in Basle, had shifted to Zurich and the manufacturing hinterlands of Argovia and Solothurn. Pension plans in the metal and machine-making sectors now represented a solid quarter of the membership.[75] These geographical and sectoral shifts reduced the influence of the Liberal-Conservative circles of the Rhine city, which had a direct impact on the SVPP's stance toward social policy. Since the debates on the Lex Forrer, machine makers and metal producers had been more supportive of social insurance programs than Basle textile and chemical entrepreneurs. The leadership of the pension lobby that had opposed the Lex Schulthess took a different position now, and the SVPP worked to entrench the supplementation idea among business circles.

The reformist stance of the Radicals and the integration of the Socialists into the government both facilitated Walther Stampfli's attempt to shape a broad consensus in favor of the AHV. On the other hand, opposition to social insurance remained strong. Alongside a reinvigorated pension lobby, free-market conservatives and trade unionists shared an unmistakable reluctance with regard to the AHV and often sided together in defense of occupational provision.

In early March 1943, the Untergruppe Altersversicherung of the Redressement National welcomed a representative of the Metalworkers' Union at one of its meetings. On this occasion, insurer Ernst Röthlisberger made it clear that, contrary to what was often assumed in labor circles, insurance companies were "not fundamentally opposed to a reasonable social insurance scheme that would cover selected occupational categories". Addressing this conservative business gathering, the Metalworkers' secretary replied that "based on practical experiences", his trade union considered "the realization of a universal old age insurance scheme in the near future a utopia".[76] The union preferred a system of jointly managed occupational pension plans that would improve pension coverage among metalworkers and put the finishing touches to the productive alliance sealed by the 1937 Peace Agreement. Negotiations on this issue had begun in late 1942 with the Federation of Machine Manufacturers and Metal Producers (Arbeitgeberverband schweizerischer Maschinen- und Metall-Industrieller).[77]

[75] For the 1933 SVPP members' list, see Werner Ammann, *Die Altersfürsorge des Bundes und die Durchführung in den Kantonen* (Basle: Helbing & Lichtenhahn, 1934). For 1943, see "SVPP Mitgliederverzeichnis per 20. März 1943", E3340 (B) 1985/102/268, SBA.

[76] Untergruppe Altersversicherung, Sitzungsprotokoll, March 9, 1943, pp. 3–4, file 5.3.2.4, AfZ-RN.

[77] On these negotiations, see Arbeitgeberverband geschäftsleitende Ausschuss, January 8, 1943, pp. 53–6, SAV.

The short-lived Swiss debate about the Beveridge Plan can be contrasted with the revival of free-market networks and neo-liberal economic thought that took place during the same period. In 1942, employers' federations shored up the ability of business circles to intervene in political campaigns by founding both the Trade and Industry Group (Gruppe Handel und Industrie), a business-friendly parliamentary caucus, and the Society for the Development of the Swiss Economy (Gesellschaft zur Förderung der schweizerischen Wirtschaft, hereafter Wirtschaftsförderung). Financed by grants from leading firms and employers' associations, the Wirtschaftsförderung was a propaganda outfit and a bridge between business federations and conservative groupings such as the Redressement National.[78]

In Switzerland, one of the most influential intellectuals of the period was neither John Maynard Keynes nor William Beveridge, but the economist Wilhelm Röpke (1899–1966). After fleeing Nazi Germany, Röpke had been hired at the Geneva Graduate School of International Studies in 1937. In the opening volume of his trilogy on the restoration of economic liberalism, *Social Crisis of our Time* (1942), Röpke anticipated Friedrich Hayek's *Road to Serfdom* (1944) in his attacks against state interventionism and the welfare state. Denouncing the Beveridge Report as an "ominous step toward collectivism, socialization, and the paralysis of the market economy", or a "radical cure for the ills of a proletarianized and mass society that would only worsen suffering while distracting attention from the roots of these diseases", Röpke favored, like insurers or the Redressement National, state-encouraged individual retirement savings accounts.[79]

The German economist considered old age pensions financed by state transfers a dangerous development, as it would mean that "the center of life, mutual aid, and community will shift from the family (its ideal and natural setting) and from other genuine communities toward the State. Everyone should realize the consequences brought by this shift if it becomes a principle and not an exception, although this one is maybe

[78] Werner, *Für Wirtschaft und Vaterland*, pp. 214–31, 392 (note 1074).

[79] Wilhelm Röpke, "Weltwirtschaft und internationale Geldordnung nach dem Kriege", *Schweizer Monatshefte*, January 1943, p. 560. On Röpke and Switzerland, see Josef Mooser, "Liberalismus und Gesellschaft nach 1945: soziale Marktwirtschaft und Neoliberalismus am Beispiel von Wilhelm Röpke", in *Bürgertum nach 1945*, ed. Manfred Hettling and Bernd Ulrich (Hamburg: Hamburger Edition, 2005), pp. 134–63 (especially pp. 139–41, 50–5). The English edition of *Gesellschaftskrise der Gegenwart* was published in 1950. On individual retirement savings accounts, see Dr. J. Wandeler (Rentenanstalt), "Private Personalfürsorge und Staatliche Alters- und Hinterbliebenenversicherung", *Neue Zürcher Zeitung*, December 18 (1st part) and December 21 (2nd part), 1943.

unavoidable given the current circumstances."[80] As this makes clear, even Röpke was aware that "current circumstances" greatly enhanced pressure in favor of state intervention.

Wilhelm Röpke's warnings about statist pitfalls and his mix of conservative social values and free-market principles found a wide audience in Switzerland. His weekly columns in the highbrow *Neue Zürcher Zeitung* became a reference-point and strengthened free-market positions against right-wing corporatism and left-wing interventionism in economic and social affairs.[81] To say the least, the mainstream ideological mindset that was emerging during the second half of the war was not a Keynesian one. Economic liberalism had always been strong in the country; however, Röpke's wartime influence heralded the postwar dissemination of free-market doctrines by the Mont-Pélerin Society. The first meeting of this famous and elite group of neo-liberal thinkers was held under Friedrich Hayek and Wilhelm Röpke's guidance on the shores of Lake Geneva in 1947.[82]

To sum up, the social policy opening of 1941–1943 was fraught with many ambiguities. The political and popular pressure in favor of social policy was unmistakable, but contradictory reform proposals and initiatives counteracted each other. In this context, the radical simplification of postwar blueprints undertaken by Walther Stampfli shaped the AHV into the cornerstone of Swiss social insurance. On the other hand, the reactivation of the pension lobby, the resilience of free-market ideology, and the growing strength of occupational provision signaled that the division of labor between employee benefits and social insurance would become a key battleground for the AHV. These issues will be dealt with in turn in the following sections.

## Walther Stampfli's progress, or the pragmatics of well-ordained postwar reform

In comparison with the protracted debates that had marred the Lex Schulthess, the making of the AHV proceeded at breathtaking speed. In May 1945, after only one year of negotiations, the Federal Council

80 Wilhelm Röpke, *La crise de notre temps* (Neuchâtel: La Baconnière, 1945 [1942]), p. 214.

81 Katharina Bretscher-Spindler, *Vom heissen zum Kalten Krieg: Vorgeschichte und Geschichte der Schweiz im Kalten Krieg 1943 bis 1968* (Zurich: Orell Füssli, 1997), pp. 30–42; Bernard Wehrli, *Le Vorort: mythe ou réalité. Histoire de l'Union suisse du commerce et de l'industrie 1870–1970* (Neuchâtel: La Baconnière, 1972), p. 291.

82 On Swiss elites and early postwar neo-liberalism, see Olivier Longchamp and Yves Steiner, "Le coup de pouce zurichois au renouveau libéral: le Schweizerische Institut für Auslandsforschung (1943–1966)", paper presented at the Centre de sociologie européenne (Paris), 2006.

published a draft of the bill that was largely similar to the final AHV law submitted to the Federal Assembly in September 1946. Even before these last parliamentary debates had taken place, a provisional old age benefits program was introduced using emergency powers to bolster assistance for the elderly poor. In December 1946, the Federal Assembly overwhelmingly accepted federal pensions. Challenged by a last stand of the conservative opponents of social insurance, the AHV finally cleared the referendum hurdle on July 6, 1947. On January 1, 1948, four years after Walter Stampfli's address on New Year's Eve 1944, the first monthly pension checks were sent to their recipients.

The establishment of social insurance coincided with a crucial reorientation period. On both the domestic and foreign fronts, the entry into World War II had proceeded relatively smoothly for Switzerland. In contrast, 1945 represented, paradoxically, the "beginning of a genuine war for the reconquest and redefinition of Switzerland's position on international markets".[83] In other words, Germany's defeat meant that Switzerland had to find new bearings in a postwar Europe dominated by the Allies. The first postwar winter was also the most difficult for the Confederation, as supply lines were briefly disrupted by the chaos that followed the fall of the Third Reich.

If the liberation of Europe did not lead to major upheavals in Swiss political equilibria – the distribution of seats in the Federal Assembly in 1948 closely approximated what it had been in 1938 – the new wind that blew across the continent was nonetheless felt in the Confederation. Having been forced underground during the war, the Communists made an impressive comeback and secured significant minorities in several cantonal elections under the appellation of the Labor Party (Partei der Arbeit). Worker militancy was on the rise, and several strikes, often demanding the extension of collective bargaining, erupted in the aftermath of the war.[84] The year 1946 witnessed the highest level of labor mobilization since the 1918 general strike (see Figure 2.2, p. 67). Between 1944 and 1947, pensions were debated as wartorn Europe gradually shifted toward a new era of confrontation, the Cold War.

Walther Stampfli was determined to avoid a second AHV failure at all costs: the introduction of federal pensions would help to cement the national community, consolidate popular confidence in political institutions, and defuse social tensions. Yet, the AHV was not intended to mean systemic change, but a careful balance between "well-ordained security"

[83] Jost, *Politik und Wirtschaft im Krieg*, p. 25.

[84] Brassel and Schiavi, "Kämpfend in den Arbeitsfrieden"; Jost, *Politik und Wirtschaft im Krieg*, pp. 263–6.

and the preservation of personal responsibility and market principles. Stampfli envisioned universal basic pensions with financing based on payroll contributions modeled on the EO. He favored the self-supporting dimension of the pay-as-you-go system, as it avoided tax increases that might have incensed fiscal conservatives. While Stampfli was also opposed to the fragmentation of pension coverage among multiple providers (the federal state, cantons, and existing occupational plans), his conception of basic benefits was compatible with the safeguarding of existing occupational schemes. Modest pay-as-you-go pensions supplemented by funded occupational schemes constituted the core of "Stampflian pragmatics".[85]

In the spring of 1944, Walther Stampfli set up a carefully selected commission of experts to ensure the success of the AHV with the help of three dedicated civil servants: Arnold Saxer, director of the Federal Social Insurance Office, Ernst Kaiser, a specialist in the actuarial dimensions of social insurance, and Peter Binswanger, a young legal expert. As Binswanger was to boast years later in an interview, the teamwork between the iron Federal Councilor and his aides was so effective that "it was impossible" for other members of the commission "to prevail against the four of us".[86]

In the AHV commission, Stampfli built a solid cross-class alliance that included representatives from the Union of Life Insurance Companies and the main business federations, as well as trade unionists and proponents of *Gesichertes Alter*. The president of the initiative committee, National Councilor Philip Schmid-Ruedin, a left-liberal Radical who headed the white-collar Association of Commercial Clerks (Kaufmännischer Verein), and National Councilor Robert Bratschi, a Socialist who presided over both the Railroad Workers' Union and the Gewerkschaftsbund, were integrated into the taskforce. The AHV commission also worked closely with the Finance Department headed by the Socialist Ernst Nobs. With the exception of Socialist and Radical representatives, the commission eschewed other political parties and replicated the technocratic apparatus that had enabled the rapid implementation of the EO. According to Walther Stampfli's biographer, "this 'triumvirate' of business and labor associations, executive branch and civil servants . . . considerably strengthened Stampfli's position during the parliamentary debates [and] shaped the compromise that could overcome the referendum".[87]

[85] Hafner, *Bundesrat Walther Stampfli*, pp. 375–80, 91–400. [86] Ibid., p. 413.

[87] Ibid., pp. 382–3. For the composition of the commission, see Binswanger, *Histoire de l'AVS*, p. 275 (note 24).

In comparison with the competing social reform initiatives launched between 1941 and 1943, the AHV accumulated key political and institutional advantages. Stampfli's "triumvirate" insulated the establishing of the AHV from the delaying tactics and institutional hurdles that social insurance had faced during the interwar period. This framework enabled Walther Stampfli to open a direct, although narrow, road leading toward the AHV.

The Catholic initiative *For the Family*, as well as the *Economic Reform and Labor Rights* and the *Right to Work* initiatives backed respectively by the Socialists and the Alliance of Independents, constituted real challenges during a delicate transition toward a new postwar equilibrium. In this context, Walther Stampfli was determined to safeguard market principles and limit state intervention in economic and social affairs. As the next section analyzes pension debates in detail, it is worth focusing here on how Walther Stampfli sidelined alternative reform proposals and submitted them to the imperatives of the AHV and to the revision of the constitutional articles that defined the economic policy of the federal government (Wirtschaftsartikeln, or Economic Articles). The "economic general" maneuvered carefully to present a tightly knit postwar policy package.

The Catholic initiative *For the Family*, infused with anti-liberal corporatist values, had the potential to torpedo the AHV and strain relations between the two main bourgeois parties, and Walther Stampfli acted quickly to defuse this. In May 1942, he had taken over the issue from his colleague Philip Etter, the Catholic Conservative in charge of the Home Affairs Department, and kept it at a safe distance from the AHV. Stampfli then exerted strong pressure on the Catholics to win their support for an official counter-proposal. Stampfli's sanitized promise to introduce family allowances and maternity leave was rushed through the Federal Assembly and overwhelmingly accepted by voters in November 1945, even before the final discussions on the AHV had taken place. After some hand-wringing, Catholic forces closed ranks behind the Federal Council. The implementation of family allowances was delegated to cantonal governments, which dampened potential federalist opposition to the AHV, while the promise of maternity benefits, a gesture toward the left, would remain in political limbo for decades.[88] The potential for

[88] On the Catholic initiative, see Stadler, "Die Initiative *Für die Familie*", pp. 116ff. On family allowances and maternity leave, see Brigitte Studer, Gaby Sutter, and Regina Wecker, *Die "schutzbedürftige Frau": zur Konstruktion von Geschlecht durch Mutterschaftsversicherung, Nachtarbeitsverbot und Sonderschutzgesetzgebung* (Zurich: Chronos, 2001), pp. 38–48. Maternity benefits were turned down several times by referenda after 1945 before being finally introduced in 2004.

damaging confrontations between Conservatives and Radicals, like those that had marred interwar debates about the AHV and were personified in the bitter antagonism between Edmund Schulthess and Jean-Marie Musy, was thus greatly reduced.

On the economic policy battlefront, Walther Stampfli took advantage of the revision of the Economic Articles to sideline competing left-leaning proposals, as well as to placate those demanding special protection for middle-class constituencies represented by the Gewerbeverband and the Farmers' Federation. The two Socialist and Independent economic initiatives remained unsuccesful. The *New Switzerland* Socialist manifesto and its accompanying initiative on *Economic Reform and Labor Rights* received only tepid support from trade unions. Moreover, the Gewerkschaftsbund was integrated into the AHV commission and followed Walther Stampfli's stance. The powerful Metalworkers' Union all but ignored the Socialist proposals, while the smaller Catholic Federation of Trade Unions leaned toward the corporatist social policies favored by the Catholic Conservative Party. In the end, the Socialists backed their own initiative only tepidly.[89] Given the marginal political weight of the Alliance of Independents, their *Right to Work* initiative was even more isolated.

The Economic Articles reinforced liberal corporatist mechanisms without ceding ground to either the left or conservative opinion. The Articles guaranteed the participation of the peak business and labor associations in political decision-making through pre-parliamentary consultations. This confirmation of the technocratic processes of the war economy was accompanied by the encouragement of collective bargaining and by promises to revise the subsidization of unemployment schemes. These two measures placated trade unions and the left. Another article allowing for Confederation intervention to protect endangered trade sectors, a concession aimed at appeasing the constituencies of the Gewerbeverband, was not made compulsory. At the same time, federal agricultural subsidies were increased and social support for farmers' families was introduced to reaffirm their integration into the bourgeois bloc.[90]

As a result of this exercise in defusing opposition, the Socialist and Independent initiatives rapidly lost ground and were turned down by popular votes (in December 1946 and May 1947 respectively), while a narrow popular majority accepted the Economic Articles on the same day as the AHV in July 1947. The blueprints for postwar reforms were reduced by Walther Stampfli's resolute use of executive power and by

[89] Kobelt, *Die Wirtschaftspolitik der Gewerkschaften*, pp. 137–57.

[90] Hafner, *Bundesrat Walther Stampfli*, pp. 336–64; Jost, *Politik und Wirtschaft im Krieg*, pp. 292–7.

the constraints of the war economy apparatus. In other words, the tracks laid for the AHV express sidelined all other alternative policy proposals, despite fierce political battles.

Before turning to the making of the AHV, a brief overview of reform proposals in both the United States and the United Kingdom will better situate Swiss debates and their postwar legacies. In late 1942, the publication of the Beveridge Report crystallized popular expectations of social reform and caught Winston Churchill off guard. The fact that the Labour Party played a larger role in both the administration of the war economy and the governing coalition helped progressive forces use Beveridge's proposals as a symbol of postwar reform. Popular support for the report accompanied the shift in British politics that would usher in the Labour electoral landslide of 1945. This change led to an overhaul of existing welfare measures and the implementation of the National Health Service in 1948, as well as the nationalization of key manufacturing sectors.[91]

Postwar social planning unfolded differently in the United States, where reform blueprints were censored by the federal administration, got bogged down in internecine departmental struggles, and, in the end, never attracted the same popular enthusiasm that the Beveridge Report did. Moreover, after 1944 a conservative political shift reinforced hostility to the reformist spirit that had marked the 1930s. In the atmosphere of "end of reform" and conservative revival that prevailed, there was little space for an encompassing welfare state. Keynesian proposals in favor of full employment were whittled down, health insurance reforms based on payroll contributions were rejected in 1948 by conservative opponents, and the Taft-Hartley Act 1946 rolled back labor rights. The war mainly furthered "indirect and disjointed forms of public policy", in other words reaffirmed a fragmented system of welfare provision. The breakthrough of the Social Security Act 1935 did not evolve into a system of "comprehensive" and "nationalizing" social insurance as it had in the United Kingdom.[92]

However, the differences between these outcomes should not be overstated. Many of the projects envisioned by Beveridge were never implemented, and Labour was replaced in 1951 by a Tory government that

[91] Brian Abel-Smith, "The Beveridge Report: its origins and outcomes", in *Beveridge and social security: an international retrospective*, ed. John Hills *et al.* (Oxford: Clarendon Press, 1994), pp. 10–22.

[92] Edwin Amenta and Theda Skocpol, "Redefining the New Deal: World War II and the development of social provision in the United States", in *The politics of social policy in the United States*, ed. Margaret Weir, *et al.* (Princeton: Princeton University Press, 1988), pp. 81–122 (quotation p. 83); Alan Brinkley, *The end of reform: New Deal liberalism in recession and war* (New York: Vintage Books, 1995), pp. 136–74, 227–64.

was much less supportive of the welfare state. Bold measures such as the nationalization of insurance companies were abandoned, and the pension system remained based on a mix of basic state pensions and voluntary occupational schemes.[93] With all their limitations and disappointing outcomes, American postwar social programs were nonetheless significant. Besides the extension of Social Security coverage and benefits that was enacted in 1949, the educational, housing, employment, and health benefits contained in the GI Bill – although disproportionately directed at the white male population – represented a massive social effort.[94]

Even before the first steps of AHV policy-making had been taken, Swiss debates on postwar social policy signaled that a turn toward a comprehensive welfare state was unlikely. In a sense, Switzerland stood halfway between the United States and the United Kingdom. First, the political situation was characterized by neither leftward nor rightward tendencies. The governing coalition dominated by bourgeois parties not only survived the war, but experienced no major changes until the end of the 1950s. The power structure that dominated in Switzerland was cemented by the reinforcement of the executive branch to the detriment of parliamentary powers and direct democracy, and was not fundamentally altered by the integration of the left in the Federal Council.

Second, although the flurry of projects that emerged between 1941 and 1943 revealed heightened public expectations of postwar reform, their overlaps and contradictions enabled Walther Stampfli to carefully delineate reform and channel social insurance down a clearly defined track. Although the Beveridge Report had no equivalent in Switzerland, the official AHV project was immensely popular and overshadowed all other reform proposals. The expansion of benefits for male citizen-soldiers and workers through the EO and corporate schemes was widened by the implementation of the AHV.

In the United States and Switzerland, a resurgence of conservatism and an enduring political stability reinforced the grip of ruling elites on the shape of the postwar settlement and contributed to restraining the potential scope of the welfare state. In both cases, basic universal pensions constituted the limited core of social provision, along with selective

[93] Rodney Lowe, "A prophet dishonoured in his own country? The rejection of Beveridge in Britain, 1945–1970", in *Beveridge and social security: an international retrospective*, ed. John Hills, *et al.* (Oxford: Clarendon Press, 1994), pp. 118–33; Pat Thane, *Old age in English history: past experiences, present issues* (Oxford: Oxford University Press, 2000), pp. 380–4.

[94] Brinkley, *The end of reform*, pp. 258–9; Ira Katznelson, *When affirmative action was white: an untold history of racial inequality in twentieth-century America* (New York: W. W. Norton, 2005), pp. 113–41.

occupational schemes and social programs, to the detriment of universal welfare measures.

The next section outlines the consensus that was reached on the AHV, and focuses on how boundaries between social insurance and occupational benefits became the object of intense negotiations between the state, business, and labor. The outcome of these pre-parliamentary negotiations not only made the AHV a social policy breakthrough, but also safeguarded private forms of provision.

## The contested boundaries of old age provision (1944–1946)

Business circles were not surprised by Walther Stampfli's January 1944 address to the nation, because early contacts regarding the AHV had already taken place between the Federal Social Insurance Office and employers' federations in late 1943.[95] By February, the mission of defining a common employers' stance on the AHV was devolved to an ad hoc commission composed of representatives from the Vorort, Arbeitgeberverband, and Gewerbeverband, and members of the Union of Life Insurance Companies and the SVPP pension lobby.[96] Several members of the Untergruppe Altersversicherung, notably Ernst Röthlisberger and Otto Steinmann, participated in the meetings of this taskforce, which signaled the close connections existing between the Redressement National and employers' federations. Depending on the context or the need, business circles used one or the other channel, or both at the same time, to achieve their aims. In contrast to labor organizations, employers not only occupied a central role in policy-making but also maintained a united front. Before sending representatives to the employers' taskforce, the Union of Life Insurance Companies acknowledged that insurers should strive to maintain a "dominant position" in the coming negotiations. Without "leading" the project or appearing to defend narrow interests, insurers wanted to put a brake on social insurance and bolster the "encouragement of private provision", especially group contracts.[97]

Responses to a survey organized in late 1943 by the Vorort and the Arbeitgeberverband to probe business opinion on social insurance

[95] Federal Social Insurance Office to Vorort and Arbeitgeberverband, November 17, 1943; Vorort to Federal Social Insurance Office, December 16, 1943, file 95.12, AfZ-SHIV.

[96] Convocation of the first meeting of the "Interne Expertenkommission der wirtschaftlichen Spitzenverbände zur Begutachtung des Volkbegehrens auf Umwandlung der LV[EO]-Ausgleichkasse in AHV-Kassen" (hereafter Expertenkommission der Spitzenverbände), February 17, 1944, file 95.1, AfZ-SHIV.

[97] Konferenz der Direktoren der VSLG, January 28, 1944, pp. 6–9, file Q127 206, ZFS.

indicated that employers' views closely matched Walther Stampfli's key positions. The predominant opinion among sectoral employers' associations and local chambers of commerce, summarized by Vorort secretary Hans Herold, were for "a compulsory insurance scheme with relatively low basic pensions".[98] Although employers refused at first to abandon their uncompromising attitude toward the use of EO funds, they agreed that pay-as-you-go financing avoided the recourse to general revenues. Financing either by direct taxation – considered too redistributive – or state-controlled funding – which might lead to an unacceptable concentration of capital in state coffers and to the crowding-out of private investment – had to be avoided at all costs. In general, employers wanted the cost of federal pensions to remain modest and not hinder competitiveness in international markets.[99] Considering the AHV in a broader perspective, Ernst Röthlisberger reminded his colleagues that such a contribution-based universal old age insurance scheme existed in only one country, the United States. Underlining the challenges that lay ahead for the AHV, the insurer added that Roosevelt had introduced Social Security without having to face the hurdles of referenda.[100]

All in all, business federations recognized the turn of the tide in the field of social policy, but their support for social insurance remained conditional. As was the case during the interwar period, financing options and the role of existing occupational plans constituted potential stumbling-blocks. In the spring of 1944, at the very moment when the preliminary results of the 1941 federal survey on occupational provision were presented to the Vorort, the latter issue was considered of the utmost importance. In a joint statement, the Vorort and the Arbeitgeberverband strongly warned the Federal Council that business circles had given a green light to a general discussion on the AHV, but that any proposal that would endanger the "will for self-help", entail excessive financial costs, or infringe existing pension plans would run into immediate and serious trouble.[101] In June 1944, Walther Stampfli similarly warned during the preparatory meeting of the AHV commission that the topic of existing pension plans "could easily become a fateful issue for the AHV".[102]

98 Vorort Vorstand, April 17, 1944, p. 20, file 1.5.3.12, AfZ-SHIV.
99 "Ergebnisse der drei Sitzungen der internen Expertenkommission der wirtschaftlichen Spitzenverbände zur Begutachtung des Volkbegehrens betreffend die AHV" [n.d., ca. April 1944], file 95.2, AfZ-SHIV.
100 Expertenkommission der Spitzenverbände, February 29, 1944, file 95.2, AfZ-SHIV.
101 Arbeitgeberverband geschäftsleitende Ausschuss, April 26, 1944, pp. 19–24, SAV. Vorort Vorstand, March 13, 1944, pp. 18–19, file 1.5.3.12, AfZ-SHIV. See also Arbeitgeberverband and Vorort to the Federal Council, April 27, 1944, file 95.1, AfZ-SHIV.
102 AHV Kleine Expertenkommission. Sitzungen zur Vorbereitung der 1. Session, June 1, 1944, p. 1, file E3340 (B)-/1/48, SBA.

Yet, in contrast to the protracted process that had plagued the Lex Schulthess, the first meetings of the commission led to a rapid convergence on key issues. Eager not to repeat old errors, various members of the commission often mentioned the failure of the interwar pension bill. From the outset, the commission limited its mandate to defining a pension scheme modeled on the EO and crossed out family allowances, disability benefits, and individual retirement savings accounts from the discussion agenda.[103]

Socialist Robert Bratschi asserted that AHV benefits had to be "generous", not least to hold off potential political radicalization at the end of the war. However, this was not the direction of the commission. Echoing Walther Stampfli's preference for a basic pension and reiterating the key concept of supplementation, Emile Marchand of Rentenanstalt explained early on that "social insurance pensions [would] never be sufficient" and that "private firms [would have to] supplement them".[104] According to a poll taken in early 1944, three-quarters of those asked to estimate the proper level of future AHV benefits envisioned monthly pensions ranging from CHF 125 to CHF 250. Yet, the commission of experts focused on much lower and more widely spread pensions, ranging from CHF 40 to CHF 125, with even lower benefits for the entry generation of pensioners. These amounts – the maximum pension representing at most one-fifth of average monthly earnings – closely matched the figures put forward by employers' federations in early 1944 and would form the basis of the benefits that were paid in 1948.[105] Introducing pensions above this basic floor would have meant a damaging confrontation with the pension lobby and fiscal conservatives, and was carefully avoided.

For business representatives and insurers, the choice for financing remained a pay-as-you-go system supplemented by modest funded reserves. Speaking of the pros and cons of this plan, insurer Emile Marchand pointed out that these two financing methods could be combined in "innumerable configurations that we can compare to a mix of milk and coffee. If we describe a pure pay-as-you-go system as 'milk' and,

[103] On *Für die Familie*, see AHV Kleine Experten kommission. Sitzungen zur Vorbereitung der 1. Session, June 1, 1944, file E3340 (B)-/1/48. On children's benefits, see Expertenkommission AHV 1. Session, July 10, 1944, pp. 10–14, file E3340 (B)-/1/49, SBA; on disability benefits and individual savings, see "Einleitende Referate der 1. Session der Expertenkommission AHV", July 10, 1944, pp. 6–8, "Anhang II: Richtlinien", file E3340 (B)-/1/49, SBA.

[104] Expertenkommission AHV 2. Session, October 16 to October 20, 1944, pp. 29, 100, file E3340 (B)-/1/50, SBA.

[105] Expertenkommission AHV 1. Session, einleitende Referate, July 10, 1944, p. 25, file E3340 (B)-/1/49, SBA. For wages, see Ritzmann-Blickenstorfer and Siegenthaler, eds., *Swiss Historical Statistics*, Table G9.

respectively, a totally funded system as 'black coffee', I would say that I would personally favor a mix that contains a lot of 'milk'."[106] In contrast, Ernst Kaiser (1906–1978), the mathematician at the Federal Social Insurance Office in charge of devising the actuarial structure of the AHV, emphasized the "social dimensions" of the pay-as-you-go structure. Kaiser underscored that payroll contributions would introduce collective solidarity between those who contributed to the AHV and those who received its benefits, and would enable the Confederation to pay pensions more quickly and more generously than any funded scheme would.[107]

These views were rarely discussed at the time by insurers and employers, who were chiefly preoccupied with containing state-controlled funding. Kaiser's insistence on pay-as-you-go showed his keen understanding of this financing system, a knowledge he gained while working with leading social security experts at the International Labor Office during the 1930s.[108] This connection was much more important than debates about the Beveridge Report, and underscored the early role of international organizations in the diffusion of social policy models and practices. The pay-as-you-go structure set up by Kaiser contributed to the success of the federal pension scheme and provided a solid financial foundation for it.

For Otto Steinmann of the Arbeitgeberverband, employers' acceptance of payroll contributions depended on taking into account existing occupational plans.[109] This issue had sparked a lively debate in the employers' taskforce. Before the first meetings of the AHV commission, insurer Ernst Röthlisberger had argued that existing plans could not simply be "integrated" into the federal AHV, as this would mean "the transformation and

106 Expertenkommission AHV 1. Session, July 10, 1944, p. 35, file E3340 (B)-/1/49, SBA. Emile Marchand had already outlined his preferences for a pay-as-you-go system during the interwar period. See Emile Marchand, *A propos de l'introduction des assurances sociales en Suisse: contribution à l'étude des diverses possibilités pour la répartition des charges* (Berne: Stämpfli, 1921).

107 Expertenkommission AHV 2. Session, einleitende Referate, October 16 to October 20, 1944, p. 45, file E3340 (B)-/1/50, SBA.

108 This experience formed the basis of Ernst Kaiser's dissertation in actuarial science, which was devoted to pay-as-you-go financing. See Ernst Kaiser, *La distribution des revenus dans la technique mathématique de la sécurité sociale* (Berne: Stämpfli, 1950). For a sample of ILO works on social insurance, see *Approaches to social security: an international survey* (Montreal: International Labour Office, 1942); Lucien Féraud, *Actuarial technique and financial organisation of social insurance: compulsory pension insurance* (Geneva: International Labour Office, 1940). Thanks to Arthur Vogt (Federal Social Insurance Office) for pointing out these references to me.

109 Expertenkommission AHV 1. Session, einleitende Referate, July 10, 1944, pp. 42–6, file E3340 (B)-/1/49, SBA.

partial destruction of private pension plans".[110] He added that the AHV would be acceptable as long as it envisioned very low or even means-tested benefits that would not encroach on the realm of occupational provision. Reiterating the position held during the interwar period by the pension lobby, Röthlisberger said that occupational plans offering benefits equal to or higher than the AHV should be able to opt out from the federal scheme to avoid "over-insurance" or a "double insurance burden". For Röthlisberger, "the postulate of the autonomy of pension plans must be based on their total liberation from the organization of social insurance, so as to preserve [their] complete autonomy and particularities".[111]

This option was not unanimously endorsed among employers. After a survey of its members, the SVPP warned that opting out might prove both risky and expensive. Recent and financially fragile pension plans would have difficulty guaranteeing the level of benefits prescribed by a federal insurance scheme. Moreover, noted a pension consultant invited to the March 1944 assembly of the SVPP, "in contrast to public pension plans, there is no guarantee that private institutions will last permanently".[112] Entrepreneurs were thus reluctant to step forward to organize basic coverage. As was the case during the interwar years when controversies over basic insurance and supplementary schemes had contributed in no small part to the demise of the Lex Schulthess, the boundaries between the AHV and occupational plans constituted a key battleground.

The final 1946 pension law offered two options for existing occupational plans: employers could choose to have their plans registered (or "recognized"), which implied that their payroll contributions and benefits would be coordinated with the AHV. The second option would allow occupational plans to continue their activities without being tied in any formal way to federal pensions. This latter solution was chosen, with a handful of exceptions, by all occupational plans. Peter Binswanger, who was one of Stampfli's trusted lieutenants and would play a key role in the postwar formulation of the three-pillar doctrine, briefly mentions in his history of the AHV that the so-called recognition issue (Anerkennung) was the most contentious one discussed by the commission: "The time devoted [to this problem] . . . has enabled the avoidance of other attempts to integrate occupational plans into the AHV, and the solution chosen has opened the path toward the 1980s legislation on occupational

110 Expertenkommission der Spitzenverbände, April 20, 1944, p. 11, file 95.2, AfZ-SHIV.

111 Ernst Röthlisberger, "Die Stellung der bestehenden Versicherungseinrichtungen bei einer AHV", April 20, 1944, p. 6, file 95.1, AfZ-SHIV.

112 *SVPP Zirkularmitteilungen*, no. 4, December 6, 1943, E3340 (B) 1985/102/263, SBA. For the discussion, see minutes of the March 30, 1944, general assembly of the SVPP, p. 10, file E3340 (B) 1985/102/253, SBA.

provision . . . in which pension plans remain legally independent of the AHV."[113] If this ex post facto conclusion is far-fetched, this forgotten chapter of the establishment of the AHV deserves more than a cursory mention.

During the first sessions of the AHV commission, National Councilors Robert Bratschi (Socialist) and Philip Schmid-Ruedin (Radical), who both represented unions whose members (railroad workers and white-collar employees) were well covered by pensions, argued that existing plans had to be fully integrated into the AHV, the same position as the *Gesichertes Alter* initiative.[114] Emile Marchand of Rentenanstalt immediately countered this and emphasized that "how and why the owner of a pension plan decides to remain outside of social insurance instead of being integrated into it will depend on the level of public pensions. If the latter remain modest, the AHV will play in many cases the role of a supplementary insurance scheme."[115] For employers, and especially insurers, the option favored by Bratschi and Schmid-Ruedin would transform existing pension schemes into mere dependencies of the Confederation. Yet, at the time when the exact parameters of the AHV were still undecided, business circles remained hostile to a complete disconnection between the AHV and existing schemes. They favored options that would, for example, have their pension plans levy AHV payroll contributions and pay AHV benefits (and substitute for the Confederation as pension providers) or receive federal subsidies to implement basic pensions while retaining their independence.

The level of and conditions for state subsidies to existing plans, the regulation of private-pension providers and their compliance with AHV rules, and the impact of private interference in AHV financial flows constituted thorny issues. Would the state allow the implementation of the AHV to be fragmented among a plurality of providers and be partly controlled by private plans? Would the allocation of public subsidies be followed by extensive regulation of existing pension plans? Would that imply a loss of employers' control of the organization and financing of pension schemes, as well as the management of the workforce?

As no suitable consensus could be reached on these questions, the issue of coordination between the AHV and pension plans was delegated to a special sub-commission in August 1944. During its sessions, Emile Marchand warned that access to subsidies might become the "fateful

113 Binswanger, *Histoire de l'AVS*, pp. 31–2; Hafner, *Bundesrat Walther Stampfli*, pp. 385–7.

114 Expertenkommission AHV 1. Session, July 10, 1944, pp. 45–6 E3340 (B)-/1/49, SBA. See also Expertenkommission AHV 2. Session, October 16 to October 20, 1944, p. 144, file 50, SBA.

115 Expertenkommission AHV 1. Session, July 10, 1944, p. 68, file E3340 (B)-/1/49, SBA.

issue" of the law. Adding that it was "a life or death issue for group insurance", he promised that the Federal Council would face "major opposition if no satisfactory solution [was] found".[116] Insurers tried to obtain public subsidies for organizing basic AHV benefits while keeping the finances and the management of pension plans for executive staff out of the reach of the federal state. This last point was not lost on Robert Bratschi, who retorted that "those who are already insured should not be disadvantaged [by the AHV]. However, no one should be advantaged or escape his duties because he is already insured and perhaps even very advantageously insured."[117] Bratschi also underlined with irony that those who relentlessly criticized state subsidies to public-sector pension plans were now demanding similar subsidies to prop up their retirement programs.

Between these two polarized positions, civil servants of the Federal Social Insurance Office tried to avoid the derailment of the whole project. Mathematician Ernst Kaiser carefully pointed out that solutions favored by insurers shattered the solidarity principle that was at the core of federal pensions. Kaiser also pointed out that the insurers' proposals would not only vastly complicate the administration of the AHV but also make its implementation more costly.[118] Arguing that the commission of experts had to report to the Federal Council by mid-1945, Robert Bratschi, Philip Schmid-Ruedin, and Walther Stampfli's trusted lieutenants convinced a majority of the special sub-commission to adjourn its debates. Despite vocal protests from insurers, the recognition issue was left unresolved, and the commission limited itself to listing options without taking a firm position. This situation vindicated Walther Stampfli's resolve not to allow the project to be hindered by delaying tactics or bickering over specific issues.

In February 1945, the Federal Council – acting on a demand originating from the Gewerkschaftsbund – gave the green light to provisional old age assistance benefits. This scheme, implemented in January 1946 through the emergency powers of the executive branch, boldly anticipated the formation of a final consensus among the members of the AHV commission and preceded the final parliamentary debates on federal

[116] "Protokolle der Sitzungen der für die Frage der bestehenden und neu entstehenden Versicherungseinrichtungen eingesetzten Subkommission" (hereafter Subkommission Versicherungseinrichtungen), September 12, 1944, p. 8, file E3340 (B)-/1/50, SBA.

[117] Subkommission Versicherungseinrichtungen, December 19, 1944, p. 8, file 3340 (B)-/1/50, SBA. See also Hans Streit, "Bemerkungen zum Bericht der eidg. Expertenkommission für die Einführung der AHV", *Schweizerische Versicherungszeitschrift* (1945), pp. 39–48.

[118] Subkommission Versicherungseinrichtungen, February 14, 1945, p. 7, 3340 (B)-/1/50, SBA.

pensions.[119] While the Federal Social Insurance Office was fine-tuning the May 1945 pension bill, business circles made a first assessment of the situation. Even those members of the Vorort who were most hostile to the idea of social insurance acknowledged that the pace of the negotiations left little space for dissent. Albert Pictet, a Geneva private banker who represented the western Switzerland Chambers of Commerce, which had traditionally opposed the AHV, conceded that "politically, it [was] dangerous to present a project that would fail in a popular vote".[120]

The conclusion of the first round of AHV negotiations coincided with the end of military operations in the European theater, a period of uncertainty about the postwar environment. The political upheavals faced by Switzerland's immediate neighbors were even echoed, albeit on a milder scale, in the Confederation. A repetition of the 1918 general strike seemed unlikely, yet the stirrings of social unrest were unmistakable: the regional electoral victories of the Labor Party, as well as increasing labor militancy, punctuated the political scene throughout 1945.

Noting that the principle of universal insurance was unassailable, Heinrich Homberger, director of the Vorort, emphasized that business federations had to focus on the financial aspects of the project. Both the Untergruppe Altersversicherung and the employers' taskforce on social insurance shared this general assessment. The latter also insisted that employers had to continue working in order to prevent unwelcome "state interference" in private pension plans. In July 1945, both employers' federations reiterated their conditional support for the AHV, but offered a reminder that the standing of existing pension plans had to be reexamined.[121] Other business representatives were less diplomatic. For insurance executive Paul Pfeil of Winterthur Life, this AHV "imposed from above" represented an "ominous step toward the nationalization of insurance" that would damage the "will for self-provision and savings among the Swiss people". Speaking in September 1945 before the delegates of the Swiss Chamber of Commerce, Hans Sulzer, chief executive of the eponymous turbine factories and president of the Vorort, spoke of the AHV in Hayekian terms, vilifying it as a "preliminary step toward dictatorship".[122]

[119] Expertenkommission AHV 3. Session, January 29 to February 2, 1945, pp. 145–58, file E3340 (B)-/1/51. See also Binswanger, *Histoire de l'AVS*, pp. 72–7.

[120] Vorort Vorstand, June 25, 1945, p. 7, file 1.5.3.13, AfZ-SHIV.

[121] Expertenkommission der Spitzenverbände, May 1, 1945, p. 7, file 95.2, AfZ-SHIV; Vorort and Arbeitgeberverband to Federal Economic Affairs Department, July 14, 1945, file 95.3, AfZ-SHIV.

[122] Paul Pfeil, "Weitere Bemerkungen zu den Berichten der Eidg. Expertenkommission für die Einführung der AHV", *Schweizerische Versicherungszeitschrift* (1945),

The Union of Life Insurance Companies considered the outcome of the negotiations on existing occupational plans highly unsatisfactory. Both Emile Marchand and Ernst Röthlisberger, the animator of the Untergruppe Altersversicherung, came together to draft a new proposal that reasserted the right of private firms to organize basic AHV coverage. This new proposal was promoted among insurers' corporate clients, circulated among key SVPP members, and endorsed by the Untergruppe Altersversicherung and the main business federations.[123] Life insurers were in fact not only interested in obtaining public subsidies from the Confederation. As Emile Marchand pointed out to his peers, allowing existing plans to act as basic pension providers enabled employers to "rein in the development of the AHV reserve fund" and limit the reach of the Confederation in pension provision. Another Rentenanstalt executive underscored that what was at stake was not a technical issue but a question of principle, which boiled down to the "division of labor between the state and the private economy".[124]

However, other insurers were more circumspect toward this attempt to enmesh private schemes within the AHV. In the summer of 1945, Hans Herold, the Vorort secretary in charge of social policy, received a memorandum from a manager of the Zurich insurance company who expressed his reservations about such options:

> Both the project of the experts' commission and the new project drafted by Professor Marchand must be described as unsocial. I am convinced that, in due time, some will reproach the [life insurance] companies for wanting to extract some profit from the situation. This proposal brings nothing other than the recapitalization of unsound plans. This will encourage certain circles to set up unreliable pension plans . . . For these reasons, one should really ask oneself whether it might not be better to leave the AHV to run its course alongside existing welfare institutions.[125]

pp. 113–16, p. 114. Hans Sulzer's declaration is quoted in Hafner, *Bundesrat Walther Stampfli*, p. 415.

123 Konferenz der Direktoren der VSLG, February 23, 1945 and Konferenz der Direktoren der VSLG, May 31, 1945, pp. 6–8, file Q127 206, ZFS. See also a report by Dr. J. Wandeler (Rentenanstalt) on this issue at the May 15, 1945 general assembly of the SVPP, file 95.2, AfZ-SHIV; Expertenkommission der Spitzenverbände, November 1, 1945, file 95.4, AfZ-SHIV and Untergruppe Altersversicherung Sitzungsprotokoll, June 7, 1945, file 5.3.2.4, AfZ-RN; *Rentenanstalt KONTAKT-BRIEF*, no. 4, June 11, 1945, file 921.111/6, SLA.

124 Emile Marchand, "Zum Problem der Berücksichtigung der bestehenden oder künftig entstehenden Versicherungseinrichtungen in der eidg. AHV", November 20, 1945, p. 11, file 95.5, AfZ-SHIV; Dr. J. Wandeler, "Zur Frage 'Volle Rückversicherung mit Saldomethode' oder 'Vorschlag Marchand'?", October 24, 1945, p. 4, file 921.111/6, SLA.

125 Unsigned memorandum from a Zurich executive to Hans Herold, July 1945, file 95.4, AfZ-SHIV.

The caution expressed by this insurance insider, as well as his preference for a clear-cut separation between the AHV and existing pension plans, highlighted the unwelcome consequences that might arise from tying occupational provision to social insurance.

As the recognition debate unexpectedly collided with the issue of pension plan regulation in the summer of 1945, such reservations sounded quite prescient. As previously mentioned, the regulation issue had been downplayed by employers during the interwar period but resurfaced at the beginning of the 1940s as questions were raised about the opaque functioning of private plans and the soundness of their finances. At the end of the war, because the nationalization of insurance companies was on the agenda in several European countries, notably in neighboring France, less guarded critiques of private provision could be heard.[126] In 1945, a pamphlet ironically entitled *The Illusion of Insurance* (*Versicherungs-Zauber*) denounced the insurance sector as the "most select, richest, and most reactionary stronghold of [Swiss] capitalism", and accused Rentenanstalt of being responsible for the endless delays that had marred social insurance since the 1920s.[127]

The regulation of existing pension plans also became a public issue in June 1945, when National Councilor Valentin Gitermann filed a motion deploring the way that pension plans could benefit from tax breaks without having to comply with any serious federal regulation. This nonconformist Socialist asked the Federal Council to ensure that firms used exempted monies properly, but also hinted that legal loopholes enabled abuses or even fraud.[128] Gitermann's motion, which was discussed in the Federal Assembly during the winter of 1945–1946, emerged in the public arena at the very moment when insurers were canvassing employers in order to launch a new offensive on the recognition issue. In other words,

[126] Gérard Glass, "Die Verstaatlichung des Versicherungswesens als internationales Problem", *Schweizerische Versicherungszeitschrift* (1946), pp. 12–15; Janick Marina Schaufelbühl, "Les nationalisations de la Libération en France et leur impact sur les investisseurs suisses", in *Les relations extérieures de la Suisse après 1945*, ed. Monique Ceni, *et al.* (Lausanne: Antipodes, 2006), pp. 15–32.

[127] Pollux, *Versicherungs-Zauber* (Zurich: Genossenschaftendruckerei, 1945), p. 5 (quotation), 31. "Pollux" was a pseudonym for Georges Bähler, a leftist engineer. See Markus Bürgi, "Bähler, Georges", in *Historisches Lexicon der Schweiz*, http://www.dhs.ch. See also "Angriffe auf privatwirtschaftliche Fürsorgestiftungen", *Schweizerische Arbeitgeber Zeitung*, November 17, 1944, as well as "Pollux Versicherungs-Phantastereien", *Schweizerische Versicherungszeitschrift* (1946), pp. 374–7.

[128] Wirz, *Die Personal-Wohlfahrtseinrichtungen*, pp. 121–7. A Ukranian Jew, Valentin Gitermann (1900–1965) had come to Switzerland as a young child and had followed there a career as a teacher and academic. His *History of Switzerland* (1941) had left reactionary circles fuming against this immigrant who dared to write about national history. See Markus Bürgi, "Gitermann, Valentin" in *Historisches Lexicon der Schweiz*, http://www.dhs.ch.

the motion could potentially throw light on the subterranean politics of private provision. Bourgeois politicians sternly dismissed the whole affair as an ideological attack against private provision, and the executive branch played down the motion by stating that it would soon present measures pertaining to the regulation of occupational provision.

Once again, the issue was deflected and would only resurface from the meandering of the federal administration after the implementation of the AHV. However, the Gitermann motion may well have damped down business enthusiasm for options that might have endangered the autonomy of pension plans by coupling them with the AHV.

In early 1946, Emile Marchand's second proposal met fierce resistance from both the Federal Social Insurance Office and labor representatives, while gradually losing the support it enjoyed among employers and the pension lobby. Confident of Walther Stampfli's support, federal civil servants reiterated the disadvantages of options that would permit existing plans to latch onto AHV money flows without facing strict controls. In the definitive report on the recognition issue, the Federal Social Insurance Office explained that these solutions would deplete the AHV reserve fund, since payroll contributions would remain with private firms instead of being immediately transferred to the federal scheme. The fact that AHV monies might be lost as a result of pension plan bankruptcies was also seen as an unacceptable prospect. Partial recognition solutions would bind social insurance to the uncertain fate of private firms. Not without irony, the Office pointed out that if insurers marketed their actuarial expertise to the owners of small pension plans bewildered by the technical complexities of these solutions, Marchand's proposal would almost inevitably mean an intrusion of the state into the workings of private plans.[129] In order to comply with Stampfli's strict timetable, civil servants firmly held their positions. Holders of occupational plans could freely choose to be fully integrated into the AHV or not, but the Federal Social Insurance Office was not going to allow private firms to tinker with the core functioning of the AHV.

The AHV commission rejected Marchand's proposal in November 1945 and then finally ditched it for good in March 1946. This unequivocal dismissal angered employers' federations and left insurers fuming against the close alliance forged by federal civil servants and trade union representatives.[130] Once again, the mix of executive power and war-economy

[129] Federal Social Insurance Office, "Die Stellung der bestehenden und neue entstehenden Versicherungseinrichtungen im Rahmen der eidgenössischen AHV", February 20, 1946, pp. 59–65, file 921.111/5, SLA.

[130] Expertenkommission der Spitzenverbände, November 1, 1945 and April 2, 1946, respectively in files 95.4, and 95.5, AfZ-SHIV.

technocracy tilted the balance in Walther Stampfli's favor. Employers were also realizing that pressing for the integration of private plans into the AHV could backfire and lead, as mathematician Ernst Kaiser pointed out, to a more probing supervision of occupational plans. Combined with the intransigence of the Federal Social Insurance Office, this threat enhanced the attractiveness of the non-recognition option that had been previously dismissed as insufficient. As the outlines of the AHV were now clearer and it became obvious that federal pensions would remain modest, employers were less preoccupied with the potential crowding-out of occupational plans by social insurance.

In the spring of 1946, life insurers declared that, given the current gridlock, their group divisions would certainly choose the non-recognition option. For the Vorort and the Arbeitgeberverband, the SVPP's position constituted a major litmus test. The leadership of the pension lobby still backed Marchand's proposal, but decided to consult its membership before taking a final position on this issue.[131] In June 1946, this internal poll revealed that only one-fifth of respondents were in favor of the solution put forward by the Rentenanstalt executive, while two-thirds found it inadequate. An overwhelming majority of members declared they would pick non-recognition.[132] For SVPP members, ensuring the autonomy of private provision took precedence over attempts to infiltrate the inner workings of the AHV. Leading corporate plans thus gave the final blow to Marchand's proposal. After acknowledging the survey results, insurers immediately switched gears and campaigned resolutely to avoid, in the words of a Vita (Zurich Life) pamphlet, "[any] amalgamation of private and governmental insurance interests and in particular any state control and intrusion into private social welfare".[133] During the fine-tuning of the AHV law, employers and insurers also took steps to reduce the attractiveness of the recognition option, so that trade unions could not claim federal subsidies to shore up, in Otto Steinmann's words, the "rotten pension plans" of the public sector.[134]

131 Memorandum [from Hans Herold?] to Heinrich Homberger, May 24, 1946, file 95.4, AfZ-SHIV. Dr. J. Wandeler (Rentenanstalt), note on the February 26, 1946 meeting of the SVPP extended committee, file 921.111/6, SLA.

132 Minutes of the June 18, 1946 general assembly of the SVPP, file 95.5, AfZ-SHIV. For an acknowledgment of the results, see also Vorort Vorstand, June 24, 1946, p. 9, file 1.5.3.13, AfZ-SHIV.

133 "Die projektierte staatliche Alters- und Hinterlassenenversicherung und ihr Verhältnis zur privaten Personalversicherung", Zurich-Vita, November 1946, p. 7, file 921.111/6, SLA.

134 For the discussions on the articles of the 1946 AHV law concerning recognition, see Spezialkommission für die Berücksichtigung der Versicherungseinrichtungen in der AHV (1947), file E3340 (B)-/1/55, SBA. For Steinmann's declaration, see Expertenkommission der Spitzenverbände, April 2, 1946, file 95.5, AfZ-SHIV.

The concept of the supplementation of the AHV by occupational provision was beginning to take a more definite shape. Two years before, in 1944, insurers had already argued that a "modest" state pension could well bolster the development of private insurance:

> We do not believe that the introduction of old age insurance will be detrimental to [insurance] companies. On the contrary, if companies act shrewdly, state insurance will serve as a propaganda device for them, as it will give to the whole nation a feel for insurance. Knowing that they will receive a modest pension, people will be keen to supplement it by contracting a supplementary insurance that companies will develop especially for this purpose.[135]

Insurers had repeatedly claimed that state pensions would form a "mere supplement" to existing private plans. Supplementation was now outlined in clearer, and more realistic, terms: the AHV would form the basis upon which insurers and employers would build occupational provision. The group division of Rentenanstalt warned that a failure of the AHV could have negative consequences for group contracts: in the absence of federal social insurance, the haphazard growth of cantonal means-tested assistance measures or insurance programs might overshadow occupational provision. In contrast, universal basic pensions were considered less of a threat to group plans.[136]

Walther Stampfli and his team had not given in to insurers' demands. On the other hand, they had offered guarantees that existing pension plans would not be endangered by the implementation of the AHV. Speaking in June 1946 before an assembly of corporate pension managers, Ernst Kaiser strived to placate them by claiming that the AHV, as a "modest basic insurance", left "considerable elbow room" for pension plans. He also guaranteed that such plans would be able to "make their choice in complete freedom" and that "no state administration [would] force them to choose recognition".[137] As during the interwar years, the delineation of boundaries between the AHV and existing pension plans had caused many qualms among business circles. The outcome of these debates avoided an entangling of federal pensions and occupational schemes, and preserved the latter's autonomy. The fact that the SVPP did not object to the options outlined by the Federal Social Insurance Office decisively insulated the AHV from a dangerous business backlash during the final run-up to the July 1947 vote.

135 C. A. Dubois, "L'assurance et l'Etat", *Schweizerische Versicherungszeitschrift* (1944), pp. 193–202, 201.

136 "Jahresbericht Kollektivversicherungen", Rentenanstalt, 1945, file 671.21/1, SLA.

137 Ernst Kaiser, "Die Bedeutung der geplanten AHV für die Pensionskassen und Gruppenversicherung", June 1946, pp. 14, 24, file E3340 (B) 1985/102/245, SBA.

## Federal pensions clear the referendum hurdle

If employers and insurers had found themselves on the defensive during the tug-of-war on the recognition issue, the left and trade unions had even less leverage on decision-making. Both the AHV commission and the Federal Assembly struck down Socialist proposals to finance pensions either through special contributions levied on wealthy individuals or the proceeds of an inheritance tax. The Socialist Party preference for higher pension benefits that adequately covered living conditions had no chance of overcoming the early consensus reached on basic pensions. The Socialists were also unable to guarantee trade union involvement in the administration of the regional and sectoral equalization funds that would oversee payroll contributions and pension benefits. Despite the Socialists' claim that the joint management of these institutions reinforced labor peace, the final pension bill left no room for systematic trade union involvement in equalization funds. Finally, attempts to integrate existing pension plans into the AHV were defeated by the employers' massive support for non-recognition.[138] All in all, the Socialist Party and the Gewerkschaftsbund were firmly integrated into Walther Stampfli's cross-class alliance in favor of federal pensions, but their proposals to shore up social insurance remained unsuccessful.

The entanglement of key industrial unions, and in particular the Metalworkers' Union, in occupational provision compounded the shortcomings of the left. Since the late 1930s, this union had been estranged from both the Gewerkschaftsbund and the Socialist Party, and was conspicuous for its lack of support for the *Gesichertes Alter* initiative. This stand-alone attitude was linked to the metalworkers' preference for both union-based and occupational provision. In 1941, the old age provision schemes of the Metalworkers' Union covered 75,000 workers. However, most of these belonged to its old age relief scheme (Fürsorgekasse), while only a minority was affiliated to its pension plan (Alterskasse).[139] While neglecting social insurance, which was seen as undermining trade union control of industrial relations, the Metalworkers' Union favored joint welfare schemes, pulling the union into an ever-tighter embrace with

[138] Marco Ferrari, *Rechtliche Stellung und faktische Bedeutung der Verbände in der Alters- und Hinterlassenen-Versicherung* (Zurich: Aku-Fotodruck, 1976), pp. 190–202; Maria Meli, "Le Parti socialiste suisse face au projet de loi et à la loi AVS", mémoire de licence de la section d'histoire, Université de Lausanne, 1974, pp. 40–60. By 1948, there were two federal, twenty-four cantonal, and eighty-two local and/or industry-wide AHV equalization funds.

[139] *Pensionskassenstatistik 1941*, p. 304; Ernst Wütrich, "Die Sozialversicherungen des Schweizerischen Metall- und Uhrenarbeiterverbandes", *Schweizerische Zeitschrift für Sozialversicherung* (1963), pp. 215–28.

corporate welfare schemes, where it exercised little leverage. To use an expression coined by Marie Gottschalk to describe similar tendencies among American labor organizations, the "institutional straitjacket" of collective bargaining and occupational schemes narrowed the metalworkers' options vis-à-vis social insurance.[140]

After the second renewal of the Peace Agreement in November 1944, collective bargaining began to spread to other manufacturing sectors and contributed to stabilizing labor relations.[141] The following spring, the Metalworkers' Union and the Swiss Federation of Machine Manufacturers and Metal Producers (Arbeitgeberverband schweizerischer Maschinen- und Metall-Industrieller, ASM) met several times to set up a joint pension scheme. Despite keen interest among the union leadership, it was obvious that the two social partners envisioned different roles for this project. For the ASM, the scheme was not meant to replace existing employers' plans, but to offer basic provision to metalworkers. In the event of a rejection of the AHV, the joint pension plan would offer a fallback position. The ASM also suggested that the metalworkers' leader, Konrad Ilg, should publicly express his support for occupational provision.[142]

Several Metalworkers' Union shop stewards cautiously pointed out that the ASM had made only vague and insufficient promises. For them, the Metalworkers' Union's disdain for the AHV gave the unwelcome impression that the union only defended its "federation interests" instead of those of the "whole working class". The metalworkers were thus in danger of being lambasted as "saboteurs" of the AHV, notably by re-emerging Communist groups. Despite these dissenting voices, the leadership kept a tight grip on its cadres. In June 1945, only sixteen members of the federation conference voted in favor of a motion pleading for immediate action by the union in favor of the AHV and for solidarity with the whole working class, and urging the abandonment of negotiations with the ASM. The leadership's motion, which only "welcomed" the idea of

[140] Marie Gottschalk, *The shadow welfare state: labor, business, and the politics of health-care in the United States* (Ithaca: ILR Press, 2000), p. 2.

[141] More than 600 collective bargaining agreements, most of them covering single firms or of local scope, were signed between 1944 and 1947. See Brassel and Schiavi, "Kämpfend in den Arbeitsfrieden", p. 63.

[142] See "Caisse paritaire professionnelle pour une assurance vieillesse dans l'industrie suisse des machines et métaux: projet de statuts", March 19, 1945; Erweiterter Zentralvorstand. Verbands-Industriekommission, Besprechungen mit Herrn H. A. Dolde (ASM), May 17, 1945, both in file SMUV 01B-001, Sozialarchiv. For the preliminary discussions on this issue, see Arbeitgeberverband geschäftsleitende Ausschuss, January 8, 1943, pp. 53–6, SAV.

the AHV, while at the same time emphasizing the need to develop jointly managed pension plans, garnered 154 votes.[143]

Although union leaders considered state insurance "much less dangerous for our old age plan than corporate plans", both the AHV and employers' pension plans were seen as competing against union-based schemes that played a key role in unionizing efforts. For Konrad Ilg, the future of joint occupational schemes depended above all on maintaining labor peace and good "contractual relations" with the ASM. Indeed, "if a combative stance emerges later in the industry, our plan will disappear into thin air".[144]

Despite the Metalworkers' Union's continuing goodwill toward employers, their hope to establish a joint pension plan was soon dashed. In October 1945, barely one month after Konrad Ilg had delivered a speech in the Federal Assembly urging the Federal Council to encourage cooperation between employers and trade unions in the fields of collective bargaining and employee benefits, the ASM abruptly pulled out of discussions about the industry-wide pension scheme. According to employers, the decision of the Federal Council to introduce, in January 1946, provisional old age assistance benefits made this solution obsolete.[145]

The abandonment of the project by the ASM underscored the ambiguities of the social partnership revered by the leadership of the Metalworkers' Union. When employers withdrew from the negotiations, they could simply fall back on their own pension plans. The constraints of the labor peace straitjacket left fewer options for the union. Despite Konrad Ilg's complaints that the AHV was being "built on workers' backs" and that trade unions had almost no say in its development, alternatives to the now defunct joint pension plan were disappointing.[146] Because of its publicly proclaimed attachment to labor peace, the Metalworkers' Union leadership depended in the end on employers' goodwill to implement joint management.

When the union realized in the summer of 1946 that AHV equalization funds dominated by employers' associations would not welcome union participation, and that union-based plans, which were closer to savings plans than genuine retirement plans, would be barred from recognition, Ilg's stance on the AHV sometimes verged on outright hostility.

143 Verbands-Konferenz, June 15, 1945, morning session, pp. 7–10; and afternoon session, pp. 2–5, file SMUV 01B-001, Sozialarchiv.

144 Erweiterter Zentralvorstand, August 30, 1945, pp. 3, 6, file SMUV 01B-001, Sozialarchiv.

145 Memorandum to the members of the Industrie-Kommission, October 22, 1945, file SMUV 01B-001, Sozialarchiv.

146 Industrie-Kommission, November 8, 1945, file SMUV 01B-001, Sozialarchiv.

Fuming that "the ring of social insurance is closing itself at the federal level and deprives the trade union of its influence", Ilg argued that "old age insurance [would] lead to very unfavorable outcomes", and that "the conclusion resulting from all this should be the rejection of the proposed scheme by the [Metalworkers'] Union".[147]

Konrad Ilg was well aware that publicly attacking the AHV would be political suicide. "Even if the law does not fulfill our wishes", Ilg conceded that the metalworkers could "not refuse the law and must support it when it faces the popular vote".[148] Besides this lukewarm support for social insurance, the metalworkers' leadership spent its energy trying, in Ilg's terms, to "rescue what could still be rescued", which basically meant scrambling to develop union-based benefits "before insurers dislodge us from this field".[149] While trying to bypass federal pensions, the union – in contrast to employers – had shunned the AHV debate and remained obsessed with the standing of its own supplementary benefits. Unfortunately, the potential for the expansion of union-based provision was limited. The union not only faced the competition of well-entrenched corporate schemes, but also the reluctance of its own rank and file to increase their contributions to the union plan, as they already had to pay into employers' plans and, soon, the AHV. All in all, the Metalworkers' Union maintained its utilitarian approach toward union-based welfare. If employers used pension plans to retain skilled workers, the union used it to lure members into its ranks.[150]

The metalworkers' hostility to the AHV was, among labor organizations, quite extreme. Public-sector unions, whose members were overwhelmingly covered by occupational plans, supported social insurance, and their leader, Robert Bratschi, actively participated in the AHV commission. In the building trade, where occupational plans were nonexistent, trade union secretary Max Weber considered the introduction of the AHV the "most pressing social policy task" of the labor movement.[151] Yet, the metalworkers' neglect of social insurance and their attachment to employment-based benefits strengthened the division of labor between basic pensions and supplementary occupational provision favored by the Federal Council and business circles. Despite many disappointments and frustrations, the Socialist Party and the Gewerkschaftsbund barely

147 Erweiterter Zentralvorstand, July 20, 1946, p. 4, file SMUV 01B-001, Sozialarchiv.
148 Erweiterter Zentralvorstand, August 31, 1946, p. 2, file SMUV 01B-001, Sozialarchiv.
149 Erweiterter Zentralvorstand, November 15, 1946, p. 1; Erweiterter Zentralvorstand, February 7, 1947, p. 2, file SMUV 01B-001, Sozialarchiv.
150 Erweiterter Zentralvorstand, August 31, 1945 and November 31, 1945, file SMUV 01B-001, Sozialarchiv.
151 Minutes of the central committee of the Gewerkschaftsbund, May 16, 1941, quoted in Hohl, *Die wirtschaftspolitischen Vorstellungen von Max Weber*, p. 319. See also Siegenthaler, *Die Politik der Gewerkschaften*, pp. 57–62.

challenged the concept of a basic AHV and towed the line drawn by Walther Stampfli. Since the 1918 general strike, the left had always, almost ritually, waved the flag of social insurance. Now that the project had finally neared completion, progressive forces were reduced to playing second fiddle in the orchestra conducted by Walther Stampfli.

Existing pension plans had been at the center of business preoccupations between 1944 and mid-1946. Although employers resented the strong-arm tactics of the Federal Social Insurance Office, the issue seemed settled and would not constitute a fatal stumbling-block for the AHV. During the last months preceding the AHV vote, the issue of the financing of social insurance was much more contentious. At the end of World War II, the dismantling of the war economy apparatus, the reimbursement of the wartime debts incurred by the Confederation, and the future of the new fiscal revenues introduced in the early 1940s had coalesced into a large debate on federal finances and fiscal policy.[152] At stake for employers in 1946 was not the general financial structure of the federal scheme, on which a wide consensus had been reached in 1944, but rather the interactions between the share of the pension financing originating from the federal budget, which had been set at around one-quarter of AHV needs, and the postwar debate on the financial and fiscal policy of the Confederation.

Following in Walther Stampfli's footsteps, Ernst Nobs, the Socialist who headed the Finance Department, spared no efforts to avoid a conjunction of social insurance and the reform of federal finances that might jeopardize the AHV. This close collaboration between the Economic and the Finance Departments contrasted with the situation that had prevailed during the interwar years, when fiscal conservatives bolstered by Jean-Marie Musy's anti-AHV maneuvers had contributed to delaying, watering down, and finally defeating the Lex Schulthess. Nobs and Stampfli devised a system in which state contributions to the pension scheme relied exclusively on proceeds from the taxes on tobacco and alcohol, as well as a large transfer from the EO reserve fund. The two Federal Councilors also resisted attempts to delay the implementation of pensions until the recovery of federal finances, and left no opportunity for proposals to finance the AHV through federal inheritance or wealth taxes. They adamantly refused to give way to demands to fix once and for all the share of AHV finances assumed by the Confederation and cantons beyond the 1968 horizon.[153]

[152] Tanner, *Bundeshaushalt, Währung und Kriegswirtschaft*, pp. 213–20.
[153] Binswanger, *Histoire de l'AVS*, pp. 79–82, 86–92, 98–100, 106–9; Sommer, *Das Ringen um die soziale Sicherheit*, pp. 220–7.

The whittling-down of the Socialists' financing proposals did not lead to major controversies. When the 1946 congress of the Gewerkschaftsbund reiterated demands for higher benefits, the introduction of a federal inheritance tax, and the integration of existing occupational plans into the federal AHV, Robert Bratschi acknowledged that the pension bill did not fulfill "all hopes, expectations, and desires", but emphasized that it took into account "the financial and economic situation, and also the political balance of power in our country".[154] Bratschi's realism was echoed by Valentin Gitermann. The author of the motion asking for better regulation of private plans noted with resignation in August 1946 that "in the current situation, it is not in our power to implement the AHV on the basis of a socialist planned economy". "For this reason", continued this rather non-conformist Socialist, "there is no sense in making extensive demands that might indeed be appropriate, but that could not be fulfilled under reigning capitalist financial conditions."[155] In autumn 1946, at the opening of the last parliamentary debates on social insurance, National Councilor Paul Graber declared before the Federal Assembly that Socialists would defend the AHV "with all [their] strength", because it constituted an "absolute political and social necessity" and because they "dreaded the consequences of its failure".[156] Socialist heavyweights maintained firm party discipline to defend the pension bill designed under Walther Stampfli's guidance. The integration of the Socialists into the governing coalition and the threat of a conservative referendum against the AHV left little room for dissent. In December, the left voted unanimously in favor of the official pension bill.

Stampfli's strong-arm tactics provoked resentment among business circles. The last debates on the financing of the AHV took place during a period marked by the return of rosier economic prospects. After the uncertainties of 1945, Swiss firms that had been unscathed by the war launched themselves on the market for European reconstruction, while banks offered new credits to governments liberated from Nazi rule.[157] In the context of this redeployment of Swiss capitalism into foreign markets, employers increasingly balked at the costs of social insurance. For the Vorort, the use of EO reserves to finance the AHV, while reducing the need for new taxes, proved that politicians tried to "circumvent

[154] Minutes of the 1946 congress of the Gewerkschaftsbund, quoted in Siegenthaler, *Die Politik der Gewerkschaften*, p. 58.

[155] *Die Volksstimme*, August 28, 1946, quoted in Meli, "Le Parti socialiste suisse face au projet de loi et à la loi AVS", p. 54.

[156] National Council Minutes, August 21, 1946, 488, quoted in ibid., p. 53.

[157] Dominique Dirlewanger, Sébastien Guex, and Gian Franco Pordenone, *La politique commerciale de la Suisse 1945–1966* (Zurich: Chronos, 2004), pp. 55ff.

financial difficulties . . . instead of solving them".[158] Similar criticisms could be heard in the Untergruppe Altersversicherung, where insurer Ernst Röthlisberger denounced the "politicization of the economy" that might occur under the influence of the AHV reserve fund. The general assembly of the Swiss Chamber of Commerce lambasted the AHV as an example of "financial adventurism". For employers, new social policy expenditures were incompatible with weak public finances, threatened price stability, and undermined the strength of the Swiss franc, which reigned supreme with the dollar in postwar international financial transactions.[159] "Instead of building a solid house for the AHV", scornfully summarized Hans Herold, "the Federal Council and Parliament have built a shack. They have put the greatest emphasis on a short construction period and on the avoidance of legal problems that could obstruct their path. The viability of this shack is limited. Its foundations are weak."[160]

The SVPP agreed that the issue of AHV finances could potentially undermine private provision, as future increases in the level of taxation might prevent employers from developing their own pension plans:

> The existence of private pension plans depends in large part on employers' willingness and capacity to contribute to these plans, and this capacity varies according to the economic situation, and, especially, the level of taxation. As public authorities can only finance their share of the AHV through fiscal means, a latent danger hovers over the post-1967 period, because [pension financing] will then depend on the current political situation. One can even imagine a new era of over-taxation during which fiscal authorities will overwhelm the private economy.[161]

Despite these hostile assessments, employers did not challenge the cross-class alliance forged by Walther Stampfli. Having supported the AHV from the beginning, albeit at times grudgingly, it was extremely difficult for them to go into reverse gear. As Werner Ammann of the Pro Senectute charity pointed out to fellow members of the Untergruppe Altersversicherung, "it is assuredly easier to 'shoot down' social insurance than to help it to clear the last hurdles". However, continued Ammann, turning down federal pensions would be both politically and financially unwise, as "in the event of its failure . . . the path of assistance will have to be followed". In the end, Ammann argued that "this piece of

[158] Vorort Vorstand, October 28, 1946, p. 3, file 1.5.3.13, AfZ-SHIV. See also Arbeitgeberverband Vorstand, November 12, 1946, pp. 105–6, SAV.

[159] See Untergruppe Altersversicherung, Sitzungsprotokoll, November 19, 1946, file 5.3.2.4, AfZ-RN, as well as "Die Schweiz: Handelskammer zur Altersversicherung und zur Budgetlage des Bundes" [n.d, ca. December 1946], file 95.5, AfZ-SHIV.

[160] Hans Herold, "Zur Finanzierung der AHV", memorandum, January 6, 1947, p. 19, file 95.5, AfZ-SHIV.

[161] *Rapport sur l'exercice 1946* (Zurich: SVPP, 1947), p. 4, file V Schweiz 2435, SNB.

legislation represents an honorable effort to find a Swiss solution. Financial qualms should not constitute a decisive factor, otherwise we will soon be confronted with an inflation of demands in this domain."[162]

Despite their misgivings, business circles were conscious that explicit opposition to the AHV was fraught with risks during a period when ruling elites were trying to ensure a favorable postwar settlement on both the international and home fronts. The defusing of tense relationships with the Allies through a combination of diplomatic agreements (the Washington Agreement on gold transactions with Nazi Germany) and goodwill actions in favor of devastated European countries (the Schweizer Spende, or Swiss Donation) accompanied the reorientation of Swiss firms on the international scene. On the home front, at a time when labor disputes briefly peaked at a level unseen since the early 1920s, the success of the AHV increasingly represented the embodiment of political stabilization and social peace.[163]

Walther Stampfli emphasized these interrelated dimensions at the February 1947 opening meeting of the official campaign committee in favor of federal pensions. In the event of a rejection of the AHV, the Radical strongman thundered that "Switzerland's reputation in foreign countries would be severely damaged because of such a lack of readiness for solidarity", and that "in Switzerland itself, a 'Black Sixth of July' would undermine popular confidence in democratic institutions".[164] Diehard opponents of the AHV were nevertheless determined to launch a referendum against the law, which had been overwhelmingly accepted by the Federal Assembly in December 1946. Although business federations were loath to appear to be opposing the AHV, they did not rein in the anti-AHV forces in their ranks. When asked in November by banker Albert Pictet if the option of a referendum would be welcomed, the president of the Vorort, Hans Sulzer, who had described the AHV one year earlier as a "preliminary stage toward dictatorship", had nodded affirmatively.[165]

Employers kept all options open. Potential opposition from farmers and trade sectors had been subdued by Stampfli's shaping of the Economic Articles, providing generous subsidies for agricultural activities, and reduced AHV payroll contribution rates for the self-employed. The task of launching the referendum was assigned to the most reactionary

[162] Untergruppe Altersversicherung, Sitzungsprotokoll, November 19, 1946, p. 2, file 5.3.2.4, AfZ-RN.

[163] Jost, *Politik und Wirtschaft im Krieg*, pp. 303–21.

[164] Walther Stampfli's speech at the "Pro-AHV Committee", February 27, 1947, quoted in Hafner, *Bundesrat Walther Stampfli*, p. 417.

[165] Vorort Vorstand, November 22, 1946, p. 10, file 1.5.3.13, AfZ-SHIV.

wing of the Vorort. Albert Pictet and Caspar Jenny, a prominent and conservative textile entrepreneur, dutifully played their roles as the usual anti-statist suspects, which enabled the Vorort to keep a safe distance from the referendum campaign. Similarly, if perpetual opponents of social insurance – mainly firebrand Catholics and federalist Liberal-Conservatives from western Switzerland – publicly headed the referendum campaign, financial and manufacturing interests, as well as such groups as the Redressement National, remained discreetly on the sidelines.[166] Insurers and the pension lobby were careful not to appear to be backing the referendum or to publicize their internal dissension over the AHV issue. The Union of Life Insurance Companies thus refused to speak out either in favor or against the referendum. The SVPP did not back the anti-AHV campaign, but criticized those who denounced the referendum organizers. Signing the referendum, the association disingenuously argued, could not be equated with rejecting the AHV, but allowed citizens to give their opinion on a major public undertaking.[167]

The final stance of the business federations toward the referendum – presented to the Federal Chancellery with 55,000 validated signatures in April 1947 – was put forward a few weeks before the decisive July vote. During the spring, the Vorort and the Arbeitgeberverband agreed that the situation was so sensitive that no efforts should be spared to avoid discordant public statements and, despite Albert Pictet and Caspar Jenny's insistent demands, refused to allow the propaganda arm of the business federations, the staunchly free-market Wirtschaftsförderung, to give full organizational and financial backing to the referendum campaign.[168]

Despite strong opposition to federal pensions, dissension was not aired publicly, as had been the case during the debates on the Lex Forrer. Moreover, and contrary to the uncertainty that had prevailed in 1931, the Vorort was confident that consulting its affiliates or organizing a special general assembly devoted to the AHV would not end up in chaotic discussions. Since the 1930s, the internal discipline of the Federation of Trade and Industry had been reinforced by statute revisions that limited the autonomy of its affiliates in their political contacts. All grievances or demands had to be approved by the Vorort before being passed on to political or administrative authorities. The dominance of the Vorort over

[166] On the referendum committee, see Binswanger, *Histoire de l'AVS*, p. 112. On Caspar Jenny, Albert Pictet, and conservative networks, see Werner, *Für Wirtschaft und Vaterland*.

[167] Konferenz der Direktoren der VSLG, December 20, 1946, file Q127 206, ZFS. See also *SVPP Zirkularmitteilungen*, no. 26, February 2, 1947.

[168] Vorort Vorstand, March 14, 1947, 9ff, file 1.5.3.13, AfZ-SHIV; Arbeitgeberverband, March 25, 1947, pp. 8–9, SAV.

its affiliates was also reinforced by its close collaboration with the federal administration during World War II and the centralizing effects of the EO equalization funds on sectoral and regional employers' associations.[169]

In a report summarizing business positions on the AHV referendum a few weeks before the vote, Vorort director Heinrich Homberger emphasized that indecision reigned among employers' associations and local Chambers of Commerce. With the exception of the metal and machine-making sector, where leading firms with well-developed corporate schemes had backed social insurance proposals since the beginning of the century, and Walther Stampfli's political fiefdom of Solothurn, few employers' associations openly backed the AHV.[170] Resistance was particularly high among eastern Switzerland and Basle textile manufacturers, who had traditionally opposed social insurance since the first vote on sickness and accident insurance. However, the textile sector had been in continuous economic decline for decades, and its influence in the Vorort was clearly waning in comparison with the metal and machine-making sector, the new powerhouse of Switzerland's export-based economy. Anti-AHV positions were also strong where banking and financial interests were well represented (Zurich and Geneva) and in Caspar Jenny's regional powerbase of Glarus.

Significantly, many manufacturing sectors and regional employers' associations signaled that they had not reached a suitable consensus on the AHV. Strong contingents criticized the financing of the AHV, but insisted that neither the Vorort nor the Arbeitgeberverband could find themselves at odds with the main bourgeois parties, which had all closed ranks behind the Federal Council. However strong their misgivings about social insurance might be, Vorort affiliates urged their representatives to avoid any public denunciation of the AHV and indicated that they would strictly follow the Vorort stance on this issue. Reporting on the position of life insurers, Heinrich Homberger stated that they "desire[d] particularly to remain above the political debate and to avoid finding themselves exposed to the danger of being considered fundamental opponents of the AHV, either because of a quarrel over the shortcomings of the law, or because of a misinterpretation of the current situation". Employers, summarized Homberger, "could not afford to be suspected of being fundamentally opposed to the idea of social insurance".[171]

169 On the 1935 statute revision of the Vorort, see Wehrli, *Le Vorort*, pp. 74–5. On the role of EO equalization funds, see Attinger, *Les caisses de compensation militaires*, pp. 138–43.

170 "Rundschreiben vom 8. April 1947 betreffend AHV" [n.d., ca. April 1947], file 95.8, AfZ-SHIV. See also Arbeitgeberverband geschäftsleitende Ausschuss, May 29, 1947, pp. 8–11, SAV.

171 Vorort Vorstand, May 28, 1947, pp. 3, 12, file 1.5.3.13, AfZ-SHIV.

The strongman of the Vorort claimed that "refusing the proposal might easily lead us toward further incursions in the free economic order". For these reasons, "outright support for the law is out of the question, but rejecting it would also not correspond to the current situation". Following the concerns of its affiliates, the Vorort had to opt for "a dispassionate confrontation of the pro and cons". Even if "the material aspects of the law (financing, integration of existing welfare institutions) called for a scathing judgment, a disavowal might open the road to a considerably worse law, after all, and the current proposal could be described as a viable foundation for the future".[172]

Unsurprisingly, this assessment was not appreciated by the referendum organizers. Albert Pictet and Caspar Jenny both fulminated that employers should not cave in before "leftist pressure" and denounced the "genuine moral terror" that characterized the campaign in favor of the AHV. A strong majority of the Vorort board brushed aside these arguments by reminding its members that employers did not have a plausible alternative to counter Walther Stampfli's project. Once again, the Vorort refused to let the Wirtschaftsförderung join the anti-AHV referendum.[173] The final public declaration of the business federations underlined that the pension bill had both "positive points" and "weaknesses", but stressed that "the great idea of the AHV [had] to be realized".[174] The fact that the Vorort and the Arbeitgeberverband kept themselves at a safe distance from the referendum and tried to rein in the Wirtschaftsförderung greatly undermined the potency of the anti-AHV campaign. At a time when business federations were highly disciplined and had powerful propaganda outfits at their disposal, a resolute opposition might have meant serious problems for social insurance. This restraint underscored Walther Stampfli's success in shaping an ironclad cross-class alliance in favor of pensions.

Stampfli spared no efforts to ensure the passage of the AHV. In addition to the official "Pro-AHV Committee" and a union-based propaganda committee, the Federal Social Insurance Office set up its own information department. Leaflets, conferences, and various appeals to vote in favor of federal pensions inundated all cantons. The union committee even shot a short documentary promoting social insurance, *Let's begin bravely* (*Lasst uns tapfer beginnen*), that was shown to packed audiences before the vote.[175] The restraint orchestrated by the Socialist and

172 Ibid., p. 12. 173 Ibid., pp. 13–15.

174 "Wirtschaftliche Spitzenverbände und Altersversicherung", *Neue Zürcher Zeitung*, June 20, 1947.

175 Binswanger, *Histoire de l'AVS*, pp. 113–14; Hafner, *Bundesrat Walther Stampfli*, pp. 416–17. For a sample of the propaganda campaign on the AHV, see "Pressedienst Pro AHV (1947)", file 95.8, AfZ-SHIV.

Gewerkschaftsbund leadership during the parliamentary debates contrasted with the full-blown mobilization of the rank and file to ensure the success of social insurance. Progressive forces, which had played a secondary role in shaping the project and whose proposals for improving the AHV had been repeatedly rejected, compensated for this by plunging into the feverish atmosphere that characterized the run-up to the vote. Trade union secretaries' insistence that industrial conflicts should not hinder the passage of the AHV played a role in curtailing the strikes that flared up in the building trade and textile industry in the aftermath of World War II.[176]

In this context, where the AHV crystallized high expectations for social reform, the opponents of social insurance faced a steep uphill struggle. The final report of the Zurich referendum secretariat emphasized the difficulties faced by the anti-AHV campaign. Volunteers collecting signatures against federal pensions had been beaten up by leftist youths in Geneva, and, with the exception of Liberal-Conservative newspapers, the press often refused to publish articles, or even paid advertisements, opposing federal pensions. The referendum committee had difficulties finding printing shops to produce and distribute its campaign material. The two secretariats based in Geneva and Zurich had received no fewer than 3,000 hostile letters pouring out abuse at the opponents of the AHV. Finally, the committee's finances had been a constant problem: the referendum had only CHF 200,000 at its disposal, or around one-fifth of the sum spent by the political machines campaigning in favor of the AHV.[177]

As in 1931, opponents of social insurance had launched an initiative proposing individual retirement savings accounts as an alternative to the AHV. However, signature-gathering for the proposal was disappointing. In a damning article, the influential *Neue Zürcher Zeitung* denounced this "baffling initiative" and warned its readers that such individual retirement accounts would undermine banking secrecy and constitute unwelcome competition in financial markets.[178]

176 Siegenthaler, *Die Politik der Gewerkschaften*, pp. 61–2.

177 Eduard Seiler, "Eidg. Aktionskomitee gegen das Gesetz über die Altersversicherung, Schlussbericht über die Referendums und Abstimmungskampagne" [n.d., ca. fall 1947], file 5.3.5.13, AfZ-RN. See also Jean F. Martin, "Rapport sur la campagne contre le projet fédéral d'AVS (Suisse romande)" [n.d., ca. fall 1947], file 5.3.5.3, AfZ-RN. The largest contributor to the referendum was the Geneva private bank Hentsch & Cie, which disbursed CHF 40,000 for the anti-AHV campaign. For documents on the finances of the referendum committee, see file 5.3.5.9, AfZ-RN.

178 "Eine neue Verwirrungsinitiative", *Neue Zürcher Zeitung*, July 1, 1947. For documents on the People's Initiative for an AHV of free Confederates (*Volksinitiative für eine AHV freier Eidgenossen*), see file 5.3.5.10/I + II, AfZ-RN.

With opponents of social insurance facing mounting odds, the AHV steamrollered its way toward a clear-cut victory. In May 1947, the Socialist initiative on *Economic Reform and Labor Rights*, nearly abandoned by its proponents and denounced by the right as Soviet-inspired, was rejected by two-thirds of voters. Despite this affront, the left and labor federations remained welded to the cross-class alliance shaped by Walther Stampfli and had to content themselves with the promises of the AHV and federal encouragement of collective bargaining. Generous agricultural subsidies and protective measures for domestic-oriented sectors further subdued potential anti-AHV opposition. By organizing a simultaneous vote on the AHV and the revised Economic Articles, the second cornerstone of his social and economic framework for postwar Switzerland, the iron Federal Councilor prodded farmers and the Gewerbeverband into line.[179]

On July 6, the final verdict was beyond appeal: with a turn-out of 80 percent, the AHV was accepted by four-fifths of voters, while the more controversial Economic Articles benefitted from the tidal wave in favor of social insurance and just scraped through with 50 percent of yes votes. A few months after this historic vote, Walther Stampfli stepped down from the Federal Council. Nominated to the board of directors of several leading corporations, Stampfli took the helm of the Von Roll foundries to lead them into the challenges of the first postwar decade. The "economic general" of World War II had accomplished his mission. The prominent executive-turned-statesman could return to where he truly belonged, namely "on the side of capital".[180]

## The postwar social policy settlement

Even though Switzerland escaped the upheaval and destruction of the two world wars that ravaged its neighbors in the first half of the twentieth century, the impact of war is unmistakable in the trajectory of Swiss social policy development. In contrast to the social and political polarization that followed World War I, epitomized by the 1918 general strike, the World War II shaping of a universal pension system represented a milestone of solidarity and a major extension of social rights. Yet, this achievement constituted an ambivalent watershed for the Swiss welfare state.

[179] "Konferenz über den eidg. Abstimmungskalender 1947", January 29, 1947 file 95.8, AfZ-SHIV. For vote results, see Ritzmann-Blickenstorfer and Siegenthaler, eds., *Swiss Historical Statistics*, Table X10.

[180] Hafner, *Bundesrat Walther Stampfli*, pp. 425–39 (quotation p. 36). For vote results, see Ritzmann-Blickenstorfer and Siegenthaler, eds., *Swiss Historical Statistics*, Table X10.

After decades of protracted debates and missed opportunities, the introduction of the AHV represented a genuine quantum leap. Thanks to astute negotiations, a damaging collision with existing pension plans had been avoided. However, by permitting occupational schemes to thrive alongside a federal scheme, the project put forward by the Federal Council entrenched a divided and bifurcated pension system. The lightning-fast implementation of the AHV also served as a preventive strike against social policy alternatives and as a dam against further postwar reforms. These outcomes resulted from a war context that temporarily removed key institutional hurdles to social insurance, decisively easing the passage of the AHV. Besides its contribution to the stabilization of industrial relations and workforce management, the EO, forerunner of the AHV, also confirmed that social insurance was not antithetical, but beneficial, to the development of occupational provision.

Business federations occupied a privileged position in the war economy apparatus, which reinforced their leverage. Yet, this close integration also increased business acquiescence toward social insurance at the very time when free-market doctrines and resistance to social policy could have jeopardized the whole project. As both an architect of federal pensions and a proponent of corporate social benefits, Federal Councilor Walther Stampfli embodied this business pragmatism.

World War II ended the foundation era of the welfare state. The introduction of the AHV transformed the role of federalism and direct democracy in social policy development. With the enactment of the AHV, the issue of pensions was firmly anchored at the national level, which left less space for federalist opposition. The choice of a self-supporting, pay-as-you-go financing structure similarly insulated social insurance from the fiscal conservative opposition that had previously been leveraged by federalist forces. Old age provision debates would now focus on the division of labor between the AHV and occupational schemes. The role of direct democracy was also transformed. Referendum politics, which had been crucial during the debates on sickness and accident insurance (KUVG) and successive attempts to implement the AHV, were replaced by the use of direct democracy, and in particular initiatives, to prod the Federal Council into action. The *Gesichertes Alter* and *Für die Familie* initiatives launched in 1941 signaled this new development, which will be analyzed at length in the next chapter.

The fact that the implementation of the AHV was not followed by the introduction of further social policy programs constitutes a crucial dimension of the limited breakthrough made by social insurance in the aftermath of World War II. Switzerland's situation in the immediate postwar period differed markedly from its neighbors'. First, the country did not experience political instability or major upheavals. On the contrary, stability was the key word: from the 1930s to the end of the 1950s, the balance of power remained unchanged in the Federal Assembly, and the integration of the Socialists into the executive branch did not alter bourgeois dominance. As the war economy apparatus and emergency powers were dismantled, the direct executive route followed by the EO and the AHV could not be replicated.

Second, Switzerland did not face pressing social and economic reconstruction, unlike many of its wartorn neighbors. In such countries as Germany or France, the overhaul of interwar welfare measures was a top priority for early postwar governments. Blueprints for reform and state intervention in the economy were abundantly discussed and fueled the postwar expansion of welfare states. The evolution of German and French pre-war pension systems toward universalism had followed a bumpy road.[181] However, in these countries, funded occupational schemes had been battered by the Depression, inflation, war, and currency instability. In France, occupational pensions abandoned funding and adopted pay-as-you-go mechanisms to become national supplementary pensions, closely integrated to the *Sécurité Sociale* and jointly managed by employers and trade unions. In postwar Germany, large firms continued to build up pension reserves for self-financing purposes, yet occupational plans played a minor role in postwar retirement incomes in comparison with the extension of universal pensions.[182] In contrast, Swiss occupational schemes that had escaped this thanks to the shield of neutrality, the stability of the Swiss franc, and the strength of the financial establishment emerged reinforced by the war. Moreover, the outcome of the recognition debate and the limited reach of trade unions in pension management meant that private welfare could develop alongside the AHV, unhindered by joint management procedures.

In the Netherlands, as in Switzerland, the development of social insurance was limited before World War II, and decentralized forms of provision had been the norm. However, the Low Countries had been invaded during the war, and reform ideas were influenced by contacts with Allied social policy plans. The aftermath of the occupation witnessed a flurry of projects to overhaul welfare measures. Despite resistance from religious conservative forces, the postwar decade saw the gradual

[181] Peter Baldwin, *The politics of social solidarity: class bases of the European welfare state 1875–1975* (Cambridge: Cambridge University Press, 1990), pp. 163–200.

[182] Emmanuel Reynaud, "France: a national and contractual second tier", in *Enterprise and the welfare state*, ed. Martin Rein and Eskil Wadensjö (Cheltenham: Edward Elgar, 1997), pp. 65–98 (pp. 69–72); Winfried Schmähl, "The public–private mix in pension provision in Germany", in ibid., pp. 99–148 (p. 137).

implementation of encompassing social welfare programs inspired by the Beveridge Report. World War II transformed the pace of development of the Dutch welfare state and made it jump into the vanguard of European welfare expansion (see Figure 0.1, p. 6).[183] Occupational old age provision remained strong in the Netherlands. However, the industry-wide plans that dominated pension coverage had no equivalent in Switzerland.

I have already mentioned the ambivalent impact of the Beveridge Report. The social and political impact of war was greater in both the United Kingdom and the Low Countries than in Switzerland or the United States. In the first two countries, further-reaching universal welfare measures figured on the postwar political agenda, which allowed social policy to catch up, as in the Netherlands, or the ground-breaking introduction of programs such as the National Health Service. Postwar social policy remained more limited in the United States and Switzerland, two countries that had experienced a smoother transition from war to peace, which facilitated the preservation of previous equilibria. The Swiss welfare state, and in particular its pension system, continued to follow a trajectory that echoed the bifurcated or divided system of social provision prevalent in the United States. At the end of the 1940s, basic pensions based on a pay-as-you-go structure constituted the cornerstone of both welfare states. Social Security remained an isolated social insurance scheme, while corporate pension plans experienced steady growth.

In the United States, the expansion of coverage and the rise of benefits that followed the 1949 Social Security Amendment rescued federal pensions from the postwar conservative resurgence. However, fiscal conservatism and opposition to the growth of the Social Security reserve fund influenced these revisions. During the 1950s, incremental improvements to federal pensions were not only considered a politically advantageous way to respond to popular demands for higher benefits, but also a means to rein in the accumulation of funds controlled by the federal state. The pay-as-you-go system "re-energized social insurance", but, as it was not backed up by further state subsidies to Social Security, it also "imposed long-term restrictions on advocates of expansion". There were few financial margins for new social insurance programs, and existing ones remained limited.[184] I have argued that Swiss business circles were

[183] Robert Henry Cox, *The development of the Dutch welfare state: from workers' insurance to universal entitlement* (Pittsburgh: University of Pittsburgh Press, 1993), pp. 67, 77, 96–127.

[184] John Myles, "Postwar capitalism and the extension of Social Security into a retirement wage", in *The politics of social policy in the United States*, ed. Margaret Weir, *et al.*

keen to choose a pay-as-you-go system to avoid both the rise of general taxation and state-based funding of social insurance. In the next chapter, we will see that the Swiss federal scheme experienced incremental growth between 1948 and 1958; but these improvements were in part due to conservative attacks on the swelling of AHV reserves.

In contrast to the slow and incremental postwar improvement of Social Security pensions, corporate benefit schemes blossomed. Confronted by an unfavorable political context for the expansion of social insurance, trade unions turned to collective bargaining to improve pensions at the company level, assuming that campaigning for corporate benefits might eventually prod employers into supporting Social Security increases. This strategy brought mixed results. Spurred on by economic growth, collective bargaining enabled unions to win new occupational benefits. However, this strategy entrenched a bifurcated system of provision that provided advantages to skilled male workers in large firms, but bypassed workers with lower qualifications, part-time employees, women, and African-Americans.[185] Employers soon learned how to get the most out of what Jennifer Klein describes as the "welfare state subsidization of welfare capitalism". Basic federal pensions were explicitly used as a floor for company plans. By deducting from company pensions the amount provided by Social Security, employers adapted their corporate plans to take advantage of public benefits. By the means of this "dovetailing" strategy, employers transformed every Social Security increase into a corresponding drop in corporate benefits.[186]

For sociologist Jill Quadagno, business motives for developing pensions were extensive:

> Corporations had numerous positive incentives to increase their pension fund, including creating large tax-free investment pools, maintaining a more flexible labor force by retiring older workers, and keeping the unions satisfied with contract negotiations. But independent negotiations for private pensions reduced whatever incentive they might have to support Social Security benefit increases. With labor's energies deflected and business uninterested, the next decade saw

(Princeton: Princeton University Press, 1988), pp. 265–84; Julian E. Zelizer, *Taxing America: Wilbur D. Mills, Congress and the state, 1945–1975* (Cambridge: Cambridge University Press, 1998), pp. 61–78 (quotation p. 81).

185 Jacob S. Hacker, *The divided welfare state: the battle over public and private social benefits in the United States* (Cambridge: Cambridge University Press, 2002), pp. 126–42; Jill S. Quadagno, *The transformation of old age security: class and politics in the American welfare state* (Chicago: Chicago University Press, 1988), pp. 153–77; Sass, *The promise of private pensions*, pp. 113–44. On trade unions, see Michael K. Brown, "Bargaining for social rights: unions and the reemergence of welfare capitalism, 1945–1952", *Political Science Quarterly* 112/4 (1997–1998), pp. 645–74.

186 Klein, *For all these rights*, p. 245.

only minor changes in public Old Age and Survivors' Insurance. These developments in the private sector impeded the expansion of the public welfare state.[187]

The next chapter will discuss how this enumeration corresponds to the factors that presided over the postwar development of the Swiss pension system, where basic pensions left ample room for voluntary occupational schemes bolstered by fiscal incentives and decentralized collective bargaining.

The American public–private pension mix was described in 1950 by Wilbur Cohen, an administrator of the Social Security Board, as a "three-layer cake" composed of federal, occupational, and individual provision: "The first layer being minimum subsistence; the second layer providing a more adequate standard supplemental to minimum subsistence; and the third 'luxury' layer being primarily a function of what the individual can do for himself".[188] In a 1949 speech, Reinhard Hohaus of Metropolitan Life also popularized the term "three-legged stool" to describe the multi-tier pension arrangement that prevailed in the United States. His reversal of the order of old age provision underscored a preference for private individual and collective provision that was characteristic of an outspoken defender of the business of social policy:

> The first in order of time is individual insurance . . . the second, a variety of employee benefit plans of which Group insurance is an outstanding American contribution; and the third, social security – designed by the government for the well-being of our fellow citizens . . . Each has its own function to perform and need not, and should not, be competitive with the others. When soundly conceived, each class of insurance can perform its role better because of the other two classes. Properly integrated, they may be looked upon as a three-legged stool affording solid and well-rounded protection for the citizen.[189]

In Switzerland, this layered or multi-tiered structure of old age provision was described as a three-pillar system, whose principle was anchored in 1972 in the federal constitution. The next chapter covers the quarter-century that followed the acceptance of the AHV and the making of this distinctive pension architecture.

[187] Quadagno, *The transformation of old age security*, p. 171.
[188] Quoted in Klein, *For all these rights*, p. 235.
[189] Larry De Witt, "Origins of the three-legged stool metaphor for Social Security", research note, Social Security Online, May 1996, available at http://www.ssa.gov/history/stool.html (October 2007).

# 4 The three-pillar doctrine and the containment of social insurance (1948–1972)

On December 3, 1972, Swiss citizens cast a decisive vote to transform the system of old age provision that had been in place since the end of World War II. The two proposals to be voted on reflected diametrically opposed projects for the future of the AHV. On one side, an initiative sponsored by the Labor Party (Partei der Arbeit, the former Communist Party) outlined an ambitious expansion of social insurance: the people's pensions (Volkspensionen). This proposal was countered by a plan designed by the Federal Council that aimed to anchor in the federal constitution the so-called three-pillar doctrine. According to this doctrine, pensioners' incomes would be ensured by a combination of universal basic AHV pensions (first pillar), supplemented by compulsory occupational pensions (second pillar), and topped up by voluntary and fiscally encouraged individual savings accounts (third pillar). This counter-proposal combined two other pending initiatives. The first, launched by the Socialists, was a more modest version of the people's pensions that demanded a better integration of the AHV and occupational schemes. The second one, launched by bourgeois politicians, insurers, and pension lobbyists, was designed as a bulwark against people's pensions and reaffirmed the three-pillar doctrine that had been developed by business circles since the early 1960s.

According to a report circulated among employers' federations in the summer of 1969, both left-wing initiatives implied an "economic and socio-political transformation" of the pension system and represented the "most important socialist challenge the bourgeoisie has confronted in decades".[1] As explained in 1971 by the Vorort, such conceptions of social insurance "went too far" and "even [overtook] what Sweden, the most extreme country in this field, envisions doing".[2] The SVPP pension lobby was more strident in its rejection of the people's pensions. According to

[1] Studienkommission Altersvorsorge, "Die AHV Initiativen der PdA und der SP", August 12, 1969, p. 15, file 95.34, AfZ-SHIV.
[2] Vorort Vorstand, November 29, 1971, p. 28, file 1.5.3.20–22, AfZ-SHIV.

this mouthpiece of leading corporate plans, the Labor (i.e. Communist) proposal envisioned "state control over existing pension plans" and was a "plundering maneuver against savings and the private sector", while the milder Socialist version would lead to the "asset-stripping" of private pension plans.[3] The influential *Neue Zürcher Zeitung* emphatically warned that the vote on the Labor proposal would "probably constitute the most fundamental social policy decision since 1948".[4]

The Labor Party initiative was heavily defeated at the polls. In June 1972, the Federal Assembly overwhelmingly backed the three-pillar concept: all governmental parties (Socialists, Radicals, Catholics, and the People's Party)[5] rejected the Communist initiative. The popular vote followed a similarly clear-cut pattern. On December 3, only 17 percent of the electorate supported the people's pensions, while the Federal Council proposal was accepted by a large majority of voters (77 percent). With the inscription of the three-pillar doctrine in the federal constitution, the pension system was locked into a framework shaped by business circles and, in particular, by insurance companies. The defeat of the people's pensions sounded the death-knell of the first and only attempt to radically transform the pension system during the second half of the twentieth century. This containment of social insurance still casts its shadow on early-twenty-first-century old age provision.

This chapter is devoted to the dynamics that led to the fierce social policy struggles that marked the end of the long postwar wave of economic growth. The politics of social insurance expansion was different from that of its early years analyzed in the preceding chapters. With the AHV now firmly entrenched at the national level, pension debates were characterized less by referendum politics and their stalling maneuvers than by the use of initiatives – no fewer than eight of them were launched between 1958 and 1970 – to prod the executive branch into improving or modifying the structure of the AHV. In contrast, the development of occupational provision had strong continuity. Factors such as tax exemptions for pension plans and decentralized collective bargaining fueled the postwar boom of the future second pillar. The quarter-century that led up to the 1972 vote also witnessed the growing financial role of funded pension assets.

The first two sections of this chapter analyze the expansion of federal pensions and occupational schemes in the decade that followed the 1947 vote. While the growth of social insurance was kept in check,

[3] *Geschäftsbericht 1969* (Zurich: SVPP, 1970), pp. 9–10, file V Schweiz 2435, SNB.

[4] C. M., "Auf dem Weg zu einer Reform der AHV", *Neue Zürcher Zeitung*, April 19, 1970.

[5] The Schweizerische Volkspartei was the 1971 successor to the Farmers', Artisans', and Burghers' Party founded in the aftermath of World War I.

occupational schemes, buttressed by social partnership and economic expansion, grew at an unprecedented pace. During this period, employers fiercely defended the autonomy of corporate schemes against state regulation. The third section explains why business circles found themselves on the defensive as the momentum for expanding social insurance accelerated at the end of the 1950s. At that point, life insurers took the lead in defining a global strategy to contain social insurance and ensure the long-term development of private benefits. These debates among employers resulted in the formulation of the three-pillar doctrine. The fourth and fifth sections delve into the controversy between the people's pensions and the three-pillar doctrine, or in other words the choice between an overhaul of pay-as-you-go social insurance or the reaffirmation of funded occupational provision.

The issues at the heart of this chapter, the supplementation of basic pensions by earnings-related schemes financed through a pay-as-you-go system or funding, preoccupied not only Switzerland but other countries too. Throughout this chapter, and especially in the final section, the "Swiss solution" is compared with pension debates that took place during the postwar decades of growth among industrialized countries. These comparisons show the distinctiveness of the Swiss pension trajectory leading to a mandatory second pillar.

## Patrolling the boundaries of the welfare state (1948–1959)

In the aftermath of World War II, employers' federations had approved financing pensions with payroll contributions supplemented by a modest reserve fund. This system reduced the share that needed to be raised through fiscal means (see Figure 4.1). As the postwar economy displayed stronger than expected growth, the monies collected through payroll contributions rapidly overtook the most optimistic estimates made in 1946 (see Table 4.1). The efficiency of the pay-as-you-go system and the meagerness of pension benefits paid to the first generation of pensioners (in 1948, average AHV pensions amounted to 7 percent of a white-collar worker's monthly wage) contributed to the swelling of the AHV reserve fund.[6] As shown below, this "excessive financing" of the AHV alarmed business circles that had always been opposed to the accumulation of monies by the state and defended private-based pension funding, echoing critics in the United States following the implementation there of Social Security.

[6] Peter Binswanger, *Histoire de l'AVS: Assurance-vieillesse et survivants suisse* (Zurich: Pro Senectute, 1987), pp. 154–6; Max Hunziker, *Der Ausgleichsfonds der schweizerischen Alters- und Hinterlassenenversicherung* (Zurich: Juris-Verlag, 1963), pp. 56–65, 113ff. For 1948 pension levels, see Nicolas Eschmann, "Damals vor 50 Jahren . . .", *Soziale Sicherheit* 6 (1997), pp. 310–13.

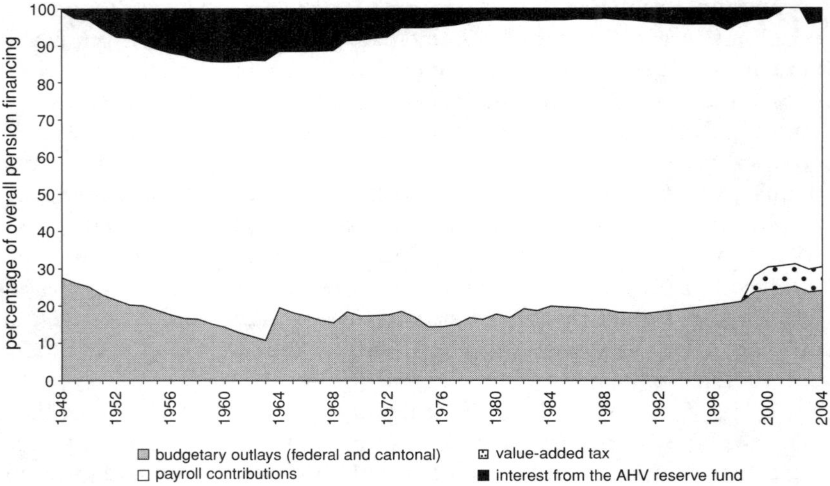


Figure 4.1 Share of payroll contributions, state outlays, and reserves in AHV financing, 1948–2004.
*Sources:* Heiner Ritzmann-Blickenstorfer and Hansjörg Siegenthaler, eds. *Historisch Statistik der Schweiz – Statistique historique de la Suisse – Swiss Historical Statistics* (Zürich: Chronos, 1996), Table P6; *Statistique des assurances sociales suisses 2005* (Berne: Office fédéral des assurances sociales, 2006), p. 93.

From the late 1930s onward, fiscal conservatives and insurers in the United States had denounced the danger of "socialized investment" through social security reserves. As in Switzerland a decade later, these controversies played a significant role in winning business approval for incremental improvements in Social Security benefits and coverage, as such measures contributed to deflating federal pension reserves.[7] In Switzerland, the business backlash against the AHV reserve fund surfaced at a time when bourgeois parties and business circles were resisting attempts to introduce more state intervention in the economy. By disentangling this complex knot of issues, this section highlights crucial features of Swiss social policy in the postwar period: incrementalism, organizational and financial fragmentation, as well as its reliance on pay-as-you-go.

[7] On the January 1937 resolution signed by Republican Senator Arthur Vandenberg and sixty life insurance directors, see Jill S. Quadagno, *The transformation of old age security: class and politics in the American welfare state* (Chicago/London: Chicago University Press, 1988), p. 120. On Social Security finances, see also Martha Derthick, *Policymaking for social security* (Washington: Brookings Institution, 1979), pp. 232–7; Julian E. Zelizer, *Taxing America: Wilbur D. Mills, Congress and the state, 1945–1975* (Cambridge: Cambridge University Press, 1998), pp. 61ff.

Table 4.1 *Payroll contributions, pension benefits, and the AHV reserve fund, 1948–1958.*

| | 1948 | | 1953 | | 1958 | |
|---|---|---|---|---|---|---|
| | in millions of CHF | in comparison with highest estimates (1946) | | | | |
| **payroll contributions** | **418** | +14 percent | **570** | +48 percent | **682** | +71 percent |
| **reserve fund** | **456** | +17 percent | **2886** | +48 percent | **4556** | +21 percent |
| **AHV expenses (pensions)** | **127** | −7 percent | **267** | +19 percent | **665** | +96 percent |

*Source:* "L'équilibre financier de l'AVS", June 7, 1947, report of the Federal Social Insurance Office, quoted by Peter Binswanger, *Histoire de l'AVS: Assurance-vieillesse et survivants suisse* (Zurich: Pro Senectute, 1987), p. 167.

The postwar reform of federal finances and the consolidation of fiscal revenues were the flagship project of the two Socialist Federal Councilors who served successively at the Finance Department between 1943 and 1954 (Ernst Nobs from 1943 to 1951 and, from 1951 to 1954, former trade unionist Max Weber). By the end of the 1950s, the bourgeois majority had seriously undermined Socialist financial reforms, and battles over the shape of public finances were intimately linked to AHV controversies. Opposition to state pension funding and increased taxation were two of the ways business sought to limit the sources of revenue available to the AHV, the cornerstone of the nascent welfare state. If the interactions between financial and social policy constituted the first backdrop to pension debates and controversies concerning the AHV reserve fund, the downfall or success of postwar social programs clearly paralleled the evolution of the AHV.

The rejection of the 1949 federal law on the prevention of tuberculosis, which was opposed by conservative forces and doctors' associations, led to the abandonment of tentative plans to introduce compulsory health insurance. Maternity coverage and family allowances made little headway after their 1945 constitutional acceptance: the latter was unevenly implemented at the cantonal level, while federal maternity benefit remained a hollow promise until its introduction in 2004. Projects for federal unemployment insurance were also rapidly shelved. The subsiding of existing unemployment schemes by the Confederation remained in place until the 1970s.[8] Yet, two social policy programs closely interacted with the AHV: the 1959 introduction of disability insurance, and the 1950s overhaul of insurance schemes compensating income loss during military duties (the EO). I untangle this complex knot of issues in the following paragraphs by focusing at first on controversies surrounding the AHV reserve fund.

During the fall 1949 general assembly of the SVPP, Peter Vieli, a prominent executive of Crédit Suisse, accused the AHV reserve fund of crowding out private investors, exerting a downward pressure on interest rates, and taking dangerous steps toward "socialization by stealth".[9] The weight

[8] On the failed postwar attempt to revise health insurance, see Jens Alber and Brigitte Bernardi-Schenkluhn, *Westeuropäische Gesundheitssysteme im Vergleich: Bundesrepublik Deutschland, Schweiz, Frankreich, Italien, Grossbritannien* (Frankfurt: Campus Verlag, 1992), p. 187; Ellen M. Immergut, *Health politics: interests and institutions in western Europe* (Cambridge: Cambridge University Press, 1992), pp. 158–63. On unemployment insurance, see Manfred G. Schmidt, *Der schweizerische Weg zur Vollbeschäftigung: eine Bilanz der Beschäftigung, der Arbeitslosigkeit und der Arbeitsmarktpolitik* (Frankfurt am Main: Campus Verlag, 1985).

[9] Peter Vieli, *La politique de placement du fonds de compensation de l'assurance vieillesse et survivants et ses répercussions sur le marché des capitaux* (Zurich: SVPP, 1949).

Table 4.2 *Different categories of savings, 1938–1969.*

| | social insurance funds (1) | AHV reserve fund | public- and private-sector pension funds | household savings | state, public- and private-sector firms | total |
|---|---|---|---|---|---|---|
| **1938** | 2.4 | . . . | 23.6 | 4.1 | 69.9 | 100 |
| **1948** | 3.5 | 21.9 | 20.6 | −7.4 | 61.4 | 100 |
| **1955** | 3.1 | 11.3 | 17.6 | 13.8 | 54.1 | 100 |
| **1960** | 3.1 | 6.8 | 19.5 | 15.6 | 55.1 | 100 |
| **1965** | 3.0 | 2.3 | 21.3 | 33.3 | 40.1 | 100 |
| **1969** | 3.2 | 1.4 | 20.9 | 28.8 | 47.1 | 100 |

(1) income compensations scheme for military service (EO), disability insurance, federal accident insurance (SUVA), as well as cantonal social security funds, public and regional health and unemployment schemes
*Source*: *Le Mois: Société de Banques Suisses*, May 1971, p. 119.

of the AHV reserve fund was far from marginal, as its share of total savings surpassed those of pension plan assets in 1948 (see Table 4.2). Switzerland was an island of political and financial stability during the troubled postwar period, and its already considerable capital accumulation was bolstered by a large influx of foreign monies. Although capital exports grew as economic opportunities reappeared in Europe, financial circles feared bottlenecks in domestic investment outlets. In this context, the sudden emergence of the AHV reserve fund in the market for long-term domestic assets was considered highly unwelcome.[10] Its size meant that pension plans and insurance companies might be, in the words of the SVPP, "directly hit by the contraction of the investment market", while the Swiss Bankers' Association feared that the federal fund would snatch from private banks large chunks of the long-term public bond market.[11]

In early 1950, business federations and conservative circles discussed several strategies to lower AHV reserves. Claiming that "reducing the

[10] Christian Gasser and Werner Meyer, *Der schweizerische Kapitalmarkt* (St. Gallen: Veröffentlichungen des Versicherungswirtschaftlichen Seminars and den Handels Hochschulen St. Gallen, 1952), pp. 86–7, 92–8, 308–18; Hunziker, *Der Ausgleichsfonds der schweizerischen AHV*, pp. 72–80.

[11] For the position of the SVPP, see *SVPP Jahresbericht 1949* (Zurich: SVPP, 1950), file V Schweiz 2435, SNB. For a business assessment of the AHV reserve fund, see the Rentenanstalt report on this issue, October 28, 1949, file 95.15, AfZ-SHIV, Studienausschuss Altersversicherung (former Untergruppe Altersversicherung), Sitzungsprotokoll October 11, 1949, file 5.3.2.4, AfZ-RN; see also Schweizerischer Bankiervereinigung (SBV) Verwaltungsrat, September 2, 1949, pp. 6–7 SBV Archiv (Zurich). Thanks to Olivier Longchamp (University of Lausanne) for providing me with this document.

accumulation of capital [by the state] is one of the core tasks of the private sector", the Redressement National launched a propaganda campaign against the reserve fund.[12] While the Vorort proposed to use a share of AHV reserves and contributions to finance the postwar renewal of the EO, the Federation of Small Employers and Trades (Gewerbeverband) lobbied to lower the AHV contributions paid by the self-employed. More outspoken critics of social insurance, such as Zurich Life executive Ernst Röthlisberger, suggested deflating the fund by either lowering overall payroll contributions or reducing the share of budgetary outlays earmarked for the AHV.[13] Yet, as Otto Steinmann of the Arbeitgeberverband underlined, transferring AHV monies to other social insurance programs or tinkering with the financial structure of the federal pension scheme would entail contentious legislative modifications.[14] Business federation solutions for the "excessive financing" of the AHV diverged, and the controversy continued unabated. In 1952, a federal commission of experts set up to survey the impact of the AHV reserve fund on financial markets emphasized that modest state funding helped avoid an increase in payroll contributions or an extension of the share covered by general state revenues, two options that were strongly rejected by employers' federations.[15] The same year, Paul Jaberg of the Schweizerische Bankgesellschaft nevertheless pointed out that "[s]uch concentrations [of capital] not only contradict our traditional decentralized state organization, but they are also extremely dangerous for the future economic development of our country".[16]

The intensity of the polemics against the AHV reserve fund decreased with the economic boom that followed the outbreak of the Korean War in 1950: the ensuing development of long-term investment outlets in hydroelectric infrastructure, highways, and railroads, dissipated investment bottlenecks and reassured financial circles. The crowding-out of private investment also appeared less problematic, as the share of AHV reserves in overall savings dropped from 22 to 7 percent between 1948 and 1960 (see Table 4.2). Business then focused more on the growth of pension assets, which reached one-third of gross domestic product in 1955 (see Table A.7, p. 303). As early as 1951, the Swiss National Bank, financial institutions, and leading pension plans signed gentlemen's

[12] Studienausschuss Altersversicherung, February 24, 1950, p. 2, file 5.3.2.4, AfZ-RN. See also Eduard Seiler, *Der Ausgleichsfonds der Altersversicherung* (Geneva: Radar, 1950).
[13] Vorort Vorstand December 8, 1949, file 1.5.3.13, AfZ-SHIV; Studienausschuss Altersversicherung, February 24, 1950, file 5.3.2.4, AfZ-RN.
[14] Otto Steinmann, *Ist die AHV überfinanziert?* (Zurich: SVPP, 1950).
[15] Binswanger, *Histoire de l'AVS*, pp. 150ff.
[16] Paul Jaberg, "Probleme der AHV", October 13, 1952, p. 11, file 95.15, AfZ-SHIV.

agreements to monitor inflation in the real-estate market, an area that was quickly becoming a preferred investment outlet for pension assets.[17] Free-marketers and conservative groups nevertheless continued to attack state-based funding during the 1950s.[18]

At that time, employers were less concerned about AHV reserves *per se* than about the general extension of social insurance, which included not only the first four revisions of the AHV but also the peacetime renewal of the EO (1952, revised in 1958) and the introduction of disability benefits (1959).

As soon as the first pensions had been paid, numerous parliamentary motions asked the Federal Council to alleviate the situation of the elderly poor, especially the first group of pensioners, who received meager transitory benefits, because they had contributed to the AHV for only limited number of years (or none at all for those who were 65 or older in 1947). The first three revisions to the federal pension program, implemented in 1951, 1954, and 1956, focused on improving these token pensions, which contributed in no small part to slowing the growth of the AHV reserve fund (see Table 4.1 above). On the revenue side, the first AHV revisions also reduced payroll contribution levels for the self-employed, a measure that satisfied the middle-class professional and trade constituencies of the Gewerbeverband.[19]

Soon social insurance gained momentum that could be neither stopped nor easily slowed down. Textile entrepreneur Caspar Jenny, a leading

[17] By 1953, 190 pension plans had signed the gentlemen's agreement. See *Rapport sur l'exercice 1951* (Zurich: 1952) and *Rapport sur l'exercice 1953* (Zurich: SVPP, 1954), file V Schweiz 2435, SNB.

[18] After 1952, the Association for the Protection of the Middle Class, Savers, and Pensioners (Vereinigung zum Schutze des Mittelstandes, der Sparer und Rentner), which campaigned in favor of AHV benefit increases instead of a bloated "State Bank", continued to criticize the AHV reserve fund. This association merged in 1954 with the like-minded Association for the Defense of Swiss Savings and Investment (Vereinigung zum Schutze des schweizerischen Spar- und Anlagekapitals), an outfit that had received financial support from insurers at its foundation. See Konferenz der Direktoren der VSLG March 5, 1943, p. 13, file Q127 206, ZFS. See also Hans Graf, Georg Renner, and Rudolf Johanni, *Bestand AHV-Ausgleichsfonds: rund 3.5 Milliarden Schweizer Franken! Noch mehr Millionen für den AHV-Fonds... und für mich? Eine Streitschrift zur eidgenössischen Altersversicherung* (Zurich/Berne, 1955); Walter Bräm and Rudolf Johanni, "Auf dem Wege zur eidg. Staatsbank", press release, January 8, 1952, file 3340 (B) 1985/102/268, SBA.

[19] Binswanger, *Histoire de l'AVS*, pp. 138–62; Jürg Sommer, *Das Ringen um die soziale Sicherheit in der Schweiz: eine politisch-ökonomische Analyse der Ursprünge, Entwicklungen und Perspektiven sozialer Sicherung im Widerstreit zwischen Gruppeninteressen und volkswirtschaftlicher Tragbarkeit* (Diessenhofen: Rüegger Verlag, 1978), pp. 287–90. On the Gewerbeverband campaign, see Alfred Gutersohn, *Das Gewerbe in der schweizerischen Wirtschaftspolitik: der schweizerische Gewerbeverband 1879–1954* (Zurich: Schweizerische Gewerbeverband, 1955), pp. 307–9.

figure of the 1947 anti-AHV referendum, bemoaned in 1952 that the ongoing controversy about the AHV reserve fund proved that social insurance would from now on become "a continual point of contention".[20] The fact that the minimum pension benefits were raised much faster than the maximum ones alarmed business federations. The diminishing ratio between the minimum and maximum AHV pension – the latter was three times the minimum pension in 1948, a ratio that had dropped to 2:1 by the mid-1950s – was considered a dangerous "leveling tendency". According to the Arbeitgeberverband, the benefits scale made the AHV less attractive to the middle-classes and pushed pensions in the direction of flat-rate benefits, such as those introduced in postwar Sweden and in the United Kingdom.[21]

Business attempts to more drastically reduce the influx of monies flowing into federal pensions or stop the leveling of AHV benefits encountered steep hurdles because of the controversies surrounding the reform of federal finances. Bourgeois parties challenged all of the Socialist attempts to expand the fiscal revenues of the Confederation, leading Federal Councilor Max Weber to abruptly walk out of the executive branch in December 1953 after right-wing forces torpedoed his financial reform proposals in a popular vote.[22] However, the contentiousness of budgetary and fiscal struggles made business unwilling to inflame the political arena further with aggressive cutbacks of AHV payroll contributions or proposals to cap federal subsidies to the pension scheme.[23]

During a 1956 meeting of the Vorort, Hans Herold, the business federation secretary in charge of social policy, pointed out that unrelenting pension increases and demands to index them to the cost of living were, in the end, adverse to the fundamental conception of the AHV as a minimum basic pension. Herold's counterpart in the Arbeitgeberverband, Leonhard Derron, added that if employers had been caught off guard by the unexpected postwar rise of AHV reserves, they should now avoid losing control of the situation. Arguments in favor of launching a referendum against the 4th AHV revision, with additional annual costs (around CHF 150 million) greater than the combined costs of the previous three

20 Vorort Vorstand, September 29, 1952, p. 12, file 1.5.3.14, AfZ-SHIV.

21 Arbeitgeberverband geschäftsleitende Ausschuss, October 14, 1952, p. 4, SAV.

22 Olivier Longchamp, "La réforme des finances fédérales suisses après la Deuxième Guerre mondiale (1945–1958)", paper presented at the Groupe de recherche économie et sciences sociales, Université de Lausanne, December 16, 2004; Jakob Tanner, *Bundeshaushalt, Währung und Kriegswirtschaft: eine finanzsoziologische Analyse der Schweiz zwischen 1938 und 1953* (Zurich: Limmat Verlag, 1986), pp. 213–28.

23 See "Sitzung der Spitzenverbände über die Frage des Finanzsystems der AHV", January 19, 1955, as well as Arbeitgeberverband to Finance Department, February 28, 1955, file 95.22, AfZ-SHIV.

AHV revisions, were not lacking. However, given the immense popularity of federal pensions, a referendum campaign "had almost no chance of succeeding".[24] While condemning the growing "politicization" of the AHV debate and the "socialization" of national wealth brought about by higher taxes and social insurance contributions, employers' federations did not oppose the 4th AHV revision accepted in December 1956 by the Federal Assembly.[25] This non-confrontational approach seemed sensible, as the burning issue of AHV costs and finances found itself ever more closely connected to the organization of income compensation for militia soldiers (EO) and disability insurance. This complex triangle of issues occupied the center stage of business attempts to patrol the boundaries of the welfare state.

As mentioned in the preceding chapter, the 1940 pay-as-you-go income compensation scheme for military service was both an organizational and financial forerunner of the AHV. In 1946, a one-time transfer of EO reserves to the AHV had jumpstarted federal pensions, avoiding a tax increase. A large political consensus existed as to the necessity of a renewal of the EO alongside the massive postwar armaments programs introduced in the wake of the Korean War.[26] EO payroll contributions had been interrupted in 1947 to make way for AHV levies, but the scheme had only dwindling reserves at its disposal to compensate for peacetime military duties, and its long-term financing remained controversial.

Keen to decrease the AHV reserve fund to avoid new payroll contributions, business federations had first lobbied politicians to transfer a share of AHV reserves to the EO. However, this option was successfully challenged by the left, which denounced this maneuver as a plundering of federal pensions and proposed instead to cover EO costs through ordinary military expenditure. Business federations and bourgeois parties were adamant in their refusal to finance militia soldiers' benefits through fiscal revenues and retreated to the option of payroll contributions.[27] This seemed the best alternative as the issue of disability benefits, which was absent from wartime social policy debates, became more pressing.

[24] Vorort Vorstand, August 27, 1956, pp. 4–7, file 1.5.3.15, AfZ-SHIV. See also Arbeitgeberverband Geschäftsführerkonferenz, April 25, pp. 4–9; and May 8, 1956, p. 8, SAV.

[25] Leonhard Derron, "Nivellierungstendenzen bei der AHV: zum vierten AHV-Revision", *Schweizerische Arbeitgeber Zeitung*, August 24, 1956; Hans Herold, "Die Alters- und Hinterlassenenversicherung am Scheideweg: ein Diskussionsbeitrag zur vierten Revision", *Neue Zürcher Zeitung*, August 31 (1st part) and September 1 (2nd part), 1956.

[26] On the postwar EO, see Sommer, *Das Ringen um die soziale Sicherheit*, pp. 260–6.

[27] On EO financing controversies, see Arbeitgeberverband geschäftsleitende Ausschuss, January 25, 1951, pp. 3–4, Arbeitgeberverband Vorstand, October 25, 1955, p. 8 and November 13, 1957, p. 7, SAV.

If postwar demands for the expansion of the AHV and the renewal of the EO were channeled through the Federal Assembly, disability benefits followed the path of direct democracy. Following the launch in 1954 of competing initiatives by the Socialists and the Communists that demanded the rapid implementation of disability insurance, the Federal Social Insurance Office and the Federal Council drafted an insurance law that emphasized the rehabilitation of disabled persons and their reintegration into the workforce. This law was implemented in 1959.[28] Beside the complexity of coordinating disability benefits with existing accident insurance and AHV pensions, their financing once again agitated business sectors.

Possible solutions included financing disability insurance through a new beverage tax, an option briefly favored by the Vorort, or by a share of existing AHV payroll contributions, a "splitting" option put forward by the Swiss Bankers' Association. Tax-based solutions, a crucial issue in the context of the reform of the federal finances, posed potential problems for fiscal conservatives.[29] Moreover, according to Arbeitgeberverband secretary Leonhard Derron, "combining the financing means of various social programs encourage[d] the emergence of a unified *sécurité sociale* [sic] system that may lead to blurring the budgets of each social program and to the use of rising state subsidies to finance them".[30] Employers' resistance to the idea of a "social pool" or the levy of a "general social security contribution à la Beveridge" corresponded to their refusal to follow the lead of more encompassing European welfare states.[31] Swiss employers resolved to shape a more loosely coordinated system of social programs.

Confronted by the challenge of delineating watertight boundaries between the AHV, disability insurance, EO benefits, and financial reform, employers' federations finally lobbied successfully for the establishment of distinct pay-as-you-go financing structures for each social insurance sector. By 1958, revenues for both the EO and disability insurance were drawn from AHV-style payroll contributions each set at 0.4 percent of wages. The choice of the pay-as-you-go system insulated social politics from attempts to raise general taxation. Reserves accumulated through disability and EO pay-as-you-go schemes were also kept apart from each

[28] On disability benefits, see Binswanger, *Histoire de l'AVS*, pp. 176–9. On the Socialist initiative, see *Protokoll über die Verhandlungen des ordentlicher Parteitages vom 12./13. Oktober 1957* (Berne: Sozialdemokratische Partei der Schweiz, 1957), pp. 143ff, file K961, Sozialarchiv.

[29] Arbeitgeberverband Vorstand, October 3, 1957, pp. 6–13, SAV.

[30] Ibid., April 2, 1958, p. 7, SAV.

[31] An expression used by Leonhard Derron, Arbeitgeberverband Geschäftsführerkonferenz, December 14, 1950, p. 5, SAV.

other and, given their small size in comparison with AHV reserves (see Table 4.2 above), did not raise major opposition. This compartmentalized financing structure, which still exists today, was compatible with general business preferences. More importantly, it ran in tandem with bourgeois parties' and employers' successful efforts to hollow out postwar Socialist financial reforms and to reduce fiscal pressure. Despite last-ditch resistance from the left, tax rates on higher revenues were capped, and the fiscal capacity of the Confederation was held in check.[32] The budgetary framework implemented in 1958 constituted a decisive step toward the consolidation of Switzerland's profile as a country with low fiscal pressure and low social expenditure.

According to historian Christine Luchsinger, the first AHV revisions and the uneven outcomes of the postwar social debates created a "patchwork" of measures that furthered "inconsistent" forms of social provision.[33] Despite business concerns about "social policy inflation", the reach of the Swiss welfare state remained limited, especially when compared with the way it developed in neighboring European countries. Contemporaries indeed acknowledged the distinctive position occupied by Switzerland's disparate and compartmentalized postwar social insurance programs.

In 1953, trade unionist Robert Bratschi, a heavyweight in the wartime AHV debate, declared in his farewell address to the Gewerkschaftsbund that Switzerland "had made important efforts since the end of World War II to maintain a leading position among nations in the social policy field". Bratschi's appreciation was not out of touch with reality, and the labor leader emphasized that a large number of decentralized occupational schemes coexisted with limited social insurance programs. Ironically, Bratschi's assessment coincided with an official declaration by the Federal Council that Switzerland could not ratify Convention 102 of the International Labour Office that defined the minimum standards of social protection. This Convention was first ratified by Sweden (1953) and the United Kingdom (1954), as well as by Norway and Denmark (both in 1955), while Switzerland finally accepted it only in 1977.[34]

[32] On the 1958 financial package, see Max Weber, *Geschichte der schweizerischen Bundesfinanzen* (Berne: Haupt, 1969), pp. 39–40.

[33] Christine Luchsinger, "Sozialstaat auf wackligen Beinen: das erste Jahrzent der AHV", in *achtung: die 50er Jahre! Annäherungen an eine widersprüchliche Zeit*, ed. Jean-Daniel Blanc and Christine Luchsinger (Zurich: Chronos, 1994), pp. 51–69 (quotation p. 59). See also Brigitte Studer, Gaby Sutter, and Regina Wecker, *Die "schutzbedürftige Frau": zur Konstruktion von Geschlecht durch Mutterschaftsversicherung, Nachtarbeitsverbot und Sonderschutzgesetzgebung* (Zurich: Chronos, 2001), pp. 138–48.

[34] *SVPP Jahresbericht 1954* (Zurich: SVPP, 1955), p. 9, file V Schweiz 2435, SNB.

From a militant, free-market perspective, economist Wilhelm Röpke, one of the standard-bearers of the postwar renovation of economic liberalism, also welcomed the distinctive features of Swiss social policy. In two lectures on the "boundaries and dangers of the welfare state" given in 1954 at the Frankfurt Chamber of Commerce and at the bicentennial anniversary of Columbia University in New York, Röpke contrasted the growth of the "excessive welfare state" taking place in western Europe with the way it evolved in Switzerland and the United States. In these countries, Röpke pointed out, a decentralized and federalist state structure, combined with the preservation of individual self-help and traditional family values, contained the "statist control over human activities" in vogue in western Europe. Röpke remarked that "the need for security and welfare" was met in Switzerland through a "colorful diversity of smaller and heterogeneous institutions that operate in a decentralized and less bureaucratic way, with a higher level of self-responsibility and spontaneity, and thus rein in the mechanized mass-assistance of a centralized welfare state".[35]

Statistical indicators confirmed this conception of a minimum welfare state "closely reined in" by private institutions. By the end of the 1950s, Swiss national-level (federal) social security expenditure as a share of gross domestic product was the lowest among western European countries.[36] A comparative study on hourly wages and social costs in eleven European countries also showed that the structure of Switzerland's overall social expenditure was unique (see Table 4.3). Payroll contributions for social insurance schemes were the lowest in the survey; however, those for voluntary, employer-based, or collectively bargained welfare measures were at the top of the sample. This distinctive public–private mix helped to maintain Swiss overall social costs slightly below the European average and thus reduce the relatively high wage levels paid by Swiss employers. The introduction of universal federal pensions, disability benefits, and EO compensation did not fundamentally transform the segmentalist labor market and welfare strategies that were created in the first half of the twentieth century. On the contrary, the division of labor between basic social insurance programs and supplementary funded pension benefits reinforced segmentalism.

[35] Wilhelm Röpke, *Grenzen und Gefahren des Wohlfahrtsstaates* (Frankfurt: Schriftenreihe der Industrie- und Handelskammer Frankfurt am Main, 1955), p. 5. See also Pierre Favre, *La Suisse est-elle socialement arriérée?* (Zurich: SVPP, 1955).

[36] See for example the data quoted by John Myles, *Old age in the welfare state: the political economy of public pensions* (Lawrence: University Press of Kansas, 1989), p. 17; Manfred G. Schmidt, *Sozialpolitik: historische Entwicklung und internationaler Vergleich* (Opladen: Leske + Budrich, 1988), p. 137.

Table 4.3 *Wage and social costs in western Europe, 1958.*

| | net wages (1) | social contributions compulsory (2) | voluntary (3) | (2) + (3) | gross wages (1) + (2) + (3) |
|---|---|---|---|---|---|
| Switzerland | **126** | **34** | **325** | **92** | **119** |
| western European (average = 100) | | | | | |
| maximum | 165 | 191 | 325 | 168 | 145 |
| minimum | 55 | 34 | 17 | 45 | 62 |

*Source:* Francesco Kneschaurek and Werner Eisenbeiss, "Die sozialen Leistungen der Arbeitgeber in verschiedenen OECE-Staaten", *Aussenwirtschaft*, no. 1–2 (1958), p. 137. Countries included in the survey: Switzerland, Denmark, United Kingdom, Sweden, Norway, Netherlands, Belgium, France, Italy, West Germany, and Austria.

Patrolling the boundaries of social insurance constituted the second facet of Swiss employers' postwar strategy focused on safeguarding the freedom of movement of the "colorful diversity" of private welfare alternatives and on using them as a bulwark against social insurance. During the 1950s, the incremental expansion of the AHV contrasted with the steady but selective growth of occupational pensions. According to the SVPP, corporate benefits allegedly enabled Swiss employers to "achieve social progress without state intervention".[37] The next section will explore the validity of this affirmation.

## Corporate benefits and postwar growth

In 1955, two-thirds of the public-sector workforce but only a quarter of the private-sector workforce were affiliated to a core pension plan. By 1970, the expansion of occupational provision had reached almost three-quarters of public-sector workers and over one-third of private ones. Overall, two-fifths of the non-farm workforce were affiliated to the second pillar of old age provision. (see Table A.2, p. 295). Leading manufacturing and financial sectors still offered the best benefits and managed most pension assets. Pension plans in the metal and machine-making sectors were the real heart of occupational provision: in 1955, they accounted for one-third of all workers insured in the private sector and one-fifth of total pension assets (see Table A.5, p. 299, and Table A.7, p. 303). Pension coverage was still underdeveloped in the building trade and among smaller firms and trade sectors.

[37] *SVPP Jahresbericht 1950* (Zurich; SVPP, 1951), p. 14, file V Schweiz 2435, SNB.

Employers held ambivalent views about surveys of pension plans. As W. Sulzer of the AIAG aluminum corporation emphasized in 1956, employers had to ensure that such statistics "should not be undertaken in order to collect materials that could bolster the idea of state regulation of private welfare institutions". On the other hand, National Councilor Josef Hofstetter (Radical), an executive at the Von Roll steelworks and a member of the SVPP, declared in 1963 that "regular surveys enable us to counter with facts the political factions that always try to exploit the alleged shortcomings of employee benefits". Insurers also argued that the surveys had to be undertaken by "neutral" authorities so that they could not be used to back up unwelcome social insurance proposals or feed information to fiscal authorities. In other words, a tension existed among business circles eager to emphasize the importance of occupational plans in overall old age provision, but reluctant to unveil their internal functioning or the allocation of their assets.[38]

Pension plans played a major role in the postwar labor market marked by growth, the influx of foreign workers, and the spread of collective bargaining. Themes such as the coordination of AHV and employee benefits, tax exemptions, state regulation of pension plans, and the growth of pension assets were key issues for employers, insurance companies, and associations such as the SVPP.

During World War II, the idea of a strict coordination of occupational pension plans with the AHV had been abandoned in favor of a non-constraining choice between autonomy (non-recognition) and formal integration (recognition). The Federal Social Insurance Office had estimated that three-quarters of those covered by core pension plans were affiliated to institutions eligible for the latter option. However, by 1955 only 7 marginal pension plans (out of more than 5,000) had chosen formal integration. Instead, most pension plans chose to use AHV pensions as a basis for enhancing the standing of corporate benefits and reducing their costs. After the introduction of the 4 percent AHV payroll contributions, an employer formerly deducting 12 percent of wages to finance its pensions would, for example, set its contribution level to 8 percent and decrease its pension expenses accordingly. By 1955, around one-fifth of

[38] W. Sulzer is quoted in the minutes of the general assembly of the SVPP, May 30, 1956, p. 6. Josef Hofstetter is quoted in *SVPP Zirkularmitteilungen*, no. 225, May 20, 1963, both documents in file V Schweiz 2435, SNB. For the insurers' point of view, see Studienkommission VSLG, April 22, 1964, p. 3, file Q128 203, ZFS. On the reluctance of business vis-à-vis the compilation of socio-economic statistics by the Confederation, see Hans Ulrich Jost, "Les contradictions entre la politique patronale et la statistique officielle en Suisse au XXe siècle", in *A tire d'ailes: contributions de Hans Ulrich Jost à une histoire critique de la Suisse* (Lausanne: Antipodes, 2005), pp. 433–46.

core public and corporate plans used this "coordinated deduction".[39] These practices echoed the "dovetailing" strategy followed in the post-war period by North American employers who used Social Security as a prop for developing their own pension plans.

Insurers used the meagerness of federal pensions explicitly as a marketing argument. Emphasizing that the "AHV has to be supplemented, as it only shields [the elderly] from dire poverty", insurance companies targeted small firms where occupational provision was often absent or underdeveloped. Rentenanstalt also underscored that group insurance had to "fill in the gaps where AHV benefits [were] insufficient".[40] Small group pension plans contributed to the fragmenting of occupational provision into a "colorful diversity" of pension plans and were considered by the Gewerbeverband as the "best way to fight back the predominance of state insurance".[41]

Once the uncertainties that preceded the introduction of the AHV had been dispelled, insurance companies massively underwrote group pension contracts, and the share of group premiums in their overall activities more than doubled between 1945 and 1965 (see Figure 2.3, p. 80). By 1955, 40 percent of all persons affiliated to core pension plans, but only 2 percent in the public sector, were covered by group plans (see Table A.2, p. 295). Despite a growing number of companies active in the group market, Rentenanstalt, Vita (Zurich Life), Winterthur Life, and Basler Life still underwrote over three-quarters of all group premiums (see Figure 2.4, p. 80). For the first time since the 1920s, Swiss providers of group insurance also made inroads into foreign markets, notably in the Netherlands, where the Pension and Savings Fund Act 1953 opened new opportunities for the development of private provision. In contrast to the Netherlands, the group division of Rentenanstalt pointed out, prospects were less rosy in such countries as France or West Germany, where the

[39] On the recognition issue, see *Pensionskassenstatistik 1941*, p. 150 and *Pensionskassenstatistik 1955*, pp. 56–60. On the practice of "coordinated deduction", see Expertenkommission der Spitzenverbände, October 1944, file 95.2, AfZ-SHIV, Alfred Matti, "Anpassung von Pensionskassen an die AHV mit gleichzeitigem Einbezug der Teuerungszulagen in die Versicherung (Methode der Koordinationsabzüge)", SVPP, June 1949, file 3.22.1, #104–106, Dokumentationsarchiv Wirtschaftsförderung, AfZ. See also Arthur Vogt, "Ernst Kaiser, der mathematische Vater der AHV", *Sécurité Sociale* 6 (1997), pp. 308–9.

[40] *De l'introduction d'assurances privées complémentaires à l'AVS dans les arts et métiers*, November 1957, file Q128 202, ZFS. Propaganda leaflet signed by the following companies: Basler Life, Vita (Zurich Life), Patria, Familia, Pax, Genevoise Assurances, La Suisse, Neuchâteloise Assurances. Dr. Martha Gut, "Unterlagen für die Geschichte der Gruppenversicherung" [n.d., ca. 1956], p. 28, file 615.642/1 SLA. See also "Jahresbericht Kollektivversicherungen", Rentenanstalt, 1947, p. 1, file 671.21/1, SLA.

[41] *Rapport du comité directeur sur l'activité de l'Union suisse des arts et métiers durant l'année 1950* (Vevey: USAM, 1950), p. 59.

expansion of social insurance hampered prospects for growth in private provision.[42]

In 1949, the SVPP "rejoiced without reservations" at the "clear and distinct boundaries" that had been set between corporate benefits and the "leveling tendencies" of social insurance. For the mouthpiece of the leading corporate plans, the "best defense against state interference reside[d] in the continuous development of private provision, which has to gain as much ground as possible in areas where state activity does not yet exert itself".[43] The SVPP strove, for example, to safeguard tax exemptions for pension plans, in particular at the cantonal level. From the 1940s on, the association undertook systematic lobbying to harmonize such exemptions in no fewer than nineteen cantons, which facilitated both the accumulation of pension assets and the opening of new plans. In Canton Valais, an alpine region that attracted metal and chemical industries such as AIAG or CIBA relying on abundant water and hydroelectric resources, the SVPP lobbied local authorities so that companies that had established production facilities in this region during the war could benefit from tax exemptions similar to those of their home cantons.[44]

New pension plan associations also emerged alongside the SVPP, and the first of these newcomers signaled the rise of independent consultants. The short-lived Association of Relief Institutions (Verein schweizerischer Fürsorgeeinrichtungen, VSF) led by Heinrich Temperli, a professor of actuarial science at the St. Gallen Business School, grouped together a handful of private pension plans from 1945 on. Business federations and insurers ignored this marginal association, while the SVPP considered it a crude marketing tool for Temperli's consulting business.[45] The VSF

[42] Foreign group contracts represented only a small fraction (5 percent in 1954) of all group contracts underwritten by Rentenanstalt. See "Jahresbericht Kollektivversicherungen", Rentenanstalt, 1954–1959. file 671.21/1, SLA.

[43] *Rapport sur l'exercice 1948* (Zurich: SVPP, 1949), pp. 3 and 6, file V Schweiz 2435, SNB.

[44] Alfred Matti, *Die Personalfürsorge der Privatwirtschaft und ihre Postulate an das Steuerrecht des Bundes und der Kantone* (Zurich: Wirtschaftsförderung/SDES, 1964), p. 2. For an overview of these actions, see *SVPP Jahresbericht* for the years 1943 to 1959, file V Schweiz 2435, SNB. On cantonal fiscal laws on occupational provision, see Graziano Lusenti, *Les institutions de prévoyance en Suisse, au Royaume-Uni et en Allemagne fédérale: placements financiers et politique sociale* (Geneva: Georg, 1989), pp. 192–3; Hans Gerold Wirz, *Die Personal-Wohlfahrtseinrichtungen der schweizerischen Privatwirtschaft. Ihre Stellung im Steuerrecht und ihre Beaufsichtigung* (Stäfa: Buchdruckerei Stäfa, 1955), pp. 41*ff.

[45] On the Verein schweizerischer Fürsorgeeinrichtungen (VSF), see file V Schweiz 1212, SNB. See also: Konferenz der Direktoren der VSLG, August 27, 1943, file Q127 206, ZFS; memorandum on a June 16, 1945 conference of the VSF, file 921.111/6, SLA; Protokoll der Gründungsversammlung der VSF vom 1. September 1945, file E3340 (B) 1985/102/245, SBA; VSF, "An die schweizerischen Fürsorgeeinrichtungen" [n.d., ca. summer 1945], file I/13.3.3.1.1, #46 and, "Statuten des VSF" [n.d., ca. summer 1945], file I/13.3.3.1.1, #50, Dokumentationsarchiv Wirtschaftsförderung, AfZ. Heinrich Temperli had participated in the 1947 anti-AHV referendum. See Heinrich Temperli to Eduard Seiler, June 25, 1947, file 5.3.6.3, AfZ-RN.

merged in 1950 with the Inter-Cantonal Association for Employee Benefits (Interkantonaler Verband für Personalfürsorge, IVP). This association, also founded in 1945, was the successor of a Berne-based committee that had lobbied during the war for tax exemptions for occupational plans. The IVP criticized the "rigidities of state insurance" and contrasted it with the "flexible solutions" offered by occupational plans. Yet, Hans Moser, administrator of the Berne municipal employees' pension plan and president of the IVP, explained that "in the same way as employee benefits strengthen both the firm and the workforce, a federal social institution may bolster the whole Confederation".[46]

This concept echoed Walther Stampfli's wartime resolve to make the AHV a symbol of national unity. The IVP also depicted occupational provision as a bridge between the public and private sectors and between workers and managers, and welcomed in its ranks both public-sector and trade union pension schemes. Prominent labor leader Robert Bratschi was invited to the founding meeting of the IVP, and metalworkers as well as white-collar trade unionists occupied seats on the steering committee of the association.[47] Such cross-class fraternization was unthinkable for the SVPP, which explicitly excluded public-sector pension plans from its ranks, or for insurance companies that considered trade union pension plans unwelcome competition. Moreover, the SVPP and the IVP did not cater for the same constituencies.

In 1949, at a time when both associations had around 400 members, two-thirds of pension plans affiliated to the IVP were based in Canton Berne. Among them, one could find many public-sector and multi-employer pension plans that had close relations with trade unions. The association acted as a bridge between linguistic regions, as another fifth of IVP affiliates were based in the less industrialized French-speaking cantons of western Switzerland. In contrast, the SVPP membership was exclusively composed of private pension plans and was strongly represented in the manufacturing and financial poles of Zurich and Basle, two regions that had only a handful of IVP members.[48] The IVP also lobbied for the investment of pension assets in the utilities and regional railways that were prominent in Canton Berne, and tried to attract small and

[46] Minutes of the foundation meeting of the Inter-Cantonal Association for Employee Benefits (Interkantonaler Verband für Personalfürsorge, IVP), June 5, 1945, p. 2, file E3340 (B) 1985/102/255, SBA. See also IVP to Federal Social Insurance Office, June 15, 1945, file 95.2, AfZ-SHIV, as well as documents in file V Schweiz 2436, SNB.

[47] Memorandum on the founding meeting of the IVP, June 1945, file 921.111/6, SLA. On the steering committee of the association, see annual reports of the IVP, file V Schweiz 2436, SNB.

[48] For the members' list of both associations, see *IVP Jahresbericht 1948* (Berne: IVP, 1949) and *SVPP Jahresbericht 1949* (Zurich: SVPP, 1950), in (respectively) file V Schweiz 2436, SNB and file V Schweiz 2435, SNB.

medium-sized firms by establishing a collective pension scheme tailored to their needs.[49] In short, the IVP represented peripheral regions and economic sectors, while the SVPP remained the reference point for large corporate plans, insurance companies, and business federations.

The expansion of corporate pension plans was closely connected to the rise of collective bargaining and the pacification of postwar industrial relations. Between 1947 and 1949, a period marked by severe currency instability and uncertain economic prospects in western Europe, employers and trade unions signed several "stabilization agreements" to stave off price and wage inflation and ensure the stability of the Swiss franc.[50] These agreements bolstered the development of corporate benefits that became part of wage packages. After a short-lived peak at the end of World War II, the number of strikes dropped precipitously in Switzerland and remained at rock-bottom levels during the following decades (see Figure 2.2, p. 67). This development was linked to the spread of industry-wide collective bargaining in machine-making, the chemicals industry, and the building trade. In 1951, already half of all workers were covered by collective bargaining agreements, yet the bargaining structure remained fragmented among a myriad local, regional, and company-level agreements. Even if the main contracts set the pace, substantial leeway was left for wage-setting at the company level. In contrast to other European countries, national-level centralized bargaining made little headway in Switzerland.[51]

The Federal Council had reaffirmed the compulsory nature of collective agreements through emergency decrees since 1941. In 1957, after complex negotiations, these ad hoc encouragements of labor peace were backed up by the introduction of a constitutional article on the compulsory character of collective agreements that left open wide margins of interpretation to their business and labor signatories. The Gewerkschaftsbund, which had unsuccessfully pushed for more interventionist measures, in the end did not oppose this modest framework. When labor

[49] See IVP annual reports for the years 1945–1954, file V Schweiz 2436, SNB.

[50] Eduard Kobelt, *Die Wirtschaftspolitik der Gewerkschaften, 1920–1950: der Einfluss einzelner Gewerkschaftsverbände und Persönlichkeiten auf die Wirtschaftspolitik des Schweizerischen Gewerkschaftsbundes* (Zurich: Chronos, 1987), pp. 158–81.

[51] Bernard Degen, "Starre Strukturen im wirtschaftlichen und sozialen Wandel: die schweizerische Gewerkschaftsbewegung in der zweiten Hälfte des 20. Jahrhunderts", in *Gewerkschaften in der Schweiz: Herausforderungen und Optionen*, ed. Klaus Armingeon and Simon Geissbühler (Zurich: Seismo, 2000), pp. 11–37, p. 15; Robert Fluder *et al.*, *Gewerkschaften und Angestelltenverbände in der schweizerischen Privatwirtschaft* (Zurich: Seismo Verlag, 1991), pp. 334–68, 447–52, 538–46; Peter J. Katzenstein, *Corporatism and change: Austria, Switzerland, and the politics of industry* (Ithaca: Cornell University Press, 1984), pp. 129–30.

organizations entered collective bargaining negotiations, they fought on a fragmented terrain where employers had the upper hand. Economic growth enabled employers to lure labor into social partnership by promising higher wages and well-developed, but selective, occupational schemes that served to reinforce bonds between workers and managers.[52] Trade unions' adherence to labor peace and social partnership represented key features of postwar industrial relations.

Although union-based provision played a marginal role in comparison with employer plans and federal pensions, trade unions' attachment to these measures compounded labor involvement in collectively bargained benefits schemes, which reinforced offhand attitudes toward social insurance. In a 1963 celebration of labor welfare schemes, a Metalworkers' Union official summarized the attitude of his organization to social insurance by asking disparagingly: "Why should we care about social security programs that might lead to a weakening of the union?"[53]

Besides the underdevelopment of social insurance, the pacification of labor relations, and the decentralization of collective bargaining, the segmentation of the working class also influenced the selective expansion of occupational provision. Pension plans favored skilled male workers and employees in leading export-oriented firms but bypassed unskilled workers and women, as well as the numerous contingents of Italian and Spanish workers hired to ease postwar labor shortages.

By the 1960s, Southern European "foreign workers" (Fremdarbeiter) represented one-fifth of the non-farm workforce, and their presence entrenched a bifurcated labor market as a growing chasm opened up between Swiss workers benefitting from stable positions, higher wages, and collectively bargained social benefits and Fremdarbeiter with temporary work permits. Seasonal or temporary workers were either barred from entering pension plans or lost some, or all, of what they had contributed to them if they left Switzerland after a few years. The bifurcated nature of the pension system thus discriminated against foreign workers and subsidized pensions for native workers. The Confederation signed

[52] Jürg Siegenthaler, *Die Politik der Gewerkschaften: eine Untersuchung der öffentlichen Funktionen schweizerischen Gewerkschaften nach dem Zweiten Weltkrieg* (Berne: Francke, 1968), pp. 78–86; Hans Fügli, *Die Sozialleistungen in den Gesamtarbeitsverträgen* (Zurich: Juris Verlag, 1952), p. 109.

[53] Ernst Wütrich, "Die Sozialversicherungen des Schweizerischen Metall- und Uhrenarbeiterverbandes", *Schweizerische Zeitschrift für Sozialversicherung* (1963), pp. 215–28 (quotation p. 228). By 1962, the Metalworkers' Union held over CHF 400 million in its various welfare schemes. Yet, the assets of its sickness plan (CHF 145 million) and unemployment fund (CHF 184 million) towered far above those of its old age relief fund (Fürsorgekasse, CHF 47 million), its savings plan (Alterskasse, CHF 8 million), and its relief fund (Unterstützungskasse, CHF 19 million).

several bilateral treaties to facilitate the transfer of social security contributions paid by foreigners in Switzerland, but occupational plans most often lacked such procedures. Labor defensiveness toward Fremdarbeiter contributed little to diminish divisions between native and foreign-born workers or to damp down anti-foreigner sentiments.[54]

The segmentation of the working class was also along gender lines. In 1955, a pension plan administrator pointed out during an SVPP assembly devoted to the issue of Switzerland's alleged social laggardness that the key difference between the Swiss welfare state and those of its European counterparts resided in the fact that the former emphasized "efficiency wages" (Leistungslohn) instead of "social security wages". According to this administrator, the generalization of universal women's suffrage in Europe had "equalized male and female wages" and forced European governments to introduce "special family support social measures".[55] Switzerland had not followed this path. Obstacles ranging from the denial of women's suffrage (universal suffrage at the federal level was refused by male voters in 1959 and only passed into law in 1971) to the lack of federal maternity leave and the patchiness of cantonal family allowances, as well as the hiring of female foreign workers, contributed to reinforcing traditional gender roles and to minimizing Swiss women's participation rates in the workforce.[56] In 1950, a survey of white-collar employees commissioned by the Association of Commercial Clerks (Kaufmännischer Verein) revealed that core pension plans covered around half of the male employees surveyed but only one-third of the women. The gender gap was only slightly narrower in banking, where two-thirds of male employees but only two-fifths of female bank employees belonged to pension plans.[57] In the overall workforce only 14 percent of women were

[54] Degen, "Starre Strukturen", pp. 20–5; Hans Mahnig, ed., *Histoire des politiques d'immigration, d'intégration et d'asile en Suisse depuis 1945* (Zurich: Seismo Verlag, 2005), pp. 89–134. The first bilateral social security treaty was signed in 1949 with Italy, the country of origin of many foreign workers. See Binswanger, *Histoire de l'AVS*, pp. 130ff.

[55] Minutes of the general assembly of the SVPP, May 12, 1955, p. 4, file V Schweiz 2435, SNB.

[56] On gender, work, and social insurance in the postwar period, see Christine Luchsinger, *Solidarität, Selbständigkeit, Bedürftigkeit: der schwierige Weg zu einer Gleichberechtigung der Geschlechter in der AHV: 1939–1980* (Zurich: Chronos, 1995), pp. 67–110; Studer, Sutter, and Wecker, *Die "schutzbedürftige Frau"*, pp. 209–32. See also Gaby Sutter, *Berufstätige Mütter: subtiler Wandel der geschlechterordnung in der Schweiz, 1945–1970* (Zurich: Chronos, 2005). For a depiction of Switzerland as an example of a "market-oriented gender policy model", see Walter Korpi, "Faces of inequality: gender, class, and patterns of inequalities in different types of welfare states", *Social Politics: International Studies in Gender, State & Society* 7 (2000), pp. 127–91.

[57] Carl Brüschweiler, *Saläre kaufmännischer Angestellter 1928–1950: Fürsorgeeinrichtungen und Ferienverhältnisse* (Zurich: Schweizerischer Kaufmännischer Verein, 1953).

affiliated to a core pension plan in 1955, as against more than two-fifths of men (see Table A.2, p. 295).

The disparity in occupational benefits also showed the limits of voluntarism. Most public-sector pension plans offered old age, disability, and survivors' benefits to their members, as did the AHV. Yet, this was not the case in the private sector, where only 13 percent of pension plan affiliates were covered for the above-mentioned risks in 1955 (this proportion would reach 30 percent in 1970, see Table A.2, p. 295). By my estimates, combined AHV pensions and occupational benefits were equal to around 70 percent of the average wage of a skilled worker in the public sector in 1955, but only 40 to 50 percent in the private sector (see Table A.6, p. 301). According to a federal survey of occupational provision, pension portability was rare among private plans, as "employers had evidently no interest in easing the departure of [their] personnel to the competition".[58] Ad hoc agreements eased portability in a handful of sectors such as machine-making, while life insurers set up rules, at the end of the 1950s, to transfer group contracts between insurance companies. However, these exceptions notwithstanding, pension portability depended on employers' goodwill.[59]

Although the issue of the regulation of pension plans had been raised since the 1920s, it never made serious inroads. It was buried in the 1936 revision of the Code of Obligations and postponed by the outbreak of war, although the issue had briefly resurfaced in 1945 in the wake of the Gitermann motion, before being sidelined during the implementation of the AHV. Between 1948 and 1958, struggles surrounding a new attempt to pass legislation in this area underscored business opposition to state interference in occupational provision.[60] These debates, which took place at the same time as those on the 1957 constitutional article on collective bargaining, underscored how business federations used social partnership to limit pension plan regulation in ways that safeguarded employers' prerogatives.

At the end of 1947, the issue of regulation re-emerged from the depths of the federal administration when the Federal Council announced that it would soon circulate the draft of a forthcoming bill addressing such issues as worker participation in pension plan

[58] *Pensionskassenstatistik 1955*, pp. 41, 49.

[59] Willy Maurer, "Der Fortschritt des Freizügigkeitsgedankens in der privaten Personalvorsorge", *Schweizerische Zeitschrift für Sozialversicherung* (1970), pp. 1–13. For the SVPP stance on pension portability, see R. Riethmann, *Möglichkeit und Grenzen der Freizügigkeit* (Zurich: SVPP, 1951).

[60] For a summary of the debate, see Lusenti, *Les institutions de prévoyance*, p. 76; Wirz, *Die Personal-Wohlfahrtseinrichtungen*, pp. 127–38.

management and the auditing of pension plan finances. In June 1948, this draft generated a tempest of negative reactions among business circles. Derided as a "centralizing" measure, an "intrusion of the state", or a "step toward socialization" it was unanimously rejected.[61] The SVPP denounced the project as a concession toward those who "defamed" pension plans and preferred class struggle instead of the encouragement of labor peace and the "factory community" (Betriebsgemeinschaft). For the Arbeitgeberverband, the lack of regulation of occupational schemes was not a problem, as it respected their inherent "diversity".[62] Labor activists were not impressed. Declaring that the absence of clearly defined pension rules could lead to protracted legal battles over welfare funds in the event of bankruptcies, they demanded "rights instead of charity" and denounced the "lordly attitude" of employers in the field of old age provision.[63]

Facing unequivocal business hostility, the legislative process rapidly lost steam, and no federal commission of experts was set up to revise the draft, which was simply passed along to several federal offices and departments.[64] Repeated Socialist and trade union demands to speed up the process went unanswered. The left briefly hoped that the ongoing revision of the federal law on labor relations (Arbeitsgesetz), which contained several articles pertaining to occupational provision, might help to solve the gridlock in which the regulatory measures were mired. However, the complete opposite happened. In December 1950, the labor law articles pertaining to occupational plans were pushed aside by federal authorities under the pretext that such issues would be better addressed by a specific legislative text.[65]

This second draft of the regulatory law again provoked a hostile response. Some employers' associations did not even bother to furnish answers to the appraisal demand that the Vorort and the Arbeitgeberverband had sent to them. The Association of Watch Manufacturers simply again sent to employers' federations a copy of its 1948 assessment of the first draft, which sternly stated that such a law "1) does not fulfill

61 According to correspondence contained in file 107.1, AfZ-SHIV.

62 Alfred Matti, "Brauchen wir eine ergänzende Gesetzgebung über das Personalfürsorgewesen?", conference at the April 13, 1948 general assembly of the SVPP, file 107.1, AfZ-SHIV. See also Arbeitgeberverband to Federal Department of Justice and Police, April 21, 1948, p. 12.

63 "Wem gehört der Wohlfahrtsfonds der Waffenfabrik Solothurn?", *Das Volk*, April 17, 1948; "Stiftung Wohlfahrtsfonds der Waffenfabrik Solothurn AG", *Das Volk*, March 8, 1949; M. Oe., "Recht statt Wohltätigkeit – Malaise um die Fürsorgefonds", *Freier Innerschweizer*, April 27, 1949. All articles in file 13.3.3.1.1, Dokumentationsarchiv Wirtschaftsförderung, AfZ.

64 Wirz, *Die Personal-Wohlfahrtseinrichtungen*, p. 141.

65 Ibid., pp. 130–1.

any need . . . 2) is inopportune . . . 3) is dangerous, as it increases state interference in the workings of the private economy". This time, the SVPP even depicted all proposals to regulate pension plans as "attempts at expropriation" that had to be "rejected" without discussion.[66] The Arbeitgeberverband, which vigorously opposed measures enabling extensive worker participation in pension management and the unions' right to scrutinize pension ledgers, emphatically underscored that federal supervision meant nothing less than the death-knell of corporate provision: "Because of this intrusive police law, a typically Swiss institution that has grown organically and that has provided outstanding contributions to the economic security of innumerable Swiss workers would be hit in its vital nerve."[67]

Having faced two unwavering rejections, the regulatory law was stillborn. During an April 1951 meeting with white-collar trade unions, business federations refused to admit that employees' pension rights were insufficiently protected. "If gaps remain in the relevant and applicable legislation", Leonhard Derron of the Arbeitgeberverband argued, "these are chiefly of a theoretical nature." Labor claims that workers were not after an inquisitive "police law" but a "social law" that would safeguard pension plan assets and employees' rights to benefits did not find a favorable ear among business federations.[68]

Despite their uncompromising public stance, employers were conscious that the "extension of legal statutes [could] not be avoided in the long run" because of the ongoing development of pension plans. Yet, they were determined to reach this through a contractual accord among social partners, with as little federal interference as possible.[69] In June 1953, a preliminary agreement praised by the SVPP as a "broad-based" framework establishing "general conditions" instead of a "special law" led to the revision of two articles related to labor contracts (art. 343 of the Code

[66] Chambre suisse de l'Horlogerie to Vorort, February 20, 1951, file 107.1, AfZ-SHIV. See also *Rapport sur l'exercice 1950* (Zurich: SVPP, 1951), p. 7, file V Schweiz 2435, SNB.

[67] Quoted from Arbeitgeberverband to Federal Department of Justice and Police, April 28, 1951, file 107.1, AfZ-SHIV. See also Arbeitgeberverband geschäftsleitende Ausschuss, March 13, 1951, pp. 7–9, SAV.

[68] Paritätische Kommission für Angestelltenfragen, April 28, 1951, p. 4. See also the minutes of a meeting between the Federal Department of Justice and Police and social partners (business federations, SVPP, trade unions), September 28, 1951, p. 3, both documents in file 107.1, AfZ-SHIV.

[69] Minutes of a joint business federations and SVPP meeting on the issue of pension plan supervision, May 5, 1953, file 107.1, AfZ-SHIV. The pension lobby IVP was not invited to these meetings. After the IVP had contacted federal authorities in June 1948 to propose its own solutions to settle the regulation issue, the association was definitively considered a troublemaker by business federations and the SVPP.

of Obligations) and to the legal form of foundations (art. 89$^{bis}$ of the Civil Code).[70] This revision confirmed such pre-existing practices as the legal separation of welfare schemes from their founding firms and heralded the abandonment of the regulatory law. This outcome was considered by the SVPP a victory for social partnership: "The energy and joy for implementing an active and progressive social policy at the corporate level are all the greater when the State does not intervene . . . to frame social life in legal clauses and to issue soulless norms that influence human relations in manufacturing firms."[71] Not coincidentally, this rapprochement between labor organizations and employers occurred precisely when the federal legislation on collective bargaining was nearing completion, having been substantially whittled down by business federations.

Employers were not in principle opposed to the idea that trade unions should jointly manage corporate pension plans. On the contrary, they described this, in the words of the SVPP, as an "adequate platform for collaborative work, [and] for a deepening of reciprocal interactions at the level of human relations".[72] Yet, the issue of joint management was only loosely addressed by the revision passed in 1953: workers had to be represented in the management of pension plans "in proportion" to the level of their contributions and should be able to choose "as far as possible" their representatives. Before the introduction of these measures, more than two-thirds of private plans already allowed their contributing members to have a say in pension matters.[73] Yet, by keeping the level of employers' contributions higher than that of employees, firms easily retained control of pension plans. This was more true in group plans, where employers delegated pension management to insurance companies in which labor had no representation at all. In the end, a "little pension sweet" was distributed to docile workers, but the vital control-switches of the plans were out of the hands of labor.[74] In contrast to Germany, where labor fought to reinforce nationwide collective agreements and workplace democracy under the slogan of "joint management" (Mitbestimmung), the Swiss left spoke more modestly of the "right to have a say" in management (Mitspracherecht).[75]

70 Alfred Matti, "Gesetzgebung über die Personalfürsorge – Stand der Vorbereitungen und grundsätzliche Betrachtungen", 1954 memorandum for the SVPP, file V Schweiz 2435, SNB.
71 *Rapport sur l'exercice 1952* (Zurich: SVPP, 1953), p. 10, file V Schweiz 2435, SNB.
72 *Rapport sur l'exercice 1951* (Zurich: SVPP, 1952), p. 13, file V Schweiz 2435, SNB.
73 *Pensionskassenstatistik 1955*, p. 25.
74 "Das Pensionskassen Zückerli", *Arbeiter-Zeitung Schaffhausen*, June 27, 1955.
75 Benno Hardmeier, "Zur problematik der Mitbestimmung", *Gewerkschaftliche Rundschau* 1965), pp. 137–45, 142–4.

Commenting on the state of negotiations on the regulation of pension plans, Max Greiner of the Federation of Employees pointed out in 1954 that despite the current fad for "human relations", ensuring fair representation of workers in the management of pension plans ranked low among employers' priorities compared with their unceasing efforts to obtain tax exemptions. In a postscript downplaying Greiner's criticism, Giacomo Bernasconi, the Gewerkschaftsbund secretary responsible for social policy and a member of the AHV federal commission, defended the compromise reached with employers by emphasizing that workers could use the future law on collective bargaining to claim their rights.[76] Given the limitations of this law, Bernasconi's uncompromising defense of social partnership showed once again the entanglement of trade unions in the web of corporate benefits spun by employers.

When the modest articles on the regulation of pension plans were submitted to the Federal Assembly in May 1955, ten years had passed since the controversial Gitermann motion, and three more would pass before their implementation. The Vorort expressed its complete satisfaction with the outcome of this protracted policy-making process, which "correspond[ed] exactly to the objectives defended by [business] federations".[77] In the words of a contemporary observer, occupational pension provision remained "only summarily regulated".[78]

The postwar expansion of the AHV and occupational provision in Switzerland can be contrasted with the situations prevailing in such countries as the Netherlands, Sweden, the United Kingdom, Canada, and the United States. In these various national contexts, one may witness the emergence of multi-tiered pension schemes that prefigured Swiss debates of the late 1960s on the three-pillar doctrine.

Since the interwar period, occupational pensions had spread in the Netherlands through the expansion of industry-wide schemes jointly managed by employers' and labor organizations. Along with the introduction of basic universal pensions in the aftermath of World War II, the growth of occupational coverage was bolstered by three governmental measures. A 1945 decree encouraged firms to join collective agreements and multi-employer pension plans, while the Industrial Pension Funds Act 1949 (Wet betreffende verplichte deelneming in een bedrijfsfonds) made adhesion to industry-wide pension schemes mandatory. Finally,

76 Max Greiner, "Zur Gesetzgebung über Wohlfahrtsfonds und -stiftungen", *Gewerkschaftliche Rundschau*, September 1954, 243–5; Giacomo Bernasconi "Nachschrift", *Gewerkschaftliche Rundschau*, September 1954, pp. 245–6.

77 Vorort Vorstand, May 23, 1955, p. 18, file 1.5.3.15, AfZ-SHIV.

78 Hans-Peter Schär, *Aufbau und Bedeutung privater Pensionskassen in der Schweiz* (Winterthur: Keller, 1958), p. 41.

the Pension and Savings Fund Act 1953 (Pensioen- en Spaarfondsenwet) increased union participation in the management of corporate plans and secured workers' rights to benefits. By that year, more than half of all workers were covered by occupational provision, the large majority of them in a few dozen multi-employer plans. More than 1,500 company plans and group contracts also operated, most of them in leading firms, but they played a minor role.[79] Dutch occupational schemes thus constituted "quasi-mandatory add-ons" to basic pensions, which differed from the Swiss case, where industry-wide plans were marginal, coverage remained fragmented at the company level or by group contracts, and, most importantly, business and labor collaboration in the establishment and management of pension plans was limited. Swiss employers were keen to control occupational benefits and were in no hurry to accede to trade union demands for encompassing social partnership.[80]

In 1959, at a time when Swedish occupational schemes covered only a very few higher-paid white-collar employees, Social Democrats introduced earnings-related secondary pensions to supplement universal basic pensions. The ATP pension funds (Allmänna Tillägspensionen, or general supplementary pensions) reinforced the solidarist path favored by employers and enhanced the mobility of the workforce by guaranteeing pension portability and vesting rights. Based on a pay-as-you-go structure, the ATP also accumulated state-supervised reserves but did not lead to the "socialization" of the economy or the takeover of private firms by state monies. In the end, assets accumulated through ATP funds "largely satisfied Swedish industry's demand for privileged access to capital from the funds and for restrictions that prevented their abuse as an instrument of Socialist control".[81] The organization of Swedish

79 Jost van Genabeek, "Collectieve pensioenregelingen 1800–2000", in *Studies over zekerheidsarrangementen: risico's, risicobestrijding en verzekeringen in Nederland vanaf de Middeleeuwen*, ed. Jacques van Gerwen and Marco van Leeuwen (Amsterdam: NEHA, 1998), pp. 883–905 (pp. 895–7); Jacques van Gerwen, *De welvaartsstaat: volksverzekeringen, verzekeringsconcerns, finaciele dienstverleners en instituionele beleggers 1945–2000* (Amsterdam: IISG/Stichting Beheer, 2000), p. 65.

80 In 1956, the Vorort politely but firmly declined the offer from the Association of Commercial Clerks (Kaufmännischer Verein) that suggested employers create a tri-partite foundation with business federations and white-collar employee unions in order to develop occupational provision in small firms and trades. See Kaufmännischer Verein to Vorort, January 17, 1956; Vorort to Kaufmännischer Verein, April 18, 1956, file 107.2, Vorort/AHV.

81 Jonas Pontusson, *The limits of social democracy: investment politics in Sweden* (Ithaca: Cormell University Press, 1992), pp. 79ff; Peter A. Swenson, *Capitalists against markets: the making of labor markets and welfare states in the United States and Sweden* (Oxford: Oxford University Press, 2002), pp. 286–92 (quotation p. 91). On Swedish white-collar schemes, see Eskil Wadensjö, "The welfare mix in pension provision in Sweden", in *Enterprise and the welfare state*, ed. Martin Rein and Eskil Wadensjö (Cheltenham: Edward Elgar, 1997), pp. 266–308.

supplementary provision along a funded but state-based second tier differed markedly from the Swiss configuration, where employers resisted attempts to either regulate or homogenize occupational coverage. The idea of pooling pension assets under the supervision of the state was absolutely foreign to Swiss employers, who had relentlessly criticized the AHV reserve funds while fighting off state regulation of private-sector pension plans.

The Swiss configuration of decentralized and voluntary-funded occupational provision more closely followed patterns that prevailed in Anglo-Saxon countries, such as the United Kingdom, Canada, and especially the United States. British occupational plans and group insurance thrived in the postwar period. In the public sector and nationalized industries, pension coverage and benefits were notably more developed than in the private sector, but overall coverage reached half of the workforce by the mid-1960s. Postwar pension regulation was confined to fiscal laws that contained new incentives for group plans. The 1957 Labour project for "national superannuation pensions" echoed the Swedish ATP scheme. However, the 1959 electoral defeat of the Labour Party presaged the implementation of a watered-down Conservative alternative, introduced in 1961, that allowed firms to "contract out" from a modest second public pension tier, or "graduated pension", if they offered similar or more generous benefits. The 1957 superannuation plan would be re-submitted a decade later, only to go under again because of another Labour electoral defeat, and be belatedly implemented in a downsized form as the State Earnings-Related Pension Scheme (SERPS) in 1975.[82]

In Canada, two alternatives were put forward to supplement the universal basic pensions introduced in 1951. On the one hand, insurers and some employers put their weight behind an extension of occupational provision as outlined by the Ontario Pension Benefits Act 1963, which ensured minimum solvency standards for pension plans, as well as limited pension portability. However, business encouragement of occupational provision was not able to fend off rising political pressure for a public supplementary pension. The 1963 Ontario law was repealed in 1964 and replaced with the 1965 Canada/Quebec Pension Plan (CPP/QPP). This earnings-related second pension tier that allowed a provincial

[82] Peter Baldwin, *The politics of social solidarity: class bases of the European welfare state 1875–1975* (Cambridge: Cambridge University Press, 1990), pp. 232–47; Leslie Hannah, *Inventing retirement: the development of occupational pensions in Britain* (Cambridge: Cambridge University Press, 1986), p. 56; Tony Lynes, "The British case", in *Enterprise and the welfare state*, ed. Martin Rein and Eskil Wadensjö (Cheltenham: Edward Elgar, 1997), pp. 309–51, 314, 334–7; Pat Thane, *Old age in English history: past experiences, present issues* (Oxford: Oxford University Press, 2000), pp. 280–4.

variant for Quebec was based on a pay-as-you-go financial structure, its modest funded reserves controlled by the federal (or in Quebec, provincial) government. The CPP/QPP did not impede the development of occupational "voluntary add-ons". On the contrary, the modesty of its benefits left "ample scope for private pensions".[83]

The British and Canadian struggles between alternative pension projects prefigured, in a sense, the Swiss controversies of the late 1960s between the three-pillar doctrine and the people's pensions. However, the supplementary "pension carve-outs" in the United Kingdom, designed to protect private occupational plans, or the co-existence of the modest CPP/QPP scheme with private "voluntary add-ons", had no equivalent in a Swiss pension mix which still bore a greater resemblance to that in the United States. The minimum pension regulation introduced in 1958 in Switzerland through the means of the Civil Code and the Code of Obligations echoed the Welfare and Pension Plan Disclosure Act enacted the same year in the United States. Described by historian Steven Sass as a "hopelessly limited law", it "required only rudimentary disclosures of trust fund activities and authorized no policing at all".[84] In both the United States and Switzerland, the continuing fragmentation of occupational provision reflected the decentralization of collective bargaining and the absence of any state-based, funded, second pension tier.

The distinctiveness of the Swiss welfare state was also a recurring topic of discussion in the context of advancing European integration. The postwar strategy of business federations and federal authorities toward Europe had been characterized by a selective "neither out nor in" attitude. Switzerland joined economic institutions such as the Marshall Plan and the Organization for European Economic Cooperation (the precursor of the OECD), and participated in European efforts to regulate coal and steel production. However, after securing access to postwar markets, Switzerland had stayed aloof from such integration projects as the Council of Europe or the Treaty of Rome, which were deemed useless or constraining for Swiss financial and manufacturing interests. At the end of the 1950s, Swiss economic elites that favored free trade and flexible

[83] Keith Banting, "Canada: nation-building in a federal welfare state", in *Federalism and the welfare state: New World and European experiences*, ed. Herbert Obinger, *et al.* (New York: Cambridge University Press, 2005), pp. 89–137, (quotation p. 109); Kenneth Bryden, *Old age pensions and policy-making in Canada* (Montreal: McGill-Queen's University Press, 1974), pp. 147–73.

[84] Jacob S. Hacker, *The divided welfare state: the battle over public and private social benefits in the United States* (Cambridge: Cambridge University Press, 2002), pp. 149–51; Steven A. Sass, *The promise of private pensions: the first hundred years* (Cambridge: Cambridge University Press, 1997), p. 192.

multilateral economic relations lobbied for a European Free Trade Area and remained wary of a European Economic Community considered excessively state-centered and protectionist.[85]

During a Vorort meeting devoted to the challenges of European integration, Hans Herold summarized in October 1962 the situation faced by the Swiss welfare state: untouched by war and inflation, unlike its European neighbors, it had been able to avoid the perils of centralization and to maintain its "well-entrenched diversity" and "strong decentralization". In this context, added Herold, the articles of the Treaty of Rome that either envisioned "income redistribution through the 'social harmonization' of social benefits according to the highest standards" or "the creation of supra-national European labor and social legislation that may serve as the cornerstone for a political unification of Europe" were unacceptable.[86] Echoing the results of the aforementioned 1958 survey on wage levels and social expenditure (see Table 4.3, p. 201), the Vorort secretary underscored that Swiss employers were "much less burdened by social programs than their counterparts in the European Economic Community".[87] The combination of high wages, low social insurance contributions, low taxation, and differentiated occupational benefits was considered a key asset that strengthened Swiss export firms in international markets and enabled them to attract much-needed foreign workers.

Leonhard Derron of the Arbeitgeberverband agreed with the Vorort that any harmonization of social policy based on "political or ideological motivations" had to be rejected, as it would lead to a "profound alteration of our economic and social order that would lead to state intervention and centralization, as well as replace contractual or company-based solutions with compulsory ones".[88] Employers always responded to those who criticized Swiss laggardness in the field of social insurance by pointing to the importance of decentralized employment-based benefits. Yet, the Swiss welfare state could not develop in splendid isolation. From the late 1950s, the expansion of social policy in neighboring European countries began to have a greater impact on Swiss domestic debates and on the shape and trajectory of the pension system.

[85] Dominique Dirlewanger, Sébastien Guex, and Gian Franco Pordenone, *La politique commerciale de la Suisse 1945–1966* (Zurich: Chronos, 2004), pp. 136–40, 163–6; Hans Ulrich Jost, Matthieu Leimgruber, and Isaline Marcel, *Europa und die Schweiz: Europarat, Supranationalität und schweizerische Unabhängigkeit* (Zurich: Chronos, 1999).

[86] Vorort Vorstand, October 29, 1962, p. 31, file 1.5.3.16–18, AfZ-SHIV.

[87] Ibid., pp. 4, 6, and 8.

[88] Ibid., p. 32. For an earlier discussion along the same lines, see Arbeitgeberverband Vorstand, October 11, 1961, pp. 7–12, SAV.

## Quo vadis AHV? The pension system at the crossroads (1959–1963)

Ten years after the payment of the first federal pensions, the momentum initiated by the first AHV revisions showed no sign of abating. On the contrary, the "politicization" of social policy expanded further under the combined pressure of direct democracy and the increasing commitment of the left to federal pensions. During the 5th and 6th AHV revisions enacted in 1961 and 1964, the pace of social policy reform accelerated markedly. This situation encouraged life insurers to initiate an inter-employer discussion on the future of the pension system. This section follows the genesis of the political answer of business circles to this changing environment, namely the three-pillar doctrine.

In the context of the booming economy of the second half of the 1950s, the development of European welfare states, especially the pension reforms enacted in Sweden (1957) and the Federal Republic of Germany (1959), cast an unfavorable light on Swiss social policy.[89] Even if business federations decried the introduction of pension-indexing in Germany as "an explosive charge that may destroy an important stronghold against inflation", neither the incremental changes brought about by the first AHV revisions nor the belated introduction of disability benefits could suppress growing impatience with the meagerness of federal pensions.[90] In late 1958, the Radical Party tried to retake its position as leader on the social policy front by sponsoring two parliamentary motions. The first (motion Guinand) demanded higher benefits for middle-class constituencies confronted with the leveling-off of maximum federal pensions, while the second (motion Dietschi) proposed new fiscal incentives and improvements in pension portability to bolster occupational coverage. Two competing initiatives – launched respectively by the Socialist Party and a committee related to the centrist Alliance of Independents – demanded better pensions, higher state subsidies for the AHV, and the regular indexing of pension benefits.[91] Inspired by the example of foreign reforms, these motions and initiatives put the AHV at the top of the political agenda during the run-up to the fall 1959 federal elections.

The increasing "politicization" of social policy was also related to a key domestic political development. The launch of the Socialist and Independent initiatives coincided with the implementation of the so-called

89 Baldwin, *The politics of social solidarity*, pp. 186–200, 212–23.
90 Arbeitgeberverband Vorstand, December 5, 1958, pp. 9–12, SAV.
91 Binswanger, *Histoire de l'AVS*, pp. 181–9. See also *Protokoll über die Verhandlungen des ordentlicher Parteitages vom 4./5. Oktober 1958* (Berne: Sozialdemokratische Partei der Schweiz, 1958), pp. 93–105, file K961, Sozialarchiv.

Magic Formula (Zauberformel) that heralded the "concordance" period of postwar politics (Konkordanzdemokratie). The Socialists did not fare well in the elections and lost five seats in the two chambers of the Federal Assembly. Yet, their 1959 program fully accepted the capitalist market economy and the "reformism of prosperity", confirming the centrist profile of the party and facilitating its re-integration into the government. One year after the 1958 defeat of their attempts to reform federal finances and after six uneasy years spent in opposition, the Socialists returned to the fold, and two of their members, Hans Peter Tschudi and Willy Spühler, were elected by the bourgeois parliamentary majority to the executive.[92] With the introduction of the informal Magic Formula that would regulate the distribution of seats in the Federal Council until December 2003, the Radicals, the Catholics, and the Socialists each got two seats in the executive branch, while the third bourgeois party, the Farmers', Artisans', and Burghers' Party, occupied the remaining seat.

The re-entry of the Socialists in the Federal Council was facilitated in no small part by the Catholic Party. The growing presence of the second bourgeois party in urban areas, away from its traditional rural strongholds, had reinforced its centrist and social Christian-Democratic wing to the detriment of more conservative currents and convinced Catholic leaders that the re-integration of the left in the government would help to more effectively challenge the Radical Party.[93]

In December 1959, a Socialist was in charge of social insurance. Hans Peter Tschudi's (1913–2002) nomination to the Home Affairs Department opened a period during which the development of the AHV would become the "display window of the Socialists' participation in the federal executive".[94] The Socialist statesman transformed the pace and scope of welfare reforms, presided over no fewer than four AHV revisions between 1959 and 1973, and attempted a major overhaul of health insurance. Yet,

[92] Bernard Degen, "Entre opposition et participation au Conseil Fédéral", in *Solidarité, débats, mouvement: 100 ans du Parti Socialiste suisse 1888–1988*, ed. Karl Lang (Lausanne: Editions d'En Bas, 1988), pp. 319–45, 338–41. On the 1950s, see Jakob Tanner, "Die Schweiz in den 1950er Jahren: Prozesse, Brüche, Widersprüche, Ungleichzeitigkeiten", in *achtung: die 50er Jahre! Annäherungen an eine widersprüchliche Zeit*, ed. Jean-Daniel Blanc and Christine Luchsinger (Zurich: Chronos, 1994), pp. 19–50.

[93] Urs Altermatt, "Die Christlichdemokratische Volkspartei der Schweiz: 1945–1999", in *Christlich-demokratische und konservative Parteien in Westeuropa*, ed. Urs Altermatt, *et al.* (Paderborn: Schöning, 2000), pp. 35–115, 74ff.

[94] Degen, "Entre opposition et participation au Conseil Fédéral", p. 341. After Walther Stampfli's return to the private sector, social policy had been administered by Federal Councilors Rodolphe Rubattel (Radical) and Philip Etter (Catholic). Because of the postwar expansion of federal social programs, the Federal Social Insurance Office had been transferred from the Economic Affairs Department to the Home Affairs Department in 1954.

the so-called "Tschudi pace" (of reform) ended on an ambivalent note, culminating in 1972 in both the largest increase in AHV benefits of the postwar period and the anchoring of the three-pillar doctrine in the federal constitution. The "Tschudi pace" thus combined both the expansion and containment of social insurance.

Tschudi's career path provides an explanation of this seemingly contradictory outcome. In his memoirs, he depicted himself as a moderate reformist. Unconvinced in his student youth by Marxism, Tschudi felt at home in the trade unionist wing of the Socialist Party and strived to obtain concrete results through social partnership. The wartime collaboration between the Socialists and the Radicals around the common goal of the AHV marked Tschudi's early political career in Basle. There, along with a group of young moderate "political border-crossers", he had mingled with centrist bourgeois politicians such as National Councilor Alfred Schaller, who had called for better occupational pension standards at the 1943 congress of the Radical Party. Alternating political mandates and a professorship in labor and social legislation at the University of Basle, Tschudi was elected to the Council of States (Senate) in 1956.[95]

In 1958, during the last parliamentary debate on the regulation of pension plans, National Councilor Hermann Häberlin (Radical), an influential politician with strong business ties, denounced the "demagogic" attempts of certain Socialist backbenchers to re-introduce binding clauses regarding worker participation in the management of pension plans in the legal measures that had been negotiated between business federations and trade unions. In contrast, Häberlin explicitly praised Tschudi's restraint on this issue. One year later, in December 1959, the bourgeois majority of the Federal Assembly elected Tschudi to the executive branch instead of Walther Bringholf, the official Socialist candidate. In contrast to Bringholf, who had committed the cardinal sin of spending his prewar political career in the ranks of the Communist Party, Tschudi offered a more reassuring profile as a moderate and trustworthy social partner.[96]

95 Hans-Peter Tschudi, *Im Dienste des Sozialstaates: politische Erinnerungen* (Berlin: F. Reinhardt, 1993), pp. 36, 39. On Tschudi's wartime activities, see Charles Stirnimann, *Der Weg in der Nachkriegszeit 1943–1948: ein Beitrag zur politischen Sozialgeschichte des "Roten Basel"* (Basle/Kassel: Friedrich Reinhardt Verlag, 1992), pp. 118–19.

96 Hermann Häberlin, "Gefahren staatlicher Bevormundung", *Neue Zürcher Zeitung*, April 9, 1958; Hermann Häberlin, "Wirtschaftsverbände und Parlament", *Schweizerische Arbeitgeber Zeitung*, April 18, 1958. On the election, see Wolf Linder, "Hans Peter Tschudi", in *Le Conseil Fédéral: dictionnaire biographique des cents premiers conseillers fédéraux*, ed. Urs Altermatt (Yens: Cabédita, 1993), pp. 500–5.

In fact, Tschudi's claim that "a strong economy form[ed] the basis for the solution to social problems" and that the development of social insurance should "take into account the contributory capacity of the economy" would not have seemed foreign to Edmund Schulthess and Walther Stampfli, the two Radical Federal Councilors who had presided over the making of the AHV. Tschudi's political career reflected the pacification of the left that had culminated in the integration of the Socialists in the governing coalition dominated by the bourgeois parties. Yet, the early actions of this politician – posthumously portrayed as a "pragmatic revolutionary" by the venerable *Neue Zürcher Zeitung* – were marked by an astute use of the combined pressures of direct democracy and administrative capacity to upgrade AHV benefits.[97] This strategy wrong-footed the business federations at first.

In November 1959, a few weeks before Tschudi's election, the Vorort and the Arbeitgeberverband outlined a common strategy toward the coming 5th AHV revision and the initiatives launched by the Socialists and the Alliance of Independents. The business federations argued that the core principle of the AHV, "namely that it should remain a basic pension supplemented by individual or collective self-provision, [was] undermined by the resolute expansion of foreign social programs".[98] Increasing the share of federal subsidies in financing the AHV, one of the key demands of the initiatives, was firmly rejected as an open door to "endless spiraling costs". According to the business federations, the Socialists, who favored this proposal, were trying to recoup the failure of their 1950s attempts to reform budgetary and fiscal policy by pushing redistributive policies through social insurance initiatives. Rising pension expenditures were considered "less a social policy [aim] than an ideological one". From the business point of view, "the more the state is involved in the organization of a social program, the more easily this can be used to pursue political goals, and the actual system can be modified without furor and violence".[99] Keen to maintain their grip on the pension system, employers were resolved to fight the expansion of the AHV:

> Both initiatives depart from the basic pension position and aim to introduce comprehensive state provision for all citizens. Moving in this direction would mean that tasks that are currently devoted to the individual and to the private

[97] Tschudi, *Im Dienste des Sozialstaates*, pp. 75, 167. For Tschudi's obituary, see "Ein pragmatischer 'Revolutionär': zum Tode von alt Bundesrat Hans Peter Tschudi", *Neue Zürcher Zeitung*, October 1, 2002.

[98] M. Fink (Gewerbeverband), "Bericht und Anträge zu den beiden AHV-Initiativen: Entwurf", Studiengesellschaft für Wirtschafts- und Sozialfragen. Sozialpolitische Kommission, November 16, 1959, p. 1, file Q128 203, ZFS.

[99] Ibid., pp. 9–11.

sector would be transferred without compelling reasons to the state. This would increase the socialization of the national income and again reduce individual freedom.[100]

In the context of the Cold War, the opposition to state-based social policy and the defense of a free economic order had strong ideological undertones. In order to counteract the two initiatives, employers were ready to accept a limited extension of AHV pensions, but without an increase in payroll contributions. For political reasons, employers also accepted the indexing of pensions as long as the bourgeois-controlled Federal Assembly could decide its scope every five years on a case-by-case basis. Despite growing misgivings, business federations were confident of their ability to secure their objectives during the pre-parliamentary phase of the decision-making process and to contain the additional costs brought about by the revision of the AHV.[101]

One year later, in early 1961, employers admitted that they had underestimated the changes incurred by the introduction of the Magic Formula. The head of the Home Affairs Department, Hans Peter Tschudi, used the political momentum created by the Socialist and Independent initiatives and approved the pension improvements outlined by the Federal Social Insurance Office. The low-cost options defended by the employers' representatives had been defeated. In March 1961, the Federal Assembly unanimously accepted the 5$^{th}$ AHV revision legislative bill, which led to the withdrawal of the two initiatives. Additional pension expenditure amounted to more than CHF 380 million, more than double the business estimates. Three months later, in a speech at the Socialist Party congress, Tschudi underlined that further improvements were necessary to solve the shortcomings of old age benefits and the "fragmentation" of the pension system. Although some Socialist backbenchers had doubts about his unwarranted optimism and, criticizing the withdrawal of the pending Socialist initiative, asked for more daring policy proposals, the bulk of the party leadership stood firmly behind Tschudi's gradualist strategy.[102] For its own part, the Vorort unambiguously characterized the 5$^{th}$ AHV revision as a defeat. The business federations had been unable to defend the aims of their November 1959 memorandum.[103]

In the aftermath of the parliamentary vote, employers briefly debated, for the second time since 1956, the option of a referendum against the new

100 Ibid., p. 19. 101 Ibid., p. 21.

102 *Protokoll über die Verhandlungen des ordentlicher Parteitages vom 3./4. Juni 1961* (Berne: Sozialdemokratische Partei der Schweiz, 1961), pp. 89, 100–1, 124–6, file K961, Sozialarchiv.

103 Vorort to affiliates of the Swiss Chamber of Commerce and Industry, March 4, 1961, file 95.23, AfZ-SHIV.

pension law. The Redressement National had urged the business federations to lead a fight against an overpriced reform that ran counter to the employers' approach. Although the Vorort and the Arbeitgeberverband shared the analysis of the conservative free-market group, they adamantly refused to launch a referendum that might provoke incomprehension among bourgeois parties, polarize the political situation, trigger further social demands from the left, and offer only a short-term solution to the expansion of social expenditure. Moreover, business federations were loath to appear publicly as opponents of the hugely popular AHV, the cornerstone of social policy. The Arbeitgeberverband pointed out that the current negative trend could only be thwarted by "a long-term and systematic information campaign".[104]

The Union of Life Insurance Companies shared this concern for a redefinition of business strategy. On the grounds that further expansion of the AHV might hinder the development of private occupational provision, and in particular overshadow group plans that represented a growing share of the life insurance market, insurers set up in February 1959 a Study Commission on Social Legislation devoted to the defense of the "free economy" perspective in social policy.[105] This study group was initiated and led by Peter Binswanger (1916–1997), director of the group division of Winterthur Life and delegate of the Union of Life Insurance Companies in the AHV Commission.

Before joining Winterthur Life in 1955, Peter Binswanger had been one of Walter Stampfli's trusted lieutenants in the Federal Social Insurance Office, where he had contributed to the writing of both the 1946 AHV law and the 1952 revision of the EO. Since commentators persist in depicting Hans Peter Tschudi as the "father of the AHV", Peter Binswanger remarks in his history of federal pensions that Tschudi was the man who brought up "the child" shaped by Walther Stampfli "into adulthood". He portrays himself as a watchful guardian who took care that the child did not go astray and remained faithful to "[the] doctrine that Walther Stampfli and himself had always defended: namely that old age and survivors' provision should rely on three pillars and not one". As the "rapid and massive development of the AHV threatened this doctrine", Binswanger joined the private sector in order to "fight this development

[104] Redressement National to Vorort, Arbeitgeberverband, Wirtschaftsförderung, and Gewerbeverband, April 6, 1961; Vorort to Redressement National, April 25, 1961; Arbeitgeberverband to Redressement National, April 25, 1961, file 95.23, AfZ-SHIV.

[105] Protokoll der Studienkommission der Fragen der Sozialgesetzgebung der Vereinigung Schweizerischen Lebensversicherungsgesellschaften (hereafter Studienkommission VSLG), February 23, 1959, file Q128 203, ZFS.

by encouraging an equally rapid development of the second and third pillars".[106]

In 1958, under the title "Quo vadis AHV?" (Where are you heading, AHV?), Binswanger published in the Radical Party political review an article warning that a reorientation of social policy was indispensable. Binswanger's resolute defense of private provision and his patient lobbying among business circles in favor of the three-pillar doctrine makes him a key protagonist of this chapter.[107] The Winterthur executive followed in the steps of lobbyists from Rentenanstalt (Georg Schärtlin, Emile Marchand) and Zurich Life (Ernst Röthlisberger), who left their marks on social policy-making since the 1920s. Under Binswanger's guidance, Winterthur Life replaced Zurich Life as the main challenger to Rentenanstalt in the group pension market (see Figure 2.4, p. 80).

In October 1961, in the aftermath of the 5$^{th}$ AHV revision, the Study Commission on Social Legislation identified two challenges that business circles would have to face in the short or medium term: the idea of people's pensions (Volkspensionen) and the prospect of compulsory occupational provision. Peter Binswanger and his peers were convinced that the benefit increases favored by the left and centrist bourgeois politicians were likely to evolve into full-blown demands for the "transformation of the AHV from basic insurance toward a people's pension covering living conditions".[108] In other words, the current development could lead to a more generous Swedish- or German-style pension system, a radical departure from the existing situation, which left ample space for supplementary private benefits.

Compulsory occupational provision designed to fill in the gaps left by the selective expansion of pension plans also ran counter to the employers' voluntary approach. Peter Binswanger emphasized that the current trend of AHV revisions had a discouraging effect, as "[m]any employers fear that employee benefits may one day become compulsory and would prefer an expansion of AHV benefits: you can feel a real resignation among employers' ranks on this subject". For life insurers who had spent decades nurturing group plans and fending off pension plan

[106] Binswanger, *Histoire de l'AVS*, p. 176. When Peter Binswanger was hired in 1955, the board of directors briefly discussed the fact that he was one-eighth Jewish. This issue was finally not deemed "a problem". See the minutes of the board of directors of Winterthur Life, August 29, 1955, quoted in Joseph Jung, *Die Winterthur: eine Versicherungsgeschichte* (Zurich: NZZ Verlag, 2000), p. 224.

[107] Peter Binswanger, "Quo Vadis AHV?" *Politische Rundschau* 10 (1958), pp. 285–90. For an appreciation of Binswanger's role, see also his Festschrift, *Begegnungen mit Peter Binswanger* (Frauenfeld: Verlag Huber, 1981), pp. 16, 20, 78–80, 93.

[108] Report by Peter Binswanger to the executive committee of the VSLG, October 16, 1961, p. 2, file Q128 203, ZFS.

regulation, the prospect of compulsory supplementary pensions and strict state supervision "would touch the vital nerve of private insurance companies".[109] According to the Study Commission, life insurers should not "retreat from their positions without fighting back" and had to vigorously defend the "division of labor" between social insurance and corporate benefits.[110] More than a decade before the 1972 vote, insurance interests had already identified the main issues that would be debated during the struggle between the three-pillar doctrine and the people's pensions alternative.

The outcome of the 5th AHV revision revealed shortcomings that could only be overcome by a long-term and comprehensive approach. In order to ensure "sound development of the AHV", Peter Binswanger suggested that insurers should initiate a debate among business federations on the future of pensions and provide decisive, albeit discreet, leadership in this matter:

> [S]uch a campaign can only be undertaken if life insurers take the initiative and supply the bulk of the effort. However, this does not mean that insurers should appear publicly as the initiators of the campaign, as this would immediately bring discredit to it. But if we provide the initial work and leadership, other groups that can do a better job with public opinion will undoubtedly join us.[111]

After securing moral and financial backing from the Union of Life Insurance Companies, the commission established positive contacts with the SVPP, the Society for the Development of the Swiss Economy (Wirtschaftsförderung), and the three business federations (the Vorort, Arbeitgeberverband, and Gewerbeverband).[112] This led to the formation in December 1961 of the Study Commission on Old Age and Survivors' Provision (Studienkommission für die Probleme der Alters- und Hinterlassenenvorsorge, SPAHV). The SPAHV, or "Binswanger study group" as it was sometimes dubbed in employers' circles, became a clearinghouse for defining common perspectives on social policy development. Despite initial opposition from the SVPP, the Inter-Cantonal Association for Employee Benefits (IVP) was also included in the study group, as it could serve as a communication channel with western Switzerland pension plans. During the next decade, the SPAHV would receive around CHF 1 million from the Union of Life Insurance Companies to finance

[109] Konferenz der Vereinigung Schweizerischen Lebensversicherungsgesellschaften (VSLG), October 20, 1961, p. 24, file Q127 206, ZFS.
[110] Studienkommission VSLG, July 14, 1961, file Q128 203, ZFS.
[111] Ibid., April 26, 1961, p. 7, file Q128 203, ZFS.
[112] Ibid., August 16, 1961, file Q128 203, ZFS.

its secretariat and various political campaigns.[113] According to Heinrich Homberger of the Vorort, strict confidentiality was a precondition for the work of the study group, as any publicity about its deliberations would enable the left to portray business federations as opponents of social insurance.[114] Peter Binswanger, initiator and president of the SPAHV, never mentions the study group in his history of the AHV.

The creation of the SPAHV was part of the response by business circles, and in particular by life insurers, to the changing political environment of the late 1950s and early 1960s. The challenges outlined by Peter Binswanger and his peers would confront employers' federations with difficult choices. Compulsory occupational pensions were deemed unacceptable in the early meetings of the SPAHV. However, this option – the present-day second pillar – would emerge as the main bulwark against the left-wing people's pensions. This strategic shift in favor of compulsory occupational pensions would prove controversial among employers. Yet, the struggle for the three-pillar doctrine that led to the 1972 vote was only in its preliminary stage in 1962. During its first years of activity, the SPAHV faced more immediate challenges.

In early summer 1962, two new pension initiatives launched by the *Beobachter*, a popular weekly, and the AVIVO, a pensioners' association linked to the Labor Party, were registered at the Federal Chancellery. This renewed use of direct democracy to bolster benefits and introduce pension-indexing triggered the negotiations for a 6$^{th}$ AHV revision.[115] Both initiatives were received coolly by the leadership of the Socialist Party, which angered some of its sections, notably in western Switzerland, that would have preferred more combative "socialist solutions" to "half measures". These dissenting factions deplored the lack of debates on policy options and their leadership's over-reliance on executive power

[113] On the foundation of the SPAHV, see SPAHV "Vereinbarung", December 19, 1961, file 95.27, AfZ-SHIV; Vorort Vorstand, December 18, 1961, file 1.5.3.16–18, AfZ-SHIV; Konferenz der VSLG, October 20, 1961, file Q127 206, ZFS; "SPAHV: Grundzüge" [n.d., ca. December 1961], file Q128 203, ZFS. On the issue of the participation of the Interkantonaler Verband für Personalfürsorge (IVP), see the invitation to the second meeting of the SPAHV, April 19, 1962, file 95.27, AfZ-SHIV; see also SPAHV Sitzung, May 10, 1962, file Q128 203, ZFS. On the financing of the SPAHV, see Konferenz der VSLG 20.10.1961, file Q127 206, as well as Konferenz der VSLG, December 12, 1969, file Q127 206, both in ZFS.

[114] SPAHV Sitzung, July 12, 1962, file Q128 203, ZFS.

[115] Binswanger, *Histoire de l'AVS*, pp. 192–200. The Association for the defense of the elderly, disabled persons, widows, and orphans (Association de défense des vieillards, invalides, veuves, et orphelins, AVIVO) had been founded in 1948 in Geneva by Roger Dafflon, a prominent member of the Labor Party (Partei der Arbeit). See Jean de Senarclens, "Dafflon, Roger", in *Historisches Lexicon der Schweiz*, at http://www.dhs.ch.

to advance social policy goals. Yet, "social security plans" and Swedish-inspired second-tier pensions found little echo in a party leadership that was committed to act within the framework of the Magic Formula, or among trade unions, which favored the expansion of occupational pensions through social partnership over social insurance.[116]

For the SPAHV, the situation was without ambiguity: the new study group not only had to respond to the two initiatives and to a new AHV revision, but also had to convince employers' federations of the necessity of agreeing on a suitable strategy to counteract future expansions of social insurance. Advancing simultaneously on these three fronts brought mixed results. Business-friendly politicians were briefed by the SPAHV, and the Wirtschaftsförderung launched a media campaign against the AVIVO and *Beobachter* initiatives.[117] The SPAHV had initially envisioned a more aggressive lobbying campaign staged by the Rudolf Farner public relations company. However, the Vorort and Arbeitgeberverband balked at this proposal and finally vetoed it, fearing that such an "Americanization" of policy-making would backfire because of Farner's staunchly conservative and anti-Communist reputation. "If it becomes known", pointed out Hans Herold, "that we have tried to use this firm in order to influence public opinion, we will lose the whole game."[118] Once again, employers were careful not to appear frontline oppositionists to social policy expansion and still favored a low-key approach.

However, business hostility to the AVIVO and *Beobachter* initiatives was unmistakable. In a scathing attack published in the newsletter of the Federal Social Insurance Office, Peter Binswanger warned that an overextension of AHV benefits would herald "social policy regression" and would "fatefully challenge" the division of labor between the AHV and occupational provision. Besides endangering the stability of the currency and fueling inflation, such social policy measures "would lead to an atrophy of the essential features, namely self-responsibility, individual autonomy,

[116] *Protokoll über die Verhandlungen des ordentlichen Parteitages vom 29./30. September 1962* (Berne: Sozialdemokratische Partei der Schweiz, 1962), pp. 92 (quotation pp. 100–2), file K961, Sozialarchiv. See also Siegenthaler, *Die Politik der Gewerkschaften*, pp. 70–1.

[117] For the briefing of the Trade and Industry Group (Gruppe Handel und Industrie) of the Federal Assembly, see SPAHV Sitzung, June 15, 1962, file Q128 203, ZFS. For these propaganda efforts, see SPAHV Sitzung, November 6, 1962, file 95.27, AfZ-SHIV.

[118] Hans Herold to Heinrich Homberger, August 21, 1962; Leonhard Derron to Peter Binswanger, August 21, 1962, both documents in file 95.27, AfZ-SHIV. Rudolf Farner (1917–1984) pioneered American-style marketing techniques in Switzerland. He was a proponent of a massive armaments build-up, including the development of nuclear warheads for the Swiss air force, and was active in anti-Communist networks. See Markus Bürgi, "Farner, Rudolf", in *Historisches Lexicon der Schweiz*, at http://www.dhs.ch.

and self-confidence, that largely contributed to immunizing our people against Communism". This type of medical imagery and ranting about the immorality of social insurance had long been peddled in Switzerland. As the Cold War was now at its height, the defense of corporate and individual provision was an integral part of an anti-Communist agenda that praised western social achievements to counter Soviet-inspired social policy.[119]

If business circles agreed that AHV pensions covering "adequate living conditions" had to be fought off with determination, it was more difficult to unite them behind a common alternative strategy. The SPAHV advised that employers should expand pension plan coverage and uphold the division of labor between social insurance and occupational provision. This aim was to be accomplished through lower group insurance premiums, tax exemptions for pension plans, and better portability of occupational benefits.[120] Needless to say, this strategy served insurers' interests, because their group divisions tried to attract small firms that had not yet developed pension benefits.

The SPAHV advocated that something be done for the worst-off pensioners and for workers who were currently not – and would probably never be – covered by occupational plans. However, in order to deflect the expansion of AHV pensions favored by the left, the alleviation of poverty among the elderly had to be achieved by means of assistance programs rather than social insurance. The SPAHV supported the development of means-tested pension supplements and indexing methods based on

[119] Peter Binswanger, "AHV – Basisversicherung oder 'Volkspension'?" *Schweizerische Zeitschrift für Sozialversicherung* (1962), pp. 120–31, 123, 30. In 1933, the respected military doctor and right-wing politician Eugen Bircher had asserted that Germany's defeat during World War I had been caused by the debilitating effect of Bismarck's social insurance policies. See Daniel Heller, *Eugen Bircher Arzt, Militär und Politiker: ein Beitrag zur Zeitgeschichte* (Zurich: NZZ Verlag, 1990), p. 37. In a similar vein, the bulletin of the Swiss Medical Association still held in 1946 that Bismarck's health insurance had constituted "a calamity that had in no small part contributed to the moral and economic decline" of Switzerland's powerful northern neighbor from the Wilhelminian Empire to the Third Reich. See Rachel Vuagniaux, "Le 'médecin libre' contre le 'bolchevisme médical': le *Bulletin professionnel des médecins suisses* et les premières tentatives de révision de la LAMA (1920–1951)", *Aspects de la sécurité sociale* 3 (2002), pp. 2–9 (quotation p. 8). On the postwar "system competition" between eastern and western European welfare states, see Raphael Lutz, "Europäische Sozialstaaten in der Boomphase (1948–1973): Versuch einer historischen Distanzierung einer 'klassischen Phase' des europäischen Sozialmodells", in *Das europäische Sozialmodell: auf dem Weg zum transnationalen Sozialstaat*, ed. Hartmut Kaelble and Günther Schmid (Berlin: Sigma, 2004), pp. 51–74 (especially pp. 53, 56–8).

[120] "Aktionsplan für die Behauptung der privatwirtschaftlichen Alters- und Hinterlassenenvorsorge" [n.d., ca. May 1962], SPAHV Sitzung, May 10, 1962, file Q128 203, ZFS; Konferenz der VSLG, September 21, 1962, file Q127 206, ZFS.

negotiated agreements instead of annual adjustments. Despite its opposition to a rise in payroll contributions, the study group was ready to accept an increase in federal subsidies to the AHV as long as this originated from consumer taxes and not from more redistributive wealth or income taxes.[121] These measures, designed to act as a fire break against the expansion of social insurance, would have lasting consequences: means-tested pension supplements and the preference given to indirect taxation in pension financing still constitute key dimensions of current pension debates.

The SPAHV guidelines were met with skepticism. For the secretary of the SVPP, the SPAHV guidelines were an unwelcome echo of Hans Peter Tschudi's appeals in favor of an expansion of social security. The idea that employers should initiate social benefit increases also provoked unease among the Arbeitgeberverband. Farsighted insurers had still to convince the business community at large of these points of view.[122] Indecision proved to be problematic. When negotiations on the 6th AHV revision began in earnest in the spring of 1963, they took place at what employers' documents described as a "stormy pace" and in a "feverish political climate" created by the prospect of federal elections in the fall.[123]

Less than a year elapsed before the acceptance of the 6th AHV revision by the Federal Assembly in December 1963. In retrospect, Heinrich Homberger of the Vorort emphasized that the Federal Council had given less weight to the usual consultation with business federations and focused negotiations at the level of the AHV Commission, a procedure that impeded coordination between the federations. Because of the Magic Formula, Homberger added, the Federal Council was "not a homogeneous body any more", and disagreements between its bourgeois and Socialist members added uncertainties to the debates on the AHV Commission.[124]

The main business federations repeatedly disagreed as to which path to follow during the revision process. Along with the Swiss National Bank, the Vorort lobbied the government to raise AHV payroll contributions

121 SPAHV, "Richtlinien für die Weiterentwicklung der kantonalen Alters- und Hinterlassenenbeihilfen", December 31, 1962, file 95.15, AfZ-SHIV.

122 SPAHV Sitzung, October 12, 1962, file 95.27, AfZ-SHIV. See also Kurt Sovilla (Arbeitgeberverband), "Das Problem einer 6. AHV-Revision" [n.d., ca. 1962], file Q128 203, ZFS; Studienkommission VSLG, November 16, 1962, p. 2, file Q128 203, ZFS; Konferenz der VSLG, December 13, 1962, p. 27, file Q127 206, ZFS.

123 Vorort Vorstand, August 26, 1963, file 1.5.3.16–18, AfZ-SHIV; *Geschäftsbericht 1963* (Zurich: SVPP, 1964), p. 5, file V Schweiz 2435, SNB.

124 Vorort Vorstand, December 20, 1963, p. 9, file 1.5.3.16–18, AfZ-SHIV.

in order to hold down inflation and reduce the possibility of increased taxation to finance the revision. Arguing that payroll contributions would be immediately re-injected into the economy through investments made by the AHV reserve fund, the Arbeitgeberverband criticized this choice, claiming it would create a dangerous political precedent and fuel further expansion demands.[125] In the end, the revision raised pensions by one-third and lowered the retirement age of women to 62 years, two improvements financed through an increase in federal subsidies to the AHV. In a final statement, the Federal Council announced that further increases in AHV benefits as well as the introduction of means-tested pension supplements remained on the political agenda.[126] Having played the role of spurring on social policy debates, the *Beobachter* and AVIVO initiatives were withdrawn by their initiators.

Employers had succeeded in fending off a rise in payroll contributions, but the outcomes of the 6th AHV revision reinforced their resolve that steps had to be taken to stop the expansion of social policy. At first, some members of the SPAHV argued that precious time had been lost in useless discussions and openly questioned the pertinence of the study group.[127] The SPAHV staved off these critics by arguing that the impending introduction of means-tested supplements, which enjoyed a wide political and public consensus, would deflect future pension increases and slow down the development of pay-as-you-go social insurance. Furthermore, the SPAHV had achieved a significant breakthrough by introducing the first officially endorsed definition of the three-pillar doctrine into the public debate. Far from being anecdotal, the efforts of the study group to set the terms of the AHV debate along a multi-pillar framework would prove to be decisive in the following years.

In April 1963, during a session of the AHV Commission, Peter Binswanger, delegate of the Union of Life Insurance Companies, successfully argued that the 6th AHV revision should clarify social policy debates by outlining the specificity of the Swiss pension system, namely its reliance on different forms of old age provision.[128] When the Federal Council presented the AHV revision to the Federal Assembly in September, the pension bill concluded with a paragraph entitled "the Swiss solution to old age provision":

[125] For these debates, see Arbeitgeberverband Vorstand, September 4, 1963, p. 7, as well as Geschäftsführerkonferenz, October 25, 1963, pp. 12–13, SAV. See also Vorort Vorstand, August 26, 1963, pp. 5–12, file 1.5.3.16, AfZ-SHIV.
[126] Binswanger, *Histoire de l'AVS*, pp. 195–200.
[127] Marc Haldy (Vaudoise Assurances) to Peter Binswanger, June 24, 1963, file 95.38, AfZ-SHIV.
[128] Studienkommission VSLG, April 18, 1963, p. 3, file Q128 203, ZFS.

Securing our population against the economic hardships of old age, death, and disability is based . . . on three forms of provision, namely individual self-provision (savings, individual insurance) and occupational provision (pension, group, and membership plans), as well as social insurance and its means-tested supplements. This distinctively Swiss system of old age provision should not be altered by the 6th AHV revision. On the contrary, we should develop social insurance so that its benefits constitute in the future a basis and an incentive for the two other forms of provision. AHV and disability benefits shall remain basic benefits that cannot alone cover the needs of the insured in case of old age, disability, or death.[129]

This reference to "three forms" of provision did not come out of the blue. Its roots were in the hybrid nature of the pension system. The wording of the section, which emphasized, first, individual provision and then occupational provision, and relegated social insurance to the last position, also echoed concepts that had recurred since the interwar period. References to the "degrees", "circles", or the "ternary nature" of old age provision had become increasingly common in postwar social policy debates, and especially in business depictions of the Swiss "enduring synthesis between private and state [welfare] measures".[130] In its 1962 annual report, the SVPP had also warned that those who attempted to "limit the development of social provision alongside three different pillars" were in the end in favor of a "revolutionary transformation of the social system" whose ultimate goal would confer to the state "a central and dominant role as sole provider of social benefits".[131] Although Hans Peter Tschudi himself had described the "three tiers" of the pension system, and some business representatives pointed out that Federal Councilor Walther Stampfli had supposedly been the first to use the expression "three pillars of old age provision" during World War II, the clause of the 1963 pension bill was the first explicit acknowledgment of this key concept in an official document.[132] The Union of Life Insurance Companies praised Peter Binswanger for having secured this clarification and

129 "Message du Conseil fédéral à l'Assemblée fédérale relatif à un projet de loi modifiant la Loi fédérale sur l'assurance vieillesse et survivants (6ème révision), du 16 septembre 1963", in *Feuille Fédérale* (Berne: Chancellerie fédérale, 1963), volume II, pp. 497–584 (quotation p. 500).

130 W. Hardmeier, *Personalversicherung und Hochkonjunktur* (Zurich: SVPP, 1962), p. 5, file 95.3, AfZ-SHIV ("three degrees"); *Rentenanstalt: Personalfürsorge*, no. 5, January 1963 ("ternary nature"); *Die Personalfürsorge-Einrichtungen der Privatwirtschaft* (Zurich: SVPP, [n.d., ca. 1959]), file K 106, Wirtschaftsarchiv ("enduring synthesis").

131 *SVPP Jahresbericht 1962* (Zurich: SVPP, 1963), p. 26. For a discussion of the three-pillar metaphor, see Matthieu Leimgruber, "Les trois piliers de la sagesse? La métaphore ternaire de la protection vieillesse en Suisse", *Aspects de la sécurité sociale* 4 (2005), pp. 2–12.

132 See Arbeitgeberverband Vorstand, May 23, 1962, p. 9 ("three tiers"), SAV; Vorort Vorstand, February 25, 1963, p. 20 ("three pillars"), file 1.5.3.16–18, AfZ-SHIV.

emphasized that "thanks to [the SPAHV] we can now rely on a clear definition of the 'Swiss solution'".[133]

However, insurers were not satisfied with this achievement. They used the lapse of time that preceded the publication of the pension bill to devise their own document praising this multi-pillar conception. In October 1963, the Union of Life Insurance Companies circulated 19,000 free copies of a brochure whose title (*The Swiss Solution to Old Age Provision*) matched that of the clause of the 6th AHV revision bill.[134] Designed to anchor the "Swiss solution" in public opinion, this text praised the Federal Council for acknowledging the distinctiveness of Swiss old age provision and pictured the three-pillar system as the embodiment of the pragmatic genius of a small, democratic, and anti-totalitarian nation: "The three pillars upon which our Swiss solution is based form an ensemble whose main characteristic resides in the fact that it does not have the rigidity of uniform solutions which might lead to the leveling of [individual] conditions and to totalitarianism."[135] Patriotic appeals to Swiss exceptionalism (Sonderfall) enabled insurers to reject alternative ways of organizing pension provision as "foreign" solutions incompatible with an allegedly immanent "Swiss way": "Solutions adopted in other countries should not be decisive for us, for Switzerland has been running its policies according to its own designs for centuries . . . Our social policy will remain faithful to our own solutions, as they are best suited to the distinctive characteristics of our country."[136]

Despite references to exceptionalism, the kernel of the text rested upon a straightforward defense of insurers' social policy concepts. The proponents of the three-pillar doctrine considered any overexpansion of the AHV a direct attack on capital accumulation, private property, and individual freedom:

> If the AHV were to expand more and more to the detriment of individual and collective provision, we would witness a corresponding diminution of the accumulation of private monies. Since private property is the basis of economic freedom, and thus of freedom itself, the consequences of such an evolution would be significant for the economy as well as for our entire social structure.[137]

The brochure even concluded that the aim of the three-pillar concept was to counter the current expansion of social insurance:

133 Konferenz der VSLG, November 11, 1963, p. 19, file Q127 206, ZFS.
134 Studienkommission VSLG, April 18, 1963, p. 3, file Q128 203, ZFS. For circulation numbers, see *VSLG. Zirkularmitteilungen*, no. 7, 1963.
135 *La solution suisse du problème de la prévoyance en faveur des vieillards, des survivants et des invalides* (Zurich: Union des Compagnies suisses d'assurances sur la vie, 1963), p. 5.
136 Ibid., p. 17. 137 Ibid., p. 18.

Whatever its shortcomings and its effects, a transformation of the AHV into an institution alone providing adequate living conditions might hardly be avoided sooner or later, notably if social security could not be provided by other means . . . [The three-pillar solution] is not only possible, but [it] also has to be preferred to an expansion of the AHV, as extensive as this might be. If one wants to think truly "socially", one can only do it by setting out to realize our distinctively Swiss solution.[138]

The "distinctively Swiss solution" depicted here demonstrated the medium-term strategy envisioned by insurers, notably their resolve to roll out a global concept that employers could use to reverse the defensive position in which they were currently mired, and then to go on the offensive.

Again using language that evoked the competition between western capitalism and Soviet Communism, Peter Binswanger asserted in October 1963 that "[t]he further expansion of the AHV is . . . no longer a social issue, but a *political issue and a question of worldview* [sic]. Those who propose an expansion of the AHV are in the end in favor of state-control and collectivism."[139] Peter Binswanger also openly admitted that the three-pillar solution suffered from "opacity" and "fragmentation", was "more demanding for each individual person", and finally appeared "less rational than a completely state-based solution". However, the insurance executive continued, this "global solution" was more efficient and "focused" than the AHV and "finally preserved a wider space for fruitful collaboration between social partners".[140]

Echoing this, the Union of Life Insurance Companies considered that, despite its soaring costs, the 6th AHV revision could be called a success, as it henceforth fixed the terms of the debate on the "Swiss solution". However, the iron framework that the insurers favored for the pension system was not yet nailed to the ground. The confrontation of ideas preceded the struggle between the three-pillar doctrine and the people's pensions. As the insurers' Study Commission of Social Legislation wrote in early 1964: "When all is said and done, our concept now permeates the whole debate. The switches have been set to the 'Swiss solution' . . . however, the final test of the 'Swiss solution' will only occur during one of the next AHV revisions."[141] A few months later, the "Swiss solution" made its

138 Ibid., p. 19.
139 SPAHV, "Thesen für die Publizistik über die AHV nach durchgeführter 6. Revision", October 24, 1963, file Q128 203, ZFS.
140 Peter Binswanger, "Die AHV als Basisversicherung oder als existenzsichernde Versicherung?" *Schweizerische Zeitschrift für Sozialversicherung* (1963), pp. 77–97 (quotation p. 86).
141 Studienkommission VSLG, January 15, 1964, p. 4, file Q128 203, ZFS.

first mass audience début in the insurance pavilion of the National Exhibition held in Lausanne. After strolling along two halls devoted to the "law of big numbers" and to "risk communities", hundreds of thousands of visitors could contemplate a wall-sized representation of Switzerland's social welfare system, depicted as an ensemble based on the "harmonious collaboration between three forms of institutions".[142]

This episode shows the shortcomings of explanations describing the three-pillar system as an embodiment of the "Swiss genius for equilibrium" or as the almost inevitable outcome of "social praxis".[143] The resolve of the SPAHV to set the terms of the debate acknowledged the strategic vision of insurers during a period marked by uncertainties as to the future of social policy fueled by the "Tschudi pace" and the increasing use of direct democracy to push forward pension expansion. This vanguard role was in no small part due to the specific position that insurers occupied at the intersection between policy-making and the business of social policy.

The development of the three-pillar doctrine was facilitated by the long-term trajectory of the pension system, and in particular the division of labor established early on between basic pensions and occupational provision. However, this doctrine was specifically designed to rein in the permanent revision process of the AHV and to safeguard occupational schemes. The early framing of the terms of the debate decisively strengthened insurers' and employers' positions when the hybrid structure of the pension system was challenged for the first time by left-wing Socialists and by the Labor Party at the end of the 1960s. However, the brainstorming and lobbying efforts undertaken by insurers through the SPAHV had no equivalent in circles on the left, which was to have dire consequences for the people's pensions.

## Uncertainties on the social policy front (1964–1967)

The mid-1960s set the stage for the struggle between the people's pensions and the three-pillar doctrine. These years witnessed the introduction of means-tested pension supplements and the enactment of the 7th AHV revision while discussions took place on the amelioration of

[142] For a presentation of the insurance pavillion, see *Assurance*, fiches d'information, volume 5, section 51/1 (Lausanne: Secrétariat de l'Exposition nationale suisse, 1964) in Archives de la Ville de Lausanne (Switzerland).

[143] Raymond Déonna, *Les tendances qui s'affrontent en Suisse en matière de sécurité sociale, et notamment d'AVS* (Zurich: SVPP, 1964), p. 19; Hans-Peter Tschudi, "Das Drei-Säulen-Prinzip", *Schweizerische Zeitschrift für Sozialversicherung und berufliche Vorsorge* (1987), pp. 1–20 (quotation p. 4).

occupational pension coverage and the economic impact of the financial assets of pension plans. The complexity of these debates echoed the uncertainties that characterized a period marked by slowing productivity, industrial rationalization, and rising inflation that together began to weigh on postwar growth. These economic problems were compounded by the ossification of the carefully crafted political equilibriums of the concordance period. The permanent governing coalition still controlled over four-fifths of the seats of the Federal Assembly. However, commentators spoke of a "Helvetic malaise" as scandals tarnished the standing of the main bourgeois parties and non-governmental parties and political movements appeared to be on the rise. In 1964, public outcry over a vast overrun of military spending on new fighter jets cost the Radical Federal Councilor heading the Defense Department his seat. In the 1967 elections, the centrist Alliance of Independents almost doubled its representation in the Federal Assembly. Lastly, the development of anti-foreigner groupings formed the backdrop to the electoral comeback of the far right and to several initiatives to rein in the number of foreign workers and the "over-foreignization" (Überfremdung) of the country.[144]

Employers and insurers attempted to rein in the expansion of the AHV, which brought mixed results. The first step in this direction was the introduction of means-tested supplements for pensioners (AHV-Ergänzungsleistungen). These tax-financed benefits were accepted by an overwhelming majority of the Federal Assembly in March 1965. As the Federal Council was preparing the bill on means-tested benefits, Leonhard Derron of the Arbeitgeberverband summarized the reasons that motivated business acceptance of these measures:

> If the AHV is to remain a basic insurance scheme, it has to be supplemented by private measures. This is not possible in all cases. These gaps can be closed by three means. One could introduce compulsory occupational provision, which would be dangerous. One could also increase the level of the lowest AHV pensions, which would be similarly dangerous. The third option remains the implementation of supplementary means-tested assistance benefits.[145]

According to the Arbeitgeberverband, pension supplements enacted at the cantonal level would help deter or deflect the expansion of federal social insurance. Means-tested assistance was meant as a temporary

[144] Peter Gilg and Peter Halblützel, "Une course accélérée vers l'avenir", in *Nouvelle histoire de la Suisse et des Suisses* (Lausanne: Payot, 1986), pp. 771–911, 786ff, 840ff. The "Mirage Affair" led to the formation of the first parliamentary investigatory commission in the history of the Confederation. Federal Councilor Paul Chaudet (Radical) stepped down in 1966 to avoid facing a difficult re-election. On anti-foreigner initiatives, see Mahnig, ed., *Histoire des politiques d'immigration*, pp. 263–73.

[145] Vorort Vorstand, January 27, 1964, p. 10, file 1.5.3.16–18, AfZ-SHIV.

measure but also underscored the inadequacy of federal pensions for a significant minority of the elderly. Despite the means tests, no less than 22 percent of pensioners received supplements in 1967. And demands for higher pensions continued unabated as rising inflation rates shrank pensions unprotected by indexing mechanisms.[146]

Keen to counter criticism of the shortcomings of the AHV, in the winter of 1966 the Union of Life Insurance Companies published a glossy brochure proclaiming that *Old Age is not a Risk Any More*.[147] Paradoxically, the results of a public opinion survey commissioned a few months later by the SPAHV revealed the gulf between this statement and public perception of the situation of the elderly: 82 percent of the persons polled declared that they worried about old age. This result was obviously linked to the fact that 74 percent of respondents (a percentage that reached 83 percent in western Switzerland) estimated that the AHV did not guarantee a decent standard of living. Moreover, 47 percent said that this statement was still valid after the addition of means-tested pension supplements. Despite constant revisions, the cornerstone of social security was seen as incomplete. When asked to situate the Swiss welfare state in international comparison, 16 percent answered that it was "superior" to its European counterparts, while around one-third estimated it of either "equal" (37 percent) or "inferior" quality (30 percent overall, but 41 percent in western Switzerland). Asked to rank the "best welfare states", respondents named Sweden (40 percent) and West Germany (17 percent), while Switzerland (6 percent) trailed behind, followed by France, the United Kingdom, and the United States. The conclusion of the survey was unequivocal: 85 percent of the people polled were in favor of a new AHV revision and supported (in order of preference) indexing mechanisms, a general rise in pensions, and the introduction of early retirement.[148]

The prospect of federal elections to be held in the fall of 1967 again spurred on social policy demands. The Catholic Trade Union Federation (Christlichnationaler Gewerkschaftsbund), whose membership had doubled between 1945 and 1965 with the influx of southern European

146 *Statistique des assurances sociales suisses 2001* (Berne: Office fédéral des assurances sociales, 2002), p. 108. On the development of means-tested supplementary benefits, see Binswanger, *Histoire de l'AVS*, pp. 202–4; Sommer, *Das Ringen um die soziale Sicherheit*, pp. 293–4. Average annual inflation rates reached 3.5 percent between 1962 and 1967, or twice the level of the preceding decade. See Heiner Ritzmann-Blickenstorfer and Hansjörg Siegenthaler, eds., *Historisch Statistik der Schweiz – Statistique historique de la Suisse – Swiss Historical Statistics* (Zurich: Chronos, 1996), Table H20.

147 *VSLG Zirkularmitteilungen*, November 22, 1966, file Q128 203, ZFS.

148 Institut für Meinungs-Forschung in Biel, "Probleme der Alters-Vorsorge in der Meinung des Publikums", 1967, pp. 16, 23–5, 29–32, 28, 36, file Q128 203, ZFS.

workers, presented an initiative in August 1966 demanding higher pensions indexed to the cost of living. The initiative also asked the Federal Council to fill in the gaps in occupational coverage among smaller firms and trade sectors and to increase workers' participation in the management of pension plans.[149] Leading trade unions such as the Metalworkers' Union did not disguise their hostility toward the proposal of this labor rival, but the issue of a mandatory second pension tier was now spelled out explicitly.[150] Almost simultaneously, the Socialist Party and the Gewerkschaftsbund called for a 40 percent rise in AHV benefits financed by an increase in payroll contributions. These proposals initiated a new social policy legislative cycle, and the Federal Council decided to launch a 7th AHV revision.[151]

For insurance executive Peter Binswanger, this revision would be the one during which "the prevailing Swiss conception . . . would experience its baptism of fire". It was time to put a "final limit" on the AHV, otherwise employers confronted with ever-increasing social costs would refrain from further developing occupational provision.[152] The insurance executive thus favored indexing mechanisms that would "depoliticize" the AHV and help fend off attempts to increase benefits or payroll contributions. Binswanger's concerns echoed similar ones in the United States. As political scientist Jacob Hacker notes, "automatic indexing" was considered during the 1960s by Republican politicians as a "*conservative* [sic] option, a means of forestalling interparty bidding over Social Security that would expand the program even faster than general price levels".[153]

The entanglement of complex pension revisions gave credibility to proponents of structural reforms. During the 7th AHV revision, parliamentary motions explicitly demanded the introduction of more generous

149 Fluder *et al.*, *Gewerkschaften und Angestelltenverbände*, pp. 96–9, 103–4; Leo Truffer, "Die schweizerische Altersvorsorge in der Sicht der Christlichnationalen Gewerkschaftsbundes", *Schweizerische Zeitschrift für Sozialversicherung* (1967), pp. 190–7.

150 Arbeitgeberverband Vorstand, April 6, 1966, pp. 23–4, SAV.

151 Binswanger, *Histoire de l'AVS*, pp. 209–15. On the Socialist and Gewerkschaftsbund perspectives on pensions, see Giacomo Bernasconi, "Probleme der 7. AHV Revision", *Schweizerische Zeitschrift für Sozialversicherung* (1967), pp. 81–91.

152 Peter Binswanger, "Die neuesten Vorstöße zur Weiterentwicklung der AHV und die Personalfürsorge", address at the May 5, 1966 general assembly of the SVPP in St. Gallen, p. 2, file V Schweiz 2435, SNB. On the need for an "end goal", see Peter Binswanger, "Grundsätzliche Betrachtung zur 7. AHV Revision", *Schweizerische Zeitschrift für Sozialversicherung* (1967), pp. 256–67, p. 260.

153 Peter Binswanger, "Zur Frage der Anpassung der AHV-Renten an den Lebenshaltungskostenindex", address to the Economic commission of the Zurich Radical Party, February 1966, p. 7, as well as Studienkommission VSLG, January 11, 1966, both documents in file Q128 203, ZFS. On the indexing debate in the United States, see Hacker, *The divided welfare state*, p. 144.

retirement benefits guaranteeing "adequate living conditions". In October 1966, minority groups within the Socialist Party once again challenged piecemeal pension reforms and denounced the "jungle of statutes" that characterized occupational provision. Criticizing the Socialist leadership's lack of interest in a real debate on social policy alternatives, Karl Gmünder, one of the fervent proponents of the people's pensions, reminded the Socialist congress that "if our comrades of 1918 had only put forward requests that seemed reachable by means of realpolitik instead of shaping new claims based on human needs, our party would have already long lost its credibility".[154] However, the majority of the party once again postponed any formal decisions on the people's pensions before the implementation of the 7th AHV revision, so as not to anger trade union proponents of collectively bargained employee benefits who had little sympathy for an extension of pay-as-you-go social insurance.[155] The people's pensions had begun their slow march toward the political arena, but the attachment of the governmental left to the three-pillar doctrine slowed the process.

The growing tangle of social policy debates generated unrest within business ranks. Since the early 1960s, Andreas Brunner (1923–1988), National Councilor (Radical) and chief financial officer of the electro-engineering firm Landis & Gyr, had been bombarding the Federal Council and the public with proposals to solve what he called the "lack of generosity" of the AHV. Brunner proposed to split AHV payroll contributions into two tiers, the first financing a flat-rate basic pension and the second devoted to individual retirement accounts. The Vorort and the Arbeitgeberverband desperately tried to silence this self-proclaimed social policy expert who launched, in the autumn of 1967, an "Action for the Reform of the AHV". Brunner's crusade provoked the ire of the left, which accused him of going after a dismantlement of AHV pensions. For annoyed insurers, Brunner's maverick proposals had "the rare gift of supplying to [our] opponents the ammunition they need against us" and they "upset public opinion and destabilize[d] members of the Federal Assembly".[156] The controversy soon transformed itself into a much publicized "war of numbers" between Brunner and the Federal Social Insurance Office. Business federations depicted the engineering executive as

154 *Ausserordentlicher Parteitag vom 22./26. Oktober 1966* (Berne: Sozialdemokratische Partei der Schweiz, 1966), pp. 184–5, 187, 197, file K961, Sozialarchiv.

155 So/He [Kurt Sovilla/Hans Herold?], "7. AHV Revision", April 25, 1966, p. 2, file 95.32, AfZ-SHIV. See also Siegenthaler, *Die Politik der Gewerkschaften*, p. 77.

156 Konferenz der VSLG, February 1, 1972, p. 23, file Q127 206, ZFS. For a biographical profile, see Renato Morosoli, "Brunner, Andreas", in *Historisches Lexicon der Schweiz*, at http://www.dhs.ch.

an unwelcome troublemaker who caused a rift in the employers' united front.[157] Although they acknowledged that the rise in AHV benefits narrowed the scope for occupational provision and led to "over-insurance" in specific sectors or firms, the business federations doubted whether transforming existing graduated AHV benefits into flat-rate pensions would reduce pressure for the expansion of social policy.[158]

In 1967, Ernst Kaiser of the Federal Social Insurance Office proposed harmonizing the financial and administrative system of the AHV into a "social pension insurance law". However, he received only token support from trade union members of the AHV Commission, and his idea was rapidly shelved.[159] Kaiser's harmonization attempts and Brunner's maverick tactics discomfited business federations, but these proposals could still be easily fended off. Such delaying tactics would prove insufficient when the people's pensions finally emerged as a potential alternative to the AHV muddle.

In January 1969, the 7th AHV revision increased pensions by 25 percent and raised payroll contribution rates from 4.0 to 5.2 percent, but again postponed automatic indexing mechanisms. Business federations did not oppose the revision, despite the fact that the rise in contribution rates strained the financial framework set up in 1947.[160] Employers were reluctant to launch a frontal attack on the cornerstone of social insurance at a time of growing political uncertainty. Moreover, the revision reaffirmed the three-pillar doctrine first outlined in 1963.

In a preliminary section of the 7th AHV revision bill entitled the "global concept according to the so-called three-pillar principle", the Federal Council reiterated its commitment to the multi-pillar approach. Ironically, this section only reversed the order ideologically favored by

[157] The Vorort archives devote an entire file to the "Brunner case", see file 95.30, AfZ-SHIV. Vorort Vorstand May 6, 1968, p. 29, file 1.5.3.18–20, AfZ-SHIV. See also Konferenz der VSLG, June 14, 1968, file Q127 206, ZFS; Arbeitgeberverband Vorstand, March 27, 1968, p. 13, SAV. On the "war of numbers" between Ernst Kaiser and Andreas Brunner, see Silvio Borner and Jürg Sommer, "Die AHV als Spielball von Experten und Interessen: Fallstudie zu den AHV-Revisionen 1948–1976", *Schweizerisches Jahrbuch für politische Wissenschaft* 17 (1977), pp. 235–75.

[158] Vorort Vorstand, September 15, 1967, p. 11, file 1.5.3.18–20, AfZ-SHIV; Arbeitgeberverband Vorstand, September 27, 1967, pp. 11–12, SAV.

[159] Ernst Kaiser, "Skizze zu einer Gesamtkonzeption der schweizerischen sozialen Rentenversicherung", September 29, 1967, file 95.32, AfZ-SHIV; "Commission fédérale AVS, sous-commission spéciale pour la 7ème révision, procès-verbal de la deuxième séance du 5 au 6 octobre 1967"; [Hans Herold], "7. AHV-Revision", [n.d., ca. 1967]. Since the early 1960s, insurers suspected Ernst Kaiser to provide expertise on social security to the Socialist Party and the Gewerkschaftsbund. See SPAHV Sitzung, November 6, 1962, file 95.27, AfZ-SHIV.

[160] Vorort Vorstand, April 1, 1966, file 1.5.3.16–18, AfZ-SHIV; Arbeitgeberverband Vorstand, August 11, 1968, pp. 16–29, SAV.

employers (individual savings, followed by occupational provision, and, lastly, social insurance) and outlined what remains the framework of the pension system today:

> On the occasion of the 6th AHV revision, we have defined and formulated a global concept of provision. According to this concept, the security of our population in the event of old age, disability, and death of the breadwinner rests on three forms of provision, namely social insurance pensions (AHV, disability insurance, pension supplements), collective occupational provision (pension plans, group plans, and membership schemes), and self-provision (savings, individual insurance) . . . This so-called three-pillar principle shall remain the guideline for the extension of social security.[161]

The piecemeal and haphazard evolution of the AHV revisions built up increasing pressure for a reassessment of the pension system. Two decades after the introduction of federal pensions, popular expectations of a "secure old age", the title of the 1941 initiative in favor of the AHV, had not been met. The boundaries between the two areas of old age provision that had prevailed since 1947 were increasingly contested and would have to be redefined or reaffirmed. These contradictory dynamics in favor of the expansion or containment of social insurance would culminate in the struggle between the people's pensions and the three-pillar doctrine.

Occupational coverage, benefits, and portability, as well as the financial significance of funded pension assets, were no less controversial than the expansion of the AHV. Occupational coverage had continued to progress since the end of the 1950s, but the expansion rate of occupational provision was slowing down. This phenomenon was explained by a federal survey of occupational provision by "redundancies made possible by rationalization measures" and by the tightening of the labor market, which "forced firms to hire a greater number of elderly workers and part-time workers" who could not join company pension plans.[162]

All in all, core pension plans would reach two-fifths of the overall non-farm workforce in 1970. Beyond this average, large gaps still existed between a well-covered public sector and a private sector where only one-third of the workforce was affiliated to a core pension plan. The gender gap in the second pillar was also important: 85 percent of male public-sector employees and 50 percent of male private-sector employees were covered by core plans. In contrast, coverage reached respectively 49 percent and 19 percent among women. The quality of occupational benefits inched forward unmistakably as more pension plans covered their

[161] "Message du Conseil fédéral à l'Assemblée fédérale relatif à un projet de loi modifiant la Loi fédérale sur l'assurance vieillesse et survivants (7ème révision), du 4 mars 1968", in *Feuille Fédérale* (Berne: Chancellerie fédérale, 1968), volume I, pp. 627–727 (quotation p. 641).

[162] *Pensionskassenstatistik 1970*, p. 13.

membership for old age, disability, and survivors' benefits (see Table A.2, p. 295). According to my estimates, the combination of AHV pensions and second-pillar benefits represented almost two-thirds of average wages in the public sector, as against only two-fifths in the private sector (see Table A.6, p. 301). Despite its postwar expansion, occupational provision still did not reach those who most needed additional benefits to supplement their meager AHV pensions. Beyond skilled workers and managerial staff, as a Rentenanstalt executive admitted, residual pockets of workers without cover could not be reached "without compulsion".[163] As in the United States, Canada, and the United Kingdom, which also relied on voluntary approaches to extend occupational provision, second-pillar coverage was reaching a ceiling.

Employers who used employee benefit programs to attract skilled workers and secure the loyalty of their workforce were reluctant to harmonize pension portability. In response to the 1958 Dietschi parliamentary motion that demanded a solution to this issue, the SVPP emphasized in 1959 that "the legislator shall not and has no rights to intervene in the free development of personnel welfare".[164] However, insufficient pension portability hindered a much-needed increase in the mobility of the workforce in a changing economic environment increasingly marked by industrial rationalization and concentration. Moreover, as the SPAHV had remarked in its first position papers, pension portability could be used to win employees and trade unions to the three-pillar system. Solutions to solve this issue became more pressing after the launch of the pension initiative of the Catholic Trade Union Confederation.

Since the 1950s, life insurers had been marketing "portable pension contracts" to their clients. This option had the support of the SVPP, whose members were loath to abandon the practice of using employee benefit programs as "golden chains" to retain a skilled workforce in a very competitive labor market.[165] On the other hand, business

[163] Hans Wyss, "AHV und Pensionskassen: Kann und soll eine Harmonisierung gefunden werden?" *Schweizerische Zeitschrift für Sozialversicherung* (1970), pp. 165–86, 168. The Federal Social Insurance Office estimated that around 600,000 workers were not covered by occupational provision in 1966; see "Message du Conseil fédéral à l'Assemblée fédérale relatif à un projet de loi modifiant la Loi fédérale sur l'assurance vieillesse et survivants (7ème révision), du 4 mars 1968", p. 642. The Arbeitgeberverband denounced this estimate as widely exaggerated and retorted that at most 165,000 workers remained without cover. See "Wie stark ist die zweite Säule?", *Schweizerische Arbeitgeber Zeitung*, September 19, 1968.

[164] *Geschäftsbericht 1959* (Zurich: SVPP, 1960), file V Schweiz 2435, SNB.

[165] Vorort memorandum on the "personal portable insurance contract" (Personalvorsorge-Freizügigkeits-Police) offered by insurers, February 11, 1970, file 92.5, AfZ-SHIV. See also *Geschäftsbericht 1965* (Zurich: SVPP, 1966), as well as the minutes of the May 5, 1966 General Assembly of the SVPP, pp. 1–4, both documents in file V Schweiz 2435, SNB. See also "Privatwirtschaft und Personalfürsorge: die Frage der Freizügigkeit",

federations continued to favor a social partnership approach. In 1964, the Arbeitgeberverband had initiated negotiations on pension portability with the Gewerkschaftsbund and the Association of Commercial Clerks. In June 1967, these negotiations ended in an agreement that safeguarded specific arrangements made in manufacturing sectors such as machine-making, and called on labor and business to "encourage the free development of occupational provision and to protect in a fair and reasonable way employees' rights when they change jobs".[166]

To placate employers alarmed by this infringement of formerly entirely voluntary portability practices, the Arbeitgeberverband argued that this solution allowed the deflection of the initiative of the Catholic Trade Union Federation and was more flexible than any legislative solution.[167] Moreover, a Wirtschaftsförderung secretary reminded business federation secretaries that it was "undeniably in employers' interest not to weaken [their] trade union partners" by refusing such a modest agreement, as it might fuel discontent among the labor rank and file and weaken moderate union bureaucracies.[168] Despite a critical assessment of the agreement, the Catholic Trade Union Federation withdrew its pension initiative in 1968.[169]

The issue of ensuring employees' rights to benefits and their participation in the management of pension plans was far from being resolved. The shortcomings of the voluntary approach encouraged alternatives based on an expansion of the AHV and would soon force employers to reconsider the idea of a compulsory second pillar, a prospect at first seen as too constricting. This shift, which is analyzed in the next section, was facilitated by a growing awareness among business circles of the need to protect the financial assets accumulated by private pension plans.

By 1970, occupational pension assets reached two-fifths of gross domestic product, up from one-third in 1955 (see Table A.7, p. 303). The financial weight of second-pillar assets clearly confirmed that Switzerland belonged to the quartet of western welfare states that relied most on funded pension provision (see Table 4.4). Before World War II, public-sector occupational plans had steadily accounted for around

*Neue Zürcher Zeitung*, May 7, 1966; Alfred Matti, "Die Freizügigkeit in der Personalvorsorge", *Schweizerische Zeitschrift für Sozialversicherung* (1967), pp. 203–17.

166 "Freizügigkeit in der Personalvorsorge", *ZSAO Kreisschreiben*, July 4, 1967 (quotation), file 92.5, AfZ-SHIV.

167 Arbeitgeberverband Vorstand, September 9, 1964 (pp. 13–17) and November 23, 1966 (pp. 18–22), as well as Arbeitgeberverband Geschäftsführerkonferenz, March 16–17, 1967, pp. 12–19, SAV.

168 Arbeitgeberverband Vorstand, May 24, 1967, p. 32.

169 Truffer, "Die schweizerische Altersvorsorge in der Sicht der Christlichnationalen Gewerkschaftsbundes", p. 197.

Table 4.4 *Pension fund assets in comparative perspective, 1970–1990.*

| as percentage of GDP | 1970 | 1980 | 1990 |
|---|---|---|---|
| Switzerland | 38 | 51 | 69 |
| Netherlands | 29 | 46 | 77 |
| United Kingdom | 17 | 23 | 55 |
| United States | 17 | 24 | 43 |
| Sweden | 22 | 30 | 28 |
| Canada | 13 | 17 | 28 |
| Australia | 10 | 9 | 19 |
| Denmark | 5 | 7 | 15 |
| Japan | 0 | 2 | 5 |
| West Germany | 2 | 2 | 3 |

*Source:* E. Philip Davis, *Pension funds: retirement-income security and capital markets. An international perspective* (Oxford: Clarendon Press, 1995), p. 55.

two-thirds of total pension assets. This proportion was reversed during the 1950s as occupational provision expanded in the private sector. In the public sector, two dozen pension plans, dominated by those of federal employees, railroad workers, and postal employees, controlled four-fifths of pension assets around 1970. Concentration was also high in the private sector, where twenty-eight leading corporations controlled around one-fifth of pension assets.[170] In 1968, the SVPP estimated that its leading members held half of private-sector pension assets (see Table A.7, p. 303). In addition, Rentenanstalt, Winterthur Life, Zurich Life, and Basler Life still controlled four-fifths of the group pension market in 1970 (see Figure 2.4, p. 80).

Since World War I, private firms had used pension plans to accumulate reserves for self-financing purposes and to lower their tax expenditure. From the 1950s on, the growth of pension assets was increasingly transforming these plans into large investors. Public-sector pension plans had no active investment policy, as they used two-thirds of their assets for self-financing and to buy public bonds, while another fifth was channeled into real estate and mortgages.[171] Real estate and mortgages

[170] Peter Hadorn, *Die Kapitalanlagen der schweizerischen Pensionskassen 1955–1970* (Basel: Institut für Sozialwissenschaften/Institut für angewandte Wirtschaftsforschung, 1974), pp. 220–1.

[171] Ibid., pp. 80 (quotation), 85, 99. See also Denis Varrin, *La prévoyance professionnelle en Suisse de 1941/42 à 1989: analyse des données statistiques (rapport de recherche)* (Lausanne: IDHEAP 1993), pp. 162–70, *Pensionskassenstatistik 1955*, p. 172.

represented over one-third of private pension fund investment. Given the high cost of land in Switzerland, real estate assets were used to lure skilled workers, as firms used pension assets to buy land and houses to provide more affordable accommodation. Private pension plans also subscribed around one-quarter of new bonds issued on the financial market. Around one-fifth of occupational assets were devoted to self-financing purposes. Because of the strength of their domestic financial market, Swiss firms used self-financing to a lesser extent than their German counterparts.[172]

The importance of real estate in pension plan investment portfolios was clearly peculiar to Switzerland. Investment in stock market shares, common for British and American pension plans, remained marginal (less than 5 percent of pension assets), as regulations strictly limited pension investment to long-term assets. Economist Peter Hadorn also underlined that the management of pension assets was rarely outsourced to professionals, that investment decisions were marked by opacity, and that a "regular monitoring of investment was lacking in most cases".[173]

In 1971, Basle economist Hermann Engler estimated that the savings accumulated by pension plans had held down inflation slightly during the postwar decades of growth.[174] According to him, the growth of these assets constituted a costly detour for pensioners, as "the more the second pillar is based on funding, the more precedence will be given to dimensions that have less priority in terms of social policy".[175] The increasing financial weight of occupational plans reinforced employers' resolution to oppose any pension reform proposals that would either limit capital accumulation or reduce the financial autonomy of second-pillar institutions. In 1970, the SVPP warned that "[t]he liquidation of [pension] assets or their concentration in a mammoth public fund [would] constitute the shortest road to State Socialism and the end of our economic system".[176]

[172] Hadorn, *Die Kapitalanlagen der schweizerischen Pensionskassen*, pp. 114, 138, 172, 217. On German firms, see Helmut Kempkes, *Die betriebliche Altersversorgung in Deutschland und in der Schweiz und ihre Bedeutung für die Finanzierung von Unternehmungen* (Düsseldorf: Stehle, 1964), pp. 88, 108.

[173] Hadorn, *Die Kapitalanlagen der schweizerischen Pensionskassen*, pp. 122 (quotation), 138, 172.

[174] Hermann Engler, "Volkswirtschaftliche Auswirkungen der drei AHV-Initiativen", April 1971, p. 12, paper presented at the St. Gallen Business School, file 95.37, AfZ-SHIV.

[175] Hermann Engler, *Deckungskapital oder Umlageverfahren: Auswirkungen der im Rahmen der Altersvorsorge stattfindenden Spartätigkeit auf die schweizerische Volkswirtschaft* (Universität Basle: Institut für Sozialwissenschaften, 1971), p. 65.

[176] *SVPP Jahresbericht 1969* (Zurich: SVPP, 1970), p. 12, file V Schweiz 2435, SNB.

In addition to the continuing gaps in coverage and to the selectivity and unevenness of occupational benefits, there existed a growing discrepancy between the role of pension plans as providers of social benefits and their role in the accumulation of capital. In both these areas, employers resolved to hold their ground and continue using corporate schemes to manage their personnel and invest pension assets. The defense of a decentralized, funded, and privately controlled second pillar against the expansion of pay-as-you-go pensions and stricter regulatory measures constituted the background to the battle that pitted the three-pillar doctrine against the people's pensions.

## Showdown: the three-pillar doctrine vs. the people's pensions (1968–1972)

The December 1972 vote on the future of the pension system crystallized several decades of social policy development and took place during a period of growing political, social, and economic turbulence. The late 1960s witnessed the closing stages of the long wave of sustained economic development of the postwar period. Rising inflation, increasing rationalization pressures, and heightened competition in international markets preceded the economic crisis of the 1970s. New social movements and political radicalization – such as the anti-foreigner initiatives and the emergence of leftist groups – formed the background to this period of transition.[177] This section analyzes the three pension initiatives (two centered on the people's pensions and one on the three-pillar doctrine) launched in 1969 and highlights the strategies deployed by insurers to ensure the success of the three-pillar doctrine – first among employers and then among the citizenry at large. The anchoring of the three-pillar doctrine in the federal constitution in 1972, the 8th AHV revision enacted in 1973–1975, and the 1982 federal law on mandatory occupational provision (berufliche Vorsorgegesetz, BVG) were the outcomes of this decisive struggle. The iron framework of the "Swiss solution" reaffirmed the standing of funded old age provision and led to the containment of social insurance.

Since the early 1960s, minority groups inside the Socialist Party had been lobbying for more encompassing social security programs. However, these proposals had met strong resistance from trade unions keen to negotiate occupational benefits with employers and from party leaders who refused to challenge Hans Peter Tschudi's gradual reformist approach. In 1965 and 1966, the congress of the Socialist Party and the

[177] Gilg and Halblützel, "Une course accélérée vers l'avenir", pp. 793–7.

general secretary of the Gewerkschaftsbund, Giacomo Bernasconi, had both publicly supported the three-pillar solution outlined in 1963.[178] The growing social policy muddle widened the chasm between moderates who supported the "Tschudi pace" and radicals who had repeatedly tried to bring the people's pensions to the fore. The global upheavals of 1968 also contributed to the emergence of bolder alternatives.

In June of that year, the congress of the Socialist Party discussed the launching of an initiative that envisioned not only people's pensions, but also the replacement of per capita health insurance premiums with payroll contributions modeled on the AHV. The left wing of the party proposed a doubling of current pension benefits, the gradual phasing-out of means-tested supplements, and the indexing of benefits. To solve the current fragmentation of the second pillar, these proposals envisioned much closer coordination between the AHV and occupational provision. Despite attempts by the party leadership to temporize, this option was adopted at the party congress, and on June 16 the Socialist leadership received a clear mandate from its base to launch an initiative designed to overhaul pension and health insurance.[179]

Two days before this vote, the Union of Life Insurance Companies acknowledged that the point of no return had been reached: "[T]he crucial struggle between the three-pillar solution and the people's pensions lies ahead of us. Of course, we do not welcome such a prospect. However, it will be easier to lead a fight against such a proposition than against a piecemeal tactic."[180] The battle ahead was difficult, but insurers were determined to spare no efforts to fight this "attempt to transform the social structure of our state".[181]

However, the preparation of the Socialist initiative took longer than expected. Delayed by trade unions keen to defend employee benefits and hampered by legal technicalities, pension and health insurance proposals were finally split into two distinct initiatives and belatedly launched in November 1969. These delays triggered competition on the left, as the Communist Labor Party tried to outmaneuver the Socialists by launching its own people's pensions initiative. In September 1968, the Federal Council had also appointed a commission of experts with the mandate to solve the shortcomings of occupational coverage and benefits.

[178] Siegenthaler, *Die Politik der Gewerkschaften*, pp. 69–77.

[179] *Ordentlicher Parteitag vom 15./16. Juni 1968* (Berne: Sozialdemokratische Partei der Schweiz, 1968), pp. 42–3, 111–13, file K961, Sozialarchiv. See also Jean Steiger, *Le deuxième pilier: Service social ou affaire lucrative?* (Geneva: Grounauer, 1978), pp. 79–80.

[180] Konferenz der VSLG, June 14, 1968, p. 14, file Q127 206, ZFS.

[181] Ibid., p. 17.

Both the Socialist and the Labor Party initiatives demanded a system of retirement benefits amounting to at least 60 percent of earnings, which would require, according to business federations, a doubling or tripling of pension expenditure. However, the initiatives differed markedly on the issue of existing occupational pensions. On the one hand, the Socialist initiative (validated in March 1970 with 85,000 signatures) proposed to combine state pensions with supplementary benefits that could be provided either by existing occupational plans offering adequate and indexed benefits and integral pension portability, or by a new federal supplementary program. Under these conditions, noted a business report, private plans would be to condemned a slow "death through attrition".[182] On the other hand, the Labor Party initiative (validated in December 1969 with 58,000 signatures) openly proposed the termination of the second pillar after the incorporation of occupational plans into an expanded pay-as-you-go system.

Both initiatives challenged the three-pillar system favored by business circles and would have hindered capital accumulation by pension funds and limited their use for personnel management. The termination of existing occupational pensions was the worst-case scenario that employers could imagine. Even if the Communist initiative had very little chance of winning in an open political contest, given the conservative balance of power in Switzerland, the prospect of more stringent regulation of pension plans and the creation of a competing federal supplementary pension tier – two dimensions present in the Socialist initiative – were already disquieting. Worse, the competition between the two left-wing proposals risked fueling further demands for social policy reforms at a time when business was facing an uncertain economic future.

In order to confront these challenges, business federations scrambled to find a common strategy. At first, divisions remained strong. In a March 1969 assessment, the Arbeitgeberverband warned that time was running out and that measures had to be taken to set old age provision on a course that would preserve free-market principles and Swiss competitiveness in international markets. While an extension of the AHV clearly represented a step toward more socialist-inspired redistribution and was detrimental to savings, the shortcomings of voluntary solutions in occupational provision had become more and more obvious. Because of the political pressure coming from the two left-wing initiatives, there was little time to close the holes in coverage. A compulsory second pillar would

182 Studienkommission Altersvorsorge, "Die AHV Initiativen der PdA und der SP", August 12, 1969, pp. 11–12, file 95.34, AfZ-SHIV.

mean higher social costs and more intrusive state regulation, a radical departure from the freedom previously enjoyed by private pension plans. However, the report continued, losing the battle against the people's pensions would undo all of the efforts undertaken to defend the three-pillar doctrine and could potentially herald the rollback of corporate benefits. A compulsory but modest and gradually implemented second pillar could safeguard employers' interests by stabilizing and depoliticizing the AHV.[183]

Although some employers' associations complained that a compulsory second pillar would encourage trade unions to push for German-style joint-management procedures and overly favored insurance companies keen to develop group plans, all agreed that something had to be done to ensure the failure of the left-wing initiatives. The Arbeitgeberverband finally backed up its support for a compulsory second pillar with political arguments. Binding together social insurance and occupational pensions in a common legislative framework would check new redistributive social policies and protect the expansion of corporate plans. Such a solution would not only secure the role of the latter in personnel management but also bolster capital accumulation. This choice was formally endorsed in May 1969 by the Arbeitgeberverband and then submitted to the other business federations.[184]

Hans Herold of the Vorort strongly disagreed with these conclusions and downplayed the urgency of the situation. In his reply to the Arbeitgeberverband, Herold explained that there was no unanimity on the left regarding the issue of pension reform and that many trade union leaders still favored the extension of pension benefits through collective bargaining. Because endorsing compulsory pension coverage closed off potential alternatives, employers should first exploit these divisions instead of surrendering to a solution that they strongly disapproved of. Herold also downplayed existing gaps in coverage and argued that any shortcomings could be improved by using a voluntary approach.[185] The Vorort finally pointed out that key manufacturing sectors with well-developed occupational plans were in favor of a compulsory second pillar, but that trades and small firms affiliated to the Gewerbeverband were reluctant, or even hostile to such a prospect.

183 "Die Alters-, Hinterlassenen- und Invalidenvorsorge", Arbeitgeberverband report, March 1969, pp. 9–10, 14–20, 24–5, 29, file 95.33, AfZ-SHIV.
184 Arbeitgeberverband Vorstand, May 22, 1969, pp. 13–16, SAV.
185 Hans Herold, "Orientierung und Aussprache über die Studie des Zentralverbandes und die damit verbundene Frage eines Obligatoriums der privaten Personalfürsorge", [n.d., ca. June 1969], file 95.34. See also Hans Herold, "Notiz über ZSAO [i.e. Arbeitgeberverband] Studie", April 24, 1969, file 95.33, AfZ-SHIV.

In June 1969, arguing that the Labor Party initiative had yet to be presented to the Federal Chancellery and that the Socialist Party was still fine-tuning the launch of its people's pension initiative, the Vorort refused to commit itself to a compulsory second pillar and underscored that it would be wiser to wait for the report of the federal commission of experts on occupational provision before taking any decisions. The two main business federations disagreed on the key issue of a compulsory second pillar, but these differences were not made public, and time remained for them to reach a consensus.[186]

In his dissenting memoranda, Hans Herold did not mention such issues as the uncertainty of the economic horizon or Switzerland's position vis-à-vis the European Economic Community (EEC). Yet, the fact that the Vorort was currently negotiating a free-trade agreement with Brussels undoubtedly played a role in the attitude of some business circles toward a compulsory second pillar. In 1971, employers would depict the current state of European integration as showing "great risks of [leaning] toward state *dirigisme* and control over the whole social policy field".[187] Because inflationary "overheating" of the economy increased pressure on the Swiss manufacturing sector to rationalize and the 1967 recession in Germany had a sobering effect on economic optimism, concerns about uncertain economic development may well have weighed in the reluctance of the Vorort to accept further rises in social costs.

Business divisions were reignited when the Redressement National reactivated its study group on old age provision (the successor to the 1940s Untergruppe Altersversicherung) to counter the left-wing pension initiatives. Although this study commission, whose members included Peter Binswanger and several other insurance and banking executives, deplored the loss of freedom that would follow the adoption of a compulsory second pillar, it strongly favored this option: "From a philosophical point of view, one may regret that another piece of freedom will be again sacrificed to the State. Yet, we have to be conscious that this intrusion

186 On the Vorort decision, see file Vorort Vorstand, June 6, 1969, pp. 6–15, file 1.5.3.18–20. See also Vorort to Arbeitgeberverband, June 30, 1969, file 95.34, AfZ-SHIV. In public, the Arbeitgeberverband only supported an "expansion of occupational pensions" and did not talk of a compulsory second pillar. See *Schweizerische Arbeitgeber Zeitung*, June 5, 1969.

187 Arbeitgeberverband Vorstand, March 1971, p. 27, SAV. The free trade agreement with the European Economic Community was accepted by popular vote on on December 3, 1972, the same day as the three-pillar system. See Dominique Dirlewanger, Matthieu Leimgruber, and Gian Franco Pordenone, "L'Allemagne a-t-elle encore besoin de la Suisse? Le capitalisme helvétique en Europe (1890–1970)", in *Bienvenue en Euroland! De l'Europe de Maastricht à l'euro* (Lausanne: Antipodes, 1998), pp. 97–136 (especially pp. 120, 129).

is ideologically much less serious than the systematic erosion of existing occupational plans that would undoubtedly follow an expansion of the AHV."[188]

This rejection of an "erosion" of the second pillar was not surprising. Group premiums represented around 40 percent of overall life insurance activities (see Figure 2.3, p. 80), and insurers knew that their companies would benefit from the implementation of a compulsory second pillar. These meetings were an incubator for an initiative launched in the autumn of 1969 by a small group of bourgeois parliamentarians. Entitled *For a Modern System of Old Age Provision*, this riposte to the people's pensions advised "the harmonious development of the AHV according to the three-pillar concept".[189]

The key aim of the bourgeois initiative was to anchor the three-pillar doctrine in the federal constitution in order to stave off once and for all further structural alterations to the AHV, or at least to establish steep hurdles against such attempts. The initiative also demanded the freezing of payroll contributions at a maximum of 8.0 percent, limitation of the share of state transfers to the AHV to one-third of total financing needs, and guarantees that only indirect consumer taxes could be used to finance this share. The text also enjoined the Confederation to fiscally encourage both compulsory occupational pension plans and new "third-pillar" individual retirement accounts, and to improve pension portability and the integration of labor in the management of pension plans. The aim was clear: pay-as-you-go social insurance had to be restricted to the benefit of private funded pension provision.

Commenting with fervor on the wide-ranging reach of the initiative, Kurt Sovilla of the Arbeitgeberverband underscored that "[i]t would be the first time since the 1847 Civil War[190] that such a line of attack encompassing all bourgeois forces will be undertaken!" For Sovilla, the initiative enabled "a closer collaboration among bourgeois forces", which was essential at a time when "the radicalization of social democratic policies under the pressure of the new left has now became more

[188] Studienkommission Altersvorsorge: "Die Alters- Hinterlassenen- und Invalidenvorsorge: Probleme und Lösungsmöglichkeiten", February 1969, p. 31, file 5.3.6.2, AfZ-RN. On the formation of the study group, see Studienkommission Altersvorsorge, file 5.3.6.1, AfZ-RN.

[189] Binswanger, *Histoire de l'AVS*, p. 217. In his history of the AHV, Peter Binswanger acknowledges that he belonged to the group that drafted the initiative. However, he remains silent on the role played by the Redressement National or the SPAHV. On the launch of the initiative, see AHV-Studienkommission (1968–1970), file 5.3.6, AfZ-RN.

[190] The November 1847 Civil War won by Radical elites over Catholic cantons that had regrouped in a "separate alliance" (Sonderbund) preceded the formation of the modern Confederation in 1848.

likely".[191] Thanks to insurers' networks, 150,000 signatures were quickly gathered during the winter of 1969–1970, and the initiative was presented to the Federal Chancellery in April 1970.[192]

As Socialists reconvened to belatedly launch their people's pensions initiative in early November 1969, the social policy field was already crowded. While the left wing of the party tried to bend the project toward a Swedish-style pension tier that would have competed against the second pillar, the party leadership, prodded by the Gewerkschaftsbund, favored the integration of existing occupational schemes into the pension system. This option was similar to pension projects that were being debated at the same time by the British Labour Party and that sought to reform the contracting-out of private plans and to introduce a new public supplementary pension (the future State Earnings-Related Pension Scheme, or SERPS, introduced in 1975).[193] Proponents of the people's pensions criticized the tepid support of the party leadership for the proposal and hinted that some Socialist heavyweights were considering abandoning the initiative to forge a more consensual solution with bourgeois politicians. In the end, the party congress overwhelmingly approved the leadership's proposals and rejected the more radical Swedish-style options that were along the lines of the competing Labor Party initiative.[194]

In the months that preceded the Socialist congress, the Arbeitgeberverband took advantage of the leverage provided by the bourgeois initiative to convince the Vorort that a compulsory second pillar would be "a prop and not a straitjacket" for private plans. The propaganda arm of the business federations, the Wirtschaftsförderung, also declared early on its support for the bourgeois initiative. In the wake of the Socialist congress, the Vorort grudgingly agreed to reconsider its position, but Hans Herold emphasized that it would neither publicly defend a compulsory second pillar nor criticize the bourgeois initiative, which had the support of the Arbeitgeberverband.[195] Given these differences between the business federations, insurers used the bourgeois initiative to rally employers around the defense of the three-pillar doctrine. As Peter Binswanger pointed out to Hans Herold in early 1970, "With their excessive demands [Socialists] have . . . contributed to the formation of unanimous support in favor of

[191] Arbeitgeber Verband Vorstand, September 3, 1969, p. 19, SAV.

[192] Sommer, *Das Ringen um die soziale Sicherheit*, pp. 315–17.

[193] Lynes, "The British case", pp. 334–7; Thane, *Old age in English history*, p. 383.

[194] *Ausserordentlicher Parteitag vom 2. November 1969* (Berne: Sozialdemokratische Partei der Schweiz, 1970), pp. 68, 77–9, 84, file K961, Sozialarchiv.

[195] Kurt Sovilla (Arbeitgeberverband), "Grundfragen bei einem Obligatorium der betrieblichen und verbandlichen Alters-, Hinterlassenen- und Invalidenvorsorge", October 31, 1969, file 95.34, AfZ-SHIV; Hans Herold to Kurt Sovilla, November 14, 1969. See also Vorort Vorstand, November 5, 1969, p. 9, file 1.5.3.18–20.

the three-pillar concept (before the launching of the non-partisan initiative many bourgeois . . . had fancied the idea of the people's pensions; they will perhaps continue to do that, but from now on will not dare any more to defend such an option publicly)."[196]

However, the "unanimous support" for the three-pillar doctrine did not translate into enthusiasm for a compulsory second pillar. The Arbeitgeberverband, the Redressement National, and the Wirtschaftsförderung had all contributed to the creation of the bourgeois initiative and actively supported it. The leading firms represented in the SVPP also supported the initiative, as their pension plans were well prepared to deal with any changes brought about by compulsion. However, according to the Vorort, the bourgeois initiative added confusion to an already tense situation and made too many concessions to Hans Peter Tschudi. While the initiative openly challenged the left-wing initiatives, Hans Herold complained that its initiators were ready to withdraw it if the Federal Council integrated their proposals in a counter-project.[197]

Between 1970 and 1972, the Vorort ceaselessly criticized the idea of a compulsory second pillar, as well as the tactics of insurers and the bourgeois initiative. Small firms that provided minimum or zero occupational coverage also feared the rise of social costs that would result from a compulsory scheme. The secretary of the Gewerbeverband summarized the situation during an SPAHV meeting by stating that the bourgeois initiative represented no less than a risky political "all or nothing". If it succeeded, the three-pillar doctrine would be firmly entrenched, but its failure might open the way to more constraints on private benefits.[198] However, these critiques remained confined to employers' meetings. Dissension over the second pillar did not undermine the consensus that existed among business circles on the necessity to confront head-on the challenge of the people's pensions.

The run-up to the December 1972 vote witnessed intense political maneuvering. Proponents of the three-pillar system followed a two-sided tactical course. As it was clear that the Labor Party had no intention of withdrawing its initiative, employers were determined to crush it in a popular vote. Terminating the Communist proposal and anchoring the three-pillar doctrine in the federal constitution would then be used as a deterrent against the Socialist people's pension project.[199] In order to

[196] Peter Binswanger to Hans Herold, February 2, 1970, file 95.31, AfZ-SHIV.
[197] See two undated reports, most probably written by Hans Herold in Winter 1969/1970: "Ist die Initiative der richtige Weg?" and "Die überparteiliche Initiative", file 95.34, AfZ-SHIV; see also Vorort Vorstand, April 23, 1970, file 1.5.3.20–22.
[198] SPAHV Sitzung, September 9, 1969, file 95.34, AfZ-SHIV.
[199] SPAHV Sitzung, January 21, 1970, file 95.34, AfZ-SHIV.

cajole the Socialists into withdrawing their initiative, an official counter-project inspired by the bourgeois initiative but giving token support to the Socialists' proposals had to be designed. In early 1970, the Federal Assembly accepted two motions presented by National Councilor Josef Hofstetter of the Von Roll foundries and Senator Robert Reimann of the Brown & Boveri engineering corporation, two members of the SVPP, who asked the Federal Council to draft such a counter-project. The members of the federal commission on occupational provision that had been convened in 1969 pushed in the same direction and voted in July 1970 in favor of a compulsory second pillar.[200]

The definition of "compulsory" had already occasioned heated debates in the commission. Trade union representatives were in favor of a second-pillar system in which "no gaps would persist", while employers argued that the compulsory second pillar would have "boundaries", or that it should not be conceived as a "thoroughly encompassing system" but only as a "supplement" to the AHV.[201] These differences of opinion were not mere wordplay. They prefigured protracted negotiations about the implementation of the compulsory second pillar that would emerge immediately after the 1972 vote and last until the acceptance of the BVG law a decade later. The commission also accepted, despite the resistance of the left, the idea of a third individual pillar and the abandonment of a federal supplementary scheme.[202]

The counter-project presented to the Federal Assembly by Hans Peter Tschudi in March 1971 endorsed the three-pillar concept and even stated that it was necessary to "put a ceiling on the state insurance program" and "prevent it from taking over or becoming a substitute for occupational plans". The counter-project remained vague on the outlines of the compulsory second pillar, hinting that its implementation would be "incremental" and subject to negotiation. As a sop toward the Socialists, the draft also argued that the AHV should cover "vital needs" and thus depart from the basic pension approach.[203] Even though it did not cap AHV payroll contributions, the draft was supported by the Arbeitgeberverband, which claimed that "for political reasons there is only *one* [sic] set of alternatives: the compulsory second pillar or the people's

200 Binswanger, *Histoire de l'AVS*, pp. 218–23.

201 Expertenkommission für die Förderung der beruflichen Alters- Invaliden und Hinterlassenenvorsorge, minutes of meeting, February 17 to February 18, 1970, pp. 9–11, file 95.31, AfZ-SHIV.

202 Arbeitgeberverband Geschäftsführerkonferenz, March 4–5, 1971, p. 10, SAV.

203 Département fédéral de l'Intérieur, "Commentaire d'un avant projet de nouvelle base constitutionnelle en matière de prévoyance vieillesse, survivants et invalidité", March 19, 1971, pp. 16, 21, file 95.35, AfZ-SHIV.

pensions". The employers' federation then convinced the Vorort to sign a joint statement in June 1971 indicating the conditional support of the two business groups.[204]

In order to reinforce the idea that federal pensions would cover "vital needs", Federal Councilor Hans Peter Tschudi launched an 8th AHV revision that proposed doubling pensions in nominal terms, as well as an extension of payroll contribution rates from 5.2 to 8.4 percent between 1973 and 1975. These measures were openly designated by the Federal Council as a way of drawing support away from the extension of benefits envisioned by the Labor Party.[205]

Despite strong reservations about this expansion of pension expenditure, the Vorort and the Arbeitgeberverband did not launch a referendum against the 8th AHV revision. Hans Herold proposed one, but his Vorort colleagues replied that the stakes were too high: "If we sustain a punishing defeat during a popular vote, it will give the green light to the proponents of social insurance and lead to an intensification of the pace toward the welfare state, so that in a few years we would face conditions similar to [those in] Sweden or Great Britain." As Peter Binswanger pointed out during a briefing of the trade and industry parliamentary caucus, the 8th AHV revision offered a "better fighting position" against the Labor Party initiative.[206] Indeed, the first benefits increase was to be implemented in January 1973, immediately after the vote that would choose between the Communist initiative and the official counter-project.

If business federations and bourgeois parties did not spare their efforts to smear the Communist initiative, the Socialist Party and the Gewerkschaftsbund also openly attacked it and supported the counter-project devised by their star Federal Councilor. The 1971 congress of the Metalworkers' Union denounced the Labor Party campaign against the second pillar as a measure inspired by "reactionary sentiments against entrepreneurs" that would "endanger the growth of the national economy".[207] Accusing the Communists of being responsible for the belated introduction of the AHV because of their opposition in 1931 to the Lex Schulthess, Hans Peter Tschudi claimed in 1972 that the promise of a "secure old age" would be realized by the mandatory second pillar and the 8th AHV revision and would thus no longer be "a distant dream".

204 Vorort Vorstand, June 28, 1971, p. 35, file 1.5.3.20–22, AfZ-SHIV.
205 Sommer, *Das Ringen um die soziale Sicherheit*, p. 323.
206 Vorort Vorstand, November 29, 1971, p. 31, file 1.5.3.20–22, AfZ-SHIV; Peter Binswanger, "Der Vollausbau der Altersvorsorge", February 29, 1972, file 95.40, AfZ-SHIV.
207 Quoted by Hans Herold, "Der bevorstehende Ausbau der Sozialversicherung, insbesondere der AHV", April 1971, p. 6, file 95.36, AfZ-SHIV.

The three-pillar system would enable Switzerland to "rank among the leading nations in the field of old age provision".[208]

Some Socialists were so thrilled by the three-pillar doctrine that they envisaged that the compulsory second pillar would enable trade unions to take control of occupational provision and that, consequently, "vast realms of the Swiss economy [would be] at the reach of trade unions and workers". This social reform would entail "either the reinforcement of traditional capitalist institutions . . . or the smooth and smiling collectivization of parts of the Swiss economy".[209] Other trade unionists remarked with foresight that the counter-project offered no such guarantees and that the second pillar might well become "the preserve of insurance companies", but they remained isolated.[210]

After the Federal Assembly endorsed both the counter-project and the 8[th] AHV revision in June 1972, business proponents of the compulsory second pillar (the Arbeitgeberverband, Redressement National, Wirtschaftsförderung, insurance companies, and the SVPP) advised employers to vote with determination for the counter-project and against the Labor Party initiative. The Vorort finally closed ranks with these organizations in late October.[211] Two weeks before the popular vote, Hans Herold darkly prophesied that because of the phasing-in of the 8[th] AHV revision, "employers would face the reality of the people's pensions in early 1973", and alleged that this revision would bring the Swiss welfare state into the European mainstream. He also emphasized that the Vorort mainly supported the compulsory second pillar for political reasons, namely because business forces had to "maintain a unified position in public". Although he would have preferred a more assertive stance against the counter-project, Herold thanked his colleagues for having let him repeatedly voice his doubts: "I do understand that from the outside the Vorort seems like a Catholic religious order. However, the fact that I have [always] been granted permission to present to you [my] divergent ideas convinces me that, in its internal workings, it is Protestant, because it allows room for freedom of thought."[212] This theologically inspired conclusion summarizes employers' unwillingness to appear

208 "Gesichertes Alter – kein ferner Traum mehr!", *Gewerkschaftskorrespondenz*, March 23, 1972, pp. 149–50.

209 *Domaine public*, March 3, 1972, quoted in Steiger, *Le deuxième pilier*, pp. 51–2.

210 Max Arnold, general secretary of the Public-Sector Employees' Union (Verband des Personals öffentlicher Dienste, VPOD), speaking at the 1972 congress of the Gewerkschaftsbund, quoted in Jean-François Marquis, "Deuxième pilier, des lendemains qui déchantent", *Page 2* 7 (1996), pp. 52–4.

211 Vorort Vorstand, October 30, 1972, p. 20, file 1.5.3.20–22, AfZ-SHIV.

212 Hans Herold, "AHV. 2. Säule" [n.d., ca. November 1972], file 95.41, AfZ-SHIV.

publicly divided in spite of their divergent appraisals of the social policy situation, and confirms their strong internal discipline.

The results of the vote came on the evening of December 3, 1972: 83 percent of voters rejected the Labor Party people's pensions initiative, while the official counter-project shaped by Hans Peter Tschudi in the framework set by the three-pillar doctrine was approved by 77 percent. In a year when citizens voted on nine referenda and initiatives (the largest number since the introduction of direct democracy in the 1870s), the turnout was the lowest (49.9 percent) for an old age insurance proposal since the incorporation of federal pensions in the constitution in 1925.[213] Yet, voter fatigue was not a determining factor. A long-term business campaign in favor of the three-pillar doctrine and its acceptance by the governmental left strongly tilted the balance toward the counter-project.

In the days following the vote, the Union of Life Insurance Companies heartily congratulated Peter Binswanger and the SPAHV for the landmark success produced by a decade of relentless lobbying for the "Swiss solution". Binswanger himself thanked Coop Life – a cooperative insurance company with close links to labor organizations – for playing a key role in winning over trade unions to the three-pillar solution. Insurers and private pension lobbyists did not share Hans Herold's gloomy perspective on the future evolution of social policy. Binswanger outlined the next steps that had to be taken for the "reasonable implementation" of the second pillar: insurers had to defend moderate solutions without ceding ground to either the Socialists, whose initiative was still pending, or to economic sectors still sparsely covered by occupational provision. State-based solutions were to be avoided to defend the existing flexible structures grounded in social partnership. One of Binswanger's main preoccupations was to make sure that "fair competition practices" would be respected between insurers, banks, and large pension plans.[214] Far from fearing the "smooth and smiling collectivization" of the economy dreamed of by some Socialists, this key inspirer of the "Swiss solution" wanted above all to avoid "mutual laceration" between the financial interests that would divide among themselves the juicy markets opened up by the compulsory second pillar and tax-free individual savings accounts.[215]

213 The votes on the constitutional article of federal pensions (December 6, 1925), the Lex Schulthess (December 6, 1931), and the AHV (July 6, 1947) had attracted respectively 61.5 percent, 75.7 percent, and 78.6 percent of all voters. See Ritzmann-Blickenstorfer and Siegenthaler, eds., *Swiss Historical Statistics*, Table X10.

214 Konferenz der VSLG, December 7, 1972, pp. 6–8, file Q127 206, ZFS.

215 Minutes of the board of directors of Winterthur Life, December 7, 1972, quoted in Jung, *Die Winterthur*, p. 227.

## The multi-pillar horizon at the end of the decades of growth

This chapter has charted the increasingly tangled development of the two areas of old age provision in the postwar decades of growth. A generation after the belated introduction of the AHV, social insurance had experienced incremental and limited expansion. This was in no small part due to the parallel development of pension plans that both benefitted from and circumscribed the expansion of social insurance. The upholding of the division of labor and the definition of clear boundaries between the two realms of old age provision constituted a key preoccupation for employers and insurers. As the momentum of social insurance expansion showed no signs of abating, and occupational provision continued to spread unevenly and selectively, a redefinition of this division of labor was needed.

The Swiss pension system did not grow in splendid isolation but was influenced by debates and controversies that agitated European welfare states. This was particularly true during the decades following World War II as the development of neighboring welfare states, in particular West Germany, fueled critics' complaints about the meagerness of AHV pensions and the shortcomings of pension plans. By the late 1960s, attempts by people's pensions proposals to challenge the "Swiss solution" and attempts to reinforce the first pillar were indirectly inspired by social democratic solutions developed in Sweden and the United Kingdom that aimed to supplement basic old age benefits with a state-controlled second pension or to bind occupational pensions more closely to social insurance.

My analysis of the inter-employer debates leading to the 1972 vote shows that business circles, and in particular insurers, realized early on that a solution had to be found to contain the AHV and fight off any reorientation of pension policy that would endanger the second pillar. Discussions were held, options were weighed, and disagreements were gradually resolved. This underscores the capacity and willingness of business circles to maintain a united front on key policy issues. Inter-employer disagreements remained strong throughout the 1960s, and business federations sometimes resented the self-serving options defended by insurers. Yet, these debates remained confined to back rooms, and employers spared no efforts to keep them out of the public eye. Combined with the entrenchment of a fragmented pension system, this long-term strategy contributed to the success of the three-pillar doctrine.

In contrast to the cumulative advantages enjoyed by the multi-pillar concept, Communist and Socialist proponents of the people's pensions faced much higher hurdles. The involvement of key trade unions with corporate welfare programs was already deep by the time of the belated emergence of the people's pensions alternative. The integration of the Socialists into the executive branch also reduced its chances. After the people's pensions had slowly made their way inside the party, they were only half-heartedly supported by the leadership and attracted little sympathy from labor organizations. Given the structural weakness of the left in Switzerland and the cleavage provoked by the open competition between the two left-wing people's pensions initiatives, the odds of breaking the cohesive front of the employers and bourgeois parties that favored the three-pillar doctrine were not encouraging.

The failure of the people's pensions underlines the incapacity of the governmental left to challenge the prevailing business-friendly orientation of the political system. In order to enter the federal executive in 1943, the Socialists had already subordinated themselves to the reigning balance of power. Fifteen years later, after the failure of their public finance proposals and an inconclusive period in opposition, the Socialists' integration into the Magic Formula confirmed their role as a junior partner in the executive coalition. Hans Peter Tschudi astutely used the political pressure of direct democracy to expand the AHV, but his reforms never went far beyond the basic framework set up during World War II. At the end of the 1960s, Socialist participation in the government led to the party endorsing the three-pillar doctrine and disciplining dissident factions on the left. For the proponents of a radical expansion of federal pensions, the 1972 vote constituted a lasting defeat. Tschudi's counter-project not only obliterated the people's pensions proposal of the Communists but also scuttled the more moderate Socialist initiative.

Yet, the challenge of the people's pensions should not be underestimated. This alternative surfaced at a critical moment in the development of the pension system, and in a turbulent political and economic context. It is doubtful whether employers would have accepted the compulsory second pillar without the pressure of both left-wing initiatives. The abandonment of the voluntary approach constituted the price that business circles were ready to pay to contain pay-as-you-go social insurance. The 8th AHV revision was the last one to approve an increase in pension benefits. As the economic situation shifted from a long wave of expansion to more troubled times, the implementation of the three-pillar doctrine also gave Swiss employers a better fighting position to limit social insurance costs at a time when, in the words of Arbeitgeberverband secretary Kurt Sovilla, "a tidal wave of social policy was rushing forward all over the western world".[216]

[216] Arbeitgeberverband Vorstand, May 18, 1971, p. 13, SAV.

Among Switzerland's European neighbors, the period 1968–1972 saw the expansion of pay-as-you-go pensions and diminishing opportunities for funded schemes. In West Germany, pension replacement rates jumped to three-quarters of workers' final wages after the reforms introduced by a coalition of Social Democrats and Christian Democrats. At the same time, a 1974 law defined a strict and binding framework for the operation of occupational pension plans, which had a negative impact on their development. In France, supplementary pensions operating on a pay-as-you-go basis were also expanded in the early 1970s to the last sectors that remained uncovered.[217] In both countries, strong political pressure from the left, as well as the long-term marginalization of funded pension schemes, continued to undermine private forms of provision. In Sweden, optional pension plans were developed in the early 1970s alongside the state-controlled ATP for white-collar workers and executive managers. However, these occupational schemes represented only a minute share of overall pension benefits, and their assets were dwarfed by the ATP funds.[218]

In the United Kingdom, intense lobbying from insurers and the reluctance of trade unions enmeshed in the management of employee benefits safeguarded contracting-out options for existing pension plans and downgraded Labour's proposal for state-based pension supplementation which had influenced the Socialist people's pension initiative of 1969. By the mid-1970s, competition between the State Earnings-Related Pension Scheme (SERPS) and private occupational schemes furthered the fragmented and "unplanned" development of the British pension system. The continuation of contracting-out gradually eroded the quality of old age benefits and overall occupational pension coverage.[219] Rather than further blurring the division of labor between public social insurance and private schemes, the 1972 Swiss vote reaffirmed the boundaries between pay-as-you-go insurance and funded occupational provision. Unlike in the United Kingdom, the compulsory second pillar also increased pension coverage, and Swiss pensioners avoided the growing pension mess that oppressed their British counterparts.

After 1972, can it still be argued that Switzerland was following a US-style trajectory in the field of old age provision? The answer is clearly negative. In both countries, a lively debate on the future of social security

217 Emmanuel Reynaud, "France: a national and contractual second tier", in *Enterprise and the welfare state*, ed. Martin Rein and Eskil Wadensjö (Cheltenham: Edward Elgar, 1997), pp. 65–98, 72; Winfried Schmähl, "The public–private mix in pension provision in Germany", in *Enterprise and the welfare state*, ed. Martin Rein and Eskil Wadensjö (Cheltenham: Edward Elgar, 1997), pp. 99–148, 132–3.

218 Wadensjö, "The welfare mix in pension provision in Sweden", pp. 291–4.

219 Lynes, "The British case", pp. 334–6; Thane, *Old age in English history*, p. 383.

and occupational provision took place during the 1960s, but their outcomes led in opposite directions. The three-pillar doctrine and the compulsory second pillar had no equivalent in the United States. The path toward occupational pension reform began in the United States in the early 1960s. The first efforts stalled in the face of fierce employer and trade union opposition, but were reactivated by the momentous bankruptcy of the Studebaker Corporation in 1964. This pension debacle heightened public concern about the reliability of corporate pension plans and fueled controversies on pension vesting, portability, and the regulation of pension assets investment.[220] Yet, the reform of occupational provision remained marginal in comparison with the 1965 introduction of health insurance for the elderly (Medicare) and the poor (Medicaid).

By the late 1960s, occupational pension reform in the United States aimed, above all, to expand coverage and safeguard benefits. The Employees Retirement Income Security Act (ERISA) 1974 constituted a "mammoth piece of legislation", but it did not integrate Social Security and occupational benefits into an explicit multi-pillar structure.[221] ERISA improved the regulation of existing defined-benefit schemes but did not lead to further extension of occupational coverage, which peaked in the mid-1970s at just below half the private workforce. In the end, ERISA did not modify the existing division of labor between basic Social Security and pension plans. Proposals to introduce compulsory affiliation to occupational pension plans found little support beyond administrative circles and died out at the beginning of the 1980s, during the first Reagan presidency.[222] The absence of a serious attempt to challenge the boundaries between pay-as-you-go Social Security and pension plans explains the continuing development of voluntary occupational provision. The outcome of ERISA might have been replicated in Switzerland if the decisive struggle between the people's pensions and the three-pillar doctrine had not taken place. Once again, the introduction of the compulsory second pillar cannot be understood without taking into account the confrontation between these two policy alternatives.

The Swiss three-pillar doctrine was also dissimilar to the Canadian system, where a public pension system mixing basic pensions (OAS) and pay-as-you-go earnings-related benefits (CPP/QPP) coexisted with occupational plans whose coverage rate remained, like that in the United Kingdom and United States, limited to the skilled and stable segments of the workforce. With the victory of the three-pillar doctrine, Swiss occupational provision had abandoned the path of "voluntary add-ons"

220 Sass, *The promise of private pensions*, pp. 179–202. 221 Ibid., p. 216.
222 Hacker, *The divided welfare state*, pp. 145–53; Sass, *The promise of private pensions*, pp. 202–26.

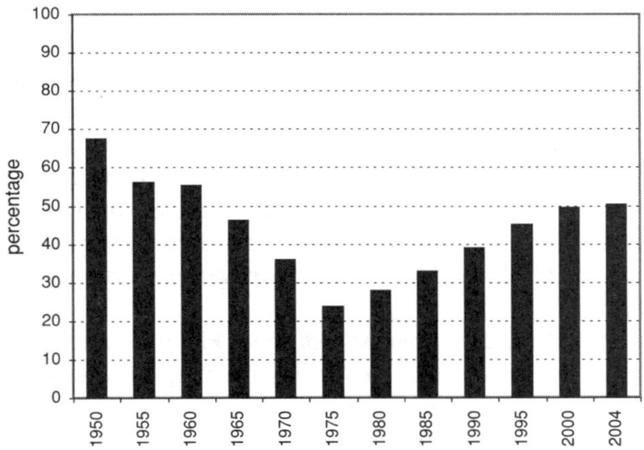


Figure 4.2 Second-pillar pension expenditure as a share of overall old age provision, 1950–2004.
*Source: Comptes globaux de la protection sociale: prestations sociales par groupes de régimes et régimes*, Table 13.1.3.3. Berne: Federal Statistical Office website: http://www.bfs.admin.ch (October 2007).

that was characteristic of North American welfare states while avoiding the path of pension "carve-outs" followed by British pension plans (see Table 0.2, p. 24). On the other hand, the new course opened by the three-pillar system could be said to echo developments taking place in the Netherlands.

The Dutch second pillar was dominated by industry-wide pension plans that covered a larger proportion of the workforce than Swiss decentralized pension plans (by the late 1960s, coverage had already reached three-quarters of the workforce) and had been submitted to stricter regulation since the 1950s. A few months after the Swiss vote on the three-pillar doctrine, the Dutch government extended the Pension and Savings Fund Act 1953. These amendments reinforced pension vesting rights, and confirmed the pre-eminence of industry-wide pension schemes. They also stipulated that social insurance and occupational benefits should reach together a replacement rate of at least 70 percent of final wages and that pension plans should regularly index benefits. This amendment reinforced the "quasi-mandatory" profile of Dutch occupational provision and made superfluous the introduction of compulsion.[223]

[223] Martin Blomsma and Roel Jansweijer, "The Netherlands: growing importance of private-sector arrangements", in *Enterprise and the welfare state*, ed. Martin Rein and Eskil Wadensjö (Cheltenham: Edward Elgar, 1997), pp. 220–65, 240; *Social Security in the Netherlands* (The Hague: Ministry for Social Affairs and Employment, 1982), pp. 66–74.

A decade before the introduction of the federal law on mandatory occupational provision (berufliche Vorsorgegesetz, BVG), the Dutch pension mix offered both higher coverage and better benefits than its Swiss counterpart. Moreover, its past history of homogeneous and industry-wide contractual expansion differed from the fragmentation that characterized the Swiss second pillar and employers' resistance to genuine union involvement in pension management. In the wake of the 1972 victory of the three-pillar doctrine, the scale and scope of the compulsory second pillar were still unresolved, and the Socialist people's pensions initiative was still pending.

From 1947 onward, the expansion of the AHV had constantly eroded the standing of occupational benefits in overall pension provision. By 1980, the AHV paid benefits to almost one million pensioners, or three times the number that benefitted from second-pillar pensions (see Table A.6, p. 301). Figure 4.2 makes clear that the share of the second pillar in overall pension expenditure had reached its lowest point in 1975: at this date, the AHV represented four-fifths of such expenditure. This trend had been visibly reversed by the end of the decade. The number of AHV pensioners and means devoted to public pensions continued to grow, but the momentum of pension expansion had resolutely shifted in favor of the second pillar. Thirty years later, on the eve of the new millennium, the AHV still constitutes the major source of income for a majority of pensioners, but the share of the second pillar in overall pension expenditure has made an impressive comeback. The epilogue will briefly outline the consequences of the significant growth in funded provision that was ushered in by the containment of social insurance.

# Epilogue
# Aging in the shadow of the three pillars (1972–2006)

In March 2004, Peter Hasler of the Arbeitgeberverband depicted an alarming landscape for the future of the Swiss welfare state. According to Hasler, unfavorable demographic trends, spiraling social expenditure, and irresponsible social demands had allegedly heralded the emergence of a "Swiss social-Moloch" that he accused of "devouring" growing portions of social wealth and impeding reasonable welfare reforms.[1] Between these lines one could almost hear a nostalgia for a time when business circles could boast of a more reasonable and frugal basis for Swiss social policy, characterized by moderate fiscal pressure and contribution rates to public programs and by free-ranging private forms of social provision.

As mentioned in the introduction, Swiss social expenditure has increased markedly during the last decade, and the graying of the population sets new challenges for the future of the welfare state. However, it is worth remembering that it is primarily the growing role devoted to *private* welfare schemes in social provision, including the transformation of occupational pension plans from voluntary to mandatory "add-ons" to the AHV, and the pre-eminence of private providers in health insurance that have fueled these rising expenditure levels. Similarly, Switzerland may now be a mainstream European welfare state in terms of overall social expenditure, but tax levels and social policy costs, key indicators of neo-liberal dogma, are still moderate in comparison with those of other western European countries.[2]

It is important to bear in mind these basic facts before focusing on the three decades that followed the victory of the three-pillar doctrine. Far from solving once and for all the struggle between social insurance and pension plans, the December 1972 vote set a new and constraining

[1] Peter Hasler (Arbeitgeberverband), "Sozialpolitik im Kreuzfeuer: Diskussion grundlegenden Fragen zur Zukunft", *Neue Zürcher Zeitung*, March 18, 2004.

[2] *Evolution de la charge fiscale en Suisse de 1970 à 2000: rapport du Conseil fédéral en réponse au postulat Vallender du 14 décembre 1998* (Berne: Chancellerie fédérale, 2003).

framework for pension politics. The first section of this epilogue shows how AHV expansion stalled as pension politics focused on the implementation of the mandatory second pillar during the 1970s and 1980s, and describes the breakneck expansion of pension fund assets. In the second section, I turn to current pension politics and outline the battles surrounding the retrenchment of the AHV and the more subterranean hollowing-out of the second pillar in the first decade of the new millennium.

## The implementation of the three-pillar doctrine

When Hans-Peter Tschudi stepped down from the Federal Council in 1973, the implementation of the three-pillar doctrine fell to his Christian Democrat successor, Senator Hans Hürlimann. The 8th AHV revision led to a doubling of pensions in nominal terms and raised payroll contributions from 5.2 to 8.4 percent of wages. However, because of the lack of indexing, pensions were immediately eroded by steep inflation rates. The freezing of AHV contribution levels put forward by the bourgeois initiative on the three-pillar doctrine was enforced *de facto*: a generation after this last increase, AHV payroll contributions remain untouched. The Socialist Party was confident that Hans-Peter Tschudi's outline for the federal law on mandatory occupational provision (berufliche Vorsorgegesetz, BVG) would be rapidly implemented and in 1974 withdrew its people's pensions initiative, which reinforced the victory of the three-pillar doctrine as economic indicators plummeted.

The recession of the 1970s and its accompanying austerity policies left their mark on pay-as-you-go social insurance and the implementation of compulsory occupational provision. Switzerland also witnessed during this period a hardening of free-market and conservative positions that pre-dated the rise of Thatcher and Reagan.[3] While the left fought for the indexing of pension benefits, a lower retirement age, and the implementation of a generous second pension tier, employers and bourgeois politicians emphasized the consolidation and downsizing of existing AHV benefits and a law on mandatory occupational pensions that would safeguard employers' prerogatives.

Emergency austerity measures introduced in 1975 to balance the budget of the Confederation led to a sharp drop in the share of general revenues in AHV finances (see Figure 4.1). For the first time since 1948,

[3] On the 1970s recession, see Michael Bernegger, *L'économie suisse sous le régime des changes flottants* (Geneva: Georg, 1988), pp. 1–10; Felix Muller, Hans Schäppi, and Jakob Tanner, *Krise: Zufall oder Folge des Kapitalismus? Die Schweiz und die aktuelle Wirtschaftskrise* (Zurich: Limmat Verlag, 1976), pp. 39–56.

federal pensions were in the red. In December 1974, both the health insurance initiative of the Socialist Party (launched in 1969) and a Federal Council counter-project were rejected after a resolute campaign led by medical associations and insurers. Despite the introduction of unemployment insurance (1976), the expansion of social insurance lost much of its momentum.[4] In the wake of the AHV deficit, a motion put forward by National Councilor Andreas Brunner (Radical) brazenly demanded an end to federal subsidies to the AHV and pension cutbacks, while far-right parliamentarians proposed to increase the retirement age for women from 62 to 65 years old. Such retrenchment proposals were considered provocative: Brunner's campaign cost him his parliamentary seat in the autumn 1975 federal elections, while proposals for a higher retirement age were dismissed as extremist.[5]

The 9th AHV revision focused on the introduction of biennial pension indexing (through a mixed index of consumer prices and wages) and consolidation measures (benefit cutbacks for married couples, taxation of post-retirement working incomes, and higher payroll contributions for the self-employed). For the first time ever, this pension package was challenged in 1977 by a referendum launched by the Gewerbeverband and the Redressement National. Both organizations opposed indexing and higher self-employed contributions, and demanded social expenditure cutbacks instead. Despite this, the AHV revision cleared the referendum hurdle in February 1978. On the same day, a constitutional initiative launched in 1975 by leftist groups proposing a general lowering of the retirement age orginally was defeated. The share of the AHV budget drawn from general revenues was returned to its pre-recession level, and federal pensions again drew surpluses.[6]

In 1979, the Radical Party made "Less state – more freedom" its election-year slogan, and employers announced that the time had come for "moderation" and a "cooling-off" period in social policy. More outspoken free-marketers suggested that the compulsory character of the AHV should be taken out of the constitution and replaced with individual retirement accounts. Preliminary negotiations on a 10th AHV revision

4 On health insurance, see Ellen M. Immergut, *Health politics: interests and institutions in western Europe* (Cambridge: Cambridge University Press, 1992), pp. 174–5. On unemployment insurance, see Manfred G. Schmidt, *Der schweizerische Weg zur Vollbeschäftigung: eine Bilanz der Beschäftigung, der Arbeitslosigkeit und der Arbeitsmarktpolitik* (Frankfurt am Main: Campus Verlag, 1985).

5 Muller, Schäppi, and Tanner, *Krise: Zufall oder Folge des Kapitalismus?*, p. 184.

6 Peter Binswanger, *Histoire de l'AVS: assurance-vieillesse et survivants suisse* (Zurich: Pro Senectute, 1987), pp. 239–48; Philipp Ischer, "Ausbau oder Konsolidierung? Der politische Diskurs der 1970er Jahre in der Schweiz im Bereich der AHV", in *Geschichte der Sozialversicherungen/Histoire des assurances sociales* (Zurich: Chronos, 2006), pp. 141–66.

focused on solving the gender imbalances in the pension structure and on early retirement, but the imperative of maintaining a "neutrality of costs" imposed a tight financial straitjacket on proposals for improvement.[7] After three decades of expansion, the pace of development of social insurance stalled. Sidelined by the contentious implementation of the BVG, the 10th AHV would only be completed in 1995, and the focus of old age provision shifted from the first to the second pillar.

The first draft of the law on occupational provision (BVG) submitted to the Federal Assembly in December 1975 aimed to follow the standards of pension schemes that offered "defined-benefit" targets rather than those of schemes that followed "defined-contribution" standards. The former offered better income security for pensioners but restricted employers' options. The draft also envisioned a central fund jointly financed by second-pillar institutions to buttress pensions for the entry generation, offer coverage for workers unaffiliated to pension plans, and ensure the indexing of BVG benefits. Once the people's pensions had been sidelined, employers' opposition to a compulsory second pillar, which had been toned down before the 1972 vote, flared up again. Small firms, poorly covered by occupational schemes, openly attacked the project, and holders of existing pension plans balked at giving up the flexibility of discretionary occupational benefits in a period of economic turbulence and heightened international competition. Insurance companies were also hostile to any state scheme competing against their group plans. After the National Council accepted the first legislative bill, intense lobbying by employers and insurers guaranteed its dismemberment in the more conservative Council of States.[8]

In late 1978, the revised BVG draft abandoned the idea of a central fund and mandatory indexing. Guidelines for trade union involvement in pension management were minimized and dropped altogether for group plans, which covered two-thirds of private-sector workers affiliated to the second pillar (see Table A.3, p. 296). Commenting on the

[7] "Weniger Staat – mehr Freiheit", *Neue Zürcher Zeitung*, October 13–14, 1979. On the shift toward neo-liberalism, see Jean-Noël Rey, *Trop d'Etat? Essai sur la mise en cause de l'Etat-protecteur en Suisse* (Lausanne: Réalités sociales, 1983), pp. 71–89. On the stalled 10th AHV revision, see Binswanger, *Histoire de l'AVS*, pp. 249–57; Christine Luchsinger, *Solidarität: Selbständigkeit, Bedürftigkeit: der schwierige Weg zu einer Gleichberechtigung der Geschlechter in der AHV: 1939–1980* (Zurich: Chronos, 1995), pp. 171ff.

[8] Giuliano Bonoli, "The institutionalization of the Swiss multi-pillar pension system", in *Rethinking the welfare state: the political economy of pension reform*, ed. Martin Rein and Winfried Schmähl (Cheltenham: Edward Elgar, 2004), pp. 102–21; Wolfgang Hafner, *Im Strudel der Finanzmärkte: Pensionskassen in der Schweiz* (Zurich: Rotpunktverlag, 2004), pp. 55–61; Jean Steiger, *Le deuxième pilier: service social ou affaire lucrative?* (Geneva: Grounauer, 1978), pp. 38–41.

parliamentary stalemate facing the BVG, the board of directors of Winterthur Life, presided over by Peter Binswanger, emphasized that "efforts to simplify the law [were] in the interest of the Company".[9] As the BVG was revised before being accepted by the Federal Assembly in 1982 and only implemented three years afterward, insurers won time to aggressively market second-pillar products.

From 1978 to 1987 occupational pension coverage jumped from one-half to over four-fifths of the non-farm workforce as employers extended existing plans, created new ones, or joined group insurance plans. The rise of coverage was especially significant for women, who had been literally left behind by the second pillar until then (see Table A.2, p. 295). The BVG preserved substantial flexibility for employers. The "compulsory domain" (or Obligatorium) of the BVG covered a wage range that started at the level of the maximal AHV pension and ran to a ceiling equivalent to three times that amount. These limits put lower-paid workers whose incomes fell below this threshold at a disadvantage and enabled employers to maintain special schemes beyond the Obligatorium ceiling for higher-paid personnel, notably reducing the redistributive features of the second pillar. In the same vein, indexing and portability remained discretionary, and a majority of employers adopted defined-contribution structures with more flexibility than defined benefits had.[10] In short, the "constraints of compulsion" largely validated the traditional features of occupational provision and formed a set of "minimum guidelines" and "half-measures".[11]

The overhaul of the second pillar improved pensions, but this resulted in more selective and less redistributive pensions than existed in countries with extensive pay-as-you-go systems, such as France and West Germany, or than in countries with more homogeneous second-pension tiers such as Sweden and the Netherlands. The fates of the first two pillars of the pension system were now increasingly linked. However, the BVG did not solve the complexity, lack of transparency, and institutional

[9] Minutes of the board of directors of Winterthur Life, December 5, 1978, quoted in Joseph Jung, *Die Winterthur: eine Versicherungsgeschichte* (Zurich: NZZ Verlag, 2000), p. 227.

[10] On the imbalances of the BVG, see Rudolf Rechsteiner, *Das 200-Milliarden-Geschäft: Pensionskassen in der Schweiz – Eine Einführung für Versicherte und Stiftungsräte* (Zurich: Unionsverlag, 1984), pp. 103–37; Martin Wechsler, *Die Einführung der obligatorischen 2. Säule: eine volkswirtschaftliche Analyse der Problematik des Bundesgesetzes über die berufliche Alters-, Hinterlassenen-, und Invalidenvorsorge (BVG)* (Basle: Zentralstelle der Studentenschaft Zürich, 1984), pp. 212, 289, 295. See also Stefan Hepp, "Mandatory occupational pension schemes in Switzerland: the first ten years", *Annals of Public and Cooperative Economics* 69/4 (1998), pp. 533–45.

[11] Graziano Lusenti, *Les institutions de prévoyance en Suisse, au Royaume-Uni et en Allemagne fédérale: placements financiers et politique sociale* (Geneva: Georg, 1989), pp. 207–8.

fragmentation of a second pillar that remained controlled by employers and still followed the subterranean politics that had been the hallmark of its century-long development. While the implementation of the BVG brought mixed results for workers, it represented a boon for financial players.

The BVG consolidated the role of pension funds as institutional investors and, far from heralding a "smooth and smiling collectivization" under workers' control, confirmed the pre-eminence of private financial interests. To avoid funding shortfalls, the BVG stipulated that employers and insurers had to guarantee a minimum rate of return of 4 percent on their pension investment. In a decade of buoyant financial growth, this rate did not represent a constraint on pension plans. Between 1978 and 1987, second-pillar assets rose from half to three-quarters of gross domestic product (see Table A.7, p. 303). By 1991, pension assets represented 40 percent of institutional investment, a very high percentage by international standards, and a few dozen of the largest pension plans controlled four-fifths of assets.[12] Delays in the implementation of the BVG left time for banks and especially insurance companies to position themselves in the market for managing pension plans and their assets. Right before the implementation of the BVG, group premiums had soared to over half of overall life insurance premiums (see Figure 2.3, p. 80). The net profits of Rentenanstalt more than trebled between 1983 and 1985, and insurers were declared the "main beneficiaries" of the corporate race toward the second-pillar bonanza. The few attempts to direct this impressive capital accumulation toward progressive goals remained inconclusive. In 1983, the union-based investment fund ASA (Anlagestiftung der Arbeitnehmerorganisationen), set up in 1976 by a Basle cooperative bank and presided over by former Federal Councilor Hans Peter Tschudi, managed a paltry 0.1 percent of overall second-pillar assets, which paled beside the other investment funds set up by leading banks.[13]

From 1987 on, a new market for banks and insurance companies opened with the introduction of voluntary individual retirement savings accounts. Contrary to the AHV and the BVG, the third pillar was not regulated by a federal law but by a patchwork of dispositions scattered

[12] Martin Anderson and Thierry Hertig, "Institutional investors in Switzerland", in *Institutional investors and corporate governance* (Berlin/New York: Walter de Gruyter, 1993), pp. 489–529 (especially p. 491).

[13] On Rentenanstalt profits, see Hafner, *Im Strudel der Finanzmärkte*, p. 147. On the role of insurers and investment funds, see Stefan Hepp, *Swiss pension funds: an emerging institutional investment force* (Berne: Haupt, 1990), pp. 137–43, 146–52; *The Swiss life insurance industry – The main beneficiary of the trend towards collective savings* (London: Morgan Stanley, 1993). On the ASA, see Rudolf Rechsteiner, *Sozialstaat Schweiz am Ende?* (Zurich: Unionsverlag, 1998), pp. 161, 202ff.

in various tax codes and regulations pertaining to insurance contracts. Estimates indicate that assets hoarded in such accounts represented 8 percent of overall pension assets (or CHF 34 billion). These tax-free savings clearly mean represented "billions lost in fiscal revenues for the Confederation".[14] The third pillar remained a gray area of fiscal privilege favoring middle-class professionals and wage earners while contributing only marginally to overall retirement needs.

The implementation of the three-pillar doctrine confirms the illusions long peddled by free-marketers and proponents of self-help. Instead of a harmonious system based on three tiers of equal importance ensuring basic provision, maintenance of living standards, and individual choice the Swiss pension system is characterized by a series of imbalances. In moving from the first to the third pillar, pension coverage becomes less universal, leaves behind low-workers, and finally remains the preserve of higher-income strata. From pay-as-you-go AHV pensions to occupational schemes and individual savings accounts, benefits become less redistributive, more unequal, and more linked to financial markets. The transparent and democratically accountable institutional structure of the first pillar is replaced by growing institutional fragmentation and opacity. These imbalances and asymmetries accompany the shift from social insurance to private provision and the various shades of gray capital.

## Toward the new millennium: austerity and the uncertain returns of gray capital

In the Thatcher and Reagan decade, the containment of the AHV, the flexible framework of the BVG, and the financialization of pension provision came together to make Switzerland a showcase for those who attacked the expansion of social insurance and preached the gospel of privatization and financial deregulation. As pension reformers called for the downsizing of public provision and the opening-up of new markets to private provision, the "three-pillar doctrine" became a key phrase for free-market enthusiasts, as well as for international organizations such as the OECD and the World Bank.[15] There was of course strong continuity between these latest appraisals and older free-market depictions of Switzerland as a welcome exception among European welfare states. The current dominance of the neo-liberal ideology means, however, that the

[14] *Statistique des assurances sociales suisses 2005* (Berne: Office fédéral des assurances sociales, 2006), p. 240 (quotation); Marie-Claude Sommer, "Prévoyance liée ou pilier 3a: enquête de l'OFAS sur les conventions bancaires et les contrats d'assurance de capitaux de prévoyance liée", *Securité Sociale*, no. 3 (2001), pp. 144–6.

[15] See the references quoted in notes 2, 3, 4, and 5 of the introduction.

containment and financialization of old age provision has now become the orthodoxy of pension reform.

Despite its envied status among pension reformers, the Swiss pension system has not escaped controversies over the sustainability of pensions that are the hallmark of a "silver age" of the welfare state characterized by economic turbulence, aging demographics, and jittery financial markets. The tug-of-war also continued between those advocating austerity measures and those emphasizing the insufficient income protection offered by the AHV and the BVG. During the 1990s, the pace of AHV revisions accelerated as Switzerland faced a new recession and an intense neo-liberal offensive. Contrasting with the first eight expansionist revisions enacted in the postwar golden age of the welfare state, the current trend of pension reform points toward consolidation and retrenchment.

Building on Paul Pierson's argument that the politics of social policy retrenchment differ from those of its postwar expansionist phase, and the fact that specific institutional configurations can protract this process, political scientist Giuliano Bonoli has described Switzerland's fragmented institutional setting as a "formidable obstacle to the neo-liberal ambitions of economic and political elites".[16] According to him, the 10th (1995) and 11th (2004) AHV revisions, as well as the 1st (2003) BVG revision, offer a mixed picture of retrenchment and selective expansion as carefully designed "quid pro quos" were agreed to by the governmental coalition to form "consensual retrenchment" packages able to leap the referendum hurdle. Other institutionalist scholars have also emphasized the simultaneity of retrenchment and the raising of Swiss social expenditure to the level attained by other European welfare states.[17]

This approach has become a mainstay of scholarship on the Swiss welfare state and has brought the Swiss case to the attention of a broader scholarly audience. However, because of their focus on the endgame of social policy development and on state forms of provision, institutionalists underestimate the long-term impact of the three-pillar doctrine and

[16] Giuliano Bonoli, *The politics of pension reform: institutions and policy change in western Europe* (Cambridge: Cambridge University Press, 2000), p. 2; Paul Pierson, *Dismantling the welfare state? Reagan, Thatcher, and the politics of retrenchment* (Cambridge: Cambridge University Press, 1994).

[17] Giuliano Bonoli, "Switzerland: adapting pensions within tight institutional constraints", in *Ageing and pension reform around the world: evidence from eleven countries*, ed. Giuliano Bonoli and Toshimitsu Shinkawa (Cheltenham: Edward Elgar, 2005), pp. 137–54. See also Silja Häusermann, "Reform opportunities in a Bismarckian latecomer: restructuring the Swiss welfare state", unpublished working paper, Political Science Department, University of Zurich, 2006; Herbert Obinger, Klaus Armingeon, Giuliano Bonoli *et al.*, "Switzerland: the marriage of direct democracy and federalism", in *Federalism and the welfare state: New World and European experiences*, ed. Herbert Obinger, *et al.* (New York: Cambridge University Press, 2005), pp. 263–306 (especially pp. 288–91).

the crucial shift from pay-as-you-go to funded provision that began in the 1970s. While underscoring that the recent increases in Swiss social expenditure are largely due to the integration of private health and pension providers into social security statistics, institutionalists tend to neglect the permanence of the subterranean politics of pensions and the financialization of social policy.

Highly visible, contentious, and protracted political battles have characterized recent AHV politics. After having been sidelined by the implementation of the BVG, the 10th AHV revision in 1995 corrected some gender imbalances by splitting couples' pensions, traditionally paid to male wage-earners, and adding education credits for women who spent years out of the workforce raising children. At the same time, the revision raised the retirement age for women from 62 to 64 years. Early retirement – a growing need for older workers facing diminishing employment prospects – was made more difficult, as it was made conditional on pension cutbacks. This reform package, forged by Socialist Federal Councilor Ruth Dreifuss, was unsuccessfully challenged by a trade union-sponsored referendum and by a constitutional initiative (1998) opposing the increase in the retirement age for women. Since payroll contributions or income and wealth taxes were ruled out as intolerable burdens on employers or taxpayers, the new value-added tax (VAT) was used to fund the AHV (see Figure 4.1, see p. 190). This method of indirect taxation was part of a wider fiscal conservative backlash against the financing of social programs through more redistributive income taxes and payroll contributions.[18]

In two influential *White Books* published in 1991 and 1995, prominent economists and business executives demanded the downsizing of the first pillar into a mere safety net, along with the replacement of the second pillar with individual retirement accounts offering more "freedom of choice". Although this wish list was not implemented, pension reform resolutely inched toward retrenchment. After calling vigorously for a "moratorium" on social policy, the Arbeitgeberverband insisted in 1998 that "social policy expansion [had to] be stopped and economies found in every existing social program".[19] The 1990s also witnessed the

[18] Bonoli, *The politics of pension reform*, pp. 101–12. On VAT, see Sébastien Guex, *L'argent de l'Etat: parcours des finances publiques au 20ème siècle* (Lausanne: Réalités Sociales, 1998), pp. 166, 174–5. 211–34.

[19] On the *White Books*, see Charles-André Udry and Jean-François Marquis, "Le renouveau de tous les dangers", in *Le livre noir du libéralisme* (Lausanne: Ed. de l'Aire, 1996), pp. 133–229, 190–3; Peter Hasler (Arbeitgeberverband), "Im Würgegriff der Anspruchgesellschaft: wider den weiteren Ausbau des Sozialstaates", *Neue Zürcher Zeitung*, August 22, 1998.

rise of the People's Party (successor to the anti-Socialist Farmers', Artisans', and Burghers' Party of 1918) whose fiscal conservatism and free-market positions constituted a spearhead for the attacks against the welfare state. Even though an official report admitted in 1995 that pensions for low and middle-income earners would have to be improved to reach the level stipulated in the federal constitution, AHV expansion was not a priority on the political agenda.[20]

Buttressed by alarmist financial and demographic forecasts and renewed AHV deficits caused by the recession of the 1990s, the 11th AHV revision aimed to secure long-term pension financing by raising the retirement age to 65 for women, scaling back widows' benefits, and shifting pension-indexing from a biennial to a triennial rhythm. This reform package, finalized in 2003 by Federal Councilor Pascal Couchepin (Radical), combined CHF 925 million of cutbacks in annual pension expenditure and a VAT increase. After its acceptance by the bourgeois majority of the Federal Assembly, the 11th AHV revision was challenged in a left-wing referendum (150,000 signatures were collected in less than a week) and an unprecedented national march against the proposed cuts. As a tit-for-tat measure, bourgeois parties and business federations campaigned against the VAT increase, because it reduced the pressure for more stringent cutbacks. In May 2004, both the AHV revision and VAT increase were rejected by strong majorities of over two-thirds of voters. This first-time rejection of a pension bill underscored the complex and protracted politics facing social policy retrenchment in the silver age of the welfare state. However, it did not lead to a reorientation of the trend toward retrenchment and the shift toward the second pillar.

In contrast to those on the AHV, debates on the second pillar have been much less contentious, and the BVG has yet to be subjected to a referendum. However, the maturing of occupational pensions and their exposure to unfavorable economic and financial situations have led to increased concern about the future of the second pillar. At the same time, criticism continues to be raised of the insufficient income protection offered by second-pillar benefits, which are playing an increasing role in old age provision despite evidence that the AHV still constitutes the key source of retirement benefits for most income categories.[21] It also

20 *Bericht des Eidgenössischen Departementes des Innern zur heutigen Ausgestaltung und Weiterentwicklung der schweizerischen 3-Säulen-Konzeption der Alters-, Hinterlassenen- und Invalidenvorsorge (3-Säulen Bericht)* (Berne: Eidg. Departement des Innern, 1995), p. 28.

21 Andreas Balthasar, *Le passage à la retraite: trajectoires, facteurs d'influence et conséquences: rapport dans le cadre du "Programme de recherche interdépartemental sur l'avenir à long terme de la prévoyance vieillesse" (IDA ForAlt)* (Berne: Office fédéral des assurances sociales, 2003), p. 158.

became clear during the 1st (2003) revision of the BVG that the institutional hurdles facing social insurance are less significant in an area where continuing fragmentation and opacity reduce accountability and enable employers to implement unilateral reforms.

The structure of the second pillar has changed since 1985. The number of pension plans has decreased dramatically as small firms have joined collective foundations (Sammelstiftungen) set up by banks and insurance companies. By 2000, the 50 largest pension plans covered two-thirds of the insured and managed half of all pension assets, while the next 2,550 pension plans (many of them group plans) covered almost all other participating wage earners. Another 9,000 pension plans had no active members and were being progressively phased out (see Table A.7, p. 303).[22] Despite drastic consolidation within the dense thicket of pension plans, the fragmentation of the second pillar remained significant. By contrast, in the Netherlands, a country with twice the population of Switzerland, 80 industry-wide pension plans (out of a total of 859 pension schemes) accounted for four-fifths of pension coverage in 2004.[23] Institutional fragmentation clearly makes second-pillar plans, and especially group plans, both costlier and more opaque than pay-as-you-go social insurance.[24] These shortcomings are even greater in collective foundations and group plans, where joint management remains at best an empty shell and employee representatives on pension plan boards have little leverage vis-à-vis insurance companies.

The combination of first- and second-pillar pensions has helped to reduce poverty among the elderly, which was still quite widespread in Switzerland in the early 1980s compared with other European countries with similar standards of economic development. Yet, the 60 percent replacement rate set as a target for combined first- and second-pillar pensions is insufficient for growing ranks of part-timers (most of them women) without adequate pensions who may see their retirement income drop below the poverty line, or for lower-paid workers who fall outside of the BVG Obligatorium. In the same vein, research has shown that the funded and tax-advantaged second and third pillars largely counter the redistributive effects of the AHV. Because of the growing number of

22 Monika Queisser and Dimitri Vittas, *The Swiss multi-pillar pension system: triumph of common sense?* (Washington: World Bank, 2000), p. 30.

23 See Table 8.6a of the *Pensioenmonitor* of the Dutch National Bank, available on the following website: http://www.statistics.dnb.nl/.

24 In 2002, the management costs of the AHV amounted to CHF 134 per person insured, against an average of CHF 499 for BVG pension plans (with amounts ranging from CHF 300 for large pension plans to CHF 600 for group plans). See *Comparaison entre l'AVS et la prévoyance économique sous l'angle économique* (Berne: Département fédéral de l'Intérieur/OFAS, 2005), pp. 47–8.

people dependent on the second pillar and of the spread of atypical work situations, demands to lower the entry threshold into the BVG and to improve second-pillar pensions (notably with indexing and portability) have been raised since the late 1980s. These proposals encountered much initial resistance from employers: only in 1993 was full pension portability introduced into the BVG Obligatorium.[25]

In contrast to its ambiguous outcomes for pensioners and continuing organizational shortcomings, the second pillar has been a source of capital accumulation. Regulations regarding pension fund investment in shares were liberalized during the 1990s, and at the peak of the last stock market bubble pension assets reached over CHF 600 billion, or 150 percent of gross domestic product (see Table A.1, p. 290). The concentration of this "gray capital" was high, because a few dozen pension plans, insurance companies, and large investment funds between them controlled two-thirds of pension assets, while funds championing socially responsible investment remained marginal players.[26] Third-pillar assets are still modest in comparison with the second pillar, yet their growth is encouraged by the demographic and financial uncertainties that plague both the first and second pillars. In a country traditionally awash with capital, the second pillar has had dubious effects on productive investment and regional development, while offering interesting prospects for financial intermediaries.[27]

25 On reducing poverty, see Martin Rein and John Turner, "How societies mix public and private spheres in their pension systems", in *Rethinking the welfare state: the political economy of pension reform*, ed. Martin Rein and Winfried Schmähl (Cheltenham: Edward Elgar, 2004), pp. 102–21. On the shortcomings of BVG benefits, see Bonoli, "The institutionalization of the Swiss multi-pillar pension system", p. 117; Kilian Künzi and Markus Schärrer, *Wer zahlt für die Soziale Sicherheit und wer profitiert davon? Eine Analyse der Sozialtransfers in der Schweiz* (Zurich: Verlag Rüegger, 2004). On early attempts to expand the BVG, see Silja Häusermann, "Flexibilisation des relations d'emplois et sécurité sociale: le cas de la réforme de la loi suisse sur la prévoyance professionnelle", mémoire de DEA, Institut des hautes études en administration publique (IDHEAP Lausanne), 2002, pp. 23–4.

26 On pension fund asset concentration, see Graziano Lusenti, *Pensionskassenanlagen 1998–2000: Ergebnisse und Kommentare zur Umfrage* (Geneva: Robeco Institutional Asset Management, 2000). For a ranking of the largest Swiss pension plans in 2001–2002, see http://www.vorsorgeforum.ch. In 2000, the "socially responsible" Geneva-based Ethos foundation managed CHF 810 million (or 0.16 percent of overall second-pillar assets, excluding group reserves). See http://www.ethosfund.ch as well as Hafner, *Im Strudel der Finanzmärkte*, pp. 121–3, 33–6.

27 For a discussion of the financial impact of pension plans, see *Comparaison entre l'AVS et la prévoyance économique sous l'angle économique*, pp. 64–5; Hafner, *Im Strudel der Finanzmärkte*, pp. 82–106; Thierry Theurillat, Olivier Crevoisier, and José Corpataux, "L'impact des caisses de pension sur les circuits de financement et de contrôle de l'économie suisse (1985–2003)", research report, Institut de sociologie/Groupe de recherche en économie territoriale (GRET), Université de Neuchâtel, 2006.

The stock market downturn of 2001–2002 wiped out 10 percent of second-pillar assets. Because their exposure to shares was more recent and less extensive than in the United States or the United Kingdom, second-pillar institutions withstood this hard ride better than their Anglo-Saxon counterparts. However, public-sector pension plans that still operated along defined-benefit lines were hit hard by a reversal that fell on them as they faced growing pension liabilities, austerity budgets, and privatization at the federal and cantonal levels. As during the 1930s, right-wing forces and employers denounced the imbalances and deficits in public-sector pension plans and pressed for benefit cutbacks, payroll contribution increases, and an accelerated shift to defined-contribution rules.[28] The financial losses sustained by pension funds may have temporarily pushed back arguments for the further financialization of pensions. However, they also reinforced concerns about the long-term viability of pension plans that were then in turn used as arguments against the expansion of BVG benefits.

Echoing the trend of recent AHV revisions, the legislative bill on the 1st BVG revision accepted by the Federal Assembly in October 2003 combined selective expansion and retrenchment. The revision improved pension coverage for low-income workers by reducing the minimum wage threshold these had to reach in order to be affiliated to the second pillar. Despite being watered down during fierce parliamentary debates (the number of people benefitting from the lower entry threshold was reduced from 300,000 to 100,000), the BVG revision received determined support from key politicians and was, finally, narrowly approved by the Federal Assembly. Many on the right would have preferred to close pension gaps through means-tested assistance instead of this extension of insurance coverage.[29] Yet, the reduction of the BVG entry threshold corresponded in the end to the long-term aim of the three-pillar doctrine – to reinforce funded occupational provision instead of pay-as-you-go social insurance.

At the same time, the revision established the BVG retirement age for all at 65 years and lowered the conversion rate used to calculate BVG pensions, which had immediate negative effects on benefits.[30] The trade-off for the selective expansion of coverage was an across-the-board cutback

[28] Heinz Zimmermann and Andreas Valda, "Ein Loch von 66 Milliarden Franken: Schätzungen zum Defizit der öffentlichen Pensionskassen", *Neue Zürcher Zeitung*, August 19, 2003.

[29] On the revision, see Bonoli, "Switzerland: adapting pensions within tight institutional constraints", pp. 151–3; Häusermann, "Flexibilisation des relations d'emplois et sécurité sociale", pp. 23–5.

[30] Let us consider the example of a worker whose BVG account reaches CHF 600,000 after 35 years of affiliation to an occupational pension scheme. At the current conversion

for future pensioners. The revision also promised to strengthen transparency and joint management procedures in collective foundations and group plans, an area that had until then been the preserve of insurance companies.

The subterranean politics of private provision have not disappeared, and wide areas of the second pillar still eschew democratic accountability. Alongside the 1st BVG revision, life insurance companies threatened to withdraw from the group pension business if the Federal Council did not lower and make more flexible the minimum rate of return (set at 4 percent in 1985) guaranteeing the growth of pension assets. Despite vociferous complaints from the left and trade unions against this so-called "Lex Rentenanstalt", the reduction was hastily implemented by means of an emergency decree that escaped the referendum mechanism. After a second round of lobbying by insurers, the rate was lowered further from 3.25 to 2.25 percent in early 2004 (the minimum rate now stands at 2.5). According to a model developed by Winterthur Life, insurance companies have also lowered the conversion rate enabling the calculation of benefits and increased payroll contributions for pensions above the Obligatorium range, resulting in cutbacks for pensioners and higher costs for employers.[31] These measures underscore how insurers can exert strong and unilateral leverage on pensions. In contrast, the fragmentation of pension coverage makes it difficult for workers and pensioners to mount effective resistance against "technical" measures that affect their benefits directly. In late 2006, the Confederation again announced for 2011 a further lowering of the conversion rate for BVG pensioners in order to take into account the lower returns of financial markets expected to take place as postwar baby-boomers retire in droves.

At the beginning of the twenty-first century, pension politics are still dominated by the tug-of-war between state-based and occupational provision, and battles over their boundaries and respective weight in old age provision. In conclusion, despite evident shortcomings and ambiguous outcomes, the force of the three-pillar doctrine remains unmistakable.

After the momentous rejection of the 11th AHV revision, the Arbeitgeberverband declared that its "politically realistic" objectives should be re-examined and called for a general rise in the retirement age and a further downgrading of pension-indexing. In a blatant example of the use of

rate of 7.2 percent, this sum translates into an annual BVG pension of CHF 43,200 (7.2 percent of CHF 600,000). With a 6.8 percent conversion rate, the annual BVG pension drops to CHF 40,800.

[31] Hafner, *Im Strudel der Finanzmärkte*, pp. 145–55. See also Markus Felber, "Ein Etappensieg für Swiss Life: Zusatzprämien im BVG-Obligatorium nicht systemwidrig", *Neue Zürcher Zeitung*, April 29, 2004.

fear-mongering over the downfall of social insurance, Federal Councilor Hans Rudolf Merz (Radical), head of the Finance Department, declared that it was time to "think the unthinkable" and discuss the possibility of "privatizing" the AHV in the medium term to save pension and disability benefits from a looming financial debacle.[32] Retrenchment and financialization are still very much on the agenda in a decade that witnessed successive rounds of austerity cuts in federal and cantonal budgets, as well as relentless pressure from right-wing politicians and business interests to reduce taxation levels. In early 2006, the second draft of the 11th AHV revision moderated cutbacks and focused on unifying the retirement age at 65 years, while introducing special pre-retirement means-tested assistance for persons who are not eligible for current early retirement options. Even before the start of parliamentary debates on this toned-down version, the Federal Office for Social Insurance warned that a 12th AHV revision centered on a complete overhaul of pensions would take place in the late 2000s, at the time when "AHV finances [would] find themselves in a critical situation".[33]

Continuing pressure on existing pensions, advocating means tests instead of social insurance mechanisms, and resistance to devoting new financial resources to federal pensions constitute a tight straitjacket restricting AHV development. At the same time, we can witness steady efforts to individualize and further financialize pensions at all levels. This shows clearly that the aim of current pension reformers is not only to continue shifting the weight of pension provision from the first to the second pillar, but also to eviscerate the few collective dimensions of the second pillar and push occupational provision toward third-pillar solutions.

Denouncing the "social romanticism" attached to the second pillar, free-market economists have argued that workers should not be forced to join "collectivist" pension plans managed by trade unions and employers but should be allowed the alternative of choosing their own plans and assume the risks of providing for their old age. The "pension plan choice" concept has been turned down by the Federal Social Insurance Office and by trade unions, but also by employers' organizations. In September 2003, the Arbeitgeberverband emphasized that such measures would "undermine employers' motivation to develop the second pillar [and] lead to a reduction of the significant monies devoted to pension provision beyond the Obligatorium". According to this employers'

32 "Arbeitgeber fordern Rentenalter 66: Einsparungen und Systemabbau bei den Sozialwerken", *Neue Zürcher Zeitung*, November 23, 2004; "Man muss das Undenkbare denken", *Tages Anzeiger*, July 7, 2004.

33 Daniela Witschard, "Motifs et buts de la nouvelle version de la 11e révision de l'AVS", *Sécurité Sociale* 2 (2006), pp. 72–8, 73.

federation, "the left might exploit this decline of corporate provision to renew claims in favor of an expansion of the AHV and the creation of a people's pension".[34] Three decades after the defeat of the people's pensions, the significance of the 1972 vote is alive in business memory, and employers' federations are uneasy about departing from the framework that has enabled them to bind trade unions to occupational provision and to contain the AHV.

Confronted by the unmet promises of the second pillar and the freezing of the AHV, voices on the left have increasingly begun to challenge, for the moment more with words than deeds, the doctrine they had embraced a generation ago. During its 2002 congress, the Gewerkschaftsbund turned down a motion demanding an immediate "exit strategy" from the three-pillar doctrine but commissioned a study group to draft proposals for improving pensions by reinforcing the first pillar. These proposals, published in February 2006 under the slogan "At last, pensions that secure existing living conditions", contain a catalogue combining radical proposals with old demands long peddled by the left. The study group proposed an increase in minimum pensions topped up with assistance supplements (AHV-Ergänzungsleistungen) granted without means-testing. These changes would be financed primarily by increased payroll contributions (which have not been raised since 1972), a federal inheritance tax (a proposal put forward since the 1920s), and an increase in VAT. Along with this, the report advised a 20 percent reduction in BVG benefits, the elimination of tax privileges for third-pillar savings accounts, and the removal of for-profit insurance companies from the second pillar.[35]

By reaffirming the solidarity and redistributive dimensions of the AHV and proclaiming the need to limit means tests and contain the financialization of pensions, the trade union study group clearly goes against the grain of current pension reform orthodoxy. However, the Gewerkschaftsbund's proposals face an uphill battle, not least because of the entrenchment of the three-pillar doctrine among its members and the increasing reliance of workers on second-pillar pensions. The 2004 referendum victory against the 11th AHV referendum has undoubtedly bolstered the morale of the left, but its effects have not lasted long and still have to be furthered by

[34] On the pension choice idea, see David S. Gerber, "Freie Pensionskassenwahl mit grossem Nutzen: von den Grenzen betrieblicher Sozialromantik", *Neue Zürcher Zeitung*, March 9, 2004; Thomas Held and Lukas Steinmann, "Plädoyer für freie Wahl der Pensionskasse: Arbeitnehmer trägt in der Altersvorsorge das Anlagerisiko", *Neue Zürcher Zeitung*, October 25, 2003. For the Arbeitgeberverband perspective, see Peter Hasler, "Keine freie Wahl der Pensionskasse: überforderte Aufsicht und ratlose Arbeitnehmer", *Neue Zürcher Zeitung*, September 2, 2003.

[35] *Endlich existenzsichernde Renten: erste Säule stärken – 3000 Franken Rente für alle* (Berne: Schweizerischer Gewerkschaftsbund, 2006).

determined action. Recent developments show that the left has still to regain the initiative in the pension domain. A Socialist popular initiative aimed at allocating a share of Swiss National Bank profits to the financing of the AHV was successfully rolled back by the right in September 2006 with the argument that it would "delay necessary reform".[36] This defeat underscored the difficulty for the left of translating a defensive victory into new, positive gains. Given their determination to shape and maintain the iron framework of the three-pillar doctrine, insurance companies are highly unlikely to abandon their century-long involvement in the business of social policy without a fight. And despite temporary setbacks, the neo-liberal drive in favor of the financialization of pensions is still a dominant trend. With the second version of the 11th, and soon the 12th, AHV revisions on the political horizon, the stage is set for the next major pension showdown to be waged in the shadow of the three pillars.

[36] Ernst Baltensberger, "Die Illusionen der Kosa-Initiative", *Neue Zürcher Zeitung*, August 29, 2006.

# Conclusion

I started this book by calling the reader's attention to how *The Economist* designated the shift from the first pillar of "crumbling" social insurance toward the third one of personal responsibility and individual, funded retirement accounts as a highly desirable course for pension reform. I also emphasized how a Swiss Re analyst boasted that the foundations of the Swiss pension system had been "properly laid", in contrast to other European "rotten social insurance systems" allegedly facing catastrophic times because of their over-reliance on pay-as-you-go programs. These metaphors underscore the importance of the semantics attached to social policy development and in particular the effectiveness of the three-pillar doctrine. If the invention of this concept cannot be attributed with certainty to any one person, its success is undeniable. What first started as the motto of the 1960s insurer-led campaign to safeguard funded occupational provision and respond to the challenge of the people's pensions has left a lasting imprint on the popular imagination and on discourses about the Swiss welfare state. It has also been picked up beyond the borders of Switzerland. The adoption of the three-pillar metaphor by free-market commentators, policy experts, and multi-lateral organizations such as the World Bank during the last decade of the twentieth century underscores the prominence of this concept in the current ideological and political offensive in favor of the financialization of pensions.

The three-pillar metaphor has indeed more appeal than the technical acronyms that litter the social policy field or the depictions of multi-tier pension configurations made up of state, enterprise, and individual solutions as "three-legged stools" or "three-layer cakes". Avoiding such trivial references, the three-pillar doctrine evokes the solid and permanent foundations of a harmonious pension design. Ironically, graphic depictions of the three pillars cannot be found on the website of the Federal Social Insurance Office, whereas such depictions often figure prominently on those of banks and insurance companies. There, images of elegant, Greek-inspired columns or Parthenon-style frontages serve as background decor to marketing second- and especially third-pillar products.[1] These temples of provision are biased. They constitute static and ahistorical representations that reflect neither the actual role of each pension pillar in pension provision nor ongoing controversies about the boundaries of each pillar of the pension system.

This book has retrieved the genealogy of this influential metaphor and deconstructed its purposes in order to chart the contested terrains of pension politics. I have systematically appraised the parallel and contrasted development of social insurance and occupational provision by weaving into a common narrative the long-term history of the various components of the pension system. This exploration has focused both on public policy areas that are usually the focus of welfare state research, and also on the more subterranean ones where private social policy deploys its off-shoots. In this process, I have revealed the blurred boundaries delineating social insurance and occupational provision, as well as their reciprocal interactions. Following these multiple fault lines has enabled me to chart the topography of Switzerland's pension system and, by extension, major features of its welfare state. It has also enabled me to assess how different sets of players and interests navigate political institutions and influence policy-making. Finally, my attempts to triangulate Switzerland's distinctive trajectory in the worlds of welfare has enabled me to question commonly held notions of comparative social policy research.

Scholars attempting to identify the main protagonists of social policy have in turn designated political institutions and the state, the left and labor, or employers and business interests as the crucial forces driving the expansion of social policy in advanced capitalist societies. This book has focused on the role of business in the shaping of a distinctive old age provision regime. Yet, it has underscored the internal complexity of each one of these three sets of forces, as well as the complex triangle that characterizes their interactions. In order to highlight the changing policy capacity of the various social groups and political forces active in the making of the pension system, I have shown how their actions evolve within a historical perspective. Apart from the study of the fault lines of public and private social provision, the exploration of the dynamic tensions between collective interests whose actions are mediated by political institutions has constituted a key site of analysis of this book.

[1] For examples, see: https://entry.credit-suisse.ch/csfs/p/rb/en/vorsorge/vor_vorsorgesystem.jsp (Crédit Suisse); http://www.swisslife.ch/slch/de/home/infocentre/ssecurity.html (Swiss Life); http://www.winterthur-leben.ch/home/vorsorge-infocenter/vic_soziale-sicherheit/vic_soz_grundlagen/vic_soz_grundlagen_dreisaeulenkonzept.htm (Winterthur insurance); http://www.ubs.com/1/g/ubs_ch/private/insurance/3_pillar_princip.html (UBS).

In particular, I have documented the modus operandi of business federations, and how inter-employer study groups and task forces contribute to shape the internal consensus and organization of collective action among Swiss capitalists. I have also charted the many tactics and channels that business circles have used to influence the development of social policy: back-room lobbying and public-education campaigns in favor of private social provision, parliamentary action, the use of referenda (or the threat of using them), and active propaganda during direct-democracy votes, and, finally, policy-making from the executive branch. Finally, I have described Swiss capitalists' relations with labor interests or with political parties. Despite internal divisions and competing interests, this book underscores the consistency and efficiency of Swiss capitalists' collective action, their close integration in the decision-making apparatus of the federal state, their capacity to translate strategic thinking into working policies, and, lastly, their ability to channel demands for the expansion of social policy into frameworks safeguarding private social programs.

The left has repeatedly generated strong support for the expansion of social rights and social citizenship. This was especially true during brief periods of intense political radicalization, such as the general strike of 1918, or during the postwar period, when the combined use of direct-democracy initiatives and executive-led policy-making made federal pensions the top item on the political agenda. Yet, the left and labor have consistently held more fragile positions, in contrast to employers. This has made it difficult for them to influence the development of social policy and has fostered their alignment toward business-friendly positions. The left has been shoehorned into a political system under perennial bourgeois dominance, while trade unions have been embedded into a system of industrial relations and collective bargaining whose vital coordinates are largely attuned to employers' preferences. While enabling the incremental growth of social benefits and occupational provision, these unfavorable configurations have in the end strengthened political cross-class alliances and patterns of social partnership that blunted attempts to expand social insurance and enhanced prospects for occupational pensions. The entrenchment of labor support for occupational provision or the reluctance felt by the Socialist leadership regarding proposals that challenged the status quo are two examples of this situation. To sum up, the left and labor had less leverage on the workings of federal social policy than bourgeois parties and employers.

In a recent article, sociologist Walter Korpi has criticized employer-centered approaches that attribute to capitalists too much of a proactive role in the development of welfare states without clearly differentiating among them between protagonists who genuinely initiate an expansion of social rights and social citizenship, consenters who merely participate in the implementation of social policy programs, and antagonists who constantly resist its expansion.[2] The shifts and tensions between these three positions are present throughout this book. Undeniable business antagonism toward social insurance surfaced at all stages of the development trajectory of the Swiss pension system. Employers opposed the development of federal social insurance for ideological and moral reasons, because it challenged existing private social arrangements, because it led to an increase in state prerogatives, or because its costs were considered too steep.

If employers were much more than simple consenting bystanders during the formation of the Swiss welfare state, their preferences and actions were undoubtedly shaped by relations with the state and the political left. Describing the role of employers in policy-making as "proactive" would be too limiting. For this reason, I prefer to describe business interests as conditional consenters toward social insurance programs. In other words, their acceptance of the extension of social rights was accompanied with caveats: as much as possible, universal social insurance had to remain a basis for the extension and preservation of selective private social programs. But consent did not mean inaction. On the contrary, it is in the key role played by employers in the delineation of the boundaries of social policy programs that we can discern the extent of their influence. By focusing on the two watersheds of 1947 and 1972, we can identify the patterns of these persistent efforts to shape social policy development in Switzerland.

The 1940s breakthrough of social insurance, in the form of the AHV/EO nexus, was shaped by representatives of leading manufacturing sectors who had experienced the tumult of two world wars, social and political radicalization, and severe economic depression. As in many other European countries, this period, described by historian Eric Hobsbawm as the Age of Catastrophe, formed the background for Walther Stampfli's push for a social security scheme that rested on a broad social and political consensus. This scheme furthered on the national stage the aims of the Peace Agreement signed in 1937 in the metal sector and sealed the wartime integration of the Socialists within the executive branch. The AHV/EO nexus also stabilized the labor market and offered a sound foundation for the welfare schemes developed by leading corporations. This strengthening of the people's community (Volksgemeinschaft) and

[2] Walter Korpi, "Power resources and employer-centered approaches in explanations of welfare states and varieties of capitalism: protagonists, consenters, and antagonists", *World Politics* 58/2 (2006), pp. 167–206.

factory community (Betriebsgemeinschaft) through a combination of basic universal social benefits and selective occupational provision consolidated the wartime productive capacity of Swiss capitalism and contributed to lay the foundations of its postwar expansion.

Pension benefits were of course centered on a core constituency of male breadwinners and disadvantaged both foreign workers and women, but their scope represented a clear break with a past in which retirement benefits had entirely remained a private, voluntary domain. Despite his staunchly corporate profile, Walther Stampfli was also a statesman groomed within the ranks of the Radical party-state, and the AHV he forged unambiguously constituted, however modest it might seem in comparison with more developed European pension systems, a keystone of the social infrastructure of the Confederation.

In contrast, the three-pillar doctrine represented a much more ambiguous construct laced with stronger anti-statist dimensions. This doctrine emerged at a time when the expansion of pensions, building on the foundations laid during World War II, had gained more and more momentum under social democratic guidance. The three-pillar doctrine, a rationalization of the bifurcated state of Swiss old age provision, was elaborated and supported by a business faction characterized by its Janus-faced attitude toward the federal state. Insurers shared their actuarial expertise with the Confederation and had recognized early on the usefulness of basic pensions as a foundation for private provision. In the end, insurers were less interested in reinforcing the social infrastructure of the federal state than in defending their stake in pension provision and opening new grazing pastures for the accumulation of financial capital. This dimension was especially important at the end of the decades of postwar growth, a time when insurance and banking activities were gaining more and more prominence in Swiss postwar capitalism in comparison with traditional leading manufacturing sectors. The answer of insurers such as Peter Binswanger to the Socialist-inspired "Tschudi pace" in AHV expansion was to weld occupational plans to social insurance and to re-channel the momentum of social policy expansion toward private solutions.

The three-pillar doctrine embedded private providers in the heart of the pension system. This had contradictory outcomes. While undoubtedly opening a trend toward more regulation, homogeneity, and fairness in occupational pension benefits, the mandatory second pillar made the expansion of social rights dependent on retirement benefits that are more opaque, selective, uneven, and costlier than social insurance pensions. Ironically, the mandatory second pillar may represent a heavier burden for certain employers, especially those who depend on insurers to set up pension provision, than an expanded AHV. However, this intricate entanglement of public and private solutions was the hefty price that business interests were ready to pay in order to contain a more redistributive, state-based pension system.

In both cases described above, business forces played a leading role in channeling popular and political pressure in favor of retirement benefits toward configurations that safeguarded private forms of provision. As Peter Binswanger of Winterthur Life asserted in 1963, "further expansion of the AHV is . . . no longer a social issue, but a *political issue and a question of worldview*. Those who propose an expansion of the AHV are in the end in favor of state-control and collectivism."[3] This candid description of the issue at the heart of the struggle between social insurance and occupational provision reminds us that it is unwise to disconnect the history of the welfare state from careful analysis of agency and power relations. Even in Switzerland, where employers concentrate much policy capacity, the outcome of pension controversies heavily depended on power relations and class struggle.

Political institutions evidently contributed to the imbalances and outcomes described above. The fragmentation of the federal political system and the hurdles of direct democracy both slowed down the momentum of social insurance and favored the selective expansion of occupational provision. This book confirms the weakness of the Swiss federal state, or rather its permeability and responsiveness, vis-à-vis the principles and objectives enunciated by business interests. It also highlights the many ways through which the federal state has facilitated the development of private social programs through proactive fiscal measures, mild regulation of pension plans, and, finally, a state mandate for occupational provision. Employer-controlled institutions such as the AHV and EO equalization funds have been integrated into the administration of federal social insurance, and firm-specific social programs have been safeguarded.

Following Peter Baldwin's recent appeal to scholars of the state to go beyond simple dichotomies of weakness and strength in their attempt to understand how states operate and intervene, the patterns unveiled in this volume underscore a specific "style of statism" based on public–private partnerships and the implementation of state tasks by organized economic interests.[4] Stated differently, this book highlights the intricacies of the entanglement between the state and civil society in an area,

[3] SPAHV, "Thesen für die Publizistik über die AHV nach durchgeführter 6. Revision", October 24, 1963, file Q128 203, ZFS.

[4] Peter Baldwin, "Beyond weak and strong: rethinking the state in comparative policy history", *Journal of Policy History* 17/1 (2005), pp. 12–33 (especially pp. 18ff).

retirement policies, which has been central to societal development during the twentieth century and will fuel much controversy in the twenty-first. By exposing the entangled configurations of pension provision, this book has not exhausted the study of the Swiss welfare state. The interpretative grid exposed in this volume is now available for further studies delving into other Swiss social programs. Health insurance, a field also much affected by struggles over the boundaries of state and private providers, or unemployment benefits, a domain where employers, trade unions, and state schemes long coexisted and competed before the setting-up of a federal scheme, represent promising fields for such further explorations.

If the analysis of the foundation, expansion, and continuing adjustment of public and private forms of social provision undoubtedly offers new perspectives to understand the Swiss welfare state, may it also contribute to renewing our understanding of the making of social policy in other industrialized countries? To answer this question, it is worthwhile considering how the study of an outsider case encourages us to reconsider the traditional ways comparisons are made.

In the worlds of welfare, the stream of comparison usually flows from the eastern to the western shores of the Atlantic. Comparative research has often judged performance according to the standard of an alleged European model and delves extensively into how the belated development of the North American welfare state, its private and market-oriented structures, and its patchiness make it so exceptional in comparison with the more favorable course followed by state-based social insurance in continental Europe. In the same vein, the current shift in favor of private social provision is often seen as the epitome of the growing prominence of an Anglo-American model and an unmistakable sign of the diminishing influence of this famed European model. In this book, I have chosen to go against the current of this established perspective in order to examine an exceptional European case through North American lenses. Recent scholarship on the interactions between public–private social provision in the United States has enabled me to generate research hypotheses that have guided my investigation of the fault lines of the Swiss pension system. From the role of private insurers in social policy, to the influence of the fiscal encouragement of private benefits, to the links between segmentalist collective bargaining and occupational pension schemes, this book confirms the portability of findings about the North American divided welfare state to the European theater.

Besides bringing closer together two exceptional cases of social policy development, I have structured my exploration of the Swiss welfare state as an extensive comparative dialogue with three other countries with well-developed occupational pension provision (Canada, the United

Kingdom, and the Netherlands). This approach has enabled me to better triangulate the distinctive features of Swiss old age provision during the various stages of its development. While these comparisons do not lead to a full-blown model or theory, they underscore the necessity to put less emphasis on the alleged Atlantic divide in social provision and more on the fault lines of public and private social provision that structure the long-term history of *all* welfare states.

During a first period running approximately from 1900 to the 1940s, all the countries mentioned in this study experienced a modest expansion of both state and occupational pensions. Limited means-tested old age provision provided by the state (as was the case in the Netherlands, the United Kingdom, and Canada) or the absence of any national pension scheme (as in the United States and Switzerland) left space for the development of the first voluntary occupational plans. With the implementation of universal state pensions – which represented either upgrades of previously existing schemes or, as in the United States and Switzerland, new ones – in the mid-century, a modus vivendi was established between the two main sources of old age provision: state social insurance provided basic benefits that were supplemented by selective occupational ones. During the decades of growth, the shortcomings of occupational schemes that nowhere covered more than a minority of workers soon led to a search for new solutions and to heated battles on the boundaries between social insurance and private provision.

In countries where occupational provision was brought closer to social insurance or better coordinated with it, the majority of the elderly finally faced better retirement prospects. This movement toward closer integration and combination took several paths (see Table 0.2, p. 24), from the quasi-mandatory extension of industry-wide pension plans in the Netherlands (early 1950s), to the foundation of a new supplementary pension plan in Canada (1965), to a state mandate for occupational provision in Switzerland (1970s–1980s). In contrast to these three countries, more disjointed pension architectures were maintained in the United States, where little coordination exists even today between Social Security and a diminishing number of pension plans, and in the United Kingdom, where each successive supplementary state pension scheme was counteracted by the opting-out of occupational schemes. Because of these developments, American and British retirees undoubtedly face a much bleaker and uncertain future than Dutch, Swiss, and Canadian ones.

Far from constituting an anecdotal narrative concerning residual forms of social provision, the study of the long-term resilience of private social schemes will help us to understand the peculiarities of national welfare state trajectories, from their foundation to their current maturing, retrenchment, and re-privatization. This book has explored in particular the influence of decentralized single-employer schemes and group pension plans. Yet, these forms of social provision coexisted in Switzerland as elsewhere with not-for-profit mutual benefit societies, trade union social programs, and other multi-employer schemes. Scholars have thus underscored the tensions between voluntary and statutory social provision in the United Kingdom, where "friendly societies" operating on a not-for-profit or for-profit basis have long competed with state-based social provision, or in the United States, where mutualist "fraternals" similarly participated in the tangled beginnings of the welfare state.[5] In France, a country too often considered an archetypical statist welfare system, *mutuelles* have long played a central role in health provision alongside family allowance funds set up and controlled by employers' federations.[6]

The history of these differentiated social schemes and their complex relations with social insurance still have to be fully integrated into our understanding of social policy development. Instead of focusing mainly on the welfare "state", it is indeed high time to reconsider the century-long collaboration, struggle, and competition between state and private social provision.

[5] See Geoffrey Finlayson, *Citizen, state, and social welfare in Britain 1830–1990* (Oxford: Oxford University Press, 1994); David T. Beito, *From mutual aid to the welfare state: fraternal societies and social services, 1890–1967* (Chapel Hill: University of North Carolina Press, 2000). For comparative perspectives, see Marcel van der Linden and Michel Dreyfus, eds., *Social security mutualism: the comparative history of mutual benefit societies* (Berne: Peter Lang, 1996).

[6] For an overview of the influence of French mutualism, see Paul V. Dutton, *Origins of the French welfare state: the struggle for social reform in France 1914–1947* (Cambridge: Cambridge University Press, 2002). See also the abundant literature listed on http://www.mutualite.fr/actualites/toutes_les_publications/livres. See in particular the titles under the heading "Histoire du mouvement mutualiste". The wealth of scholarly studies now available on *mutuelles* is in no small part due to a conscious effort by the Fédération nationale de la mutualité française (National Federation of French Mutual Schemes) to encourage research into the "social economy" perspective at the very moment when French insurance companies are developing private supplementary health and retirement benefits.

# Appendix
# A statistical overview of the second pillar

Before the 1982 law on occupational provision (berufliche Vorsorgegesetz, BVG), federal pension surveys (Pensionskassenstatistik) were undertaken for the years 1941–1942, 1955, 1966, 1970, and 1978. The 1941–1942 survey also contained retrospective information reaching back to 1911, while two surveys published in 1929 by the Federal Social Insurance Office and the Employers' Federation (Arbeitgeberverband) offered an overview of public- and private-sector pension plans existing in 1925. The annual reports of the Federal Private Insurance Office also gave basic information on group contracts since the early 1930s. Yet, the changing scope of the surveys – in particular the gradual elimination of informal savings and relief schemes from postwar pension surveys (see below) – hindered comparisons.[1] Even after the passage of the 1982 BVG, data on the second pillar remained, as statistician Stéphane Rossini noted, "surprisingly poor" in comparison with its financial assets and its spread among workers. At a time when occupational pension plans covered almost 3 million workers and managed CHF 160 billion in assets, only two full-time employees of the Federal Statistical Office were responsible for gathering data.[2] After the 1987 pension survey, pension statistics were first reorganized on a biennial (1992–2002) and then on an annual basis from 2004 onward. As this book was going to press, a wealth of additional data on the current situation of pension plans was finally made available on the website of the Federal Statistical Office.[3]

This appendix offers a century-long overview of data on second-pillar institutions, with specific focus on the pre-BVG period. I chart in particular the evolution of the number of pension plans, the growing role of

[1] For an attempt to synthesize the surveys, see Denis Varrin, *La prévoyance professionnelle en Suisse de 1941/42 à 1989: analyse des données statistiques* (Lausanne: Cahiers de l'IDHEAP, 1993).

[2] Stéphane Rossini, *Les institutions de sécurité sociale en Suisse: panorama statistique 1915–1990* (Berne: Office fédéral de la statistique, 1992), p. 46.

[3] The latest pension surveys are available on the website of the Federal Statistical Office: http://www.bfs.admin.ch/ (theme 13: Social Security).

Table A.1 *Pension plans in the public and private sectors, 1865–2004.*

| | public and private sectors (1 + 3) | (2 + 4) | | public sector 1 | 2 | | private sector 3 | 4 | |
|---|---|---|---|---|---|---|---|---|---|
| | **all pension plans** | **of which core plans** | *group plans as a percentage* | **all** | **core** | *group* | **all** | **core** | *group* |
| **1865** | 124 | . . . | | . . . | | | . . . | | |
| **1880** | 140 | . . . | | . . . | | | . . . | | |
| **1903** | 147 | . . . | | 57 | . . . | | 90 | 46 | |
| **1911** | . . . | 103 | *17* | . . . | 60 | . . . | . . . | 43 | . . . |
| **1920** | . . . | 343 | *31* | . . . | 103 | . . . | . . . | 240 | . . . |
| **1925** | 1,220 | . . . | . . . | 169 | | | 1,051 | | |
| **1930** | . . . | 1,145 | *58* | . . . | 248 | . . . | . . . | 897 | . . . |
| **1941** | 4,031 | 2,123 | *69* | 756 | 356 | *40* | 3,275 | 1,767 | *74* |
| **1942** | 4,617 | . . . | . . . | . . . | . . . | . . . | . . . | . . . | . . . |
| **1946** | 6,667 | . . . | . . . | . . . | . . . | . . . | . . . | . . . | . . . |
| **1955** | 9,791 | 5,222 | *76* | 883 | 546 | *58* | 8,908 | 4,676 | *78* |
| **1966** | 13,304 | 9,023 | *68* | 328 | 296 | *36* | 12,976 | 8,727 | *69* |
| **1970** | 15,581 | 10,367 | *81* | 577 | 499 | *63* | 15,004 | 9,868 | *82* |
| **1978** | 17,060 | 10,412 | *86* | 643 | 563 | *70* | 16,417 | 9,849 | *87* |
| **1987** | 15,179 | 4,237 | *33* | 224 | 178 | *16* | 14,955 | 4,059 | *34* |

| | | | | | | | | | |
|---|---|---|---|---|---|---|---|---|---|
| **1992** | 13,689 | 3,457 | *40* | 162 | 133 | *8* | 13,527 | 3,324 | *41* |
| **1996** | 11,572 | 3,075 | *68* | 168 | 141 | *14* | 11,404 | 2,934 | *71* |
| **2000** | 9,096 | 2,599 | . . . | 147 | 126 | . . . | 8,949 | 2,473 | . . . |
| **2004** | 2,935 | 2,307 | *35* | 109 | 108 | *6* | 2,826 | 2,199 | *36* |

core plans = company-based "insurance plans" and group pension plans managed by life insurance companies (Versicherungseinrichtungen). From 1987 onward, this category encompasses registered pension plans offering benefits under the federal law on mandatory occupational provision (BVG)

all pension plans = core plans + various relief institutions (Fürsorgeeinrichtungen) providing discretionary benefits, such as welfare funds (Wohlfahrtsfonds) and savings plans (Spareinlegerkassen). From 1987 onward, most of these relief institutions were not registered as BVG institutions.

*Sources:* For **1865, 1880, and 1903**, see Alfred Gutknecht, "Versicherungswesen, d: Die gegenseitigen Hilfgesellschaften" in *Handwörterbuch der schweizerischen Volkswirtschaft, Sozialpolitik und Verwaltung* (Berne: Verlag Encyclopädie, 1911), pp. 1249ff; Tadeusz von Dymowski, *Die Alters- und Invaliden-Versicherung in der Schweiz: eine Studie über die Sozialversicherung* (Zurich/Leipzig: Rascher, 1915), pp. 139ff; for the number of core plans in **1904**, see K. Stoll, "Die Alters- und Invalidenvorsorge für die kaufmännische Angestellten in der Schweiz", *Schweizerische Blätter für Wirtschaft und Sozialpolitik* (1904), pp. 141–2. For **1911, 1920, 1930, 1941**, see *Pensionskassenstatistik 1941*. For **1925**, see *Pensionskassenstatistik 1925a*. The Arbeitgeberverband survey counted 982 private pension plans but estimated that this total represented 85 percent of all private pension plans. For **1942–1946**, see *Pensionskassenstatistik 1941*, p. 98. For **1955 onward**, see *Pensionskassenstatistik* for the corresponding year.

group pension plans, and the development of pension coverage in both the public and private sectors among various manufacturing and service sectors, as well as among men and women employees. I also present estimates of average occupational pension benefits and data on the financial assets accumulated by second-pillar institutions.

## Core pension plans and relief institutions (Table A.1)

Before the 1980s, federal pension surveys considered two forms of old age provision as genuine or, according to my denomination, *core pension plans*. These so-called insurance plans (Versicherungseinrichtungen) encompassed "autonomous" or single-employer pension schemes (autonome Pensionskassen) set up by leading corporations and large public authorities (the Confederation, cantons, and cities), as well as group pension plans (Gruppenversicherungen) managed by insurers. These two kinds of plans which defined insured risks and benefits according to actuarial rules were contrasted with more informal types of provision described as *relief institutions* (Fürsorgeeinrichtungen). Under this denomination, one could find various welfare funds (Wohlfahrtsfonds) and savings schemes (Spareinlegerkassen) that most often did not follow actuarial rules and offered discretionary benefits hardly comparable with those of single-employer and group pension plans.[4]

In the following tables, I make a clear distinction between core pension plans and other relief institutions. This is a decisive step to better grasp the reach of the second pillar. While relief institutions were marginal in the public sector, informal pension schemes often operated side by side with formal retirement plans in the private sector. As workers could be affiliated to both types of plans in the same firm, this led to systematic overestimates of pension coverage. Relief institutions offering only token benefits were gradually excluded from federal pension surveys, but this dense thicket of haphazard welfare measures continued to distort attempts to get a clear view of the main constituent parts of the second pillar. For these reasons, I have decided to focus my estimates of pension coverage on core plans.

Table A.1 shows clearly that group pension plans represented a large proportion of core plans. As most group contracts covered small and medium-sized firms, they contributed to the fragmentation of pension coverage into thousands of plans. However, as most group plans were

[4] *Pensionskassenstatistik 1941*, pp. 4–5, *Pensionskassenstatistik 1955*, pp. 10–12. See also Graziano Lusenti, *Les institutions de prévoyance en Suisse, au Royaume-Uni et en Allemagne fédérale: placements financiers et politique sociale* (Geneva: Georg, 1989), pp. 171–7.

managed by a handful of insurance companies (Rentenanstalt, Vita [Zurich Life], Basler Life, and Winterthur Life, see Figure 2.4, p. 80), this form of pension provision underscored the key role of leading insurance companies in the shaping of the second pillar. Group pension plans indeed covered a significant number of workers, especially in the private sector (see Table A.3, p. 296). Only a minority of core plans were registered under the 1982 BVG. Many of them, among them countless small group plans, either merged, discontinued their operations, or were "frozen" and have now been closed. The fragmentation of Swiss occupational provision thus hides a core constituted by the largest pension plans of the public and private sector, and by the group plans managed by leading insurance companies.

## Membership-based and union pension schemes

Besides core and relief pension institutions, pension surveys also mention the existence of membership insurance schemes (Mitgliederversicherungseinrichtungen). This category encompassed pension schemes set up in the printing trade, union-based old age plans organized by the Metalworkers' Union, the transport workers' association, or the Association of Commercial Clerks (Kaufmännischer Verein), as well as retirement and savings schemes for nurses or professional associations (lawyers, doctors). While some of these plans were similar to other single-employer plans or functioned as mutual benefit societies, others were group pension plans set up by the Coop Life, a Basle-based cooperative insurance company. Most membership insurance schemes were hardly comparable to core pension plans: they mostly offered lump sums that supplemented other old age benefits, or served as a kind of portable pension for those who switched job while remaining in the same sector.[5] In 1941, around 100 membership insurance schemes covered 243,000 workers and professionals. The 1955 pension survey indicated that out of 474,000 persons covered by 144 such schemes, only 304,000 were affiliated to proper pension schemes. By 1970, membership insurance schemes still covered 200,000 workers. As their modest benefits were in no way comparable to those of core pension plans, membership insurance schemes were excluded from pension surveys after

[5] *Pensionskassenstatistik 1941*, pp. 73–90, *Pensionskassenstatistik 1966*, p. 7. See also "Message du Conseil fédéral à l'Assemblée fédérale concernant l'attribution à la Confédération du droit de légiférer en matière d'assurance-invalidité, vieillesse et survivants, et la création des ressources nécessaires à la Confédération pour les assurances sociales, du 21 juin 1919", in *Feuille Fédérale* (Berne: Chancellerie fédérale, 1919), volume IV, pp. 1–234 (especially pp. 74–6).

this date.[6] These schemes accounted for a minute fraction of pension assets (barely 2 percent of private pension assets in 1955, see Table A.7, p. 303), and one may reasonably assume that most of their members – notably in the machine-making, transport, and service sectors – were also affiliated to employer-based plans. Membership insurance schemes can thus be considered as double counts, and so I have omitted them from Table A.1 (p. 243), as well as from my estimates of pension coverage.

## Occupational pension coverage (Tables A.2, A.3, A.4, and A.5)

Table A.2 offers a century-long overview of pension coverage. Affiliation to core pension plans reached one-fifth of the non-farm workforce in 1941, but over two-thirds of public employees at the federal and cantonal level, as well as in large cities. Right before the introduction of the BVG, occupational pension coverage reached three-quarters of public-sector employees, but still only half of private-sector ones. The postwar decades also witnessed a qualitative improvement in occupational benefits as a growing number of pension plans, mimicking the AHV, insured their members against the three risks of old age, disability, and death (i.e. widows' and orphans' benefits). Once again, public plans offered much better conditions to their workforce. In 1955, almost all of them already covered these three risks, whereas this was the case for only half of private-sector workers affiliated to pension plans. This gap narrowed perceptibly during the 1970s, as private-sector employers overhauled their occupational plans to make them compatible with the impending BVG. After decades of incremental expansion, the quantum leap of occupational provision took place during the 1980s, in particular between the 1982 passing of the BVG and its implementation in 1985. Two decades after its introduction, the second pillar steadily reached around four-fifths of the non-farm workforce.

6 *Pensionskassenstatistik 1941*, pp. 304–5; *Pensionskassenstatistik 1955*, pp. 77–9, *Pensionskassenstatistik 1970*, p. 7. There were 25 membership insurance plans in 1911, a number that increased to 47 in 1920, 66 in 1930, and 97 in 1941. The biggest plans were then those of the Metalworkers' Union (75,000 affiliates), transportation firms (40,600), the printing trade (11,600), and the service and banking sectors (10,700). Several other plans covered professionals, doctors, and nurses from the medical sector (90,000), as well as a handful of civil servants (5,600).

Table A.2 *Occupational pension coverage as a percentage share of the non-farm workforce, 1903–2004.*

| | | public and private sectors | | | | public sector | | | private sector | | |
|---|---|---|---|---|---|---|---|---|---|---|---|
| | | all plans | core plans | men in core plans | women in core plans | core | men | women | core | men | women |
| **1903** | | 8.2 | . . . | | | . . . | | | . . . | | |
| **1911** | | . . . | 5.1 | | | 33.2 | | | 1.3 | | |
| **1920** | | . . . | 11.1 | | | 37.4 | | | 6.7 | | |
| **1925** | | 21.4 | . . . | | | . . . | | | . . . | | |
| **1930** | | . . . | 18.3 | | | 66.5 | | | 11.1 | | |
| **1941** | | . . . | 22.4 | 27.6 | 13.0 | 59.7 | 64.3 | 39.6 | 15.6 | 18.8 | 10.6 |
| **1955** | | 47.7 | 31.8 | 40.1 | 13.9 | 67.4 | 92.6 | 27.4 | 25.8 | 30.8 | 11.7 |
| | (b) | | 20.2 | | | 66.4 | | | 12.5 | | |
| **1970** | (a) | 54.3 | 40.2 | 56.3 | 23.2 | 72.0 | 84.8 | 49.1 | 34.6 | 51.0 | 19.1 |
| | (b) | | 35.5 | | | 70.7 | | | 29.3 | | |
| **1978** | (a) | 59.8 | 49.7 | 64.6 | 28.9 | 74.4 | 87.5 | 54.3 | 44.4 | 59.7 | 23.2 |
| | (b) | | 47.0 | | | 74.0 | | | 41.2 | | |
| **1987** | | 98.1 | 84.1 | 91.5 | 72.2 | | | | | | |
| **1992** | | 89.3 | 79.6 | 88.6 | 67.2 | | | | | | |
| **1996** | | 83.1 | 77.2 | 86.1 | 65.4 | | | | | | |
| **2000** | | 82.6 | 77.9 | 92.4 | 70.1 | | | | | | |
| **2004** | | 80.0 | 77.1 | 83.6 | 69.1 | | | | | | |

(a) excluding double counts
(b) employees affiliated to pension plans covering the *three risks* covered by the AHV (old age, disability, and death)
*Sources:* Tables A.3 and A.4

Table A.3 *Workers and employees affiliated to pension plans, 1903–2004.*

| | | workers and employees affiliated to pension plans, in thousands | | | | | | | | | | | | | | |
|---|---|---|---|---|---|---|---|---|---|---|---|---|---|---|---|---|
| | | public and private sectors | | | | | public sector | | | | | private sector | | | | |
| | | all pension plans | core plans | *of which affiliated to group plans (as a percentage)* | men affiliated to core plans | women affiliated to core plans | all | core | *group* | men | women | all | core | *group* | men | women |
| **1903** | | 61.0 | . . . | | . . . | . . . | . . . | . . . | | . . . | . . . | . . . | . . . | | . . . | . . . |
| **1911** | | . . . | 58.0 | | . . . | . . . | . . . | 45.0 | | . . . | . . . | . . . | 13.0 | | . . . | . . . |
| **1920** | | . . . | 129.0 | | . . . | . . . | . . . | 63.0 | | . . . | . . . | . . . | 66.0 | | . . . | . . . |
| **1925** | | 262.0 | . . . | | . . . | . . . | 112.0 | . . . | | . . . | . . . | 150.0 | . . . | | . . . | . . . |
| **1930** | | . . . | 236.0 | | . . . | . . . | . . . | 112.0 | | . . . | . . . | . . . | 124.0 | | . . . | . . . |
| **1941** | | . . . | 294.0 | *18* (c) | 233.0 | 61.0 | . . . | 120.0 | *1.8* | 105.0 | 15.0 | . . . | 174.0 | *29* | 128.0 | 46.0 |
| **1955** | | 848.4 | 566.0 | *30* | 444.8 (d) | 92.6 (d) | 204.5 | 172.4 | *2.1* | 153.3 | 24.8 | 643.9 | 393.6 | *42* | 291.5 | 67.8 |
| | (b) | | 360.0 | | | | | 170.0 | | | | | 190.0 | | | |
| **1970** | (a) | 1,382.0 | 1,023.0 | *42* | 914.0 | 214.2 | 280.0 | 274.0 | *2.2* | 215.0 | 62.2 | 1,102.0 | 749.0 | *57* | 699.0 | 152.0 |
| | (b) | | 904.0 | | | | | 269.0 | | | | | 635.0 | | | |
| **1978** | (a) | 1,581.0 | 1,314.0 | *43* | 1,057.3 | 290.9 | 359.0 | 350.0 | *2.0* | 249.2 | 100.8 | 1,222.0 | 964.0 | *58* | 808.1 | 190.1 |
| | (b) | | 1,243.0 | | | | | 348.0 | | | | | 895.0 | | | |
| **1987** | | 3,265.7 | 2,800.3 | *57* | 1,888.9 | 911.3 | 473.7 | 468.8 | *0.6* | 295.9 | 172.9 | 2,792.0 | 2,331.5 | *44* | 1,593.0 | 738.4 |
| **1992** | | 3,432.0 | 3,058.6 | *43* | 1,974.4 | 1,084.1 | 555.0 | 533.7 | *0.2* | 320.4 | 213.3 | 2,877.0 | 2,524.9 | *52* | 1,654.0 | 870.8 |

*(cont.)*

| | | | | | | | | | | | | | | | | |
|---|---|---|---|---|---|---|---|---|---|---|---|---|---|---|---|---|
| **1996** | 3,135.0 | 2,911.3 | *53* | | 1,847.9 | 1,064.3 | 548.0 | 548.3 | *0.4* | 312.9 | 235.4 | 2,587.0 | 2,363.0 | *65* | 1,535.0 | 828.9 |
| **2000** | 3,226.0 | 3,039.5 | *49* | | 2,021.8 | 1,204.2 | 523.0 | 511.3 | *0.2* | 268.6 | 254.1 | 2,703.0 | 2,528.2 | *59* | 1,753.2 | 950.1 |
| **2004** | 3,214.4 | 3,098.1 | *39* | | 1,849.8 | 1,248.3 | 527.9 | 527.7 | *0.3* | 250.1 | 277.6 | 2,686.5 | 2,570.4 | *47* | 1,599.7 | 970.7 |

(a) all pension plans: *including* double counts; core plans *excluding* double counts

(b) employees affiliated to pension plans covering the three AHV risks (old age, disability, and death)

(c) group plans *excluding* double counts

(d) 1955 onward: men + women in core plans ≠ overall core plan coverage because of the inclusion of double counts

*Sources:* For **1903**, see W. Grütter and A. Alder, "Pensionskassen" in *Handbuch der schweizerischen Volkswirtschaft* (Berne: Benteli, 1939), pp. 221–5; Alfred Gutknecht, "Versicherungswesen, d: Die gegenseitigen Hilfgesellschaften" in *Handwörterbuch der schweizerischen Volkswirtschaft, Sozialpolitik und Verwaltung* (Berne: Verlag Encyclopädie, 1911), pp. 1249ff; for **1911, 1920, 1930, 1941**, see *Pensionskassenstatistik 1941*; for **1925** see *Pensionskassenstatistik 1925a* and *Pensionskassenstatistik 1925b*; for **1955–2004** see *Pensionskassenstatistik* for the corresponding year.

Table A.4 *Non-farm workforce 1903–2004.*

| *(in thousands)* | | | | public sector | | | private sector | | |
|---|---|---|---|---|---|---|---|---|---|
| | total | men | women | total | men | women | total | men | women |
| **1903** (a) | 743.6 | | | | | | | | |
| **1911** (b) | 1,140.3 | | | 135.4 (c) | | | 1,004.9 | | |
| **1920** (d) | 1,158.3 | | | 168.3 | | | 990.0 | | |
| **1925** (e) | 1,222.9 | | | | | | | | |
| **1930** (d) | 1,287.5 | | | 168.5 | | | 1,119.0 | | |
| **1941** (d) | 1,313.9 | 843.1 | 470.8 | 201.1 | 163.2 | 37.9 | 1,112.8 | 679.9 | 432.9 |
| **1955** (f) | 1,778.7 | 1,110.6 | 668.1 | 255.9 | 165.5 | 90.4 | 1,522.8 | 945.1 | 577.7 |
| **1970** (g) | 2,547.3 | 1,622.9 | 924.4 | 380.3 | 253.5 | 126.8 | 2,167.0 | 1,369.4 | 797.6 |
| **1978** (i) | 2,643.4 | 1,637.3 | 1,006.1 | 470.3 | 284.8 | 185.5 | 2,173.1 | 1,352.5 | 820.6 |
| **1987** | 3,328.0 | 2,065.0 | 1,263.0 | | | | | | |
| **1992** | 3,842.0 | 2,229.0 | 1,613.0 | | | | | | |
| **1996** | 3,773.0 | 2,145.0 | 1,628.0 | | | | | | |
| **2000** | 3,904.0 | 2,187.0 | 1,717.0 | | | | | | |
| **2004** | 4,020.0 | 2,214.0 | 1,806.0 | | | | | | |

(a) decennial federal census for 1900 (*Eidgenössische Volkzählung*, hereafter *EVZ*) data on workers (unselbständige Erwerbstätige), not including the self-employed, or agricultural and forestry workers.
(b) *EVZ 1910.*
(c) data reconstructed with *EVZ 1910.* Census categories taken into account: Ea, Da185, Da188, Da189, Ec204 (hygiene and health police); 3/4 of Ed (teaching); 4/5 of Ee (religious professions). The number of employees working in hospitals, asylums, and penitentiaries could not be estimated.
(d) *EVZ 1950.*
(e) average workforce estimated with *EVZ 1950.*
(f) average workforce estimated with *EVZ 1950* and *EVZ 1960.*
(g) *EVZ 1970.*
(i) *EVZ 1980.*
*Sources:* For **1903–1978**, see decennial federal census (*EVZ*) data on workers (unselbständige Erwerbstätige), not including the self-employed, or agricultural and forestry workers. For **1987–2004**, see worforce survey (Statistique de la population active occupée, SPAO), Federal Statistical Office website: http://www.bfs.admin.ch.

Besides the uneven spread of pension coverage in the public and private sectors, Table A.2 also highlights the considerable gender gap in occupational provision. At the end of the 1970s, only one-third of women were affiliated to a core pension plan, as against two-thirds of men. This gender gap began to close only with the implementation of the BVG, which was concomitant to the increase of Swiss women in the overall workforce. This late affiliation of women to the second pillar explains why they represent an overwhelming share of pensioners with low BVG benefits and, by extension, the majority of the elderly poor.

Table A.5 *Occupational pension coverage in manufacturing and service sectors, 1911–1950.*

| | 1911 | 1920 | 1930 | 1941 | 1955 |
|---|---|---|---|---|---|
| *private-sector average (as a percentage)* | 1.3 | 6.7 | 11.1 | 15.6 | 25.8 |
| *coverage in each activity sector (as a percentage)* | | | | | |
| **I** | | | | | |
| Metals, machine-making | 1.0 | **15.9** | **26.6** | **29.8** | **40.9** |
| Chemicals | . . . | **37.8** | **68.3** | **55.6** | **60.4** |
| Banking | **1.6** | **54.4** | **56.7** | **67.3** | **59.6** |
| Insurance | **40.8** | **50.8** | **57.2** | **53.5** | **52.7** |
| Utilities (water, gas, electricity) | 1.1 | **17.6** | **102.7** | **97.8** | **95.0** |
| Private transport firms | **9.2** | **18.7** | **24.6** | **31.6** | **41.1** |
| **II** | | | | | |
| Paper, rubber, leather | . . . | 2.4 | 8.6 | **20.4** | **41.1** |
| Watch-making | 0.3 | 0.4 | 1.4 | **16.3** | **30.2** |
| Textiles and clothing | 0.6 | 4.8 | **11.0** | **17.2** | **26.8** |
| Food, beverages, and tobacco | . . . | 3.7 | **11.8** | **16.9** | 25.2 |
| **III** | | | | | |
| Printing trade | **3.0** | 3.2 | 7.5 | 12.6 | 20.8 |
| Commerce, retail, distribution | **4.9** | **8.1** | 8.8 | 13.6 | 17.9 |
| Wood, stone, and cement | . . . | 1.3 | 3.6 | 5.6 | 16.0 |
| Building trade | . . . | . . . | 0.1 | 0.3 | 3.0 |
| Catering/tourism | 0.2 | 0.2 | 0.6 | 0.7 | 0.8 |
| *NB*: bold type indicates sectors with above-average rates of coverage | | | | | |
| | **1911** | **1920** | **1930** | **1941** | **1955** |
| *share of each sector in overall occupational coverage (as a percentage)* | | | | | |
| **I** | **33.6** | **64.6** | **61.3** | **55.4** | **49.2** |
| Metal, machine-making | 7.0 | 31.5 | 32.0 | 31.9 | 31.6 |
| Chemicals | 0.0 | 9.3 | 9.2 | 7.5 | 6.4 |
| Banking | 1.2 | 12.1 | 8.0 | 5.9 | 3.2 |
| Insurance | 9.4 | 4.0 | 3.6 | 3.4 | 2.4 |
| Utilities (water, gas, electricity) | 0.7 | 1.2 | 4.0 | 2.9 | 1.9 |
| Private transport firms | 15.2 | 6.4 | 4.5 | 3.8 | 3.7 |
| **II** | **15.0** | **20.1** | **24.2** | **28.5** | **23.9** |
| Paper, rubber, leather | 0.0 | 0.6 | 1.3 | 2.7 | 2.8 |
| Watch-making | 1.4 | 0.3 | 0.7 | 4.4 | 5.2 |
| Textiles and clothing | 13.6 | 15.9 | 15.9 | 14.1 | 10.3 |
| Food, beverages, and tobacco | 0.0 | 3.3 | 6.4 | 7.2 | 5.5 |
| **III** | **44.1** | **12.4** | **11.7** | **13.3** | **15.7** |
| Printing trade | 3.7 | 0.8 | 1.3 | 1.7 | 2.1 |
| Commerce, retail, distribution | 39.4 | 10.3 | 8.1 | 9.1 | 9.2 |
| Wood, stone, and cement | 0.0 | 1.1 | 1.9 | 2.1 | 2.9 |
| Building trade | 0.0 | 0.0 | 0.1 | 0.2 | 1.3 |
| Catering/tourism | 1.0 | 0.2 | 0.3 | 0.2 | 0.2 |

*Sources:* For **non-farm workforce: 1911**, see *EVZ 1910*, volume 7, tables 2–3, 10–17; **1920–1941**, see *EVZ 1950*, volume 25/II, Table 6; **1955**, see average 1950–1960 according to *EVZ 1950* and *EVZ 1960*, volume 27/I, Table 7; for **occupational coverage: 1911–1941**, see *Pensionskassenstatistik 1941*, Table 4b; **1955**, see *Pensionskassenstatistik 1955*, Table 1.

Table A.5 retraces the expansion of core pension plans in 15 sectors that amounted to over 90 percent of the private non-farm workforce and accounted for a similar proportion of overall private occupational pension membership. In a first tier of leading industrial sectors (machine-making and metal; chemical and pharmaceuticals), financial services (banking; insurance), and sectors that followed the standards of public-sector pension plans (utilities; transport firms), pension coverage was consistently higher than in the private sector as a whole. Occupational coverage only overtook the average during the 1940s in a second tier of crafts-based industries such as the paper, rubber, and leather industries, as well as watch-making. Coverage also progressed slowly in the powerhouses of nineteenth-century industrialization (textiles and clothing), which were characterized by lower capital intensiveness than the machinery and metal sectors. Along with watch-making and textile factories, food-processing, tobacco, and beverage firms employed many women. This contributed to lower pension coverage levels, as pension plans favored male workers with stable and long-term job contracts. A last tier clearly trailed behind the others in terms of occupational pension coverage: the printing trade – where coverage in joint labor–employer membership pension schemes often replaced core plans – the commerce, retail, and distribution sectors, and, finally, wood, stone, and cement factories. In the building trade and in catering/tourism, affiliation to occupational pension plans remained almost non-existent before the 1950s.

### Occupational pension benefits (Table A.6)

Estimating the level of benefits provided by occupational pension plans is a difficult undertaking. Differences between manufacturing and service sectors, or between white-collar employees and blue-collar workers, qualify any estimate. The smallness of pensioners' cohorts before the late 1940s also leads to overestimates of average benefits, as these early cohorts must have been composed of higher-income wage earners. With all these cautionary remarks in mind, Table A.6 sizes up the level of pensions – I have left out lump sums that were paid by relief institutions – paid by core plans before the introduction of the BVG. Unsurprisingly, this table shows that public-sector pensions were superior to private ones. However, these estimates should also take into account the wide differences in benefits that existed among various manufacturing and service sectors. Benefits in banking, insurance, chemicals, or machine-making towered far above those offered in the textile, food-processing, or watch-making industries. Unfortunately, only the 1925 and 1941 pension surveys enable such a break-down of occupational pension benefits. Pensioners were also more

Table A.6 *Average AHV pensions and occupational pension benefits, 1925–1978.*

| | as a percentage of a skilled worker's average monthly wage | | | | | | average monthly amounts (CHF) | | | pensioners in thousands | |
|---|---|---|---|---|---|---|---|---|---|---|---|
| | AHV + second pillar | | | second-pillar pension | | | | | | | |
| | public sector (1) + (2a) | private sector (1) + (2b) | AHV pension (1) | public sector (2a) | private sector (2b) | | skilled male worker wage | AHV pension | second-pillar pension | AHV | second pillar |
| **1925** | n/a | n/a | n/a | 57 | 28 | | **291** | n/a | **125** | n/a | **24.3** |
| | | | | | | | | | *167–82* (b) | | *16.4–7.9* (b) |
| | | | | | *railroad* (a) | *57* | . . . | | *176* | | 15.6 |
| | | | | | *insurance* | *64* | 517 | | *333* | | *0.10* |
| | | | | | *banking* | *44* | 517 | | *227* | | *0.50* |
| | | | | | *chemicals* | *33* | 302 | | *101* | | *0.45* |
| | | | | | *machines* | *31* | 297 | | *91* | | *1.60* |
| | | | | | *textiles* | *21* | 250 | | *52* | | *3.28* |
| | | | | | *food, beverages, tobacco* | *15* | 300 | | *45* | | *0.71* |
| | | | | | *watch-making* | *15* | 287 | | *44* | | *0.14* |
| **1941** | n/a | n/a | n/a | 72 | 48 | | **312** | n/a | **189** | n/a | **71.0** |
| | | | | | | | | | 226–151 (b) | | *50.7–20.3* (b) |
| | | | | | *banking* | *80* | 581 | | 465 | | 1.2 |
| | | | | | *insurance* | *45* | 581 | | 264 | | 0.6 |
| | | | | | *chemicals* | *56* | 335 | | 186 | | 1.3 |
| | | | | | *machines* | *41* | 312 | | 127 | | 5.5 |

(*cont.*)

Table A.6 (*cont.*)

| | as a percentage of a skilled worker's average monthly wage | | | | | | average monthly amounts (CHF) | | | pensioners in thousands | |
|---|---|---|---|---|---|---|---|---|---|---|---|
| | AHV + second pillar | | | second-pillar pension | | | | | | | |
| | public sector (1) + (2a) | private sector (1) + (2b) | AHV pension (1) | public sector (2a) | private sector (2b) | | skilled male worker wage | AHV pension | second-pillar pension | AHV | second pillar |
| | | | | | *food, tobacco* | *35* | 345 | | 120 | | 2.3 |
| | | | | | *textiles* | *24* | 270 | | 65 | | 4.2 |
| | | | | | *watch-making* | *13* | 316 | | 42 | | 0.3 |
| **1955** | **69** | **50** | 13 | 56 | 37 | | **616** | **80** | **287** | **461.6** | **110.8** |
| | | | | | | | | | *348–226* (b) | | *71.2–39.6* (b) |
| **1970** | **63** | **44** | 20 | 43 | 24 | | **1,430** | **290** | **478** | **888.7** (c) | **196.4** |
| | | | | | | | | | *608–347* (b) | | *91.0–105.4* (b) |
| **1978** | **70** | **51** | 32 | 38 | 19 | | **2,698** | **858** | **765** | **1,000.5** | **306.4** |
| | | | | | | | | | *1,024–505* (b) | | *112.1–194.3* (b) |

(a) including federal railways
(b) breakdown between the public (left) and private (right) sectors
(c) 1969

*Sources:* For **average AHV pension**, data kindly made available by Nicolas Eschmann of the Federal Social Insurance Office; for **pensioners**, see *Swiss Historical Statistics* Table P8 (excluding partial pensions, as well as beneficiaries of widows' and survivors' benefits); for **average second-pillar pensions/pensioners**, see: **1925** *Pensionskassenstatistik 1925a*, p. 44, *Pensionskassenstatistik 1925b*, appendix VI; only core plans have been taken into account for the period **1941–1978**. For **1941**, see *Pensionskassenstatistik 1941*, tables 23 and 28; **1955** *Pensionskassenstatistik 1955*, tables 4, 26, 27; **1966** *Pensionskassenstatistik 1966*, tables 10, 11, 16, and 17; **1970** *Pensionskassenstatistik 1970*, tables 10, 11, and 17; **1978** *Pensionskassenstatistik 1978*, tables 22.3, 22.4, 24.2, and 24.3; average second-pillar pension = total old age, disability, and survivors' benefits paid divided by the number of recipients of such pensions. These estimates do not include retirement lump sums or other one-off cash benefits; for **average monthly wages**, see: Ritzmann-Blickenstorfer and Siegenthaler, *Swiss Historical Statistics*, Table G9 (hourly wages of a skilled worker, according to SUVA statistics). Calculation method: monthly wage = [hourly wage × no. hours worked/week × 52 weeks]/12 months. For **hours worked/week**, see *Swiss Historical Statistics*, Tables F27a and F27b. Exceptions: banking and insurance: for **1925**, see Mario König, Hannes Siegrist and Rudolf Vetterli, *Warten und Aufrücken: die Angestellten in der Schweiz, 1870–1950* (Zurich: Chronos, 1985), p. 140; **1941** *Swiss Historical Statistics*, Table G12, monthly wages for a skilled employee.

Table A.7 *Pension fund assets, 1922–2004.*

| | total (1) + (2) + (3) | | *in millions of CHF* | | | | | |
|---|---|---|---|---|---|---|---|---|
| | *as a percentage of GDP* | *in millions of CHF* | group reserves (1) | public sector (2) | | private sector (3) | | |
| **1922** | ... | ... | ... | ... | | | **≈ 200** | |
| | | | | | | *SVUSAI* | | *20* |
| | | | | | | *SVUSAI (1929)* | | *200* |
| **1925** | *≈ 12* | **> 1,000** | ... | **600** | | | **380** | |
| | | | | | | *by sector (sample = 339.7)* | | |
| | | | | | | *banking* | | *88.2* |
| | | | | | | *textiles, clothing* | | *87.5* |
| | | | | | | *metal, machine-making* | | *72.2* |
| | | | | | | *chemicals, pharmaceuticals* | | *35.5* |
| | | | | | | *food, beverages, and tobacco* | | *22.5* |
| | | | | | | *insurance* | | *17.6* |
| | | | | | | *retail, distribution* | | *16.2* |
| **1937** | *26* | **1,900–2,100** | **200** | **1,000** | | | **700–900** | |
| | | | | *Confederation plans* | *500* | *SVUSAI* | | *320* |

(*cont.*)

Table A.7 (*cont.*)

| | total (1) + (2) + (3) | | in millions of CHF | | | | | |
|---|---|---|---|---|---|---|---|---|
| | *as a percentage of GDP* | *in millions of CHF* | group reserves (1) | public sector (2) | | | private sector (3) | |
| **1941** | *29* | **3,100** | **400** | **1,400** | | | **1,300** | |
| | | | | *core plans* | *1,340* | *core plans* | | *1,000* |
| | | | | *relief institutions* | *40* | *relief institutions* | | *200* |
| | | | | | | *membership insurance schemes* | | *70* |
| | | | | | | *by sector (sample = 991.2)* | | |
| | | | | | | *banking* | | *217.9* |
| | | | | | | *metal, machine-making* | | *206.0* |
| | | | | | | *retail, distribution* | | *141.5* |
| | | | | | | *textiles, clothing* | | *133.9* |
| | | | | | | *chemicals, pharmaceuticals* | | *113.8* |
| | | | | | | *food, beverages, and tobacco* | | *96.4* |
| | | | | | | *insurance* | | *81.7* |
| **1955** | *35* | **9,400** | **1,100** | **3,500** | | | **4,800** | |
| | | | | *core plans* | *3,360* | *core plans* | | *3,700* |
| | | | | *relief institutions* | *170* | *relief institutions* | | *1,100* |
| | | | | *Confederation plans* | *1,500* | *membership insurance schemes* | | *179* |
| | | | | *main cantonal/city plans* | *1,000* | *by sector (sample = 3637.8)* | | |
| | | | | | | *metals, machine-making* | | *1,006.9* |
| | | | | | | *retail, distribution* | | *610.5* |
| | | | | | | *banking* | | *563.5* |
| | | | | | | *chemicals, pharmaceuticals* | | *482.9* |
| | | | | | | *textile, clothing* | | *451.2* |
| | | | | | | *food, beverages, and tobacco* | | *298.8* |
| | | | | | | *insurance* | | *224.0* |

Table A.7 (*cont.*)

| | total (1) + (2) + (3) | | *in millions of CHF* | | | | | | |
|---|---|---|---|---|---|---|---|---|---|
| | *as a percentage of GDP* | *in millions of CHF* | group reserves (1) | public sector (2) | | | private sector (3) | | |
| **1970** | *41* | **37,100** | **4,600** | | **12,600** | | | **19,900** | |
| | | | | *Confederation plans* | | *4,500* | *SVPP (1965)* | | *6,000* |
| | | | | *main cantonal/city plans* | | *3,800* | *SVPP (1968)* | | *8,500* |
| **1978** | *54* | **81,800** | 12,000 | | 24,700 | | | 45,200 | |
| **1987** | *74* | **188,300** | 33,500 | | 51,400 | | | 103,400 | |
| **1992** | *92* | **312,800** | 56,100 | | | | 256,700 | | |
| **1996** | *116* | **425,700** | 77,400 | | | | 348,300 | | |
| **2000** | *149* | **603,500** | 110,600 | | | | 492,900 | | |
| **2002** | *130* | **561,900** | 121,400 | | | | 440,500 | | |
| **2004** | *132* | **602,900** | 118,700 | | | | 484,200 | | |

*Sources:* For **pension assets**, see: **1922** "Zusammenschluss von Unterstützungskassen und Stiftungen", *Soziale Informationen*, nos. 11–12, 1922. The pension assets of the first half-dozen SVUSAI members represented around 10 percent of all private pension assets; **1925** *Pensionskassenstatistik 1925a*, p. 43. Public pension assets including private transport firms; private pension assets include insurance companies' plans and "other funds", *Pensionskassenstatistik 1925b*, appendix C; **1929** (SVUSAI) "An die Nationalrätliche Kommission zur Beratung des Bundesgesetzes über die AHV", open letter of the SVUSAI, Basle, November 12, 1929, p. 9, file V Schweiz 3234, SNB; **1937** Hans Christen, "Die finanzielle Lage der Pensionskassen", *Schweizerische Zeitschrift für Volkswirtschaft und Statistik* (1938), pp .61–8; W. Grütter and A. Alder, "Pensionskassen" in *Handbuch der schweizerischen Volkswirtschaft* (Berne: Benteli, 1939), pp. 221–5, (SVUSAI) Pension assets for eighty-three SVUSAI pension plans (sectors: textiles and clothing, food, metal and machine-making, banking and insurance); **1941** *Pensionskassenstatistik 1941*, pp. 263, 300–1, 383; **1955** *Pensionskassenstatistik 1955*, pp. 172–3 (core plans), 175, 188–9, 191; Hans Gerold Wirz, *Die Personal-Wohlfahrtseinrichtungen der schweizerischen Privatwirtschaft*, pp. 77, 23–50; **1970–2004** *Pensionskassenstatistik*, various years. For large public plans, see Peter Hadorn, *Die Kapitalanlagen der schweizerischen Pensionskassen 1955–1970* (Basle: Institut für angewandte Wirtschaftsforschung, 1974); **1965, 1968** (SVPP) *Zirkularmitteilungen SVPP*, no. 256, August 31, 1965, sample of 563 SVPP plans; Harald Schulthess, "Ergebnisse der Enquête über die Vermögensanlage in den Wohlfahrtseinrichtungen unseres Verbandes", June 1971, file Q124 203, ZFS, *SVPP Zirkularmitteilungen*, no. 328, May 1971; for **group insurance reserves**, see *Die privaten Versicherungsunternehmungen in der Schweiz* (Berne, Bundesamt für Privatversicherung: 1931–2006); for **GDP**, see: **1925–1941** Thomas David and Heiner Ritzmann-Blickenstorfer, "Gross domestic product in Switzerland, 1891–1950. A new estimation", unpublished working paper, University of Lausanne, 2002; **1948–1990** *Swiss Historical Statistics*, Table Q6a. **1990–2004** National accounts, Swiss National Bank website: http://www.snb.ch.

numerous in the public sector, where pension plans had been introduced several decades before private ones, before the late 1960s.

After the introduction of the AHV, the level of occupational benefits decreased. This development can be explained by the following factors. First, as pensioners' cohorts rose significantly, the "average" pension was less skewed in favor of higher-paid income strata. This trend also illustrated the growing coordination of AHV and occupational benefits. Between 1955 and 1978, the combined replacement rate of first- and second-pillar benefits ranged between half and two-thirds of average wages, albeit higher levels were reached in the public than in the private sector. Once again, in the absence of studies on specific sectors, and without a thorough reappraisal of unpublished data that might be available at the Federal Statistical Office, these rough estimates have to be considered with caution.

### Pension plan financial assets (Table A.7)

Table A.7 combines data about public- and private-sector pension plans, and group insurance mathematical reserves to give a comprehensive perspective of the financial assets of the second pillar. During the first half of the twentieth century, second-pillar financial assets were dominated by public plans, and notably by the two retirement plans set up in the aftermath of World War I for railroad workers, postmen, and federal civil servants. During the interwar period, public-sector pension assets represented around two-thirds of overall assets. However, private plans were catching up rapidly. By the mid-1950s, they had taken the lead and, by 2000, controlled around two-thirds of second-pillar assets. Table A.7 also makes clear how core plans largely outstripped relief institutions and membership-based pension plans in terms of financial assets.

Pension assets were traditionally concentrated in a minority of large plans. Throughout the century, the two occupational plans of the Confederation represented between one-third and half of overall public second-pillar assets. Asset concentration was lower in the private sector. Leading corporate plans held a sizable amount of private pension assets. In 1925 or 1965, to take only two examples, less than 8 percent of private pension plans – all of them members of the SVUSAI/SVPP pension lobbies – controlled half of occupational assets. An overwhelming proportion of group insurance reserves were in the hands of the leading life insurance companies active in the group market (see Figure 2.4, p. 80). These reserves amounted to 12 percent of overall occupational financial assets in 1941, a share that rose to 15 percent in 1978, and stabilized at around one-fifth of overall assets after the introduction of the BVG.

# Sources and references

This book makes extensive use of primary documents and records originating from the archival resources listed below. Full citations for any secondary work referred to in any chapter can be found in that chapter's endnotes. A complete bibliography will be made available upon request to the author.

## ARCHIV FÜR ZEITGESCHICHTE (ZURICH)

Historisches Archiv des Schweizerischen Handels und Industrie Vereins

| | |
|---|---|
| 1.5.3 | Vorstandsprotokolle des Vorortes, 1921–1972 |
| 92 | Personalvorsorge Erwerbersatz, 1955–1973 |
| 95 | AHV/AHV Revisionen, 1943–1972 |
| 107 | Private Sozialpolitik, 1950–1958 |

Historisches Archiv Redressement National/Aktionsgemeinschaft Nationaler Wiederaufbau

| | |
|---|---|
| 5.3 | AHV/Pensionskassen, 1929–1970 |

Nachlass Rudolf Grob

| | |
|---|---|
| II BVH | Bund für Volk und Heimat, various correspondence, 1929–1931 |

Dokumentationsarchiv Wirtschaftsförderung/Société pour le développement de l'économie suisse

IB wf-Archiv CD-ROM #I, call numbers:

| | |
|---|---|
| 3.22 | Schweizerischer Verband für (privatwirtschaftliche) Personalfürsorge privatwirtschaftlicher Unternehmungen |
| 13.1.1 | Sozialpolitik, Überblick (Wohlfahrt; Sozialleistungen der Privatwirtschaft, Arbeitsrecht), 1937–1953 |
| 13.3.3.1 | Sozialpolitik, Sozialversicherungen, Personalvorsorge, Überblick |

## HISTORISCHES ARCHIV RENTENANSTALT/SWISS LIFE (ZURICH)

| | |
|---|---|
| 310.31 | Schw. Lebensversicherungen Gesellschaften AHV, 1918–1939 |
| 312.6/1 | Kritik am Versicherungswesen, 1935–1942 |
| 317.2/1 | Steuerfragen, 1925–1939 |
| 615.601/1 | Blätter für Angestellten- und Arbeiterfürsorge (1921–1945), Kontakt-Briefe (1944–1958) |
| 615.621/1 | Außendienst – Kollektivversicherungen, 1922–1969 |
| 615.642/1 | Gruppenversicherungen. Orientierung und Geschichte 1932–1956 |
| 676.21/1 | Verwaltung – Jahresberichte Kollektivversicherungen, 1923–1969 |
| 68.100 | Verwaltung – Eidgenössische Steuern |
| 921.111/1 | 1945 – Zeitungsausschnitte, Druckschriften, Referendum |
| 921.111/5 | 1946 – die Stellung der bestehend. und neuen Versicherungsform technische Erläuterung zur vollen und zur teilweisen Rückversicherung |
| 921.111/6 | 1943–1952 – AHV Anerkennung |

## SCHWEIZERISCHES BUNDESARCHIV (BERNE)

| | |
|---|---|
| E 3340 (B) | Bundesamt für Sozialversicherung |
| -/1 | Expertenkommission AHV (1944–1945) |
| | Expertenkommission über die Berücksichtigung der Versicherungseinrichtungen |
| 1985/102 | Korrespondenz |

## SCHWEIZERISCHER ARBEITGEBERVERBAND ARCHIV (HISTORICAL ARCHIVES OF THE SWISS EMPLOYERS' FEDERATION, ZURICH)

Protokolle des Vorstandes, 1922–1972
Protokolle des geschäftsleitenden Ausschusses, 1922–1972
Protokolle der Geschäftsführerkonferenz, 1922–1972

## SCHWEIZERISCHE NATIONALBIBLIOTHEK (BERNE)

| | |
|---|---|
| V Schweiz 3234 | Schweizerischer Verband der Unterstützungskassen und Stiftungen für Alter und Invalidität (SVUSAI), 1925–1941 |
| V Schweiz 2435 | Schweizerischer Verband für privatwirtschaftliche Personalfürsorge (SVPP), 1941–1997 |
| V Schweiz 2436 | Interkantonaler Verband für Personalfürsorge (IVP), 1944–1997 |

## SCHWEIZERISCHES SOZIALARCHIV (ZURICH)

| | |
|---|---|
| K 961 | Sozialdemokratische Partei der Schweiz. Ordentliche Parteitagen, 1888– |

| | |
|---|---|
| 368 | Betriebliche Sozialpolitik, 1918– |
| 61.5 ZA | Pensionskassen (Zeitungsauschnitte), 1918– |
| SMUV 01B-001 | Historisches Archiv Schweiz. Metall- und Uhrenarbeiterverband (SMUV), 1944–1946 |

## SCHWEIZERISCHES WIRTSCHAFTSARCHIV (BASLE)

| | |
|---|---|
| D 11 | Basler Volkswirtschaftsbund, 1918–2002 |
| K III 2E | Gruppenlebenversicherung, 1920–1966 |
| K 106 | Schweiz. Verband für privatwirtschaftliche Personalfürsorge, 1925– |
| M | Private Wohlfahrtseinrichtungen, 1905–1982 |
| HS 245 | Referendumskommittee gegen die Kranken- und Unfallversicherungsgesetz 1912 |

## ZURICH FINANCIAL SERVICES CORPORATE ARCHIVES (ZURICH)

| | |
|---|---|
| Q124 203 | Pensionskassenstatistik, 1932–1978 |
| Q127 206 | Protokolle der Konferenz der Direktoren der schweiz. Lebensversicherungs-Gesellschaften/Konferenz der Vereinigung Schweizerischer Lebensversicherungs-Gesellschaften (VSLG), 1919–1972 |
| Q128 202 | Unterlagen Broschüre “private AHV Ergänzung”, 1957–1958 |
| Q128 203 | Konferenz der Vereinigung Schweizerischer Lebensversicherungs-Gesellschaften, Kommission für soziale Fragen, 1961– |

# Index